The Origins of European Integration

Bringing together political, diplomatic, economic, cultural, and contemporary history, this book explores why and how European integration came to pass. It tells a fascinating story of ideals and realpolitik, political dreams and geographical realities, and planning and chaos. Mathieu Segers reveals that the roots of today's European Union lie deep in Europe's past and encompass more than war and peace, or diplomacy and economics. Based on original archival and primary source research, Segers provides an integrated history of the beginnings of European integration and the emergence of post-war Western Europe and today's European Union. *The Origins of European Integration* offers a broad perspective on the genealogy of post-war Western Europe, providing readers with a deeper understanding of contemporary European history and the history of transatlantic relations.

Mathieu Segers is Professor of Contemporary European History at Maastricht University and academic director of Studio Europa Maastricht. He is general editor of *The Cambridge History of the European Union* and has previously held positions as a research fellow at Harvard University and at the University of Oxford. His book *The Netherlands and European Integration, 1950 to Present* was awarded the Dutch PrinsjesBoeken prize for best political book in 2013. Segers is a member of The Netherlands Scientific Council for Government Policy.

The Origins of European Integration

The Pre-history of Today's European Union, 1937–1951

Mathieu Segers
Maastricht University

Shaftesbury Road, Cambridge CB2 8EA, United Kingdom

One Liberty Plaza, 20th Floor, New York, NY 10006, USA

477 Williamstown Road, Port Melbourne, VIC 3207, Australia

314–321, 3rd Floor, Plot 3, Splendor Forum, Jasola District Centre, New Delhi – 110025, India

103 Penang Road, #05-06/07, Visioncrest Commercial, Singapore 238467

Cambridge University Press is part of Cambridge University Press & Assessment, a department of the University of Cambridge.

We share the University's mission to contribute to society through the pursuit of education, learning and research at the highest international levels of excellence.

www.cambridge.org
Information on this title: www.cambridge.org/9781009379410

DOI: 10.1017/9781009379380

© Mathieu Segers 2024

This publication is in copyright. Subject to statutory exception and to the provisions of relevant collective licensing agreements, no reproduction of any part may take place without the written permission of Cambridge University Press & Assessment.

First published 2024

A catalogue record for this publication is available from the British Library.

Library of Congress Cataloging-in-Publication Data
Names: Segers, Mathieu, author.
Title: The origins of European integration : the pre-history of today's European Union, 1937–1951 / Mathieu Segers.
Description: Cambridge, United Kingdom ; New York, NY : Cambridge University Press, 2023. | Includes bibliographical references and index.
Identifiers: LCCN 2023023084 (print) | LCCN 2023023085 (ebook) | ISBN 9781009379410 (hardback) | ISBN 9781009379427 (paperback) | ISBN 9781009379380 (ebook)
Subjects: LCSH: European federation – History – 20th century. | Europe – Economic integration – History – 20th century. | European Union – History – 20th century.
Classification: LCC JN15 .S424 2023 (print) | LCC JN15 (ebook) | DDC 321/.040940904–dc23/eng/20230718
LC record available at https://lccn.loc.gov/2023023084
LC ebook record available at https://lccn.loc.gov/2023023085

ISBN 978-1-009-37941-0 Hardback
ISBN 978-1-009-37942-7 Paperback

Cambridge University Press & Assessment has no responsibility for the persistence or accuracy of URLs for external or third-party internet websites referred to in this publication and does not guarantee that any content on such websites is, or will remain, accurate or appropriate.

Contents

Acknowledgements	*page* vii
List of Abbreviations	xi
Prologue	1
Introduction	11
1 The Genealogy of Western Europe	13
1.1 Approach and Context: Blueprints of Hope	17
1.2 Planning Europe	25
1.3 Renewing Historiography	31
1.4 Outline of the Book	38

Part 1 Beyond Americanisation (1937–1947)

2 In Search of a Programme for the West	49
2.1 Human Rights: A Franco-American Grand Narrative	54
2.2 Neoliberalism and Ecumene	60
2.3 Tackling the Social Question	64
2.4 Mixed Economies and Ordoliberalism	71
3 Re-conceptualising Capitalism and Democracy	77
3.1 Fighting the Ghosts of 'Après-Guerre'	81
3.2 'The Irrepressible Supremacy of Ideas'	85
3.3 Inventing European Christian Democracy	88
3.4 'Voices in the Night'	93
4 The Great Escape	102
4.1 Illusions and Experiments	106
4.2 Two-Step Move in Multilateralism	111
4.3 Grand Engineering: Banking without Banks	119
4.4 The Vicissitudes of Multilateralism	126

Part 2 The Making of European Integration (1947–1951)

5 The Marshall Plan: Western Europe as a Unit — 133
5.1 Marshall's Message and the Failure of the ITO — 135
5.2 An Island in the West — 138
5.3 Dealing with the German Problem — 142
5.4 'Coined Freedom' — 146

6 British Preoccupations and Ecumenical Politics — 150
6.1 Bevin's Grand Design — 150
6.2 The Delusion of 'Western Union' — 154
6.3 The Spiritual Dimension — 158
6.4 The Emergence of a Continental West — 163

7 Reality Check: The OEEC and 'Integration' — 168
7.1 Transatlantic Action on Intra-European Trade — 169
7.2 The Challenges of Convertibility — 175
7.3 The German Re-entry — 179
7.4 Launching European Integration — 187

Conclusion

8 Eclipsing Atlantis — 199
8.1 The Narrowing of Community — 200
8.2 Europeanisation — 202
8.3 Political and Spiritual Shifts — 205
8.4 Arsenal of the Free World — 208

Epilogue — 210

Bibliography — 216
Index — 231

Acknowledgements

This book is the result of more than ten years of research. The history of that research is like any other history: it is a story of ideas and ideals. But it is also a story of the often brutal confrontation between those ideas and ideals and the reality of researching and of life in general. To stay grounded on my own two feet in that confrontation – and thus to be able to write this book – I relied on the indispensable support of others.

The support and help I received in the research for this book go back a long way. The pre-history of the research that underpins this book began more than ten years ago, when I was preparing the European diaries of Max Kohnstamm for publication (published in Dutch in 2008 and 2011), a project that was a result of the research I conducted for my dissertation (on the West German position and the French–German dynamic during the negotiations for the Treaties of Rome). During my research for these publications, I obtained many new and deeper insights into the early history of European integration through the diaries of Kohnstamm, who was the right-hand man of Jean Monnet for many years. What struck me most was the whirlwind of ideas for post-war Europe that existed at the time, meticulously documented by Kohnstamm.

What stuck in my mind from this research was just how chaotic that whirlwind was and the sheer number of different and contradictory ideas that were circulating at the time. Many of those ideas we now no longer – or barely – know about. Countless such ideas ended up being unsuccessful; and many were not as new as they seemed or only consisted of superficial rhetoric – from hopeful words to despairing language. Plenty of ideas were self-contradictory or contradicted other ideas; and many were in-depth and impressively well thought out on a philosophical level as well as the policy level. Above all, I was impressed by how this chaotic storm of ideas drove the history of European integration. It became clear to me that, without an understanding of this storm of ideas characterising the history and pre-history of the beginning of European integration, it was an illusion to think that one could fathom anything about the history of European integration.

There was one more thing that struck me. It was evident that all these ideas needed to have people sponsoring and supporting them – among the population, in intellectual and political circles, among economists and planners, etc. But what I had not realised sufficiently until then was that many of the ideas for European integration had been sustained by ecclesiastical networks. This was something that received little attention in the historiography that I came across, while it is clear from Kohnstamm's diaries that such networks played a key role in the process of selecting and combining ideas for the future of post-war Europe.

I am deeply grateful to Max Kohnstamm – not only for his diaries and for his generosity in the final years before his death in 2010 in giving me access to his personal papers and in providing background explanations but also and above all for his guidance and friendship, which were a never-ending source of inspiration and insight for me.

I was able to really get started on the research underpinning this book during a research fellowship in the autumn of 2013 at the Department of Politics and International Relations of the University of Oxford, under Professor Anne Deighton in particular. This fellowship laid the foundation for a key pre-study for this book: the article 'Eclipsing Atlantis: Trans-Atlantic Multilateralism in Trade and Monetary Affairs as a Pre-History to the Genesis of Social Market Europe (1942–1950)'. This article was published in a special issue of the *Journal of Common Market Studies* in 2019 (57, 1) entitled 'Rethinking the European Social Market Economy', which I co-edited together with Rutger Claassen, Anna Gerbrandy, and Sebastiaan Princen. I also received valuable feedback on earlier drafts of my article from the participants in the STOREP conference in June 2015 in Turin, from my colleagues at the international conference on 'Free Trade and Social Charges in 20th Century Europe' in November 2015 at the University of Padova, and from those who attended the preparatory conference for the *Journal of Common Market Studies* Special Issue at the Maastricht University Campus in Brussels in December 2017.

These pre-studies were also essential ingredients for the Blueprints of Hope research project funded by the Dutch Research Council (Nederlandse Organisatie voor Wetenschappelijk Onderzoek, NWO 360-52-190, *Blueprints of Hope: Designing Post-War Europe; Ideas, Emotions, Networks and Negotiations*; see the Prologue for more details). This book synthesizes the research conducted within the framework of this ambitious project. I am heavily indebted to the work of the larger research team of the Blueprints of Hope project. It was a great joy to direct and steer this interdisciplinary project together with Beatrice de Graaf (PI) and Peter-Ben Smit and to work with such excellent researchers as

Acknowledgements

Trineke Palm, Jorrit Steehouder, and Clemens van den Berg. I am thankful to them for their academic good fellowship. The wide-ranging and in-depth international archival research conducted by the latter two during their Ph.D. projects forms the core of the larger Blueprints research project and deserves the highest praise.

During my research, I was also able to benefit in many ways from working together with the staff at a number of archives, many of whom enabled me to examine items that were otherwise difficult to access. My thanks for that valuable cooperation go to Ruth Meyer Belardini and Jean-Marie Palayret of the Historical Archives of the EU in Florence, Françoise Nicod of the Jean Monnet Foundation for Europe in Lausanne, the Dutch Ministry of Foreign Affairs, the Archive for Christian Democratic Policy in Sankt Augustin, The National Archives in Kew, Surrey, the Diplomatic Archives at the Quai d'Orsay in Paris, the Dutch National Archives in The Hague, the German Federal Archives in Koblenz, the Political Archive of the Federal Office in Berlin, the archives of the International Institute of Social History in Amsterdam, the Wilhelm Röpke Archive at the Institut für Wirtschaftspolitik at the University of Cologne, the Bodleian Archives in Oxford, the KADOC Archives in Leuven, the Chatham House Archives in London, and the recently launched Europa Archive in Maastricht.

Discussing and exchanging ideas with colleagues play an indispensable role in sharpening one's analyses and critically assessing one's sources, and in that regard I am very grateful to have had the opportunity to be one of the general editors of *The Cambridge History of the European Union* together with my friend and colleague Steven van Hecke. This endeavour, which began in 2016, has been extremely enriching for my own work in recent years. I want to thank all the contributors to *The Cambridge History of the European Union* for their scholarly comradeship.

The list of colleagues who further helped me and stimulated my thinking is almost endless. For various reasons, I would like to say a special thank you to Christine Neuhold, Rianne Letschert, Ernst Hirsch Ballin, Kenneth Dyson, Carole Fink, Corien Prins, Anne Deighton, Albert Kersten, my *Doktorvater* Bob Lieshout, Bart Stol, Elmar Hellendoorn, Caterina di Fazio, Annelies van Rijen, Frits van Oostrom, Joep Leerssen, Erik Jones, Georges-Henri Soutou, Hanns Jürgen Küsters, and my colleagues at Studio Europa Maastricht, the Faculty of Arts and Social Sciences of Maastricht University, and The Netherlands Scientific Council for Government Policy.

I am heavily indebted to two anonymous reviewers who meticulously read through an earlier draft of the manuscript for this book and provided me with countless constructive comments, corrections, and suggestions that significantly improved this book. Michael Watson, Liz Hanlon, Liz Friend-Smith, Sari Wastell, and Linda Randall formed the team at Cambridge University Press & Assessment that steered, guided, and facilitated this book project. I could not have wished for a better team. In addition, I had Gioia Marini, the best editor imaginable, who thoroughly edited the original manuscript I sent in for publication.

Lastly, to Sofia, Orfeo, Gloria, and Marèl – my family: thank you for your love.

Mathieu Segers

Maastricht, May 2023

Abbreviations

Benelux	Customs union of Belgium, the Netherlands, and Luxembourg
CDU	Christian Democratic Union
CEEC	Committee of European Economic Cooperation
CJDP	Commission for a Just and Durable Peace
DNA	Nationaal Archief, Dutch National Archives, The Hague
ECA	Economic Cooperation Administration
ECE	United Nations Economic Commission for Europe
ECSC	European Coal and Steel Community
EEC	European Economic Community
EKD	*Evangelische Kirche in Deutschland*
EPU	European Payments Union
ERP	European Recovery Programme
EU	European Union
FRG	Federal Republic of German (West Germany)
GATT	General Agreement on Tariffs and Trade
HAEU	Historical Archives of the EU, Florence
IEPS	Intra-European Payments Scheme
IMF	International Monetary Fund
ITO	International Trade Organisation
MPS	Mont Pèrelin Society
NATO	North Atlantic Treaty Organization
NWO	Nederlandse Organisatie voor Wetenschappelijk Onderzoek
NWR	Nachlass Wilhelm Röpke, Institut für Wirtschaftspolitik Cologne
OEEC	Organisation for European Economic Cooperation
TNA	The National Archives, Kew, Surrey
UDHR	Universal Declaration of Human Rights
UK	United Kingdom
UN	United Nations
US	United States
WCC	World Council of Churches

Prologue

The more secure and enduring peace appears to be, the more difficult it becomes to imagine a better world.[1] When freedom and stability have been won, the desire to escape reality inevitably wanes. This mental metamorphosis reflects the complex working of the human capacity for both oblivion and memory.[2] Fairly soon after the experience of horror and despair – fairly soon after the war, in other words – collective feelings start to change below the surface of politics and rhetoric. Passionate programmes of action, conceived in the darkest moments of threat and violence, begin to fade. This goes hand in hand with the inevitable clouding over of the true history of war and terror. The urge to imagine a better world is extinguished and morphs into more easy-going and less radical ways of thinking. The 1940s, the strangest decade encapsulating both war and peace, was no exception.

The discarding of overly ambitious visions of a new and better world began as early as 1943, when the first signs appeared that a victory over Nazi Germany was within reach. When the time was ripe to transform grand designs and ideas into actual policies, directly after the Second World War, the 'Atlantic imagination' of a 'better world',[3] on which wartime hopes in the West had thrived, was already losing much of its power. After all, it is often when futures are least likely to be realised that 'imagining a different world is an act of defiance, a rejection of the likely in

---

[1] This statement is inspired by the Polish philosopher and sociologist Zygmunt Bauman, who in the last year of the twentieth century put forward this endemic historical question about the human ability to imagine: 'If freedom has been won, how does it come about that human ability to imagine a better world and to do something to make it better was not among the trophies of victory?' By asking this question, Bauman drew attention to the interaction between imagination and freedom, the dynamics of which form an enduring puzzle at the heart of European history (Zygmunt Bauman, *In Search of Politics* (Cambridge: Polity Press, 1999), p. 1).

[2] Aleida Assmann, *Der europäische Traum. Vier Lehren aus der Geschichte* (Munich: C.H. Beck, 2018).

[3] Alan S. Milward, *The Reconstruction of Western Europe 1945–51* (London: Methuen & Co., 1984), p. 55.

the search for the necessary'.[4] Just as in 1919, the activist imaginative spirit, which thrived on 'the wartime revulsion' and led to political activism for a more peaceful and just international system, 'soon eased itself back into the comforts of the years of peace'.[5] After the end of the Second World War, Europe's statesmen rather swiftly regained their habitual fixation on the national interest and 'economic nationalism'.[6] This tendency was further induced by the experience of 'the inadequate settlement' after the First World War and the depression and war that followed, which 'had eroded the basis of international cooperation'. In other words, a recurrence of the inter-war years was not at all unthinkable in 1945.[7]

This tendency of history to repeat itself did, however, have its counter-forces. Indeed, the disruptive decade of the 1940s also stands out as a uniquely successful incubator period of new thinking, most notably concerning new world orders. From this perspective, the 1940s was a period in which politicians, intellectuals, men of business, and policy-makers alike 'sought to imagine the shape of the world to come'.[8] They did this within the practical, political, and moral framework of what became an unparalleled pan-Western exercise in planning aimed not merely at imagining a better world but actually creating it. The countless ideas and policies generated in this process of 'imagination in action' were increasingly channelled into institutions of the Western world as the Cold War started to unfold. Some of the ideas generated in this pan-Western exercise brought forth highly successful and durable policies of international cooperation that are still the principal foundations of today's multilateral order.

The challenge these planners faced was to transform American ideas – on the promotion of liberal-capitalist international trade, for example – 'into more tangible form' through practical policies based on planning.[9] Initially, this conversion of American ideas into the practices of international cooperation, and the organisation of something like 'planned

---

[4] Jay Winter, *Dreams of Peace and Freedom. Utopian Moments in the Twentieth Century* (New Haven and London: Yale University Press, 2006), ch. 4.
[5] David Mitrany, *A Working Peace System* (Chicago: Quadrangle Books, 1966 [1943]), 'Author's Foreword, 1966', p. 14.
[6] Alan Milward, *The European Rescue of the Nation-State* (London: Routledge, 1994), p. 38.
[7] John Gillingham, 'From Morgenthau Plan to Schuman Plan', in Jeffry M. Diefendorf, Axel Frohn, and Hermann-Josef Rupieper (eds.), *American Policy and the Reconstruction of West Germany, 1945–1955* (Cambridge: Cambridge University Press, 2004), pp. 112 and 119.
[8] Or Rosenboim, *The Emergence of Globalism. Visions of World Order in Britain and the United States, 1939–1950* (Princeton and Oxford: Princeton University Press, 2017), pp. 2–3 and 25.
[9] Volker R. Berghahn, *Europe in the Era of Two World Wars. From Militarism and Genocide to Civil Society, 1900–1945* (Princeton and Oxford: Princeton University Press, 2006), pp. 135–6.

Prologue 3

capitalism',[10] was achieved mainly in the fields of monetary policy, trade, and financial-economic affairs. The positive image of the planners' work was soon boosted by a unique success story of growth, welfare, and general progress during the first two post-war decades in Western Europe, when 'the material standard of living for most people improved uninterruptedly and often very rapidly'. Alan Milward even goes so far as to say that 'nothing in the history of western Europe resembles its experience between 1945 and 1968'.[11] This unique experience, which essentially centres around a transatlantic story of state intervention, sets apart the post-war period after 1945, especially its first three decades, the so-called *trente glorieuses*.[12]

The societies on the continent's Western rim together succeeded in blending and reconciling a myriad of highly rational and idealistic schemes for post-war national and international society. And in doing so, they were also able to translate this mix of ideas and ideals into feasible and coherent policies that buttressed the highly successful and stable welfare states of Western Europe. These international policies were conceived in numerous European, mainly transatlantic, networks through which the European diaspora remained involved in building the post-war future of the old continent. In concert, these often-overlapping networks, knitted together in a trans-Western Republic of *Policy* Letters (as a contemporary version of the *Respublica literaria* that flourished in the age of Enlightenment in Europe and the Americas). This 'European Republic of Planning' built a time and a space within which Europe managed to pull off something extraordinary.

The fact that this extraordinary historical experience occurred in parallel with the very visible work of the planners strongly suggested a causal relation between the two phenomena. It was as if the institutional products of planning had their own history, and as such, to certain extent, could single out post-war Western Europe from its own history. This simultaneity was intoxicating.

On a deeper, more metaphysical level, it may even have felt as if by this new simultaneity the old simultaneity of dogmatic ideology and apolitical rationalism, the simultaneity of horror and glory, the simultaneity of the vicissitudes of Romanticism and Enlightenment,[13] these unfathomable

[10] David W. Ellwood, *The Shock of America. Europe and the Challenge of the Century* (Oxford: Oxford University Press, 2016), p. 185.
[11] Milward, *The European Rescue*, p. 21.
[12] Thomas Piketty, *Capital in the Twenty-First Century* (Cambridge, MA, and London: Harvard University Press, 2014), pp. 136–55; Gillingham, 'From Morgenthau', p. 112; Milward, *The European Rescue*, p. 21.
[13] See Isaiah Berlin, 'The Bent Twig: On the Rise of Nationalism', *Foreign Affairs*, 51 (1972), 11–30, and 'European Unity and its Vicissitudes', in *The Crooked Timber of Humanity. Chapters in the History of Ideas* (London: John Murray, 1990 [1959]);

contradictions in European history had been overcome at last. It might have felt as if this very European *'Skandal der Gleichzeitigkeit'*, 'scandal of simultaneity', in the words of the German writer Hans Magnus Enzensberger,[14] which had set the century up to then in such wild and sinister shades, was finally countered. Indeed, it might have felt as if the confusion of the inter-war years was exchanged for the lucidness of planning, introducing a long overdue harmonisation of the endemic contradictions in European history through a new simultaneity (that of planning and prosperity), restoring hope and confidence on the continent. Given the profound uniqueness of this period in Western Europe, historiographers rank its planners as miracle makers, even in retrospect.[15]

Against the *mise en scène* of the history of the second half of the twentieth century, the legacy of these leading planners acquired a mythical quality. As the post-war decades progressed, much of the miracle makers' planning culminated in a series of *political* victories of freedom and democracy over totalitarianism and dictatorship that prefigured the fall of the Berlin Wall, the implosion of the Soviet Union, and triumph in the Cold War. It is no wonder, then, that the Western world became high on the buzz of the end of history.

According to the British historian Norman Davies, the First World War had marked the beginning of a period of 75 years in which Europe 'was divided by the longest of its civil wars'.[16] This period of darkness only ended in 1990 with the signing of the peace treaty between Germany and the four victorious powers from the Second World War. It was this treaty that put an end to the order of Yalta and Potsdam and finally re-united Germany, laying the foundations for the end of the Cold War and the reunification of Europe. It was only then that Europe's 'longest civil war' came to an end. The order of pan-European peace that replaced it explicitly built on the multilateral order of the post-war Western world and its ideals and policies of international cooperation and human rights, and vividly exists, albeit struggling, until this day–proving that there was no end to this history at all. This book is devoted to the effort to re-discover

---

Mathieu Segers, 'European Integration and Its Vicissitudes', *Inaugural Lecture*, 7 December 2018 (Maastricht: UM).

[14] Hans Magnus Enzensberger, *Hammerstein oder der Eigensinn. Eine deutsche Geschichte* (Frankfurt: Suhrkamp, 2008).

[15] Richard N. Gardner, 'Sterling-Dollar Diplomacy in Current Perspective', *International Affairs*, 62, 1 (1986), 21–33; Mathieu Segers, 'Eclipsing Atlantis: Trans-Atlantic Multilateralism in Trade and Monetary Affairs as a Pre-History to the Genesis of Social Market Europe (1942–1950)', *Journal of Common Market Studies*, 57, 1 (2019), 62. Key figures in this 'epistemic community' of transatlantic planners were, for instance, John Maynard Keynes, Paul Hoffman, James Meade, and Jean Monnet (see chapter 1).

[16] Norman Davies, *Europe. A History* (London: Pimlico, 1997), p. 14.

this history of the origins and beginnings of the present-day Europe of European integration. The re-discovery begins with entering the virtual *European Republic of Planning* that was so real and central in that pre-history of the European Union (EU) of today.

The progress made in the second half of the twentieth century in Western Europe – in particular the unprecedented stability and prosperity in the region – was neither evident in 1945 nor an automatic consequence of the horrors of the Second World War. While the Western Europe that was to emerge in the first post-war decades started to take shape in the mid-1940s, this 'new Europe' was not created during or after the Second World War. Instead, crucial pieces among the wreckage of the first decades of the twentieth century formed its central building blocks.[17]

The post-war developments in Western Europe were strongly linked to the inter-war years, when processes of 'de-globalisation', 'nationalisation', and a transnational 'turn to private corporatism' shook up the societal and political order,[18] while possibilities for 'one-worldism' and lofty pacifism were being explored by 'a new elite of policy experts' inspired by American examples and their potential for global scale-up, most notably President Roosevelt's New Deal.[19] The ordinary people of inter-war Europe, however, were not really interested in the grandiose blueprints of the elites. Matters of individual security, food, housing, and clothing simply took precedence.[20] These were the evident priorities in the lives of many Europeans. This situation made European societies fundamentally insecure and uncertain and desperate for stability and security, a persistent collective feeling that had kicked in after the beginning of the Great War.

The uncertainty that accompanied the above-mentioned parallel developments – the increasingly *nationalist* focus of governments in parallel with *transnational* talk of a world government – did not arise in a historical vacuum. According to the Romanian–British policy expert and scholar David Mitrany – the father of functionalism and champion of post-war

---

[17] See Kiran Klaus Patel and Wolfram Kaiser, 'Continuity and Change in European Cooperation during the Twentieth Century', *Contemporary European History*, 27, 2 (2018), 168; Jorrit Steehouder, 'Constructing Europe. Blueprints for a New Monetary Order 1919–1950', Ph.D. thesis, Utrecht University (NWO 360-52-190), 2022, pp. 41ff.

[18] Andrew Preston and Doug Rossinow (eds.), *Outside In. The Transnational Circuitry of US History* (New York: Oxford University Press, 2017), pp. 1–2; Mark Hewitson and Matthew D'Auria (eds.), *Europe in Crisis. Intellectuals and the European Idea, 1917–1957* (New York and Oxford: Berghahn, 2012), p. 13; Poul F. Kjaer, 'The Transnational Constitution of Europe's Social Market Economies: A Question of Constitutional Imbalances?', *Journal of Common Market Studies*, 57, 1 (2019), 146.

[19] Ellwood, *The Shock*, p. 182.

[20] Andrew Shennan, *Rethinking France. Plans for Renewal, 1940–1946* (Oxford: Oxford University Press, 2001 [1989]), p. 13.

functionalist planning – it was during the nineteenth century that two political trends emerged that 'moved on two and opposite lines'. The first line enhanced 'the enfranchisement of the individual, the person becoming a citizen' (anchored in the Renaissance, humanism, and anti-totalitarianism). The second line led to 'the enfranchisement of national groups through states of their own' – a process that would radically intensify during the first five decades of the twentieth century, when Europe's nation-states became more ethnically homogeneous, often as a result of very violent politics.[21]

Mitrany stressed that it was the task of post-war Europe 'to reconcile these two trends'.[22] Indeed, this may have been the key challenge of the post-war era in Western Europe, given that the uncertainty mentioned above persisted into the first post-war years. It confronted the planners of the post-war West with the dilemma endemic to the multilateral management of interdependence. The 'two trends' identified by Mitrany continued unabated in a geopolitical and geocultural context marked by unremitting ambiguity. On the one hand, this context was characterised by nation-states that were increasingly becoming culturally homogeneous. On the other hand, it was coloured by the phenomenon of economic, political, and cultural 'Americanisation', especially in the Western Europe of Paris and Berlin.[23] At the same time, segments of Western European societies increasingly became spellbound by the United States (US) and its films, its music, its automobiles, its stimulation of the senses, its money.[24] This attraction was also increasingly exploited by American elites intent on 'export[ing] the "American Dream" to the world'.[25]

This cultural-commercial trend was mirrored in new political visions. The backdrop of Americanisation allowed the idea of an 'Atlantic Community' to win relevance in Western Europe. This imagined Atlantic Community was conceived of as a vast transnational region in

---

[21] Tony Judt, *Postwar. A History of Europe since 1945* (London: Pimlico, 2007), pp. 27–8; Ido de Haan, 'The Western European Welfare State beyond Christian and Social Democratic Ideology', in Dan Stone (ed.), *The Oxford Handbook of Postwar European History* (Oxford: Oxford University Press, 2014), pp. 305 and 312.

[22] Mitrany, *A Working*, pp. 26–7.

[23] In the capitals of Western Europe – and in Paris in particular – a growing number of Americans fell in love with Europe, just as an earlier generation had done in the 1920s; see Brooke L. Blower, *Becoming Americans in Paris. Transatlantic Politics and Culture between the World Wars* (Oxford and New York: Oxford University Press, 2013).

[24] Philip Gassert, 'The Spectre of Americanization: Western Europe in the American Century', in Dan Stone (ed.), *The Oxford Handbook of Postwar European History* (Oxford: Oxford University Press, 2014), p. 184.

[25] Inderjeet Parmar, *Foundations of the American Century. The Ford, Carnegie, and Rockefeller Foundations in the Rise of American Power* (New York: Columbia University Press, 2014), pp. 33 and 31–96.

which 'the rimlands of the Atlantic Ocean [were] sites of exchange'. This transatlantic region – both a geographical region and an intangible region encompassing shared values, ideas, etc. – even had the potential to enable the cultures of the West to transcend their national boundaries by interacting in this geographical and spiritual sphere.[26]

It was the outbreak of the war against Hitler's Germany that allowed this idea to truly catch the mood of the time, as the concept of the Atlantic Community could be easily linked to Allied cooperation, in particular to the politics and policies that sprang from the strongly intensified Anglo-American partnership but also to the drafting of plans for post-war Europe by the European exile governments in wartime London.[27] Nonetheless, the translation of this 'easy link' into a concrete and coherent grand design ultimately failed. As a result, the visionary concept of an Atlantic Community was put on the back burner and turned into a transatlantic politico-economic incubator space facilitating the international cooperation of open societies and promoting 'liberalism as a pan-Western exercise' but remaining 'unguided by overall strategy'.[28]

Writing this history often entails describing how exigencies and utter chaos upstaged elaborately thought-out decision-making; unveiling the continuities between the post-war Western European order and its dark, pre-1945 history; shedding light on the endemic doubts and moral struggles lingering in the background of the political scenery; finding the blueprints and grand designs that never came to fruition, the plans that failed or that were merely erected as halfway houses, or the initiatives set in motion by largely unforeseen developments; and, last but not least, reconstructing the twists and turns that are often obscured by the Anglo-Saxon, pro-European glitter and glory added ex post facto that have coloured the scenery of the post-war West.

It is a historian's duty to try to see beyond these blinding lights on that well-known, star-spangled historiographic main stage of the post-war West. These two elements of the scenery – the illuminated and the obscure – are two sides of the same history of European integration. Seen from this perspective, that history is not the history of a 'surprising

---

[26] William O'Reilly, 'Genealogies of Atlantic History', *Atlantic Studies*, 1, 1 (2004), 66–84.
[27] Steehouder, 'Constructing Europe', pp. 73–135; Martin Conway, 'Legacies of Exile: The Exile Governments in London during the Second World War and the Politics of Post-War Europe', in Martin Conway and José Gotovitch (eds.), *Europe in Exile. European Exile Communities in Britain 1940–45* (New York and Oxford: Berhahn, 2001).
[28] Berghahn, *Europe*, p. 6; Gassert, 'The Spectre', p. 196; Gillingham, 'From Morgenthau', p. 111.

outcome of the Second World War',[29] but rather a more nuanced story that starts long before the Second World War.

This history is also the story of a nearly perfect match between the 'Old World' of Europe and the 'New World' as represented by the United States, a match that was based on the model of supply (from the US) and demand (from Europe). The United States supplied Europe with practical policies during the Second World War, geopolitical clout both during and after the war, and material needs in the immediate post-war years. More importantly, the Americans also fulfilled a deep craving among Europeans for fresh hope through their unabashed self-confidence based on their country's economic abundance and geopolitical and military power. The United States portrayed itself as a beacon of hope for the world, a 'City upon a Hill' (this expression was originally cited by John Winthrop on 21 March 1630 at Holyrood Church in a speech to the first group of Massachusetts Bay colonists who embarked on the ship *Arbella* for Boston; on 9 January 1961, President-Elect John F. Kennedy quoted the expression during a speech).

The first glimmers of this hope were planted in Europe in the early 1940s, during the first years of the Second World War. By the time of the Allied campaign to liberate Italy in the autumn of 1943, many in Western Europe were utterly unable to go on without the hope supplied by the living example of optimism in the form of the United States.

Nonetheless, the false hope aroused in Europe by Woodrow Wilson during the First World War (see chapter 1) resurfaced in the Second World War in another form. By then, the rather desperate hope for and belief in the goodness of the Americans – deliberately reinforced by the Americans themselves – were so strong among Europeans that the Americans could be viewed as the lifesavers of Europe. These 'open, vigorous, 2 x 2 = 4 sort of people, who want yes or no for an answer', in the words of the British philosopher Isaiah Berlin,[30] had a contagious can-do spirit. This was also the beginning of the phenomenon of the 'Americanisation' of the world. America was not only a dominant and victorious power in geopolitics, it also became 'the suggestive image of a rich and democratic society, and ideal for many to emulate ... a force of attraction'.[31] In spite of the repulsion inherent in any attraction, for Europe, the pull overpowered the push time and again, harking back as

---

[29] Martin Conway, *Western Europe's Democratic Age, 1945–1968* (Princeton: Princeton University Press, 2020), p. 22.

[30] Isaiah Berlin, *Flourishing. Letters 1928–1946*, 31 July 1940 (London: Chatto & Windus, 2004), p. 323.

[31] Federico Romero, *The United States and the European Trade Union Movement, 1944–1951* (Chapel Hill and London: University of North Carolina Press, 1992), preface.

Prologue

it did to the Old World's earlier experiences forging a transatlantic community, most notably the failure to do so after the First World War.

This history, in essence – and like all histories – is a story about 'a sign of a sign', to use the wording of the Italian writer Umberto Eco: the common characteristic in the flood of the planner's blueprints was an omen of hope, reflecting the search for ideas and the collective emotions of the time. In other words, that history has been a history of ideas and emotions that both harks back to earlier times and continues until today.

**

The present study synthesises research conducted as part of the ambitious 'Blueprints of Hope' research project funded by the Dutch Research Council (NWO),[32] and is heavily indebted to the work of the larger research team of the 'Blueprints of Hope' project. It was a great joy and inspiration to co-direct and co-steer this interdisciplinary project together with Professor Beatrice de Graaf (PI) and Professor Peter-Ben Smit (who was a partner in setting up this interdisciplinary research project from the very beginning, within the framework of the Institutions for Open Society research programme of Utrecht University).

Thanks to our collaboration, we managed to bring together different relevant trends and perspectives in the study of contemporary European history and European integration history, such as: (1) the focus on the ideas and collective emotions, a recent trend in the historiography of international relations, as for example expressed in the work of De Graaf, concerning the mapping of collective security cultures in Europe and beyond, in the nineteenth century,[33] (2) the role of ecclesiastical actors, especially within the ecumenical movement, in the history of European integration, as contributed to the project by Smit, and (3) the state of the art research in contemporary European history and European integration history (to which all three of us contributed from our respective specialisms and disciplines).[34]

In our supervisory tasks, the three of us were greatly helped and assisted by the Post-Doc of the team, Dr Trineke Palm, who played an essential role in much of the day-to-day coordination within the team, and was crucial in fleshing out concepts, methods, etc., for the project in general. Palm's own pioneering research work and political science approach – on the role of

---

[32] NWO 360-52-190, *Blueprints of Hope: Designing Post-War Europe; Ideas, Emotions, Networks and Negotiations*, executed at Utrecht University.

[33] Beatrice de Graaf, *Fighting Terror after Napoleon. How Europe Became Secure after 1815* (Cambridge: Cambridge University Press, 2020); Beatrice de Graaf, Ido de Haan, and Brian Vick (eds.), *Securing Europe after Napoleon. 1815 and the New European Security Culture* (Cambridge: Cambridge University Press, 2019).

[34] For instance reflected in Segers, 'Eclipsing'.

emotions in the history of European integration (as an 'affective glue')[35] – found its way into this book.

The wide-ranging and in-depth international research done by Jorrit Steehouder and Clemens van den Berg during their Ph.D. projects, which were at the core of the larger 'Blueprints research project', deserves special mention here. Their work in the international archives (from a transnational perspective) – among others in the archives of the Organisation for European Economic Cooperation (OEEC) and many of its members (Steehouder), relevant European private paper collections, such as those in the archives of the Fondation Jean Monnet in Lausanne (Steehouder), the Historical Archives of the EU in Florence (Steehouder), relevant British and American archives and private paper collections (Steehouder and Van den Berg), as well as in the archives of the World Council of Churches (WCC) in Geneva (Van den Berg) – not only unearthed a wealth of new primary sources, but also enabled them to make truly new combinations of archival sources and draw new insights from these sources. The results of their archival work are reflected in two excellent Ph.D. theses.[36] The results of the research of Van den Berg and Steehouder are reflected in this book, most notably in sections 2.2, 3.4, and 6.4 (Van den Berg), and sections 5.4 and 7.1 (Steehouder).

---

[35] Dorien Lanting and Trineke Palm, '"Change the Heart, and the Work Will Be Changed": Pius XII's Papal Blueprints for Europe', *Contemporary European History*, 31, 1 (2021), 1–13; Trineke Palm, 'Interwar Blueprints of Europe: Emotions, Experience and Expectation', *Politics and Governance*, 6, 4 (2018), 135–43; Martijn Kool and Trineke Palm, 'Crafting Emotions: The Valence of Time in Narratives about the Future of Europe in the Council of Europe (1949)', *Journal of Contemporary European Research*, 17, 4 (2021), 463–81.

[36] Steehouder, 'Constructing Europe'; Clemens van den Berg, 'European Believers. Ecumenical Networks and Their Blueprints as Drivers of Early European Integration, 1933–1954', Ph.D. thesis, Utrecht University (NWO 360-52-190), 2022.

Introduction

1   The Genealogy of Western Europe

Contemporary European history has its origins in the interweaving of people and regions both distant and nearby. The tragedies and success stories that ensue from this reality encapsulate a pan-European history of life and death, of prosperous societies, and of lethal strife. That history is, first and foremost, a history not of nations but of people and their actions, ideas, and emotions, and as such, it is a history of a community. The present book focuses on one European community that became influential and eventually rose to prominence in the international political arena: what I call 'the Europe of European integration'. By reconstructing the 'take-off' in European integration,[1] the book analyses what still counts as 'one of the more surprising outcomes of the Second World War': the emergence of a 'smaller Europe' in the form of post-war Western Europe,[2] built around the historic exercise of Franco-German reconciliation and driven by the process of European integration but without the active participation of the United Kingdom (UK).

The two core questions this book tries to answer are *how* this happened and *why* the history of European integration unfolded in the way it did. In answering these questions, the research explicitly takes on board the broader geopolitical and institutional positioning of post-war Western Europe in the 'Atlantic Century'. During this period of emerging American leadership in international affairs – starting roughly around the time of the American intervention in the First World War – the United States not only gradually accepted the leadership of the free world, it also offered Western Europe protection under the umbrella of an 'Atlantic Community'.[3] The latter manifested itself in an increasingly active way, inviting the people and nation-states located in this Atlantic

---

[1] Ernst B. Haas, 'The Challenge of Regionalism', *International Organization*, 12, 4 (1958), 440–58; see also Ernst Haas, *The Uniting of Europe: Political, Social and Economical Forces 1950–1957* (Notre Dame: University of Notre Dame Press, 1958).
[2] Conway, *Western Europe's Democratic Age*, p. 22.
[3] Ronald Steel, *Walter Lippmann and the American Century* (New York: Vintage, 1981), pp. 110–13 and 339.

sphere into a community 'bound together in mind and in deed'.[4] Indeed, it was this new transatlantic community – and its dense networks of politics, elites, and money in particular – that, more than anything else, shored up the devastated, war-traumatised, and uncertain Europe of the post-war era. These transatlantic realities offered material and moral comfort, which were indispensable for the reconstruction and resurrection of Europe. Moreover, this new community offered a world of rational policies and democratic politics – based on a restoration of values rooted in Christianity and the Enlightenment – that was immediately familiar to Europeans.

These shared mores fortified the two most resilient beacons of freedom: capitalism and democracy. As such, this transatlantic community transcended national borders,[5] while at the same time respecting the concept of the nation-state as the basic model for a new world of cooperation aimed at peace, stability, and prosperity for all. This community of 'liberal' states and societies was perceived from the outset as 'the progeny of Western Christendom'.[6] The central actors in this book are the movers and shakers of this community and their actions and thinking, their passions and beliefs. It is through them that the book reconstructs this crucial chapter in the genealogy of post-war Europe.

In tracking the emergence of a European community within a wider transatlantic framework of Western partnership and kinship, the focus of this study is on the political choices and political processes – and the ideas and beliefs behind them – that gave Western Europe its unique post-war shape and form. However, such a study would remain woefully incomplete without the psychological dimension, given that in the case of a community, power is fundamentally a psychological tool. Moreover, it is precisely within international politics – where uncertainty is the norm and elaborate calculations for the future are near impossible – that this psychological dimension of power manifests itself,[7] as it remains largely unchecked by (hierarchical) rules and regulations.

Essentially, European integration is a political phenomenon; researching it hence implies researching politics and thus power, from hard power to

---

[4] Kenneth Weisbrode, *The Atlantic Century. Four Generations of Extraordinary Diplomats Who Forged America's Vital Alliance with Europe* (Cambridge, MA: Da Capo, 2009), pp. 1–10 ff; Geir Lundestad, *'Empire' by Integration. The United States and European Integration, 1945–1997* (Oxford: Oxford University Press, 1998).
[5] Conway, *Western Europe's Democratic Age*, pp. 17 and 21.
[6] Ross Hoffmann, 'Europe and the Atlantic Community', *Thought*, 20 (1945), 25–34; Walter Lippmann, *The Political Scene. An Essay on the Victory of 1918* (New York: Henry Holt and Company, 1919), pp. 21 and 46–7; O'Reilly, 'Genealogies'.
[7] Hans J. Morgenthau, *Politics among Nations* (New York: McGraw Hill, 1993 [1948]), p. 30; Jonathan Mercer, 'Rationality and Psychology in International Politics', *International Organization*, 59 (2005), 77–106.

soft power, from the power of weapons and money to the power of ideas and emotions. Furthermore, great uncertainty reinforces the natural inclination of any group to close itself off from the outside world. In many ways, uncertainty was a dominant factor in post-war Western Europe. This makes the history of the Europe of European integration difficult to enter and prone to post facto explanations that cover up the original uncertainties and vagueness.

Indeed, the history of European integration is made difficult to navigate by the thick mist surrounding its final goal. That vagueness makes ideal types seem much more realistic than they actually are. This dialectic between vagueness of destination and the (false but tantalising) clear-cut elegance of (federal) blueprints still colours today's debate on the 'future of Europe', as it did in the decisive pre-history of the integration process and ever since. Moreover, this dialectic not only triggers much teleological debate about the future of Europe and European integration and the deterministic models in which it is framed (a federation, confederation, super-state or nation-state), it also stirs collective emotions of hope and fear, progress and decline, universal ideals and individual realities, estrangement and tradition, welfare and decadence, reconciliation and guilt, resurrection and remorse.

Above all, however, it makes it difficult to analyse and better understand the history of this process, which can only be achieved if historical facts, both physical and psychological, can be clearly distinguished from the rhetoric surrounding the final goal – and that is no simple task. Attempts to do so have a chance of succeeding only if they include a study of the primary sources: sources that can tell us something about the circumstances, ideas, and emotions prevailing at moments when decisions were made to initiate and take steps towards European integration – or not.

Notably, and despite all the blueprinting up until today, the 'normal' situation in the history of European integration comes close to one of chaos. In the midst of the unpredictable circumstances that such a situation generates, emotions, coincidence, and (alleged) intrigues or conspiracies have often been more decisive than policy choices made on the basis of rational considerations or economic cost-benefit calculations. This makes the history of European integration in the first place political (and thus psychological): it is about the art of achieving what is possible in unforeseen circumstances. In these circumstances, it is often difficult to predict how political processes will develop, especially if there is great uncertainty and when a large number of widely varying actors, often representing conflicting interests and emotions, is involved. Some of the individuals, networks, and organisations playing a part in the history of European integration have had a better command of the 'art of the possible' than others and formed influential intellectual alliances and policy coalitions that steered the history of post-war Western Europe.

By considering the above-mentioned (collective) psychological dimension of the history of European integration, this study strives for sharper identification of the shifts in coalitions that took place around specific ideas and concepts, as well as their narratives, that eventually induced the change that empowered the surge in Europe's post-war integration – and, like any fundamental change in society, responded to the dominant feelings of the time, the zeitgeist. To reconstruct that inner world of ideas and emotions, we must also examine the often-hidden dynamics at work in the collective or individual 'intellectual' struggles and dilemmas of the time,[8] as they played an important role in shaping the community's institutional form and external image.

Indeed, this way of writing history essentially concerns 'not imagination' nor 'logic' but 'thought', as Benedetto Croce has put it.[9] In concrete terms, this means digging up not just historical facts but also the relevant genealogies concerning post-war Western Europe and the wider transatlantic community it was a part of. Given this ontological position, navigating the history presented in this book implies orienting oneself in the flood of often-interconnected blueprints for international organisation, for regional groupings, for international governance, for transatlantic cooperation, for multilateral monetary and/or economic management of the international economy, for post-war societies and order, for European cooperation and integration, etc., that emerged in the period under study (with a special focus on the 1940s). Many of these blueprints were products of planning: policy-programmes rather than rhetoric or politics. Despite their apolitical look and feel, however, these blueprints, somewhat paradoxically, got *en vogue* as a token of hope, reflecting ideas and emotions that preoccupied post-war European society, including the harsh lessons of history that Europe ought to learn.

---

[8] As such, this research approach is associated with a recent trend in the study of international relations that redirects the searchlight of historical research towards the sphere of feelings, community, and emotions. This new tendency is sometimes associated with more discursive approaches to the study of international relations and/or the 'emotional turn' in international relations. See Beatrice de Graaf, 'A New Perspective on the European Security Culture after 1815', *Confronti* (Bologna: Società editrice il Mulino, 2019), 627–34, and 'Bringing Sense and Sensibility to the Continent: Vienna 1815 Revisited', *Journal of Modern European History*, 13, 4 (2015), 447–57.

[9] Benedetto Croce, *History as the Story of Liberty* (Indianapolis: Liberty Fund, 2000 [1941]), pp. 8–20.

1.1 Approach and Context: Blueprints of Hope

In the history and pre-history of European integration, one conclusion proves inescapable: none of the parties involved – the governments of the (future) member states, European institutions in the making, the business community, national and transnational pressure groups, lobbies, political parties, networks, individuals, etc. – have been able to control the process of European integration, nor its birth pangs, let alone to dominate it, not even for a short time. The process has been uncontrollable from the very beginnings, even for the United States. This history is full of drama. Much of that drama, however, is hidden away in technical policy dossiers and associated blueprints; behind their dry and rational exterior, the most unpredictable battles have been fought out, often high on individual and collective emotions. To become an insider in that history, one must plunge into the dossiers and become familiar with technocracy, such as the economic and monetary methods and techniques, and grand designs of experts and intellectuals that buttressed the policies and planning. Indeed, reading between the lines in relevant policy dossiers reveals unexpected facts, and often a deeper understanding of the political processes behind them.[10]

It is from that perspective that this book builds on multinational and transnational archival research, often focused on policy dossiers (disclosed via original archival research and/or primary source collections, memoirs, diaries, and published results of archival research within the rich body of scholarly literature on the history of European integration and twentieth-century West). As such, the book reconstructs how decisions were reached in specific key policy domains (such as trade and monetary policy) at critical junctures in the history of Western Europe such as the 'fall of France' in the spring of 1940, the signing of the Atlantic Charter in August 1941, and the launch of the Marshall Plan in June 1947.

In presenting the results of the research conducted, this study systematically shifts (roughly as per part of the book) between the following levels of analysis, or layers of the history under study – starting at the deepest layer: *first*, the layer of (Western European) society expressed through collective memory and the flaws and emotions inherent in that, mirrored in the zeitgeist, or mood of the time (Introduction); *secondly*, the layer of intellectual history – a history of ideas – focused on the *Respublica literaria* of that time, within which ideas for the post-war European and world order were floated within a broad and loose epistemic community of scholars, intellectuals and journalists, and from which plans and designs fed into the worlds of politics and policy (Part 1); *thirdly*, the layer of policy history,

---

[10] See Mathieu Segers, *The Netherlands and European Integration, 1950 to Present* (Amsterdam: Amsterdam University Press, 2020), preface.

concentrated on (influencing) decision-making through international negotiations – via the transatlantic elite-network-hubs that propped the emerging 'Republic of Planning' – and steered and inspired the political decisions that eventually would shape post-war Europe.[11]

To be sure, the first layer entails the 'psychological level' and encapsulates the realm of collective mental life, in which ideas, plans, and narratives are charged with emotions, essentially through experience and expectation.[12] As such, the present study adheres to the criticism of the German historians of European integration, Kiran Patel and Wolfram Kaiser, who have pointed to the excessive emphasis on what they call 'core Europe' in the existing historiography on European integration – referring to the European Coal and Steel Community (ECSC) as the exclusive (West European) precursor of today's EU.[13]

In addition, this book tries to unlock the history of European integration in a new way: to open the complex genealogy of Western Europe and the Europe of European integration by using the conceptual key of blueprints. These blueprints enable us to unveil the 'who', 'where', 'when', and 'how' of the coming about of the transnational coalition(s) in Atlantic Europe. These coalitions (of Western elites) steered the post-war history of Western Europe. In turn, however, these decisive processes of coalition formation were both induced and facilitated by what can best be described as an ongoing 'battle of the blueprints'. This battle is at the core of the main argument of this book: the decisive transnational coalition that was to enable the take-off of European integration was facilitated by discussions about Europe's post-war future, a battle of blueprints that went on and on during the preliminary and early stages of European integration. This continuous battle of blueprints, its interim outcomes, and interim scores guided and refined the formation of the transnational coalitions that would lead the way to European integration. That happened through convergence – within the battle – into a pragmatic and growing transatlantic and Western European consensus about the institutional design, practical planning, and moral embedding of the future Europe.

---

[11] I am gratefully indebted to one of the anonymous reviewers of the manuscript of this book for the suggestion to make this division in 'layers of history' explicit in the Introduction.

[12] Reinhart Kosseleck, *Vergangene Zukunft: Zur Semantik geschichtlicher Zeiten* (Frankfurt: Suhrkamp, 1988).

[13] To counter this overly teleological way of looking at the history of European integration, Patel and Kaiser propose to learn from Reinhart Kosseleck's notion of historical time (Patel and Kaiser, 'Continuity and Change', 172; Palm, 'Interwar Blueprints'). Most recently, Patel has argued that the focus on 'core Europe' is ultimately unproductive, because the evolution of European integration can only be explained if it is related to the other relevant international organisations (Kiran Klaus Patel, *Project Europe: Myths and Realities of European Integration* (Cambridge and New York: Cambridge University Press, 2020)).

The research approach applied in this study is based on the central assumption that discussions about policy-blueprints are often characterised by imperfect information and take place in a setting in which anarchy rules and an actor's positions and allies remain unclear. This is the 'normal condition' of international politics in general and the process of European integration more specifically. Under such conditions, ideas and identity may 'produce emotions that create trust' and may even help to surmount the obstacles to collective action,[14] thereby facilitating institutional reform and policy change. This process is a result of inter-elite persuasion,[15] an essentially psychological process that drives redefinitions of interests by the actors involved.[16] In other words, this mechanism of persuasion sets in motion a process of change – or continuity perceived as change. Emotions play a key role in this act of persuasion, since 'emotion can be important when using brute force; it is always important when the objective is persuasion'.[17]

During the preliminary and early stages of European integration, the formation of a decisive transnational coalition that was to enable its take-off was facilitated by discussions about Europe's post-war future. Gradually, these discussions converged into a pragmatic and growing transatlantic and Western European consensus about the institutional design, practical planning, and moral embedding of this future Europe. It was this crystallisation (of convergence) that underpinned the post-war Western Europe that eventually materialised, shaped by the outcomes of specific battles over competing blueprints. Moreover, these 'battles of ideas' at the heart of Western Europe's reconstruction[18] were based on practical, spiritual, and religious vocabularies of renewal and hope. In parallel with the growing consensus on the shape and aim of Western European reconstruction, these vocabularies in turn converged into what can be called a 'grand narrative'.[19] During the crucial 1940s, this grand

---

[14] Mercer, 'Rationality', 95. Here, trust is understood as an 'emotional belief', that is a 'generalization about internal, enduring properties of an object that involve certainty beyond ["hard" or natural science-like] empirical evidence'.

[15] Mark M. Blyth, '"Any More Bright Ideas?" The Ideational Turn of Comparative Political Economy', *Comparative Politics*, 29, 2 (1997), 229–50, and 'Powering, Puzzling, or Persuading? The Mechanisms of Building Institutional Orders', *International Studies Quarterly*, 51 (2007), 761–77.

[16] Judith Goldstein and Robert O. Keohane (eds.), *Ideas and Foreign Policy: Beliefs, Institutions, and Political Change* (Ithaca: Cornell University Press, 1993).

[17] Jonathan Mercer, 'Emotional Beliefs', *International Organization*, 64 (2010), 22; see also Kool and Palm, 'Crafting Emotions'.

[18] Craig Parsons, *A Certain Idea of Europe* (Ithaca and London: Cornell University Press, 2003), pp. 1–37.

[19] For recent research on the analysis of narratives and its importance for the study of international history, politics, and policy, as well as on the key role that emotions and ideas play in this, see among others: Simon Koschut, 'Speaking from the Heart: Emotion

narrative emerged primarily within the framework of the Anglo-Saxon partnership,[20] while its paramount intellectual anchors were to be found in the two great democratic revolutions of the modern Western world: the American Revolution and the French Revolution (see chapter 2).[21]

This grand narrative responded to what was needed on the ground. There it was clear what 'the great task after the war' would be: to secure the 'willing co-operation of Germany in the economic reconstruction of Europe on a basis of the recognition of the rights and interests of all people involved',[22] as Charles Guillebaud, the author of an analysis of Germany's economic recovery, explained in a speech in September 1940. He was thinking ahead to the end of the war. To begin with, this implied reconciling the political system of nation-states with a wide-ranging form of international cooperation and coordination. At the same time, it also required a credible guarantee of individual and collective security in war-traumatised Europe as well as a delicate balance between protecting international trade and capital flows and safeguarding human rights – that is, a balance between the interests of consumers, producers, and citizens. The ideas on how to accomplish this, and how to legitimise it politically and publicly, came mainly from the United States and continental Europe, France in particular.

In all this, new vocabularies of renewal and hope were urgently needed to bring the planning of the post-war order in line with the zeitgeist, the mood of the time. This was even more pressing since 'to contain moods' was rapidly becoming 'a prime requisite of leadership' in international politics.[23] Indeed, any narrative – the 'heart and soul of policy debates'[24] – had to extend its power of persuasion to the public realm to be successful. And the mood of the time in Europe was dominated by an overwhelming societal 'desire' for stability[25] and more specifically for peace, prosperity, progress,

---

Discourse Analysis in International Relations', in Maéva Clément and Eric Sanger (eds.), *Researching Emotions in International Relations* (New York: Palgrave Macmillan, 2018); Vivien Schmidt, 'Discursive Institutionalism: The Explanatory Power of Ideas and Discourse', *Annual Review of Political Science*, 11, 1 (2008), 303–26; Mark McBeth and Elizabeth Shanahan, 'Introducing the Narrative Policy Framework', in Michael Jones, Mark McBeth, and Elizabeth Shanahan (eds.), *The Science of Stories* (New York: Palgrave Macmillan, 2014).

[20] Andrew Williams, *Failed Imagination? The Anglo-American New World Order from Wilson to Bush* (Manchester: Manchester University Press, 2007), pp. 1–5.

[21] See Mary Ann Glendon, *A World Made New. Eleanor Roosevelt and the Universal Declaration of Human Rights* (New York: Random House, 2002), pp. xvii–xviii.

[22] Keith Tribe, *Strategies of Economic Order. German Economic Discourse 1750–1950* (Cambridge: Cambridge University Press, 1995), pp. 241–2.

[23] Chatham House Archives, London, Yale Study, June 1948, last page.

[24] Jones, McBeth, and Shanahan (eds.), *The Science*, p. 249.

[25] This relation between incentives and desire is derived from Chomsky (Mercer, 'Rationality', 95).

and social cohesion. Europe's demand for peace and stability was fulfilled by the steadily increasing American supply of military, economic, and moral leadership which in concrete terms translated into a set of public policy best practices that originated in the New Deal but essentially focused on economic growth to overcome the material and social disasters of war in Europe.[26] The 'historical meaning of the experience was not to be found inside it, but outside, in the steady build up of progressive social policy in Europe'.[27]

Hence, this transatlantic match between European demand and American supply was also the product of a deeply emotional affair: American planning satisfied a burning desire in traumatised Europe. In general, one could perhaps even say that 'faith in planning' became 'the political religion of post-war Europe'.[28] The so-called 'planners' – leading policymakers, intellectuals, and politicians of the time – were the saints of this political religion. Together, they created a new and alternative Republic of Letters, what one could call a European and transatlantic 'Republic of Planning'. All sorts and conditions of planners are the central actors in this book, the drivers of the story of the origins of European integration.

Soon after the war, the idea that building a West European 'unit' would be impossible without some sort of spiritual unity gained ground. That notion was another reflection of the mood of the time. The pressing political and societal demand for some kind of spiritual community or community feeling was a trans-European phenomenon, manifesting itself in all free nations of Western Europe, that could not be ignored. Maybe, the longing for renewed hope – something to believe in, something to counter the fear bred by war – was the dominant emotion of that time. In this atmosphere of collective longing, the uniting potential of Christianity in Europe was an increasingly prominent force while the churches got more actively engaged in discussions on reconstruction and the post-war order. These developments were matched by the steady growth of the ecumenical movement, which led to the founding of the World Council of Churches in Amsterdam in 1948, just three months after the Congress of Europe held in The Hague (which despite the wariness of the national governments was an event of substantial political impact that marked a collective longing). These events were part of a broader ecclesiastical movement in the wider West.

---

[26] See Ellwood, *The Shock*, pp. 176ff. As Kiran Patel has stated concerning the global impact of the New Deal: 'it was the war that made the New Deal', and, as such, made the New Deal an appealing tenet of the new American claim to global leadership (Kiran Klaus Patel, *The New Deal. A Global History* (Princeton and Oxford: Princeton University Press, 2016), pp. 271 and 274).

[27] Rodgers cited in Ellwood, *The Shock*, p. 181. [28] Judt, *Postwar*, p. 67.

Towards the end of the Second World War, the Catholic Church – after a long and painful silence on the horrors of the Nazi age – had reactivated itself internationally through a pro-democracy and human rights programme, seizing the opportunities offered by the growing societal force of Christian religion and the unprecedented popularity of the new Christian Democratic political parties. On the Anglo-American side of the Atlantic, the church had already anticipated the 'space for discourse on European unity' in the late 1930s and early 1940s. This all went hand in hand with a narrowing of political focus on the countries of the West and Western Europe, those that could be made safe for democracy – and, by extension, capitalism. Moreover, this line of reasoning implied a clean break with socialism 'as a system' and won overwhelming credibility during the Cold War build-up, within the context of the Christian-inspired and anti-communist Truman Doctrine.[29] It also became the guiding principle of the first governments of West Germany under the Christian Democrat Konrad Adenauer.[30] Moreover, it effectively meant the end of the 'One World' approach in US foreign policy, and a further reorientation towards practical and regional internationally (US-led) coordinated economic liberalism in Europe with a keen eye for the social question. The latter was bolstered by US charity, also because leading intellectual voices were advocating concentration on the economy as the key area in which US foreign policy could have a decisive impact. Finally, this all seemed in tune with the mood of the time. And a special time it was. This time after the war that Europe knew so well from not that long ago.

After the unmatched horrors of the Great War, American President Woodrow Wilson's call for a 'worldwide settlement' gained traction at the Paris Peace Conference. Hopes were high that, as the British commentator and writer H.G. Wells had put it already during the first year of the Great War, this war would be 'the war that will end war'.[31] At Versailles in 1919, the 'Big Four' powers – the United States, the United Kingdom, France, and Italy – knew all too well 'that there had never been an attempt at a worldwide settlement'; indeed, as historian Margaret MacMillan wrote in 2013, 'there has never been one since'. While the post-Great War period was unique in that the populations of the warring states were

---

[29] Melvyn P. Leffler, 'The Emergence of an American Grand Strategy, 1945–1952', in Melvyn Leffler and Odd Arne Westad (eds.), *The Cambridge History of the Cold War*, vol. I (Cambridge: Cambridge University Press, 2010), p. 76; see also Van den Berg, 'European Believers', p. 169.

[30] Mathieu Segers, *Deutschlands Ringen mit der Relance. Die Europapolitik der BRD während der Beratungen und Verhandlungen über die Römischen Verträge* (Frankfurt etc.: Peter Lang, 2008), ch. 2.

[31] H.G. Wells, *The War That Will End War* (London: Frank & Cecil Palmer, 1914).

ready and keen to embrace universalism and world peace, MacMillan noted that, if anything, the Treaty of Versailles made the Great War into 'the war that ended peace'.[32] In other words, the peace settlement of 1919 failed to 'make the world safe for democracy' (a phrase Wilson used on 2 April 1917 in a speech before Congress to obtain permission to declare war against Germany, which he obtained four days later: the moment the United States became definitively involved in European and world politics). What Wilson had achieved was quite the contrary.

By the time Wilson was bypassed as presidential candidate for the 1920 elections, his 'Fourteen Points' outlining his principles of peace had already been dead in the water for quite a while. Wilson's proactive and idealistic vision for world cooperation became buried under the essentially reactive and opportunistic cost-benefit reasoning enshrined in the agreements of the Versailles Peace Treaty. This was also 'an illustration of how ill-defined Wilson's ideas were as practical politics'.[33]

A young American journalist named Walter Lippmann was covering the events at Versailles, and two conclusions he drew from the Paris Peace Conference proved to be highly relevant in the post-Great War era. Viewing international politics from a long-term perspective and tapping into the emotions of the time, he concluded that 'men will prefer a violent hope to a terrible despair'. His second assessment pertained to Wilson's failed attempt to mould a morally better world order: 'he [Wilson] has an ideal; but has he a program?'[34] The question was clearly rhetorical.

The brute reality on the ground in Europe tore down the American-inspired aspirations for a better world and relegated them to naïve utopianism, ultimately symbolised by the fate of the League of Nations, which proved to be tragically dysfunctional in the inter-war years. Europeans turned a deaf ear to the politics of reconciliation touted by politicians such as Gustav Stresemann and Aristide Briand.[35] What re-emerged was a Europe of conflict, violence, uncertainty, and poverty. It was a Europe that was plunging into even greater darkness than before, transfixed by a feverish search for an escape. This was the Europe of the Spanish Civil War and of Pablo Picasso's *Guernica* (1937), the mural-sized painting portraying the suffering of people and animals during the bombing of the eponymous city by German and Italian fighter aircraft. This was the Europe of rampant poverty and gloom, which Lippmann had implicitly

---

[32] Margaret MacMillan, *The War that Ended Peace: The Road to 1914* (New York: Random House, 2013).
[33] Williams, *Failed Imagination?*, pp. 19–21 and 38–44.
[34] Lippmann, *The Political Scene*, pp. xi and xiii.
[35] Henri Kissinger, *Diplomacy* (New York: Simon & Schuster, 1994), pp. 266–88.

warned about in his coverage of the Paris Peace Conference. This was the Europe that was captured by the German–Swiss painter Paul Klee in his painting *Europa* (1933): a goddess still, but one of wild despair and expressionism.

But this Europe of the inter-war years was also (and maybe more than anything else) the Europe of Ernest Hemingway: 'the *banlieu* of Paris', the continent a mere background to the Paris of the 1920s, the city of Josephine Baker, F. Scott Fitzgerald, and Cole Porter. Their Paris was an electrifying city full of sex, booze, and jazz; the city of light and its exciting shades, the city as *A Moveable Feast* (the title of Hemingway's Parisian memoir), where arty-intellectual youngsters from across the Atlantic were 'like iridescent flies caught in the black web of an ancient and amoral European culture', as Sinclair Lewis, one of Hemingway's fellow travellers, put it.[36] This was something very different from the American dream. The intellectual and physical environment of the *années folles*, however, was coloured by the sinister aftermath of the unprecedented devastation of the Great War. The Europe these Americans loved was a traumatised Europe, dangerously insecure and wild. Its war fever would not leave them untouched.

A new generation of American descendants of well-to-do East Coast families came to know Europe while living there during the inter-war years, often travelling together with the intellectual American avant-garde in Paris. It was this generation of Americans that fell in love with the struggling old continent, and it was this emotional attachment that explains why key figures among these Americans – who were to take up influential positions in government and business during the 1940s – pushed passionately for a brighter European future after the Second World War. Indeed, the outlook of their generation would carry the 'American century' along with an emerging, 'altogether new, emblematic, Atlantic world, bound together in mind and deed'.[37] Politically, their activism had its origins in the direct involvement of the United States in the post-First World War peace negotiations, then also labelled 'America's geopolitical coming-out party'.[38]

---

[36] Sinclair Lewis cited in Curzio Malaparte, *The Skin* [*La Pelle*] (n.p: Pickle Partners Publishing, 2015 [1949]), ch. 1; Ernest Hemingway, *A Moveable Feast* (London: Arrow Books, 2011 [1964]); Mathieu Segers, 'Flags and Bones. The Europe of Malaparte', *European Review of Books*, 2 (2022), 76–91.
[37] Weisbrode, *The Atlantic Century*, p. 10.
[38] Nelson D. Lankford, *The Last American Aristocrat. The Biography of Ambassador David K.E. Bruce* (Boston: Little, Brown and Company, 1996), pp. 42–3.

1.2 Planning Europe

The American point of view on the Second World War was that it was the Great Depression and the devastating inequality, nationalism, and racism it had unleashed that was at the root of the extraordinary violence that ravaged Europe during Hitler's war. This meant that the work of the many American diplomats, policymakers, journalists, businessmen, and politicians involved in the American mission of 'building Europe' boiled down to a dual battle against both poverty and the collapse in international coordination. This mission eventually culminated in the Marshall Plan in 1947 – the programme Wilson did not have. This was no coincidence. These Americans sensed what Lippmann had formulated back in 1919:

> The continent is still there, most of the population is still there, to be sure, but Europe as a diplomatic system is hopelessly gone. Its organization is broken ... Only small groups of far-seeing men have comprehended ... that this is what the 'Victoire intégrale' would mean; that victory would compel us to make a new framework for human society.[39]

It was up to the Americans to create this new framework, together with those Western Europeans who were far-seeing and fit enough – but in that order, with America in the lead. This plot twist, that the Americans took the lead in rebuilding Europe, had already been foreshadowed in Wilson's lofty words, but 'practical politics' had been lacking at that time. It would take another war before the United States was ready to fully take on the transatlantic assignment to 'make a new framework for humanity'; to rally the forces of the free world around the belief that the Europe of the first post-war era could be buried for good; and to mobilise political, societal, and religious forces around a programme of practical politics to realise this ideal.

For it to stand a chance of being realised, it was clear that this new Western world would have to be 'post-European'. Many had understood already in the inter-war period the necessity of some form of global or transnational planning under American aegis. As this would be the only way to make that 'new framework for human society' that had been promoted by American presidents, presidential candidates, and ministers from Woodrow Wilson to Wendell Willkie and Sumner Welles in different variants of the One World approach.[40]

---

[39] Lippmann, *The Political Scene*, pp. 6–7.
[40] Wendell L. Willkie, 'One World', and Sumner Welles, 'Blueprint for Peace', *Prefaces to Peace* (New York: Simon & Schuster/Doubleday, etc./Columbia University Press, 1943), pp. 9–148 and pp. 418–37; Veronika Heyde, 'Amerika und die Neuordnung Europas vor dem Marshallplan (1940–1944)', *Vierteljahreshefte für Zeitgeschichte* (Munich: Oldenbourg), 58, 1 (2010), 116; Rosenboim, *The Emergence*, p. 4.

But it was only after the failure of Wilson's leadership, the bogging down of the League of Nations, the devastation wrought by the Great Depression, and the outbreak of the Second World War that it became obvious that this 'new framework' could not simply be based on the allure of the 'New World' of America. It was crucial that the Europeans themselves promote and defend the new transnational policies of international organisation, mobilising the commitment of their fellow Europeans to embrace a radically different post-war experience than the one twenty-five years earlier. To American analysts, it was immediately obvious that making this work would be no walk in the park, to say the least.[41] Or to put it in more cynical terms: to be acceptable, real European unity (in the sense of an America-like federation for instance) was not allowed to exist.[42] This was the harsh dictum on a continent of warring nation-states. It also was one of the key lessons of the failure of Wilsonian idealism in 1919: any new post-European Europe must also, somehow, resemble an old Europe. Mobilising Europeans was impossible without a dash of pretence, (nostalgic) hints to the past, and a shot of conceptual vagueness (not exactly the '2 x 2 = 4' kind of approach; see Prologue). In practice, this meant that post-war Europe was still to be based on its nation-states (no matter how worn out and discredited they may be) and their traditions (no matter how dark these may have been). Moreover, the 'new Old World' of post-war Europe would remain an ongoing experiment in new and more just forms of capitalism and democracy, oscillating between the past and the future, the national and the supranational.[43]

It is this experiment that forms the wider context of the present research into the origins of the take-off in European integration from 1950. The period under study runs from the mid-1930s to the 1950s, a period marked by a myriad of discussions about the future order of Europe, many of them wide-ranging and inherently transnational. In essence, they boiled down to the classic question 'What is Europe?' Typically, these mid-twentieth-century discussions about Europe's future generated numerous blueprints for international organisation, regional groupings, transatlantic cooperation, and European integration. In many ways, the 'creative reconstructions' of political and societal order,[44] which sprang

---

[41] Nationaal Archief, Dutch National Archives (DNA), The Hague, 2.21.408 (Nalatenschap Beyen), B.2.2.2.1, 71, 'Anglo-American Relations in the Post-War World', Yale Institute of International Studies, May 1943, pp. 5ff; see also Weisbrode, *The Atlantic Century*, p. 104.

[42] Pierre Melandri, *Les États-Unis face à l'unification de l'Europe 1945–1954* (Paris: Pedone, 1980), p. 26.

[43] Perry Anderson, *The New Old World* (London and New York: Verso, 2009).

[44] Orfeo Fioretos, *Creative Reconstructions. Multilateralism and European Varieties of Capitalism after 1950* (Ithaca: Cornell University Press, 2011).

from the exchange of views that these blueprints spawned, defined the political and institutional directions taken in post-war Europe, not least because many of these reconstructions were designed explicitly to mobilise hope for political and societal action.

The planner's blueprints were a token of hope. A hope that hinged on the United States – radiating success and power during the period (largely overlapping the entire twentieth century) that would become known as the 'American century'[45] – or more precisely: that hinged on the American willingness to activate itself as a guiding force in European affairs. That hope was deemed allowable because it bordered reality. However, by becoming actively involved in the rebuilding of Western Europe, the United States was forced to confront a complex and fundamental question of foreign policy. At the end of the 1940s, it became increasingly clear that the responsibility for reconstruction in Western Europe that the US had taken on would not be a short-term undertaking. On the contrary, it probably meant the start of a long-term relationship with Western Europe. That forced Washington to take part in an unknown world of international organisations, multilateral dynamics, and regional partnerships – a world in which the American 'get up and go' attitude often had completely different effects than expected. Time and time again, it became clear that the US had little or no grip or influence on the cooperation between Western European countries. It sometimes drove policymakers in Washington to despair.

This situation would present the US with policy issues that called for a clear perspective on the future of Europe. As the implementation of the Marshall Plan and the European Recovery Programme (ERP) progressed, new policy issues kept coming to the fore. Should the Marshall Plan be seen as the first step in a long road towards European unification sponsored by the US, or as little more than cement for the Cold War alliance? Crucially, from 1949 the latter was established via the North Atlantic Treaty Organization (NATO), which was practically (militarily) and psychologically (offering security) essential to reassure the Western Europeans about the US commitment to their future (of democracy and capitalism). Could the Cold War alliance and European unification be combined in a transatlantic community, or was this simply wishful thinking? If American engagements overseas should be of a temporary nature, as the founding fathers had advised, how could the task the Americans had set themselves of 'building Europe' be anything other than a quick fix in response to international circumstances? Contrary to what is often

---

[45] Ellwood, *The Shock*, pp. 22ff.

claimed today, the policymakers in Washington remained undecided on how to answer these questions.[46]

Nonetheless, as the post-war era unfolded, one thing soon became more and more clear in Washington. In the end, the answers to all these questions depended on how one interpreted a matter of a higher order than the problem of Western Europe: the Cold War. At the time, it was far from evident how long this phenomenon would persist and what would come after it. Here, too, understandably, the Americans had no clear idea of how to answer these questions. It is in this space of the unknown where they lost the Europeans. Paradoxically, and in contrast to dominant historiography, the American attitude in the Cold War remained too hesitantly static in a peculiar way: too traditionally black-and-white, too 'either–or', instead of the 'and–or' or even the 'and–and' that would eventually steer the project of European integration. To the Americans, the European 'and–and' approach (liberalism *and* socialism, individual *and* community, enlightenment *and* romanticism, federation *and* nation-state, etc.) was rather alien. They considered this approach vague at best, and hypocritical and risky most often.

However, to the Europeans, looking for and–and solutions to the pressing problems of the time corresponded to an emerging, and very European, post-war practice: to push ideas, plans, and blueprints because of their qualities of reconciliation and tolerance, and because of their association with Christian virtues promoted both through trendy movements such as ecumenism and classical religious doctrines such as those of Irenicism. This association of planning with Christendom also included Christian-inspired 'third ways' for liberal democracy, advanced by a very diverse group of prominent European intellectuals and politicians, often associated with the popular conservative movement of Christian Democracy, but at the same time also including staunch liberals from all over Western Europe. Crucially, in its practical (policy) translations, the 'European way' of post-war societal and international design centred more around an ideological 'and–and' than the 'either–or', pushed by the United States because of the Cold War news of the day.

Against many odds, the 'better world' envisaged during the inter-war decades and the war years did build the foundation for stability, prosperity, and well-being in post-war Western Europe. Moreover, despite the global aspirations often simmering below the surface in post-war planning, this new reality of free societies, progress, and international cooperation remained a strictly Western affair for more than four decades, crafted from ideas of an 'Atlantic civilisation' and a distinct and coherent Western unity – or even

---

[46] See Leffler, 'The Emergence', pp. 67–89.

The Genealogy of Western Europe

union – and identity.[47] However, when the time was ripe to put such ideas into practice in post-war Western Europe, this 'Atlantic imagination' of a 'better world'[48] had already lost much of its power. In its place, a messier Western European variant emerged, morally indebted to its American precursors (including the One World movement) yet focused in practical terms on devising a European method of American-inspired socio-economic and financial-economic planning, a European style of state intervention, inter-state coordination, and supranational organisation.

If there was a clean historical break with the post-First World War past after 1945, it was reflected in the modern phenomenon of economically legitimised state intervention elaborated in projects of *planning*. The credibility of planning offered a fresh solution to the political problems that had torn Europe apart in the first decades of the twentieth century. Planning had been at the very core of the 'imagination in action' that characterised the wartime Western world, and during the 1940s, planning even evolved into something much bigger than a set of policy instruments to organise society. It became a mission, a belief, a movement, a kind of pseudo-religion. It became the binding mission that drove the Western quest for a resilient, free world: 'if a democracy was to work, if it was to recover its appeal, it would have to be *planned*';[49] and primarily economically planned, focused on the battle against unemployment and on providing 'welfare for all'.[50]

In taking on this mission, the leading planners designed a society that was more organised than the inter-war societies had been when Europeans had experimented with a mix of wild capitalism (in the form of laissez-faire economic policy) and even wilder politics. These experiments had only led the continent into economic depression and societal unrest. Given this dark historical backdrop, it was felt that the adventures of the inter-war years had to be avoided at all costs. Planners now took the lead, presenting themselves as unsullied by political ideology. They helped politicians build their promised 'better world' of prosperity and multilateralism by drawing up a programme of practical politics that the Western world had lacked. This earned them political trust, and it made their claim that rational policies of

---

[47] In the 1966 publication of his influential pamphlet *A Working Peace System* (first published in 1943), David Mitrany starts off the reworked introduction as follows: 'When this short study was first published in the summer of 1943, there was great confidence in the unity which had grown up during the war, and [we] were thinking mainly of how to consolidate that unity and expand it' (Mitrany, *A Working*, p. 25).
[48] Milward, *The Reconstruction*, p. 55. [49] Judt, *Postwar*.
[50] Diane de Bellefroid, 'The Commission pour l'Étude des Problèmes d'Après-Guerre (CEPAG), 1941–1944', in Martin Conway and José Gotovitch (eds.), *Europe in Exile. European Exile Communities in Britain 1940–45* (New York and Oxford: Berhahn, 2001), pp. 124–9.

international cooperation could prevent disaster even more convincing and thus appealing. The most prominent of the planners even presented themselves as 'statesmen of interdependence' – as apolitical experts operating within an emerging international order based on the cooperation of free and open societies, social justice, and the practical and material benefits of functionalism (in Mitrany's sense of the word) and market expansion, cheap production, and mass consumption.[51]

The key challenge these planners faced was to translate lofty American ideas such as the promotion of free trade and 'an Atlantic Community of institutions and values' into 'more tangible form' through practical policies based on planning.[52] Initially, this conversion of American ideas into Atlantic and Western European practices of international cooperation and organisation was achieved mainly by promoting and managing economic interdependence in the fields of monetary policy, trade, and financial-economic affairs. Moreover, and rather soon in the day, it turned out that the Europeans were particularly effective in 'selectively appropriating whatever it was that the United States cared to send over'.[53] It has been this polysemic European way of adapting to the American power, abundancy, and seduction that was at the very heart of the 'Americanisation' of Western Europe.[54]

Be that as it may, the work undertaken by the planners of post-war Western Europe was soon given a powerful boost by the success story – unparalleled in history – of economic growth, prosperity, and general progress. As the British historian Alan Milward has noted, 'nothing in the history of western Europe resembles its experience between 1945 and 1968 . . . the material standard of living for most people improved uninterruptedly and often very rapidly'.[55] In combination with the geopolitical and ideological black-and-white logic of the Cold War, this makes it seem – ex post facto – as though the early post-war rationalist planners had triumphed. This influential perception, however, is false because it obfuscates the origins of European integration. We now know from historical research that any image of European integration as a predominantly economic or otherwise purely rational affair is fundamentally incomplete. This notion forms the starting point for the historical research that underpins this book, which mirrors relatively recent developments in the historiography of European integration.[56]

---

[51] François Duchêne, *Jean Monnet. The First Statesman of Interdependence* (New York and London: Norton, 1994); see also John Foster Dulles quoted in Berghahn, *Europe*, p. 136.
[52] Berghahn, *Europe*, pp. 135–6.   [53] Ellwood, *The Shock*, p. 9.
[54] Victoria de Grazia, *Irresistible Empire: America's Advance through Twentieth-Century Europe* (Cambridge, MA: Belknap Press and Harvard University Press, 2005).
[55] Milward, *The European Rescue*, p. 21.
[56] For a useful and complete overview of the historiography concerning European integration, see Kiran Klaus Patel, 'Widening and Deepening? Recent Advances in European Integration History', *Neue Politische Literatur*, 64 (2019), 327–57.

1.3 Renewing Historiography

General accounts still consider European integration to be, first and foremost, a reflection of the national interests of the most powerful states and their corresponding policy choices in the 'geopolitical', 'socio-economic', or 'commercial' realms. This rationalised vision on the process of European integration was boosted by the revisionist 'economic' explanations for European integration that became dominant during the 1990s. This revisionist turn in the historiography was carried by two path-breaking monographs: *The European Rescue of the Nation-State* (1992) and *The Choice for Europe* (1995) respectively written by the British historian Alan Milward and the American political scientist Andrew Moravcsik – a self-proclaimed follower of Milward.[57] Both Milward and Moravcsik, in their own stylised way, positioned themselves as new realists, debunking the explanations that had dominated the research for decades. They did this in two ways. First, they dismissed the overly impressionistic functionalist theories (which had identified a *sui generis* deepening and widening dynamism in the process of European integration that was driven by its unique supranational institutions). Secondly, they challenged the classic challengers of the functionalist theories, the so-called *traditional realists*, who based their explanations on the (geo)political: the hard power of states and their geopolitical and security calculations (relegating the supranational institutions of European integration to products and/or proxies of geopolitical power relations in Europe, the West and the world).

In contrast to this classic juxtaposition of supranationalism versus intergovernmentalism, the revisionism of Milward and Moravcsik dismissed both the often-inherently teleological analyses of the functionalists (stressing the (rationally) inescapable spill-over of supranationalism from one (economic) sector to the other, and from one region to the other), and the fixation on geopolitics and hard power of the traditional realist. While siding with the latter regarding the primacy of the nation-states in the making of European integration, Milward and Moravcsik pointed to the *economic* national interest of the member states as the decisive rationale in the making of the Europe of European integration. In doing so, they triggered a year-long scholarly debate between explanatory theories for the phenomenon of European integration, pitting economic factors (socio-economic and/or commercial in nature) against geopolitical factors (the calculus of national interest based on power political relations

---

[57] Milward, *The European Rescue*; Andrew Moravcsik, *The Choice for Europe. Social Purpose and State Power from Messina to Maastricht* (London: UCL Press, 1995), for Moravcsik as a follower of Milward, see p. 88.

between nation-states). This led to a long-drawn-out abstract discussion over the decisiveness of economic or geopolitical factors, mainly based on highly deductive theories.[58]

The current historiography is impregnated with these polarisations: between the traditional realist (stressing the importance of geopolitics and security over economy) and the revisionist realists (claiming that it was the other way around), and between (neo-)functionalist explanations of the 'why' of European integration (centred on European integration's unique supranational institutions) and more intergovernmental approaches (concentrated on the nation-state as the locus of action). As of the mid-1990s, Andrew Moravcsik has been the main driver in these debates, which he sharpened, retailed, and revived.[59] As such, Moravcsik's contributions to the scholarly debate on the history of European integration stimulated multidisciplinary discussion and inspired new research. However, this went at the cost of nuance in Moravcsik's writing of history and the quality of empirical evidence – eventually he produced too rigid a commercial economic rationalisation of the history of European integration (for the sake of the power of his theoretical claim) that proved unable to resist the seduction of an almost purely rational ex post facto reading of the history.[60]

Moreover, varieties of intergovernmentalism share comparable problems in their efforts to capture the institutional dynamics of the process of European integration, as this system contains normative features, transnational dynamics, fragmented national governments, the caprices of public support for European integration, non-state actors, and (non-rational) beliefs and emotions, ranging from personal preoccupations and religious belief to faith in planning.[61] This book aims to tackle the 'two main weaknesses' that Wolfram Kaiser and Brigitte Leucht had already registered in 2008 (and have worked on since then) but still

---

[58] For an influential traditional geopolitical explanation, see Hanns-Jürgen Küsters, 'West Germany's Foreign Policy in Western Europe 1949–58', in Clemens Wurm, ed., *Western Europe and Germany* (Oxford and Washington, DC: Berg, 1995).

[59] Andrew Moravcsik, 'Liberal Intergovernmentalism and Integration: A Rejoinder', *Journal of Common Market Studies*, 33, 4 (1995), 611–28, and 'De Gaulle between Grain and Grandeur' (parts 1 and 2), *Journal of Cold War Studies*, 2 (2000) and 3 (2000), 3–43 and 4–68, and 'Preference, Power and Institutions in 21st Century Europe', *Journal of Common Market Studies*, 56, 7 (2018), 1648–74.

[60] Robert Lieshout, Mathieu Segers, and Anna van der Vleuten, 'De Gaulle, Moravcsik, and *The Choice for Europe*. Soft Sources, Weak Evidence', *Journal of Cold War Studies*, 6, 4 (2004), 89–139.

[61] See Mareike Kleine and Mark Pollack (eds.), Special Issue: 'Liberal Intergovernmentalism and Its Critics', *Journal of Common Market Studies*, 56, 7 (2018), 1491–696; Liesbet Hooghe and Gary Marks, 'Is Liberal Intergovernmentalism Regressive? A Comment on Moravcsik', *Journal of European Public Policy*, 27, 4 (2020), 501–8.

characterise much of the historiography of the origins of European integration today: the historiography's unduly state-centric scope and the neglect of the 'embedded nature of ideas and their role in the creation and evolution' of European integration.[62]

European integration never was the result of a preconceived plan; rather, it consisted of a complex mix of messy procedures, political games, lofty ideals, and, above all, heated differences of opinion. Ad hoc decision-making, crises, and even utter chaos have been constants in its history. This complicated reality has induced scholars to zoom in on European integration's infamous modus operandi of 'muddling through' in order to better understand what is going on in the integration process. But this has come at a cost. Most importantly, the resulting focus on the institutional ways and means and the outcomes of inter-state bargaining has meant that ideas about Europe's future have mostly been treated as reflections of the interests of specific states or institutions, an approach that has led to distorted images of this history.

The present study aims to help counterbalance this situation in the historiography. As such, it joins the growing body of scholarly literature that is introducing new combinations of approaches to the study of European integration and discovering new links in the history and pre-history of European integration. This study seeks to make an important contribution to the existing historiography by integrating three insights from the emerging revisionist literature into a new comprehensive approach.

One new insight derived from the recent revisionist literature is that the governments involved in initiating European integration were unable to control what emerged out of the widely popular idea of European unification. Once the genie was let out of the bottle, European integration took on a life of its own, penetrating domestic politics and causing deep splits within cabinets and parliaments, cutting across conventional political camps and stirring up heated debates between federalists, confederalists, isolationists, nationalists, and so on. The lack of national control over this process of integration led to the formation of unorthodox transnational coalitions, lobbies, and networks. Moreover, the transatlantic and European

---

[62] Wolfram Kaiser and Brigitte Leucht, 'Informal Politics of Integration: Christian Democratic and Transatlantic Networks in the Creation of ECSC Core Europe', *Journal of European Integration History*, 14, 1 (2008), 35–49, and 'Transatlantic Policy Networks in the Creation of the First European Anti-Trust Law: Mediating between American Anti-Trust and German Ordo-Liberalism', in Wolfram Kaiser, Brigitte Leucht, and Morton Rasmussen (eds.), *The History of the European Union: Origins of a Trans- and Supranational Polity 1950–72* (Abingdon: Routledge, 2009), pp. 56–73; Wolfram Kaiser, Brigitte Leucht, and Michael Gehler (eds.), *Transnational Networks in Regional Integration: Governing Europe 1945–83*, Studies in EU Politics Series (Houndmills, Basingstoke: Palgrave Macmillan, 2010).

34   Introduction

negotiations that prepared the ground for the revolutionary first steps of European integration involved both state and non-state actors from the very beginning, which meant that the drafting of plans and the formation of coalitions occurred across national frontiers and that state and non-state institutions worked together. This was, in essence, its own 'polity' in the making[63] – the importance of factoring in the transnational and polity dimensions has been underscored by relatively recent studies of diplomatic history, as well as by research within the neo-functionalist tradition in political science research.[64] Influencing the integration process thus presupposed access to this polity. Moreover, there was a certain degree of 'transnationalisation' of European politics and policies already from the prehistory and the earliest days of European integration. This has not been given sufficient attention in the historiography. This study aims to correct this.

The second new insight is the need to delve deeper into the past to understand the origins of European integration. The state-centric and issue-specific historiography mentioned above impedes efforts to understand transatlantic and trans-European path dependencies, intellectual foundations, policy planning, and issue linkages from a more diachronic perspective. In the rare cases in which these phenomena have been studied over a longer period, the scope has been limited to either intellectual history or institutional path-dependency or issue linkage within and between certain policy domains[65] – of which the latter two typically remain limited to the traditional timeframe of European integration, meaning post-1950 or even post-1990.[66] Obviously, this is a major shortcoming in the existing literature. For instance, because long-term institutional consequences may well have been 'by-products' of decisions taken for short-term reasons inherent in specific issue linkages (of earlier episodes) or spin-offs of older ideas. Three notable, yet specifically focused,

---

[63] Kaiser, Leucht, and Rasmussen (eds.), *The History*; see also Anne Boerger-De Smedt, 'Negotiating the Foundations of European Law, 1950–57: The Legal History of the Treaties of Paris and Rome', *Contemporary European History*, 21, 3 (2012), 339–56.

[64] See, for instance, Weisbrode, *The Atlantic Century*; Mathieu Segers, 'Preparing Europe for the Unforeseen, 1958–63. De Gaulle, Monnet and European Integration beyond the Cold War: From Cooperation to Discord in the Matter of the Future of the EEC', *International History Review*, 24, 2 (2012), 347–70; Arne Niemann, *Explaining Decisions in the European Union* (Cambridge: Cambridge University Press, 2006).

[65] Hewitson and D'Auria (eds.), *Europe in Crisis*; Paul Pierson, 'The Path to European Integration: A Historical Institutionalist Analysis', *Comparative Political Studies*, 29, 2 (1996), 123–63.

[66] Wayne Sandholtz and Alec Stone Sweet (eds.), *European Integration and Supranational Governance* (Oxford: Oxford University Press, 1997); see also Lykke Friis, '"The End of the Beginning" of Eastern Enlargement – Luxembourg Summit and Agenda-Setting', *European Integration Online Papers*, 2, 7 (1998).

exceptions to this state of affairs in the literature are the exemplary overview work by Kenneth Dyson,[67] and the broad general histories of contemporary Europe by David W. Ellwood and Stella Ghervas.[68]

It is essential and urgently needed for historians to go back beyond 1950, beyond 1945, and even beyond the Second World War to the interwar period and the First World War in order to widen their diachronic scope of research.[69] It is telling in this regard that the interlinkage of the process of European integration with the history of decolonisation up till now has been scarcely researched as integral part of European integration,[70] while key powers in the history of European integration, like France and the United Kingdom, were colonial empires at the time and thus preoccupied with the challenges, problems, and (colonial and racial) outlook of empire. Although the 'complex double process of decolonisation, and the building of a new world and European order' only really came to impact European integration as of the mid-1950s during the negotiations on the Rome Treaties – most notably the establishment of the European Economic Community (ECC) – and therefore falls outside the scope of the present study, the dimension of colonial empire is key in understanding the positioning of France and the United Kingdom in matters of post-war world and European order.[71]

In French government circles, for instance, the appeal of a concept like Eurafrique (based on the Franco-African common market) went further than geo-economic benefits. It also alluded to new possibilities to hold the *Union française* (the French empire in Africa) together in post-colonial times by connecting it to schemes of European (market) integration. As such, the concept of Eurafrique could not only open up the resources of the African colonies to Western Europe (widely seen as a matter of necessity in government circles of the West in the 1940s and 1950s),[72] it also could keep alive the (French) ambition of a French-led European power bloc next to and relatively independent of the United States and the Soviet Union.[73]

---

[67] Kenneth Dyson, *Conservative Liberalism, Ordo-Liberalism, and the State. Disciplining Democracy and the Market* (Oxford: Oxford University Press, 2021).

[68] Ellwood, *The Shock*; Stella Ghervas, *Conquering Peace, from the Enlightenment to the European Union* (Cambridge, MA: Harvard University Press, 2021).

[69] Hewitson and D'Auria (eds.), *Europe in Crisis*.

[70] Important exceptions are: Marie-Thérèse Bitsch and Gérard Bossuat (eds.), *L'Europe Unie et l'Afrique* (Brussels: Bruylant, 2006); Peo Hansen and Stefan Jonsson, *Eurafrica. The Untold History of European Integration and Colonialism* (London: Bloomsbury Academic, 2014).

[71] Anne Deighton, 'Brave New World? Brave Old World?', *Contemporary European History*, 28, 1 (2019), 31.

[72] See Segers, *Deutschlands Ringen*, p. 310.

[73] Yves Montarsolo, *L'Eurafrique: contrepoint de l'idée d'Europe. Le cas français de la fin de la deuxième guerre mondiale aux négociations des traités de Rome* (Aix en Provence:

Eventually, the idea of Eurafrique took the institutional form of a European fund and built an essential part of the package of compromises that underpinned the EEC treaty. The final deal on the Eurafrique fund was as follows: of the total of 581 million dollars that would be deposited into the fund, 511 million would be allocated to the French overseas territories. The Netherlands, Belgium, and Italy would receive 35, 30, and 5 million dollars, respectively. Luxembourg and the Federal Republic of Germany (FRG) would get nothing. The FRG would, however, be a net contributor to the fund, paying 200 million dollars.[74]

For the UK, the question of empire was as essential. But it chose a radically different course compared to the French: during the second half of the 1940s the UK decided to exclude itself from a more united Europe because it prioritised its ties to the British Commonwealth (based on Winston Churchill's famous 'Three Circles' party conference speech of 1948).[75]

The 'new Europe' of cooperation and integration was not created after the Second World War; instead, post-war developments were deeply rooted in the inter-war years, if only because it was ultimately the Great War that plunged Europe into a period of seventy-five years of war, unrest, and division that only ended in 1990 with the Treaty on the Final Settlement with Respect to Germany allowing the two German states to reunite (see the Prologue). This study is an effort to reconstruct this fragmented history of the Western world in the twentieth century of which post-war Western Europe was – and still is – an integral part.

The third new insight that has emerged from recent historiography is the conviction that in order to understand how European integration developed the way it did, historians must delve beneath the surface of day-to-day politics, diplomacy, and the development of institutions. On that deeper level, it becomes apparent that European integration was drawn from a relentless 'battle of ideas' over Europe's future. It was not the

---

Publications de l'Université de Provence, 2010); Anne-Isabelle Richard, 'The Limits of Solidarity: Europeanism, Anti-Colonialism and Socialism at the Congress of the Peoples of Europe, Asia and Africa in Puteaux, 1948', *European Review of History*, 21, 4 (2015), 519–37; Hansen and Jonsson, *Eurafrica*, pp. 71–146; Guia Migani, 'Europe, Decolonization and the Challenge of Developing Countries', in Mathieu Segers and Steven van Hecke (eds.), *The Cambridge History of the European Union*, vol. I (Cambridge: Cambridge University Press, 2023), ch. 3.

[74] Segers, *The Netherlands*, p. 136.
[75] Deighton, 'Brave New World?', 33. As Deighton stresses, this speech of Churchill 'set the framework for strategic thinking about the place of the UK in the world ... The UK, Churchill argued, was the only country at the centre of the three great interlocking circles of Europe, the United States and the Empire-Commonwealth. A British commitment to one circle alone would destroy the whole structure of the free world and its ability to fight communism. The argument was that the UK's international leadership could only be guaranteed by sustaining its pivotal balance between the three circles.'

result of a preconceived plan but the product of never-ending battles over such plans – battles that were fuelled by ideas and ideals that crossed national frontiers as well as political parties. This ceaseless competition between different concepts, plans, and blueprints is key to understanding what happened and why. And yet the unsuccessful grand designs are largely neglected in the depictions that dominate the historiography. This study hopes to paint a more complete picture of these ideational dynamics and struggles than is usually presented in scholarly works on European integration.

Another way in which this study aims to enrich the existing literature on European integration is the addition of two innovative conceptual elements. The first element is the introduction of the more psychological sphere of emotions – both at the personal level and the collective level – into the study of the historical phenomena and events surrounding European integration. This book has tried to dig beyond the political rhetoric, the policy plans, the international negotiations, and the formation of coalitions to examine the mood of the time. Also analysing the (collective) emotions at play enables one to understand how Europe was able to transition from its intoxication with ideology in the first four decades of the twentieth century to a more positive, can-do attitude following the Second World War and how this played out in the realms of politics, policies, and society.

The second element, which is closely related to the first, is a key aspect of the early stages of European integration that is often overlooked: the role of the leading ecclesiastics. Representatives from most of Europe's mainstream churches actively participated in many of the public, political, and diplomatic discussions about Europe's future – discussions in which spiritual notions of a common destiny and a collective mission were explicitly mentioned. The active involvement of the church was made possible through the trans-European and transatlantic networks of Christian Democracy, which became a vital political force in all free societies of post-war Europe. In particular, those churches that were more ecumenically oriented considered 'Europe' a proper topic for their sermons. Political, technocratic, and clerical networks overlapped in an emerging world of transatlantic cooperation that fostered friendships and partnerships that were pivotal in the post-war West. Many architects of the post-war West became acquainted with each other and with each others' ideas in a desire to interconnect their work – from pulpit to bully pulpit – in a cogent pan-Western and pan-European societal road map and narrative.

Surprisingly, these vast networks have yet to be studied in a systematic fashion, as the interconnectedness of the world of the churches and the process of (re)building Europe has been largely ignored in historiography.[76] The World Council of Churches is a prime example: its intimate relationship with European integration has remained uncharted until now.[77] Notable exceptions to this situation are the recent monographs by Giuliana Chamedes and Sarah Shortall. Both books have served as rich sources of information and inspiration for the present study.[78]

1.4 Outline of the Book

The remainder of this book is divided into two parts. The first part is devoted to the pre-war, war, and direct post-war years of 1937 to 1947. The second part assesses the run-up to and take-off in European integration within the context of the emerging Cold War. It covers the years 1947 to 1951, including the launch of the European Coal and Steel Community. Together, these two parts tell the story of the making of the Europe of European integration. Central to this story are the movers and shakers in the politics and policies of the developing transatlantic community that would lead and steer the post-war West.

Western Europe after the Second World War was fundamentally different from anything it had been before. This could be seen as a historical vindication in that Europe was given a 'second chance' to take up the grand challenge of creating a new, transatlantic 'framework for human society'. The leading designers and planners of the post-war West were able not only to learn from their own sobering experiences of the 1920s and 1930s, but they also had recourse to the preparatory work carried out by the bureaus of the League of Nations and its academic

---

[76] The mainstream historiography of European integration has referenced very few relevant church-historical sources such as Katharina Kunter, '"Zurück nach Europa". Kirchen und Christen als politische und gesellschaftliche Faktoren im demokratischen Transformationsprozess Tschechiens', *Kirchliche Zeitgeschichte*, 19, 1 (2006), 145–58; Beatrice de Graaf, *Über die Mauer. Die Kirchen, die Friedensbewegung und die DDR* (Münster: Agenda Verlag, 2007); Hans-Ulrich Reuter, 'Die Europäische Ökumenische Kommission für Kirche und Gesellschaft (EECCS) als Beispiel für das Engagement des Protestantismus auf europäischer Ebene', dissertation Universität Hannover, Stuttgart/Hannover, 2002; Jurjen A. Zeilstra, *European Unity in Ecumenical Thinking, 1937–1948* (Zoetermeer: Boekencentrum, 1995); Lucian N. Leustean, *The Ecumenical Movement and the Making of the European Community* (Oxford: Oxford University Press, 2014); Sergei A. Mudrov, 'European Integration and the Churches', in Mathieu Segers and Steven van Hecke (eds.), *The Cambridge History of the European Union*, vol. I (Cambridge: Cambridge University Press, 2023), ch. 26.

[77] See Wolfram Kaiser, *Christian Democracy and the Origins of the European Union* (Cambridge: Cambridge University Press, 2007).

[78] Giuliana Chamedes, *A Twentieth-Century Crusade. The Vatican's Battle to Remake Christian Europe* (Cambridge, MA: Harvard University Press, 2019); Sarah Shortall, *Soldiers of God in a Secular World. Catholic Theology and Twentieth-Century French Politics* (Cambridge, MA: Harvard University Press, 2021).

and non-governmental partners. The moribund committees and bureaus of the League – which found themselves increasingly orphaned in a Europe under the spell of fascism, nationalism, and Nazism – formed a breeding ground for what would turn out to be an 'epistemic community in the making'. Indeed, with the benefit of hindsight, the broad, loose, and diverse community of internationally oriented and universalistic inspired people, scattered over and around the League's committees and secretariats, can be seen to have been a kind of 'training centre' for the post-war years of reconstruction.[79] It was here that thinking was focused on practical and implementable plans. And, what was more, this community was pro-Western *avant la lettre*, before the unfolding of the Cold War. Lippmann's prediction back in 1919 – that 'a new Europe will emerge from this war ... the only question is whether it will be organized at Paris or disorganized from Moscow' – rang increasingly true as the 1940s progressed, albeit with a delay of almost three decades.[80]

Moreover, the building blocks were there for Paris to fashion a 'new Europe'. In inter-war France, the preparatory work for a 'new framework for human society' had not stood still. On the contrary, the challenge of translating Wilson's universal ideals into practice had been taken up in France by the Republic's most realistic and creative minds, such as René Cassin and Jean Monnet, who helped to establish the institutional and legal structures of human rights and European integration, respectively. They were not alone but rather part of a highly diverse collection of people scattered across the transatlantic community all working on building a 'better world' through planning and practical politics. These people included internationally well-connected planners like Monnet and Cassin; economists, intellectuals, scholars, socialist trade unionists, and other political influencers like John Maynard Keynes, Friedrich Hayek, Walter Lippmann, David Mitrany, John Foster Dulles, James Meade, Lionel Robbins, Barbara Wootton, Louis de Broukère, André Philip, Karl Polanyi, Paul-Henri Spaak, Luigi Einaudi, Raymond Aron, Wilhelm Röpke, Alexander Rüstow, and Ludwig Erhard; diplomats, bureaucrats, businessmen, and policy advisors like Miriam Camps, Paul Hoffman, and Richard Bissel in Washington; Hervé Alphand and Robert Marjolin in Paris; internationally oriented Benelux policymakers such as Hubert Ansiaux, Robert Triffin, and Max Kohnstamm; and German ordoliberals like Alfred Müller-Armack and Walter Eucken. And as this

---

[79] Patel, *The New Deal*, p. 292; Patricia Clavin, *Securing the World Economy: The Reinvention of the League of Nations, 1920–1947* (Oxford: Oxford University Press, 2013).
[80] Lippmann, *The Political Scene*, p. x.

book emphasises, this community also included influential ecclesiastics, especially ecumenical networkers, and lobbyists like Reinhold Niebuhr; WCC President Willem Visser 't Hooft; Dietrich Bonhoeffer of the *Bekennende Kirche* ('Confessing Church'); and William Temple, the Anglican archbishop of York and later Canterbury as well as leading figures in the Catholic resistance and promotors of Catholic social teaching and 'personalism', such as the editors and the entourage of the (clandestine) journal *Témoignage chrétien* and Jacques Maritain. These groups and individuals formed a web through their interpersonal and professional connections. It was through this web that the foundations of post-war Western Europe were built.

Numerous plans for a new and more just world order emerged in this extraordinary time and place – the early post-war years of Western Europe. They were seen as blueprints of hope that were built upon four new precepts for creating a better society, both domestically and internationally. These four precepts sprang from the initial Wilsonian-inspired approaches to the new world order in the context of the harsh realities of the inter-war years.

The first precept was that to preserve 'the independence of the mind', it was necessary to defend 'the individual against the depredations of the state'. Thus, totalitarian regimes like Nazi Germany or Stalinist Russia were defined 'a threat to world peace' and served as examples of what was to be avoided at all costs. In the bleak spring of 1946, in the ruined auditorium of Cologne University, the aged mayor of the city and future chancellor of Western Germany, Konrad Adenauer, would explain 'the deepest lying reasons for our having fallen' by claiming that:

> Our nation has made an idol of the state and raised it onto the altar. The dignity and value of the individual have been sacrificed to this idol. The conviction of the state's omnipotence – that the state and the power assembled in it takes precedence over all other values, including the enduring and eternal values of humanity – rose to dominance in Germany.[81]

This historic fatal mistake was not to be repeated. To shield the free world against this threat, the 'principle of transnational jurisdiction' was indispensable.[82] Or, as Adenauer put it in 1946: 'This conception of the state as the most powerful, indeed as the all-powerful, entity and of the

---

[81] Konrad Adenauer, 'Rede in der Aula der Universität zu Köln', 24 March 1946 (Konrad Adenauer Stiftung), reprinted in English in Mathieu Segers and Yoeri Albrecht (eds.), *Re: Thinking Europe. Thoughts on Europe: Past, Present and Future* (Amsterdam: Amsterdam University Press, 2016), pp. 178–9.
[82] Winter, *Dreams*, ch. 4.

primacy of its rights over the individual's right to dignity and freedom, stands in contradiction with natural law as Christianity understands this.'[83]

The second precept was the pressing need to focus on the social question.[84] This was deemed crucial and entailed more than simply combating hunger and poverty. Social cohesion was needed to buttress individual freedom, capitalism, and democracy so that they would be resilient enough to weather any potential storms of totalitarianism and nationalism. This task of achieving social cohesion went beyond the bounds of the state. Post-war European leaders like Adenauer and Robert Schuman – who were behind the blueprint for the European Coal and Steel Community in 1950 – agreed that for European democracy to endure, it had to be a Christian democracy so as to ensure that both the state and the market would serve the individual and not vice versa. The concept of human rights, according to Schuman, was a Christian one.[85] Modern democracy, including its state planning and market planning, had to include not only 'rationality and scientific progress but also morality, faith, myth, and religion'.[86] The Christian churches thus had a role to play here, albeit one that had to be embedded in the rule of law of a democratic-capitalist welfare republic.[87]

The third precept was the notion that if the planning for social policies were to succeed, it had to be done on an international scale. As Mitrany put it in 1943, 'the more we have of national planning the more we must have international planning'. The new designs for international cooperation revolved around 'completing the state' – first and foremost in the social domain – rather than replacing it.[88] This was in fact a realist approach. A functionalist like Mitrany was not a federalist but a planner of international affairs. His planning was functional in principle, practical, and essentially materially oriented because 'sovereignty cannot in fact be transferred effectively to a formula [or] any grandiose juridical gesture [but] only through a function'. Mitrany was convinced that only 'functional cooperation may be a means of persuading the Powers ultimately to make the wide sacrifices in national sovereignty which the preservation of peace will

---

[83] Adenauer, 'Rede in der Aula der Universität zu Köln'.
[84] See, for instance, Susan Howson and Donald Moggridge (eds.), *The Wartime Diaries of Lionel Robbins & James Meade 1943–45* (New York: St Martin's Press, 1990).
[85] Milward, *The European*, p. 328; Konrad Adenauer, *Erinnerungen 1945–1953* (Stuttgart: DVA, 1963); Segers and Albrecht (eds.), *Re: Thinking Europe*, pp. 31–3 and 177–84; Segers, *The Netherlands*, pp. 77–9.
[86] Rosenboim, *The Emergence*, p. 9.
[87] Philip M. Coupland, 'Western Union, "Spiritual Union", and European Integration, 1948–1951', *Journal of British Studies*, 43 (July 2004), 372–5.
[88] Charles Maier, *In Search of Stability* (Cambridge: Cambridge University Press, 1987), pp. 129 and 140; Mitrany, *A Working*, pp. 29ff; Rosenboim, *The Emergence*, pp. 24 and 35; Segers, 'Eclipsing', 61–4.

demand'. The democratic dynamism needed to pull this off in a politically sound manner worked both ways: 'a gradual transfer of sovereignty from the ruler to the people, the people in their turn gradually entrusting its exercise to a central authority. Therefore, the democratic tests have all along been expressed in a selection of policy and of ultimate control of its execution.' Mitrany stressed that many 'tasks and activities could or should be made matters of common concern' and that doing this was essential, since 'international society' – a prerequisite to winning the peace and forging social cohesion – 'will grow precisely in the measure in which we do join together', through 'the exchange of knowledge and of the fruits of expertise', to which he added: 'Nothing could be more barren and confusing, therefore, than the habit of mind which, in the words of Dr. Reinhold Niebuhr, "thinks that we lack an international government only because no one has conceived a proper blueprint of it. Therefore, they produce such blueprints in great profusion."' (Mitrany, thus principally sat on another end of the intellectual spectrum than those, who he called, 'pure constitutionalists', who – again in Niebuhr's words – 'have a touching faith in the power of a formula over the raw stuff of history'.)[89]

The final precept was that to be truly international in a functionalist sense – that is to say, focused on practical goals of universal ideals in an anti-totalitarian, post-ideological, and feasible manner[90] – the planning of multilateral cooperation had to be regional. More than anyone else, it was the internationally well-connected Monnet who brought functionalist thinking out of its inter-war incubator mode into the practical politics and policies of post-war regional cooperation. During the war, Monnet became a member of the Comité Français de Libération Nationale (1943–4) and worked for the British government on its elaboration of the American Victory Program.[91] For the record, Monnet's intimate knowledge of the Anglo-Saxon world sometimes caused a few raised eyebrows, especially those of General de Gaulle, the leader of the 'Free French' and the first prime minister of post-war France (who, nevertheless, had appointed Monnet to a key position after the war; from 1946, Monnet headed the Commissariat Général de Plan de Modernisation, the influential and powerful unit within the French government apparatus charged with modernising the French economy – a crucial step if France was to once again play its role as a great power).

---

[89] Mitrany, *A Working*, pp. 31, 29, and 115 n. 3; see also Ghervas, *Conquering Peace*, pp. 256–7.
[90] Heyde, 'Amerika', 131 and 134; Rosenboim, *The Emergence*, pp. 29 and 34.
[91] Duchêne, *Jean Monnet*, p. 103.

However, the great mission Monnet had established for himself in those years went far beyond Allied planning and restoring French grandeur. He himself described it as 'changing the existing order' in Europe.[92] In his eyes, that could only be achieved by striving for European integration, but one step at a time and *functionally*, through economic cooperation between Western European states per sector. This meant that while Monnet's agenda may have been one of continuity, it was also revolutionary in a key way: the limited functional cooperation had to be anchored in supranational institutions. This was how Monnet proposed to give form to Mitrany's goal 'to complete the state'.

This book traces the story of the inception of European integration. It highlights the crucial plans and blueprints for a new and more just Europe and a better society, as well as their main carriers and promotors. The story is told in two parts covering six episodes.

The first part of the book covers the period from the pre-war years to the early post-war years (1937 to 1947). Within this part the first chapter (chapter 2, 'In Search of a Programme for the West') sets the scene for the history of plan-making and blueprint-drafting in the Western hemisphere before, during, and after the Second World War, in which the United States, the United Kingdom, and France were the leading political and intellectual powers. It delves into four great ideational projects of this period: (1) human rights, (2) the invention of a Christian-inspired liberalism, (3) solving the 'social question', and (4) the why and how of 'mixed economies'. During the period 1937–47, these projects were gradually taken on by the leading politicians, policy-makers, and intellectuals of the 'free world' (of transatlantic cooperation), as they were considered key for the creation of a more stable and just order, both in the national and in the international sphere, than the order that had come about after the First World War. These four projects, moreover, were not only interlinked, but they also shared the overarching outlook of anti-totalitarianism and – in their own way – aimed for what could be called 'ideational reconciliation': the merging of the universal and the personal in the Universal Declaration of Human Rights (UDHR), a transatlantic-inspired ecumene, a combination of the ideologies and economic theories of socialism and liberalism. This produced a myriad of plans and counter-plans for institutional structures, (federal) organisations, and policies for post-war Europe.

The following two chapters reconstruct how the (collective) emotions, the political and economic practices, and the geopolitical and

---

[92] Europe Archive Maastricht, Maastricht, Private Papers Max Kohnstamm, Jean Monnet to René Pleven, 3 September 1950.

societal circumstances of those war times guided Western Europe to a path of deeper international and regional cooperation focused on free trade and valuta convertibility. During exile and occupation, European governments fleshed out plans and schemes for post-war cooperation, first of all in the domains of socio-economic and the financial-economic planning, in greater (practical) detail. These exercises were emotionally charged and driven by the lessons of the post-war period after the First World War and the war against Hitler's Germany – a learning from history in which the churches played a leading role and co-prepared the political ground for the popularity of a new and hugely influential conservative political family in Western Europe: Christian Democracy (chapter 3, 'Re-conceptualising Capitalism and Democracy'). Initially, however, the step from grand designs and lofty models for a post-war Western order that could 'win the peace' to the practices of policies of cooperation was taken via the grand institutional engineering in the Atlantic world, most prominently through the 'system' envisioned in Bretton Woods. However, the original ideas of Bretton Woods soon proved practically unfeasible, which complicated global ambitions as well as the proper build-up of Atlantic-wide institutions – and pushed Western Europe to think and act 'beyond Americanisation' (chapter 4, 'The Great Escape').

Part 2 of the book turns to the period of the take-off of European integration in the context of the emerging Cold War (1947–51). In this period, the Americans, the British, and the Western Europeans get their hands dirty in actions of institution building aimed at making a more stable and just post-war European order, centred around new and deeper forms of European and international cooperation. This part of the book is about the history of 'the making of European integration'. It does this through a reconstruction of the main economic, (geo)political, and ideational forces that enabled European integration to take off as of the spring of 1950. Moreover, this part of the book tries to uncover deeper layers (of psychology and belief) in this history through three crucial sub-histories. The first sub-history traces how the coming about and the workings of the Marshall Plan gradually illuminated an institutional, economic, and political pathway for integration in Western Europe (chapter 5, 'The Marshall Plan: Western Europe as a Unit'). The second sub-history shows how the gradual (self-)outmanoeuvring of the United Kingdom in matters of European cooperation happened to that country and the West, and how this worked as a catalyst for regional European integration and 'the emergence of a continental West' (chapter 6, 'British Preoccupations and Ecumenical Politics'). The third sub-history explains how – against the background of the beginnings of the Cold War and growing British aloofness in European affairs – 'the (West) German re-entry' became the driving force in the process of emerging European integration. This development crystallised first in the OEEC, subsequently through the European Payments Union (EPU), and finally in the launch of the ECSC. This process was not only political and economic in nature, but also to great extent intellectual via the deep influence of (German) ordoliberalism in the politics of the FRG and Christian Democracy in Western Europe (chapter 7, 'Reality Check: The OEEC and "Integration"').

The concluding chapter of the book summarises the main findings of the present study and puts these in the wider conceptual and historiographical framework of this introduction (chapter 8, 'Eclipsing Atlantis'). This concluding chapter goes back to the central question of the present study and shows how and why the developments in the transatlantic management of economic and monetary affairs created decisive political momentum for bold Franco-German (supranational) initiatives in European integration, and which transatlantic and European ideational and emotional undercurrents co-steered this development. It also highlights the increasingly central role of Western Germany in this. Lastly, the epilogue to this book zooms in on a telling and difficult conversation between two highly influential friends in the transatlantic Anglo-Saxon epicentre of this extraordinary period in the history of the West and Europe. In doing so, the epilogue, in a more essayistic way, reflects upon the conclusion of this book.

Part 1

Beyond Americanisation (1937–1947)

2   In Search of a Programme for the West

The new world war of the 1940s confronted European politics for the umpteenth time with a familiar challenge: could a peaceful and stable Europe be established with international help, or would it fall into disarray again as had happened after the First World War? Seen from the West, this question increasingly entailed a choice – just as in 1919 – between, on the one hand, order imposed by Washington, London, and Paris (in that order) and, on the other, disorder spawned by Berlin and Moscow. There were, however, two crucial differences from 1919. First, the West now included an actively engaged United States, a superpower with a political appetite for global leadership. In 1945, US President Truman presided over the greatest military and economic power the world had ever known. As summed up neatly by Melvyn Leffler: US GDP had been increased by 60 per cent during the war, total earnings by 50 per cent. By the end of 1942, the US was producing more arms than all the Axis states combined (in 1943 the US made almost three times more armaments than the Soviet Union). Moreover, the US had two-thirds of the world's gold reserves, three-fourths of its invested capital, half of its shipping vessels, and half of its manufacturing capacity. US GDP was three times that of the Soviet Union, and more than five times that of the United Kingdom. And the US was completing the atomic bomb.[1]

Secondly, Washington had something new to offer this time around: a tangible policy, one that was modelled on the best practices of the New Deal. By the beginning of the 1940s, it had become clear that the New Deal could be seen as a global paradigm of what policy was able to create[2] – a global paradigm of the American can-do mentality. And this policy could be deployed relatively easily in Europe,[3] given the already existing foundation of the Anglo-American partnership that had buttressed the American war effort.

---

[1] Leffler, 'The Emergence', p. 67.   [2] Patel, *The New Deal*, pp. 271–98.
[3] Ellwood, *The Shock*, p. 181.

In 1943, David Mitrany, one of the intellectuals at the forefront of functionalist planning and, what could be called, the policy approach in international relations, explained that the institutions of the New Deal had 'revolutionized the American political system' and that 'in many of its essential aspects – the urgency of material needs, the inadequacy of the old arrangements, the bewilderment in outlook – the situation at the end of the Second World War will resemble that in America in 1933, though on a wider and deeper scale'. This made the functionalist policy approach adopted in the New Deal 'the best, perhaps the only, chance for getting a new international life going'.[4]

Policy has always been associated with rationalism and a problem-solving attitude. It is seen as progressive yet essentially apolitical – and thus allegedly unemotional. This apolitical outlook inherent in policy was especially appealing and comforting in the 1940s, as the brute facts confronting Europeans led to the conviction that politics should not be allowed to run wild again. New bureaucracies and state planning would build a trustworthy fortress against the evils of polarisation and fragmentation, enabling societies to contain their feelings and sentiments by means of reason and moderation. The 'policy approach' offered a form of purifying therapy, after the incomprehensible horrors of war. Moreover, a suchlike approach was by far preferred over radical new political experiments.[5] This 'policy therapy' gained enormous influence, as it was able to offer what was being demanded: political modesty mixed with a convincing rationalism that was strongly driven by a new idealism. It was something new in which to believe.

Nonetheless, many of the policies and societal plans conceived by the functionalists could equally be categorised as plain escapism. The influential economist Joseph Schumpeter, for one, thought so. Schumpeter was a prominent member of the staunchly liberal 'Austrian School' of economics of his time. The Austrian School, which also included well-known economists like Ludwig von Mises and Friedrich Hayek, was renowned for its highly deductive approach to societal problems, as it assumed that all social phenomena were the result of the motivations and actions of individuals. From this perspective, strictly (inductive) empirical approaches were considered inadequate to understand social phenomena. In public debates on societal issues, the Austrians of Schumpeter's time positioned themselves as arch defenders of individual freedom and spontaneous social order, which was best fostered through the competition that was inherent to the market mechanism. Using deductive arguments, they tirelessly showed that this was more vital and

---

[4] Mitrany, *A Working*, pp. 56–7. [5] Maier, *In Search*, pp. 123–9.

'just' than any planned alternative. Coming from this academic background, Schumpeter would continuously warn against a new fatal attraction during the 1940s. He claimed that the overwhelming desire for a post-fascist utopia went hand in hand with an obsession with policy, which offered an alternative that was just as seductive and make-believe as fascism was.[6]

Schumpeter's warnings, however, were largely unnecessary. Right from the beginning, when the first plans for the post-war West were being designed during the war years in sessions of 'purifying policy therapy', the liberal 'counter-planners' were actively involved as rather constructive co-conceivers of these projects. This even included some from the Austrian School who were the most visible public denouncers of socialism as well as Keynesianism, most notably several members of the diverse community of academic neoliberals who founded the Mont Pèlerin Society (MPS) in 1947. Many of them were involved in the active co-designing of post-war socio-economic policy and planning, especially in Western Europe (this has been largely overlooked in the existing Anglo-Saxon historiography).[7]

Among these members were several leading German ordoliberals who became hugely influential in shaping and fine-tuning the blueprints for European integration driven forward by people from outside Germany like Jean Monnet, who was an archetypical planner. During the 1930s and 1940s, distinguished German ordoliberals like Walter Eucken, Alfred

---

[6] Joseph Schumpeter, *Capitalism, Socialism and Democracy* (London: Allen and Unwin, 1981 [1942]), pp. 409–20. According to Schumpeter, this implied that new political and societal fixation on policy and planning would lead to a blind 'march into socialism'. See chapter 6.

[7] Most of the relevant scholarly literature on the history of neoliberalism still heavily leans on the 'clash' between socialism and Keynesianism on the one hand and (neo-)liberalism on the other and/or treats the (neo-)liberal school that was emerging since the 1930s as a 'bastion-phenomenon' or 'intellectual silo' created against the tide of the time, which was predominantly pro-Keynesian, socialist, and pro-planning. This includes the following leading, well-researched, and insightful works: Angus Burgin, *The Great Persuasion. Reinventing Free Markets since the Depression* (Cambridge, MA: Harvard University Press, 2012); Daniel Stedman Jones, *Masters of the Universe. Hayek, Friedman, and the Birth of Neoliberal Politics* (Princeton and Oxford: Princeton University Press, 2012); Nicolas Wapshott, *Keynes–Hayek. The Clash that Defined Modern Economics* (New York and London: Norton, 2011); Janek Wasserman, *The Marginal Revolutionaries. How Austrian Economists Fought the War of Ideas* (New Haven and London: Yale University Press, 2019); and to a certain extent this also includes (albeit it concerns itself with a slightly different theme): Quinn Slobodian, *Globalists. The End of Empire and the Birth of Neoliberalism* (Cambridge, MA: Harvard University Press, 2018). Important exceptions to this trend are Kenneth Dyson, *States, Debt and Power: 'Saints' and 'Sinners' in European History and Integration* (Oxford: Oxford University Press, 2014), and Philip Mirowski and Dieter Plehwe (eds.), *The Road from Mont Pèlerin. The Making of the Neoliberal Thought Collective* (Cambridge, MA: Harvard University Press, 2015), especially the contributions by François Denord and Ralf Ptak.

Müller-Armack, Alexander Rüstow, Wilhelm Röpke, and Ludwig Erhard all embarked on a feverish quest for a liberal international order that went beyond the laissez-faire approach, as the latter had proved incapable of coping with economic depressions or preventing war. When the war ended and the emphasis shifted to 'on-the-job policymaking', however, these German ordoliberals turned out to be even more unorthodox and pragmatic in combining insights and instruments from planning and even socialism than the leading figures of the Austrian School like Hayek and Robbins had been in their explorations of federalist models for a new democratic international order in the late 1930s and early 1940s (see section 2.4).

Within the ranks of the neoliberals, however, there were few who saw or knew about this pragmatic intellectual openness. Indeed, in public appearances and in their many publications, neoliberals took pains to keep under cover this intellectual rapprochement between their philosophy on the one hand and socialist-inspired planning and welfare policy on the other through their highly stylised 'either–or' rhetoric of anti-Keynesianism and Cold War anti-socialism. Crucially, the intellectual black-and-white elegance of the stylised contradictions between neoliberalism and Keynesian socialism has obscured much of the key role that German ordoliberalism – the more hybrid strand within Mont Pélerin liberalism – has played in what was to become a megaproject of planning: the post-war uniting of Western Europe. Indeed, from its very inception, European integration has been modelled along the lines of the ordoliberal concept of the 'social market economy' (*soziale Marktwirtschaft*), which would become the distant *finalité politique* for the Europe of European integration.[8] Up to the present day, the social market economy remains the guiding concept for the European Union. Its origins are in the late 1940s, when this concept was engineered on a West European scale by German ordoliberals in the wake of the Marshall Plan and the West German *Wirtschaftswunder* (see chapters 7 and 8).

Be that as it may, post-war European integration was preceded by years of failed attempts to achieve a deeper and more durable form of cooperation in Western Europe. Much of this failure can be ascribed to the unresolved German question hovering over post-war Europe. It was only with the largely American-inspired Western European approach within the context of the Cold War that this European conundrum was reassessed in such a way that it did not hinder but instead induced

---

[8] See the preamble of the Treaty on European Union (the 'Lisbon Treaty'); see also Brigitte Leucht and Katja Seidel, 'Du Traité de Paris au règlement 17/1962: ruptures et continuités dans la politique européenne de concurrence, 1950–1962', *Histoire, économie et société*, 27, 1 (2008), 35–46.

Western European cooperation and even integration. What was essential in this shift towards the creation of the Federal Republic of Germany as an integral part of post-war Western Europe and a vital partner in its establishment was the implementation of the new creed of mainly German liberal and ordoliberal policy engineers. Part 2 of this book is devoted to that episode in history, which only really began in 1948 after the Marshall Plan was up and running and the Cold War had unequivocally started defining post-war politics and geopolitics.

This was not the whole story, however. There was a second key factor holding back the projects of Western European integration during the 1940s. Before the ordoliberal architects and engineers could really test and refine their blueprints of the post-war institutions of Western multilateralism and European integration, it was essential not only to deal with the German question in an innovative way (by creating the FRG) but also to address another uneasy paradox in the Western approach towards international organisation. This was the contradiction that the transatlantic endeavours into unchartered territories of international organisation were underpinned by universal ideals linked to the so-called One World approach towards international cooperation that in effect ruled out projects of regional cooperation such as Western European integration. The One World principle seriously limited steps to design the post-war West until well into the 1940s. In other words, as a matter of principle, any serious liberal experiment in capitalism and democracy had to promote universal ideals. This made the whole idea of Western European integration highly problematic.

During the early 1940s, it became horrifyingly clear that while the world could become many things, becoming 'one' was not among the options. The bitter lesson of the early 1940s, moreover, was that utopias based on a world-spanning federation were either futile or dangerous.[9] Last but not least, it was becoming painfully clear that the sovereignty of the nation-state, together with the interlinked concept of 'balance of power' (which still served as a 'substitute for thought'), was an essential part of the problem. After all, balance-of-power rules and practices – principally unchanged since the eighteenth century – were never written down nor had been a solution to war (quite the contrary).[10] This was borne out almost every day in the nitty-gritty of the post-war day-to-day Western politics of cooperation, which remained severely hindered by

---

[9] See, for instance, DNA, 2.21.408 (Nalatenschap Beyen), B.2.2.2.1, 71, 'Anglo-American Relations in the Post-War World', Yale Institute of International Studies, May 1943; Steehouder, 'Constructing Europe'.

[10] Paul Schroeder, *The Transformation of European Politics, 1763–1848* (Oxford: Clarendon Press, 1994), pp. 6ff; De Graaf, *Fighting Terror*.

national preoccupations, despite the rhetoric on the historic need for truly transnational approaches. These realities made it already obvious during the war that fighting totalitarianism and putting the individual above the state came with the mind-cracking question of how to match these liberal assignments with a Europe rife with national interests that would probably outlive the war. In other words, the key question was how the free world could be/remain a real and credible alternative, while the traditional European system of nation-states was there to stay at the same time.

In the context of the war against Hitler's Germany and its fascist partners, any realistic liberal assignment could not be about a utopian idea of one united world of peacefully cooperating nations, nor could it be about abstract, all-explanatory economic systems or theories. It was all about the forging of an American-led wartime alliance – a united West – and, within its specific institutional structures, the re-emphasis of human rights. It was a re-emphasis because this liberal assignment harked back to the failure of the world to set things right after the First World War. This task of prioritising human rights was left to Western Europe and more specifically to France.

2.1 Human Rights: A Franco-American Grand Narrative

It was during the International Exposition of Art and Technology in Modern Life held in the Palais de Chaillot in Paris from 25 May to 25 November 1937 that Pablo Picasso's *Guernica* was first displayed. And it was on the steps of this same Parisian palais some ten years later – on 9 December 1948 – that the French-Jewish jurist René Cassin (1887–1976) signed the Universal Declaration of Human Rights in the name of France. In so doing, Cassin enabled humanity to rise from the ashes of its fierce and lethal struggle against totalitarianism, fascism, and war. On that historic occasion, he proclaimed the following:

> Our declaration is the most vigorous, the most essential of protests of humanity against the atrocities and oppression which millions of human beings suffered throughout the centuries and more particularly during and between the two last world wars. In the midst of this torment, heads of state, Pres. Roosevelt, Pres. Benes, both no longer with us, proclaimed the meaning of this crusade, and in the name of France, then imprisoned and gagged, I had the honour at the international conference held at St James Park on 24 Sept 1941, to join my voice to theirs, in order to proclaim that the practical consecration of the essential liberties of all men is indispensable to the establishment of a real international peace.[11]

---

[11] Cassin cited in Winter, *Dreams*, ch. 4. This statement by Cassin, by the way, contained an apt summary of the 'spiritual' Western Union which the British minister of foreign affairs, Ernest Bevin, tried to launch that same year (see chapters 6 and 7).

This boiled down to a renewal of 'the French Republican tradition', which had been severely 'injured' by the war and the Vichy regime but which still remained 'intact'.[12] Cassin himself phrased this as follows: all of Vichy's reforms 'are built on sand, as long as the enemy occupies our country'.[13] During the war, the proto-government of the 'Free French' – established under the leadership of General Charles de Gaulle in London after the fall of France in May 1940 – embodied this continuity (see chapter 3).

From a more general European perspective, this moral and historical anchoring of France's adherence to the UDHR, so aptly and lucidly summarised by Cassin in 1948, reflected the extent to which the postwar European nation-states were institutionally embedded in the wider West, its ideals of freedom, and its practical politics of multilateralism. This wider West was a Christian world, as had been stressed so penetratingly and consistently by leading voices in the Catholic French resistance, such as the US-exiled Thomist philosopher Jacques Maritain and the clandestine journal *Témoignage chrétien*, which was rooted in a trans-European ecumenical network (see further chapter 3). During the war, church voices like these had prepared the ground for a transnational and interconfessional understanding of human rights as a 'spiritual project', which went beyond 'the logic of secular political taxonomies'.[14] As Sarah Shortall has highlighted, Maritain gave a comprehensive summary of this approach in his contribution to the 1947 United Nations Educational, Scientific and Cultural Organisation report on the philosophical grounds for human rights, which was produced in the run-up to the UDHR. In this text, Maritain claimed that 'the declarations of the eighteenth century' ought to be completed 'by a statement of the rights of man, not only as a human and a civic personality, but also as a social personality' – a call that harked back to statements of Maritain from the early 1940s that emphasised 'the social rights of the working person', the need to complement civil and political rights with the right to a fair wage, unemployment benefits, and the right to organise in trade unions.[15] This work by Maritain was a crucial element in the backdrop against which the Vatican, after the war, had been adapting to the 'legal-moral language' of human rights, even up to the point at which the Catholic Church adapted it as its own in the form of 'Christian

---

[12] Jay Winter and Antoine Prost, *René Cassin and Human Rights. From the Great War to the Universal Declaration* (Cambridge: Cambridge University Press, 2013), pp. 85 and 146ff; see also Peter Lindseth, *Power and Legitimacy: Reconciling Europe and the Nation-State* (Oxford: Oxford University Press, 2010).

[13] Cassin cited in Shennan, *Rethinking France*, p. 55.

[14] Shortall, *Soldiers of God*, p. 134.

[15] Maritain quoted in Shortall, *Soldiers of God*, pp. 134–5.

human rights'. Of course, this also was part of the growing partnership between Pope Pius XII and the American government in their increasingly joint (Christian) battle against communism.[16]

It was no coincidence, however, that this reconciliation of state and individual, of moral values and practical policies, came from France and was brought about by Cassin, the father of the UDHR. This megaproject, which more than anything would develop into the soul of the post-war West, did not come as a bolt from the blue – it was the fruit of decades of zealous thinking, drafting, and work. Cassin, who was responsible for the full draft of the UDHR, had been a dedicated delegate to the League of Nations from 1924 to 1938. Having served as a soldier in the First World War, Cassin knew what it was that he was working so hard to achieve. Following the end of that war, he founded the French Federation of Disabled War Veterans. From that base, Cassin developed into a dedicated legal-political advocate for peace and social rights, soon forming the Union Fédérale, a pacifist political organisation for war veterans. During the Second World War, Cassin was at the intellectual epicentre of the Free French government in London promoting French wartime interests by keeping alive France's republican tradition and its universal outlook (see also chapter 3). In 1968, Cassin received the Nobel Peace Prize for his lifetime's work.

Back in 1930, at the Academy of International Law in The Hague, Cassin began outlining his vision of how best to stifle 'the pretensions of state sovereignty': by establishing 'a new system' that juxtaposed the law of domicile with the law of citizenship, arguing that each had 'merit as a basis of political rights' and stressing the non-uniqueness of nationality.[17] According to Cassin, it was jurisprudence that had to follow events and not the other way around. In inter-war Europe, which had fallen under the spell of ideological struggles, it was therefore paramount 'for the pendulum to move back towards the claims of domicile over nationality'. This implied a fundamental 'commitment to internationalism' to protect 'vulnerable minorities stalked by powerful nationalist movements in states worried about their ethnic composition'. He also stressed the need 'to establish the standing of the individual within international law itself'. Cassin's argument was in line with the Declaration of the International Rights of Man adopted by the Institute of International Law in New York in October 1929.

Crucially, Cassin did not believe that nationality had to be abolished as a principle of law but rather that it needed an antidote to prevent it from being taken to the extreme (for example, in the case of totalitarianism). In

---

[16] Chamedes, *A Twentieth-Century Crusade*, pp. 237–41.   [17] Winter, *Dreams*, ch. 4.

his strategy of complementing the state with international institutions in order to improve its functioning – in this case in the domain of justice – Cassin was on the same page conceptually as his compatriot Jean Monnet, the planner and functionalist in the Mitrany tradition.[18] He was also very close intellectually to activist welfare state economists like William Beveridge when it came to postulating the essential 'how' and 'why' of international cooperation between the nation-states of the twentieth century. Another striking resemblance between these men was their deeply felt urge to translate lofty goals into the practice of policy as rigorously as possible yet without neglecting 'constitutional ethos'.[19] The translation of ideals into practical and legal structures was deemed crucial in the effort to safeguard the credibility of those ideals – or, in the phrase often used in those days, 'to win the peace'.

This broad move towards a more functionalist approach in the politics of international cooperation united jurists, policy planners, and economists behind what became a shared liberal assignment for the post-war West. This assignment crystallised in the wider historical context mainly constructed by the Americans during the Second World War, in which the Wilsonian ambition 'to make the world safe for democracy' had not died but had taken on more tangible institutional forms of international organisation. The most notable manifestation of this ambition was probably the post-war construction of an international and European legal order. Indeed, the post-1950 process of European integration and establishment of a 'social market economy' was a constantly evolving component of this process of becoming 'embedded' in the international legal order based on human rights, including social and economic rights. This legal embedding took its cue from the 'Four Freedoms' that President Roosevelt had outlined on 6 January 1941 – freedom of speech, freedom of worship, freedom from want, and freedom from fear – to prepare his country for more involvement in the Second World War, as 'no realistic American can expect from a dictator's peace international generosity, or return of true independence, or world disarmament, or freedom of expression, or freedom of religion – or even good business'.[20] Roosevelt's famous speech embodied the American war spirit of the time. Even those who loathed Roosevelt's New Deal, such as the founder of the *Time* and *Life* magazines Henry Luce,

---

[18] Eric Roussel, *Jean Monnet* (Paris: Fayard, 1996), p. 914.
[19] Lindseth, *Power*; Peter Lindseth, 'Equilibrium, Demoi-cracy, and Delegation in the Crisis of European Integration', *German Law Journal*, 15, 4 (2014), 529–67; Koen van Zon, 'Assembly Required. Institutionalising Representation in the European Communities', Ph.D. thesis, Radboud University, Nijmegen, 2019, pp. 49–50.
[20] Franklin D. Roosevelt, (6 January) 1941, 'The Four Freedoms', in Andrew J. Bacevich (ed.), *Ideas and American Foreign Policy* (Oxford: Oxford University Press, 2018), pp. 230–5.

urged the US government to assume the mantle of world leadership and be 'the powerhouse of the Ideals of Freedom and Justice'. They urged Roosevelt to come to the rescue of the United Kingdom and more generally to create an 'American Century'.[21]

It was shortly after making this famous speech that Roosevelt met secretly with Churchill in August 1941 off the Newfoundland coast to forge an Anglo-American wartime alliance, giving birth to what came to be known as the Atlantic Charter. In the Charter, the United States and the United Kingdom declared that: (1) both countries would not seek territorial gains, (2) territorial adjustments must be in accordance with the wishes of the peoples concerned, (3) all people had a right to self-determination, (4) trade barriers were to be lowered, (5) global economic cooperation and social welfare were to be promoted, (6) the signatories would work towards establishing a world free of want and fear, (7) the signatories would strive for freedom of the seas, and (8) aggressor nations would be disarmed and there would be a common disarmament after the war.[22]

While the Atlantic Charter was significant largely for its securing of American support for the United Kingdom in the war, the concept of the Four Freedoms offered a durable and solid moral foundation on which to base transnational institutions and structures aimed at protecting the fundamental rights of individuals in the nation-states of the West. At the regional level, it also paved the way for new trans-European institutions for the furthering of fundamental rights (initially as an exclusive task of the Council of Europe, founded in 1949,[23] as a follow-up to The Hague Congress of 1948, but later defined in greater detail in the European Convention on Human Rights and Fundamental Freedoms, as drafted in 1950 by the Council of Europe).[24]

All in all, this embedding of Western Europe's future in the moral framework of the promotion of human rights – inspired by universal ideals, put into practice on the European continent, and shouldered by the Americans – was a prerequisite for an additional, and equally demanded, embedding of Western Europe's liberal order in the social

---

[21] Henry Luce, 'The American Century', in Andrew J. Bacevich (ed.), *Ideas and American Foreign Policy* (Oxford: Oxford University Press, 2018), pp. 235–42; Gassert, 'The Spectre', p. 186.
[22] The Atlantic Charter, 14 August 1941.
[23] The Council of Europe was founded on 5 May 1949 by the Treaty of London, when the statute was signed by ten states: Belgium, Denmark, France, Ireland, Italy, Luxembourg, the Netherlands, Norway, Sweden, and the United Kingdom. Turkey and Greece joined three months later. Paul-Henri Spaak was elected as the first president of the assembly.
[24] Ernst Hirsch Ballin, Emina Cerimovic, Huub Dijstelbloem, and Mathieu Segers, *European Variations as a Key to Cooperation* (Cham: Springer, 2020), p. 37; Kjaer, 'The Transnational', 147–8.

security of the (national) welfare state. This further cushioned Western Europe's corrupted and traumatised, yet intact, nation-states. In the same year that Roosevelt proclaimed his Four Freedoms, Luce heralded the 'Atlantic Century', Roosevelt and Churchill signed the Atlantic Charter, and the English Anglican Archbishop William Temple introduced the notion of the welfare state into the British public discourse. All these public statements contrasted a liberal post-war world of democratic welfare states with the German *war*fare state and the bleak outlook of German hegemony over Europe.[25] Alongside the emerging American engagement with the future of the free world, this functioned as a crucial source of inspiration in the drafting of plans for post-war welfare states by the governments in exile in London.[26]

These new twentieth-century ambitions of the Western world were developed in response to both the First and Second World Wars. The victorious (Anglo-Saxon) states of the West were leading this broader transatlantic and trans-European development. Their undertaking was realistic and credible, because it rested on broadly shared geopolitical, political, material, and moral interests in the West, which also enabled the respective national narratives of the West to become part of a shared grand narrative. At the core of this grand narrative was the synthesis of the two great modern democratic traditions of the Enlightenment: the French and American Revolutions of the late eighteenth century.[27] This synthesis came about under the pressure of two world wars over the course of the first half of the twentieth century, and it maintained the duality that characterises both republican traditions: intense patriotism and a ferocious form of universal idealism. This was precisely what Cassin had managed to reconcile in his guiding draft of the UDHR. Translated into universal terms from an emotionally appealing Western – essentially Franco-American – grand narrative, the UDHR embodied a new conception of modernity that was indispensable for creating a pluralist yet coherent democratic order in the post-war world. Indeed, as Jay Winter summarises: 'the only way to restore French political culture, he [René Cassin] believed, was to restore its international standing as the carrier of the central messages of the French Revolution. And at the core of those ideas, at their very heart, was the concept of human rights.'[28]

---

[25] DNA, 2.21.408 (Nalatenschap Beyen), B.2.2.2.1, 71, 'Anglo-American Relations in the Post-War World', Yale Institute of International Studies, May 1943; O'Reilly, 'Genealogies', 69–72 and 74.

[26] See DNA, 2.21.408 (Nalatenschap Beyen), B.2.2.2.1, 71; De Haan, 'The Western', p. 301; Winter and Prost, *René Cassin*, p. 143; Steehouder, 'Constructing Europe', pp. 108–9 and 118.

[27] See O'Reilly, 'Genealogies', 67 and 78.

[28] Winter, *Dreams*, ch. 4; see also Rosenboim, *The Emergence*, p. 8.

It was this same underlying grand narrative that enabled Western Europe to unlock a future of international cooperation, spawning the embryonic beginnings of what would become the Europe of European integration.

2.2 Neoliberalism and Ecumene

What stands out as a major driver in this pre-history of European integration – an idea that was also reflected in the Anglo-American politics of the Atlantic Charter – is the reinvention of free markets following economic depression and war.[29] This was the force of the 'great persuasion' of individual freedom coupled with a reinvention of liberalism in what came to be known as neoliberalism.[30] It was a force that often alluded to a deeper Christian heritage as its ethical basis. Indeed, the 'great persuasion' of neoliberalism existed by the grace of its essentially metaphysical nature. Perhaps that was the crucial thing that made it superior in the longer run to the newest trends in societal engineering such as Marxism and Keynesianism, especially to the presumed amorality of the latter.

Leading continental European economists and social scientists from the ranks of German ordoliberalism such as Wilhelm Röpke and Alfred Müller-Armack (see sections 2.3 and 2.4) believed that Western civilisation had come under severe threat in the years following the First World War and the Great Depression due to the Keynesian policies and obsession with planning that the caprices of capitalism had triggered. From a broader perspective, beyond the angle of economic theory, these neoliberals and ordoliberals addressed the societal crisis of their time roughly along the lines of the cultural pessimism presented by Oswald Spengler in his bestselling monograph *The Decline of the West* at the end of the First World War. Like Spengler, they located the root causes of this crisis in Western civilisation in the modern phenomenon of secularisation. Not surprisingly, the champions of neoliberalism from the old continent had intimate trans-European intellectual ties with 'religious-conservative streams', both of which considered democracy often an issue of secondary importance. Through these networks, neoliberal intellectuals played an active and influential role in Christian Democratic politics in continental Western Europe and in West Germany in particular in the first decade after the Second World War.[31]

What these neoliberals seemed to offer were forms of societal innovation and renewal based on continuity instead of the ground-breaking

---

[29] Romero, *The United States*, ch. 1, section 1.
[30] Burgin, *The Great Persuasion*, pp. 87–123.
[31] Ralf Ptak, 'Neoliberalism in Germany. Revisiting the Ordoliberal Foundation of the Social Market Economy', in Mirowski and Plehwe (eds.), *The Road*, especially pp. 103–5.

state-led experiments that the socialist and communist revolutions were promoting and implementing. Moreover, in their decisive move into active post-war politics, neoliberals could build on a particularly strong and coherent political-intellectual power base that was truly transatlantic in a unique and ecumenical way. This uniqueness largely stemmed from the fact that its key networks had already been created before the Second World War. One such network was the select group of leading transatlantic liberal economists and intellectuals who met for a seminar in Paris at the end of August 1938 to discuss the crisis faced by capitalism and democracy – the renowned Walter Lippmann Colloquium (for more detail, see next section).

But economists were not the only ones in search of practical politics and a concrete programme to battle the totalitarian and nationalist tendencies that infected their times. During a conference in Oxford in July 1937, the precursors of what would later become the World Council of Churches (WCC) decided upon more active measures to pursue their goals of practical politics by promotion an international, largely Protestant-inspired, transatlantic-oriented cooperation among churches. The Oxford meeting became a decisive moment for the ecumenical movement, marking it as an anti-totalitarian force with a special focus on the social question. This can be seen as the logical next step within a broader movement in the Christian churches initiated as far back as 1931 in the social programme set out by Pope Pius XI in his encyclical *Quadragesimo Anno*, which had been entirely devoted to 'the social question'. The encyclical's title referred to the forty years that had passed since Pope Leo XIII's encyclical *Rerum Novarum* which had concentrated 'On the Condition of Workers' (see next section for more details on these encyclicals).

It was telling that prominent figures in the ecumenical movement had already rejected Nazism in the early 1930s – the coming about of this stance and its legacy is fleshed out in detail in the thesis 'European Believers' of Clemens van den Berg. In 1933, Willem Visser 't Hooft, who would become the first secretary-general of the WCC, was the first ecumenist to qualify Nazi Germany as 'totalitarian', a strongly negative term that had been developed by Catholic intellectuals in the late 1920s.[32] He also condemned the *Gleichschaltung* (the Nazification of all cultural institutions) and the acceptance of the 'Aryan paragraph' (excluding Jews and those married to Jews from the clergy), proclaiming that the boycott of the Jews was 'a moral and political mistake'. Visser 't Hooft was not alone. The adoption of the Aryan paragraph by *Reichsbischof* Ludwig Müller

---

[32] Chappel, cited in Van den Berg, 'European Believers', p. 45.

prompted the so-called *Kirchenkampf*, which caused a schism in the *Reich* church and divided the German Protestant churches into two opposing camps: the so-called 'German Christians', generally accepting Müller's authority, and the 'Pastors' Emergency League' (founded in 1933 by Gerhard Jacobi, a Berlin pastor), which in 1934, under the leadership of Martin Niemöller (of the Berlin-Dahlem parish), transformed into the 'Confessing Church' (*Bekennende Kirche*), that defended the autonomy of regional churches against central government interference and started to hold its own synods.[33]

Within the transatlantic world, the ecumenical movement developed into an increasingly prominent voice against Nazism. Because of that, the movement also created something of an international home for the Confessing Church (George Bell would meet the German resisters Bonhoeffer and Hans Schönfeld in Sigtuna in Sweden in the summer of 1942). At the Oxford meeting in July 1937, it was agreed that a World Council of Churches would be established based on a merger of the conference on Faith and Order chaired by Charles Brent of the Episcopal Church of the United States and the conference on Life and Work chaired by Nathan Söderblom of the Lutheran Church of Sweden. These conferences had taken place in Edinburgh and Oxford respectively earlier that year. It had been the latter that had attracted those who wanted to translate their church work into more societally meaningful action. In the 1930s, the Universal Christian Council for Life and Work was one of the younger organisations that had emerged from a broadly shared vision of closer cooperation between the multitude of Christian church denominations in existence; compared to established organisations with a comparable objective, such as the World Student Christian Federation, which started in 1895, the International Missionary Council and the Faith and Order movement, both launched in 1910, and the World Alliance for International Friendship through the churches, which had been established in 1914, Life and Work, founded in 1925, was still a newcomer in the early 1930s. Life and Work was largely the project of one man: Nathan Söderblom, the archbishop of the Lutheran Church in Sweden. Söderblom was convinced that cooperation between churches should not be limited to the level of doctrine (Faith and Order) or mission but should also involve joint ventures in practical issues. The central issue at stake for him was how Christianity could be applied to the social questions of the day.[34]

---

[33] Vissert 't Hooft, cited in Van den Berg, 'European Believers', p. 45.
[34] Van den Berg, 'European Believers', pp. 37, 73–81, and 88–92.

The urgency of this question was emphasised in historically unprecedented ways by the horrors unleashed upon the industrialised societies of the modern world by the Great Depression, with people losing their livelihoods, suicides hitting record highs, and the general feeling being one of pending doom.[35] Life and Work responded to these events by organising study conferences on the issue of unemployment, most notably in Basel in 1932. However, when the final report on the Basel conference was sent to George Bell, the bishop of Chichester who held the rotating presidency of the Life and Work Council, Bell refused to sign the report. He thought it was too one-sided in its focus on economic aspects, arguing that one should first properly rethink one's view of the nature of humanity and society before moving into the realm of economics (note that Bishop Bell was a controversial figure in English cultural life and was denied high promotion because of his critical stand on the bombing of Germany).[36]

Subsequently, Bell stepped up his networking and expanded the Life and Work movement to include prominent figures in the ecumenical movement such as J.H. Oldham, the former missionary in India who represented the International Missionary Council; Visser 't Hooft, the secretary-general of the World Student Christian Federation; and Henry-Louis Henriod and Dietrich Bonhoeffer on behalf of the World Alliance for International Friendship through the churches. Most of them gathered in Oxford in July 1937, with the notable exception of the Germans. Those who attended included high-profile figures like the Swiss theologian Emile Brunner; Max Huber, lawyer, member of the Permanent Court of International Justice in The Hague, and president of the International Committee of the Red Cross; Marc Boegner, president of the Protestant Federation of France; and the influential American lawyer John Foster Dulles, who was well connected in the highest circles of Washington and was at that moment a passionate supporter of world federation. During the conference, Dulles asserted that while the peace treaty of 1919 had indeed given voice to a 'world opinion opposed to the war', it had not changed – 'not by an iota' – 'the underlying conditions which have always made war inevitable'.[37] In his capacity as an associate of the Federal Council of Churches of Christ in America, where he was appointed to head the Commission for a Just and Durable Peace (CJDP) in December 1940,

---

[35] See Hewitson and D'Auria (eds.), *Europe in Crisis*, Introduction.
[36] Van den Berg, 'European Believers', p. 39.
[37] John Foster Dulles, 'The Problem of Peace in a Dynamic World', in *The Universal Church and the World of Nations*, The Official Oxford Conference Books, vol. VII (Chicago: Willet, Clark & Company, 1938), p. 154, cited in Van den Berg, 'European Believers', p. 89.

Dulles would become a key player in connecting the ideas of the ecumenical movement to the practical politics of international cooperation in the post-war West.[38]

Dulles cautiously walked the middle ground between the isolationists and interventionists who were at loggerheads in the United States after the definitive outbreak of the Second World War. The interventionists were led by Reinhold Niebuhr who, together with thirty-one other prominent church leaders, issued a statement in January 1940 calling upon the American government to abandon its neutrality. With conflict and violence ravaging Europe once again, they argued that what was ultimately at stake was not power but freedom. Although Dulles also signed this manifesto, in private he was more reluctant, as he believed intervention alone would be futile without a radical change in what he had called the 'underlying conditions'. And in Dulles's opinion, changing the underlying conditions meant changing the system of international relations and international organisation into one that was more supranational. In this regard, his thoughts echoed those of his long-time friend from France, Jean Monnet.

In general, the men who had gathered in Oxford in 1937 all agreed that the church's vision on transforming human society would only have an impact if the churches were prepared to get political: 'when nation-states encroached on national churches to subdue them to a political ideology, it was up to those same churches to muster the responsibility to resist this and boldly claim their independence'.[39] And this is indeed what they did. Bell's beliefs on this matter, for instance, were so strong that he regularly published opinion pieces in *The Times* or appeared on BBC Radio to share his views with the broader public, both at home and overseas. He was not alone. In the face of the spread of fascism and Nazism, the pressing liberal assignments of the time – to defend the open society against its totalitarian enemies and fight for a more just social order – were taken on in many parts of Europe and the transatlantic world in the late 1930s.

2.3 Tackling the Social Question

In 1936, the world witnessed the birth of a new coalition of fascist nations following an agreement signed between Hitler and Mussolini in October (in a follow-up to the stationing of Nazi troops in the demilitarised

---

[38] Mark G. Toulouse, 'Working toward sohn Foster Dulles and the F.C.C., 1937–1945', *Journal of Prebysterian History*, 61, 4 (1983), 393–410.
[39] Van den Berg, 'European Believers', p. 39.

Rhineland in March) and the signing of the so-called Anti-Comintern Pact between Japan and Germany in November (which Mussolini would join a year later). It was also the year in which the already fragile inter-war European order was rocked by the outbreak of the Spanish Civil War in July after right-wing army officers took up arms against the democratically elected government. In response, France and the United Kingdom opted for non-intervention and a naval blockade of Spain. The United States chose to keep aloof. Mussolini thereupon thanked the democracies for their 'impartiality' by sending planes and troops to aid the fascist coup under the leadership of General Francisco Franco, while the Spanish government turned to Moscow for help.

Against this backdrop, the influential American star journalist Walter Lippmann initially joined the non-intervention choir of the leading Western nations, urging 'a hands-off policy', as even he 'was less interested in saving Spanish democracy than in quarantining the conflict'. Lippmann's assessment of the situation soon started to shift, however. A year later, in 1937, Lippmann returned from a two-month summer trip to Europe 'heavy with pessimism'. He captured his European impressions in October of that year: 'I came away from Europe with the feeling that the Western democracies were amazingly complacent, distracted, easy-going and wishful. If the democracies *are* decadent, then the future of the Old World is once more in the hands of the warrior castes, and the civilian era, which began with the Renaissance, is concluded.' In other words, it was precisely the 'defence of the Atlantic world' – of which Lippmann, like no other, was the ultimate champion – that was more urgent than ever.[40]

In the summer of 1938, Lippmann travelled to Europe again with the main purpose of promoting the French translation of his bestselling book *The Good Society* (retitled *La cité libre*), which argued that democracy and its open society were being dangerously challenged by totalitarianism and ought to be defended by Enlighted (i.e., Western) political willpower to build a better and more just society that tackled the social question. In Paris, Louis Rougier, a French philosopher and professor at the University of Besançon, organised a special event to celebrate and discuss Lippmann's new book. More than an academic, Rougier was a 'political activist' who supported the centre-right in France 'both against radicalism and communism, and against monarchism and fascism'. As such, Rougier was a leading advocate of new liberal solutions for the political-societal crisis that was destabilising France's Third Republic after the collapse of the left-wing Popular Front government of Léon Blum, which had failed to radically transform France's economic structures. Rougier

[40] Steel, *Walter Lippmann*, pp. 337–41.

sought ways to overcome the fierce polarisation of French politics between the left and the right – with communists and fascists as its respective extremes – by reconciling the opponents of the Popular Front experiment with disillusioned socialists based on an up-to-date liberal programme. This reconciliation of left and right, however, came off the ground only in France, where in 1939, the Centre International d'Études pour la Rénovation du Libéralisme was founded, as a follow-up to the Colloque Walter Lippmann. This institute brought together classical liberals, neoliberals, corporatists, and disabused planning advocates, as well as leading businessmen and the leaders of the labour union Confédération Génerale du Travail, among whom, for instance, Christian Pineau (who would be minister of foreign affairs in the left-wing government of Guy Mollet, and in that capacity would negotiate the Treaties of Rome (1957), which established Euratom (the European Atomic Community) and the European Economic Community (EEC), still the foundation of today's EU).

The networker Rougier used his contacts in France, Switzerland, and Austria to organise a five-day 'Walter Lippmann Colloquium' in August 1938 with the aim of initiating 'an international crusade in favour of constructive liberalism' to seek an answer to 'the crisis of capitalism'. Initially, Lippmann had been hesitant to accept the invitation, as he learned that Rougier envisioned prominent roles at the event for André Maurois, the historian and writer and later member of the Free French government who had written the preface to the French edition of Lippmann's book, and Paul Baudouin, the director of the Banque d'Indochine. Both men were financing fascist movements such as the Parti Populaire Français, and Lippmann therefore was reluctant to associate himself with them. Lippmann had met Rougier only once before, in Geneva with the Swiss academic-diplomat William Rappard, Ludwig von Mises, and Wilhelm Röpke. In the end, Lippmann was willing to accept the invite under the precondition that it would be a 'restricted and closed conference'.[41]

In fact, it was Röpke who had written to Lippmann after receiving the proofs of Lippmann's book from Friedrich Hayek in the summer of 1937, suggesting there be 'in one form or another, a discussion among the few people in the world whose thoughts in these matters have reached the necessary degree of maturity'. Others who joined the Walter Lippmann Colloquium were Friedrich Hayek and Ludwig von Mises, a handful of influential French corporate managers (including Ernest Mercier,

---

[41] François Denord, 'French Neoliberalism and Its Divisions. From the Colloque Walter Lippmann to the Fifth Republic', in Mirowski and Plehwe (eds.), *The Road*, p. 47.

director of the French Petroleum Company), the influential French intellectual and publicist Raymond Aron, the senior French civil servant Jacques Rueff (one of the trustees of the Rockefeller Foundation and later a key financial advisor to President de Gaulle) and Robert Marjolin (who later became the general secretary of the Organisation for European Economic Cooperation), and the German ordoliberals Rüstow and of course Röpke, whose research project at that moment was on 'international economic disintegration' and was being funded by the Rockefeller Foundation. The participants were no strangers to each other, for apart from being in regular contact in academic settings, their networks often overlapped. The International Studies Conference, for instance, was a network of international experts focused on the study of international relations that had been meeting annually since 1928. The American coordinating committee for the International Studies Conference was the Council on Foreign Relations, which had Lippmann and John Foster Dulles among its members.[42]

After almost five days of talking and brainstorming, the Walter Lippmann Colloquium had generated much discussion and an abundance of disagreement among its participants – for instance along the obvious fault lines between the industrialists and the economists on issues of monopoly – but not much else. The planned 'international congress in 1939 on the same subjects' – for which the Colloquium was meant to be the steppingstone – never took place.[43] Nonetheless, the historical significance of the Walter Lippmann Colloquium lies in the two fundamental ways in which it shaped the intellectual beginnings of the Europe of European integration after the Second World War.

First, if there was one thing that came to the surface at this curious event in Paris, it was the emergence of a schism within liberalism, a parting of ways between the promotors of a rather traditional form ironically coined 'radical libertarianism' and the proponents of a new liberalism that could be seen as a 'third way' between socialism and laissez-faire economics. The first group of liberals was led by Mises and Hayek of the Austrian School and was firmly embedded in the Anglo-Saxon communities and institutional structures of their academic lives in transatlantic exile (Mises had emigrated to the US while Hayek was living in the UK in the 1930s and 1940s). The second group was inspired by the relatively new school of German ordoliberalism and the crucial role they envisioned for a strong state that could and should guarantee order and intervene in certain situations to ensure an enduringly free society. Crucially, this division – which became apparent at the Colloquium – foreshadowed the parting of ways

---

[42] Slobodian, *Globalists*, pp. 76–7.   [43] Denord, 'French Neoliberalism', pp. 46–9.

between the Anglo-Saxon liberals and the continental European liberals that would manifest itself in the process of European integration and leave the United Kingdom outside the Europe of integration (see Part 2).

Secondly, by bringing leading liberals of the free world together around a coherent set of principles and an agenda for action, albeit prematurely, the Walter Lippmann Colloquium became the inspiration for the founding of the Mont Pèlerin Society in 1947. It was at the Colloquium that a first rough agenda for neoliberalism was sketched out. Boiled down, it consisted of two central principles and one general notion. The first and uncontested principle was that the price mechanism represented the best and only instrument to adequately manage and maximise human expectations in a society based on freedom. The second principle was that a juridical framework installed by the state was indispensable for guaranteeing market order and the working of the price mechanism in the long run. Competition required dedicated institutions: the state must create the juridical framework within which competition is allowed to operate freely. Underneath the surface of this second principle, however, there was a sliding scale of state intervention that stretched from the bare minimum (as espoused by traditional liberalism) to targeted state interventions and welfare state provisions designed to counter socio-economic misfortune (advocated by the more avant-garde liberals, including the German ordoliberals).[44]

The single most important signal emanating from the Colloquium, however, was the general notion that liberalism had to reinvent itself if it were to survive. As Rüstow formulated it during the event: 'the responsibility for the decline of liberalism' had to be sought 'in liberalism itself', and consequently, 'the solution' had to be sought 'in a fundamental renewal of liberalism'. This notion was fully in tune with Lippmann's warning about the 'fallacy of laissez-faire' and his call for a 'renovation of liberalism' (including the idea of welfare state projects paid for by taxing the wealthy). But the general notion as formulated by the participants of the Colloquium went even further, extending to the recognition of what the Austrians, along with Lippmann, identified as the 'illusion of control', that is, the realisation that it was simply impossible to fully steer and tame the economy.[45]

This general notion formed the core of what can be called a renewed liberal conscience. It became the guiding light in liberalism's self-acclaimed struggle 'against planning', which would result in a flurry of counter-planning in the name of a natural and spontaneous economic order. These 'new creed' liberals fought to counteract the crypto-totalitarian

---

[44] See Denord, 'French Neoliberalism', p. 47; Slobodian, *Globalists*, p. 79.
[45] Rüstow cited in Denord, 'French Neoliberalism', p. 49; Slobodian, *Globalists*, pp. 79–80.

societal straitjackets derived from socialism, communism, and Keynesianism and their over-the-top projects of planning (which, paradoxically, would lead these liberals into the realm of planning after all, especially in post-war Western Europe). When Lippmann concluded in *The Good Society* that 'social control can never be regarded as even an approximation to the kind of mastery which men have ascribed to God as the creator and ruler of the universe',[46] he mirrored the standpoint of the upcoming leaders of European liberalism such as the German ordoliberals Röpke and Müller-Armack and the Italian liberal economist Luigi Einaudi (see next chapter) who tried to anchor their analyses and policy prescriptions for a new and more resilient liberal order within a more sociological, metaphysical, and Christian-inspired approach towards pressing societal issues.[47]

As a matter of fact, European neoliberals such as Röpke – a Protestant – and Einaudi were intellectually on the same wavelength as Pope Pius XI in his encyclical *Quadragesimo Anno* that had been devoted to 'the social question'. The title of the encyclical referred to the forty years that had passed since the encyclical *Rerum Novarum*, 'On the Condition of Workers'. According to Pius XI, that 'peerless' encyclical of Pope Leo XIII had 'laid down for all mankind the surest rules to solve aright that difficult problem of human relations called "the social question"'. Leo XII had had 'the great courage to defend the cause of the workers whom the present age had handed over, each alone and defenseless, to the inhumanity of employers and the unbridled greed of competitors'. In this endeavour, Leo had 'sought no help from either Liberalism or Socialism, for the one had proved that it was utterly unable to solve the social problem aright, and the other, proposing a remedy far worse than the evil itself, would have plunged human society into great dangers'. Moreover, as Pius stressed, Leo's encyclical impelling 'peoples themselves to promote a social policy' had unquestionably 'become ... a standard to the nations'. In *Quadragesimo Anno*, Pius now took Leo's work to the next level, referring to still very urgent challenges posed by the 'social question' in the 1930s, and among others pleading for wages 'to be regulated and established' so as to ensure that 'the worker must be paid sufficient to support him and his family' and to strive for 'adjustment to the public economic good' and to prevent 'an excessive lowering of wages, or their increase beyond due measure, [which] causes unemployment': 'this evil ... which has plunged workers into misery and temptations, ruined

---

[46] Lippmann cited in Slobodian, *Globalists*, p. 80.
[47] See Wilhelm Röpke to Benedetto Croce, 7 April 1943, and Wilhelm Röpke to Alfred Müller-Armack, 29 September 1950, Wilhelm Röpke, *Briefe. Der innere Kompass, 1934–1966* (Erlenbach and Zurich: Rentsch, 1976), pp. 67–9.

prosperity of nations, and put into jeopardy the public order, peace, and tranquillity of the whole world'.[48]

All in all, according to the text of *Quadragesimo Anno*, 'two things', for which Leo XIII already had called in *Rerum Novarum*, were especially necessary to re-recognise 'the human dignity' of the worker: 'reform of institutions and correction of morals'. To achieve these goals, 'economic life', 'again', had to be 'subjected to and governed by a true and effective directing principle'. This, however, was something that 'the economic dictatorship which has recently displaced free competition can still less perform', as 'it cannot curb and rule itself'. Hence, 'loftier and nobler principles – social justice and social charity – must, therefore, be sought whereby this dictatorship may be governed firmly and fully'.

After Röpke read the text – some twelve years after it had been published – he wrote to his friend Rüstow about how pleasantly surprised he had been by the content of the encyclical, which, according to him, came down to a programme of 'redemption of the proletariat' coupled with 'the resurrection of a proper market economy, against monopoly and the economy of serving special interests',[49] with special attention to the dimension of international organisation.

International organisation was a matter of central concern in *Quadragesimo Anno*. And there was a reason: 'since the various nations depend on one another in economic matter and need one another's help, they should strive with a united purpose and effort to promote by wisely conceived pacts and institutions a prosperous and happy international cooperation in economic life'. There was, however, more to it. International organisation was also crucial to ward off the dangers inherent in the year-long festering '"capitalist" regime – that has invaded and pervaded the economic and social life ... and is unquestionably impressing on it its advantages, disadvantages and vices' leading to a situation in which 'wealth is concentrated ... [and] an immense power and despotic economic dictatorship is consolidated in the hands of a few'. This concerned 'three kinds of conflict' in particular: 'First, there is the struggle for economic supremacy itself; then there is the bitter fight to gain supremacy over the State in order to use in economic struggles its resources and authority; finally there is conflict between States themselves', not only because of the pursuit of the national interest, but 'also because they seek to decide political controversies that arise among nations through the use of their economic supremacy and strength'. Pius's conclusion was far from

---

[48] *Quadragesimo Anno*, 'On Reconstruction of the Social Order' (1931), sections 2, 10, 22, 27, 70, 71, and 74.
[49] *Quadragesimo Anno*, sections 77, 83, and 88.

comforting for the world he lived in, a world in which 'the ultimate consequences of the individualist spirit in economic life' were that 'free competition has destroyed itself; economic dictatorship has supplanted the free market'. And as to international relations, 'two different streams have issued from the one fountain-head': economic nationalism 'or even economic imperialism', and 'a no less deadly and accursed internationalism of finance or international imperialism whose country is where profit is'.[50]

That Röpke had found nothing on 'corporatism' in the text made the pleasant surprise complete.[51] In short, the encyclical prescribed almost exactly what Rüstow and he were after.[52] The intellectual affinity of these German ordoliberals to Catholic social teaching would bring them close to the continental European political current of Christian Democracy during the immediate post-war years, in particular its trans-European and pro-European integration outlook.[53]

2.4 Mixed Economies and Ordoliberalism

Just as the contraposition between liberalism and socialism (and between neoliberalism and corporatism) – which was often exaggerated by academics, politicians, and public figures – was put aside after the war in the practice of actually building a viable post-war order, the contrived contraposition between liberalism and planning dissipated quickly in the translation of ideals into policy. In order to survive by reinventing itself, liberalism could not afford to ignore the teachings of its intellectual adversaries. The further the neoliberals took their antagonism to planning, the more they had to acknowledge that to actualise their ideals, it was necessary to address what was called 'the social question' in practical terms, that is, through welfare policies instead of leaving the matter to the devastating caprices of laissez-faire economics. The leading economists of the Austrian School at the time, however, such as Schumpeter and Hayek, were extremely reluctant to write openly about this. If they addressed it at all, they did so in very obscure terms. Far more often, they preferred uncomplicated ideational elegance over practicability and real-world problem-solving.

[50] *Quadragesimo Anno*, sections 89, 103, 105, 108, and 109.
[51] Note however that the text of the encyclical made explicit reference to the maxim that 'those in power should be sure that the more perfectly a graduated order is kept among the various associations ["subordinate groups"], in observance of "subsidiary function", the stronger social authority and effectiveness will be the happier and more prosperous the condition of the State' (*Quadragesimo Anno*, section 80).
[52] Wilhelm Röpke to Alexander Rüstow, 13 May 1943, Röpke, *Briefe*, p. 69.
[53] Markus Lingen, 'Müller-Armack, Alfred' (Konrad Adenauer Stiftung: www.kas.de); Wolfgang Tischner, 'Wilhelm Röpke' (Konrad Adenauer Stiftung: www.kas.de).

Nobody exposed this opportunistic weakness in the early Austrian-inspired neoliberalism of the 1930s and 1940s more tirelessly than the British economist and public intellectual Barbara Wootton. Wootton methodically presented her critique in her 1945 book *Freedom under Planning*,[54] a direct riposte to the 1944 bestseller *The Road to Serfdom* written by her friend and colleague Hayek. The socialist-oriented Wootton, who by and large shared Hayek's analysis but had identified specific points in his research she disagreed with, personally wrote the following to Hayek: 'I wanted to point out some of these problems ... but now that you have exaggerated it I must turn against you.'[55]

Wootton abhorred the rather one-dimensional, either–or perspective – either free trade or planning, either freedom or totalitarianism – that Hayek had employed in what would become one of the most influential books of the post-war West. Like Hayek's London School of Economics colleague Karl Mannheim, the Hungarian sociologist who was a lasting inspiration to her, Wootton believed a laissez-faire approach was inherently unable to provide the societal conditions for political liberty, and she thus found fault with Hayek's dogmatic hammering home of free trade as the remedy for everything. Moreover, she shared the conclusion of Keynes, a family friend, that supranational institutions should regulate and steer an increasingly interdependent international economy. Building on an eclectic collection of scholarly and empirical sources ranging from Fabianism and socialism to liberalism and having engaged in practical policies and politics herself – by assisting William Beveridge in piecing together the Beveridge Report on full employment, for example, and by helping H.G. Wells formulate his universal declaration of the 'Rights of Man' – Wootton was convinced of the necessity for social scientists and economists to be pragmatic.

The first domain that called for this pragmatism was the domain of welfare policies which, according to Wootton, should be focused not so much on issues of ownership of industry and production (as Marx had argued) but rather on 'just and equal distributive measures' that have a real impact on the daily lives of ordinary citizens. Furthermore, the socialism she promoted was 'politically acceptable only in a democratic system upholding civil and political liberties as basic values'.[56] Obviously, this vision brought her close to the British Labour Party. From 1938, Wootton joined the political organisation Federal Union, as she felt that

---

[54] Barbara Wootton, *Freedom under Planning* (Chapel Hill: University of North Carolina Press, 1945).
[55] Wootton cited in Wapshott, *Keynes–Hayek*, pp. 202–3.
[56] Or Rosenboim, 'Barbara Wootton, Friedrich Hayek and the Debate on Democratic Federalism in the 1940s', *International History Review*, 36, 5 (2014), 894–900.

the acute social and economic problems of her time could no longer be solved nationally but instead required a transnational approach of some sort. What she missed in the federal movement of those days, however, was an 'actual blueprint applicable to the complex economic world' as she put it in 1939. This was what she worked on, also inspired by what she called 'the New Deal experience'.[57]

The Federal Union was founded in 1938 when Oxford and Cambridge graduates Charles Kimber, Derek Rawnsley, and Patrick Ransome, concerned about the looming possibility of war, started a petition to create a world federation to ward off global conflict.[58] The movement received support from an impressive number of leading British politicians, intellectuals, and opinion makers including Ernest Bevin, William Beveridge, and the archbishop of York, and the well-known and well-connected economists Lionel Robbins, James Meade, and Hayek. By June 1940, the Federal Union had over 12,000 members in over 250 local branches and had founded the Federal Union Research Institute to provide scholarly grounding for their arguments. It also launched its own news outlet and grew into a political force to reckon with, wielding real influence up to the level of the prime minister. Shortly after its foundation, Wootton became a leading member of the Federal Union.

Robbins, Beveridge, Hayek, and Wootton travelled to Paris in April 1940 – two months before France's capitulation to Nazi Germany – to try to bring the ideas of European economic federalism to the next level. The endeavour ended without a successful outcome, as too many entrenched differences of opinion – especially on free trade, the planning of social welfare, and the governance code of a federal economic authority – meant that the participants were unable to get beyond a general call emphasising the importance of federation. As a second-best alternative, Wootton turned to backing Keynes's plan for a global bank to be known as the International Clearing Union with its own international currency, the bancor. This would be part of the British input to the 1944 Bretton Woods Conference (officially called the United Nations Monetary and Financial Conference). In her view, this offered a clear blueprint for supranational economic regulation and planning. What it lacked, however, was a clear social component.[59]

After the trip to Paris, Hayek concluded that establishing a world economic federation was a pipe dream and thus retreated from playing an active role in the Federal Union. From this point on, he refrained from

---

[57] Wootton cited in Rosenboim, 'Barbara Wootton', 898 and 899.
[58] Andrea Bosco, *June 1940, Great Britain and the First Attempt to Build a European Union* (Newcastle upon Tyne: Cambridge Scholars Publishing, 2016), pp. 2–3.
[59] Rosenboim, 'Barbara Wootton', 907 and 910.

exploring the possibilities of economic planning, as planning inherently meant limiting liberty and thus was, in his view, a form of totalitarianism that spelled the beginning of the end of Western civilisation, which had liberalism at its core. In other words, from 1940 onwards, Hayek definitively sided with the general conclusion of that other Paris event – the 1938 Walter Lippmann Colloquium – which had endorsed the price mechanism and market competition. He thereby abandoned the call for economic federation issued by the Federal Union and no longer partnered with Wootton and other pro-federal economists and social scientists but exclusively sided with his fellow neoliberals, with whom he would establish the Mont Pèlerin Society in 1947.

A key intellectual force that was present at both the Walter Lippmann Colloquium and the birth of the Mont Pèlerin Society was German ordoliberalism, which was most prominently represented by Wilhelm Röpke. This well-connected Swiss-based economist from Lower Saxony was the international mouthpiece for the German defenders of free enterprise who tirelessly worked on blueprints of legal frameworks designed to guarantee respect for property and the law, protect free competition, and encourage monetary prudence. They were convinced that only a free market and the process of price correction through deflation could lead the way to a new and stable – and more self-organised – order. At that moment in European history, their mission often seemed at odds with the predominantly Keynesian interventionist policies of planning, government lending, and price fixing.

German ordoliberals thought along the same lines as their kindred spirits from the Austrian School when it came to their aversion to what they labelled the new 'proletarianisation' of the masses, which they saw unfolding because of Keynesian welfare politics. Just like the Austrians, the ordoliberals 'identified the welfare state as an expression of proletarianized social structure' and warned against the emergence of a 'government by the masses that demand welfare protection and employment guarantees'. This was a sign of what they called a 'weak state', which they felt had to be avoided. In the ordoliberal view, a weak state and socio-economic chaos caused by class conflict were two sides of the same coin. To the German ordoliberals, the solution was obvious: a strong state. According to their vision of 'state-centric neoliberalism', economic freedom was 'ordered freedom' and was indispensable for creating a truly free market. A strong state was 'the political form' of a free market. Only through free markets – through competition, entrepreneurship, and enterprise – could a realistic route towards 'dissolving entrenched social relations' be built, the issue at the top of the ordoliberal societal agenda.

To be sure, there was more to ordoliberalism than markets alone. In terms of economic solutions to societal problems, the ordoliberal route lay somewhere in between the Keynesian welfare state (an expression of 'mass emotion and mass passion') on the one hand and laissez-faire liberalism – a 'superstitious belief' that ignored the social consequences of capitalism – on the other. The best possible social policy according to ordoliberals was sustained economic growth. And this was where the responsibility lay with the state. Ordoliberals believed the state ought to be the 'organiser of market liberty', but crucially, they felt the state should do so in a depoliticised way. This depoliticised policymaking is *the* distinctive feature of the ordoliberal strong state. Although this clearly set them apart from Keynesianism because, as one ordoliberal put it, 'for the sake of market liberty we reject the socialisation of the state, and demand the "etatisation" of society',[60] it did bring them close to the planners of policy. This was despite the utter aversion of ordoliberals like Röpke to the 'eternal Saint-Simonism' of these 'collectivist society-engineers' whom they suspected of trying to realise a *Zivilisationshölle* (civilisation hell) characterised by a total 'instrumentalising' and 'functionalising' of people.[61]

Despite this antagonism between the German ordoliberals and the so-called planners, it was inevitable that the two camps would end up working together. After all, no matter how different their philosophical outlook might have been, from the moment they gained real influence in post-war politics and policies, it was clear that they would meet on the common ground of apolitical and policy-oriented approaches to tackle the societal challenges of the time. Moreover, the ordoliberal conviction that the state was the only credible 'organiser of market liberty' evolved into the post-war ordoliberal ambition to create what Alfred Müller-Armack described as a 'social market economy' in West Germany. Indeed, Müller-Armack's description continues to fire up the European imagination to the present day, as it clearly sets apart the 'European way of life' from the harsher Anglo-Saxon versions of the contemporary experiment with capitalism and democracy.

Seen from this longer historical perspective, the German ordoliberals had tapped into the zeitgeist of post-war Western Europe and were offering what substantial parts of the societies of Europe, politically traumatised as they were, demanded and longed for. Their apolitical

---

[60] Werner Bonefeld, 'Freedom and the Strong State: On German Ordoliberalism', *New Political Economy*, 17, 5 (2012), 633–45; Sara Warneke, *Die euroäische Wirtschaftsintegration aus der Perspektive Wilhelm Röpkes* (Stuttgart: Lucius & Lucius, 2013), pp. 16–35; Wilhelm Röpke, *Civitas humana. Grundfragen der Gesellschafts- und Wirtschaftsreform* (Bern and Stuttgart: Paul Haupt, 1979 [1944]), pp. 69–88.

[61] Röpke, *Civitas*, pp. 136–7.

'liberal interventionism' focused neither on revolution nor on *ancien régime* but on an active role for the state in devising a more responsible and humane society[62] rooted in religiously inspired conservatism. This agenda of social-liberal adaptation – by adding the prefix 'social' to 'market economy' – soon allowed them to move into key positions as co-designers of post-war Western Europe. Although the Austrian School still set the tone during the immediate post-war years, once the Federal Republic of Germany was established in 1949, the ordoliberals' practical and political influence in Western Europe began to outshine that of the Americans, the Keynesians, and the Austrians.

In summary, while the Keynesian planners and the neoliberals (together with the ordoliberals) remained *intellectually* far apart, in *practice* they increasingly joined forces in the post-war challenge of building a better and more stable world order. This seemingly improbable collaboration evolved in ways that people like Wootton could not have foreseen. To begin with, inside most Western diplomatic circles it had become clear already during the war that a world federation was not only impossible but also undesirable (in June 1943, the 'Advisory Committee on Postwar Foreign Policy' to the US government concluded that a European order of nation-states (separate from the UN) was to be preferred over the creation of a united and independent post-war Europe).[63] In parallel with this realisation came a convergence in views that would lead to the compromise of 'mixed economies' – that is, free markets combined with the international and supranational coordination of trade and monetary policies. Historians often ignore the key roles played by German ordoliberals and the Christian church in this process of convergence – most notably the ecumenical movement and the transatlantic study committees it inspired, such as the Commission to Study the Bases of a Just and Durable Peace under the chairmanship of Dulles. Cutting across political and ideological lines as well as national borders, the ordoliberals and the church succeeded in bringing together the nations of the Western world to pursue a moral and practical, policy-oriented agenda of peaceful and democratic cooperation that would ultimately result in the process of European integration. Much of the thinking and preparatory work for this post-war endeavour was conducted during the war years by a unique network – built up in exile – of government officials and an inner circle of planners.

---

[62] Mirowski and Plehwe (eds.), *The Road*, p. 12; Bonefeld, 'Freedom', 645.
[63] Heyde, 'Amerika', 126ff.

3 Re-conceptualising Capitalism and Democracy

The international congress envisioned by the participants of the Walter Lippmann Colloquium never took place. Nonetheless, in the wake of the Colloquium there had been a rather lively correspondence between some of the participants. In September 1938, for example, Wilhelm Röpke and Alexander Rüstow sent a memorandum to Lippmann outlining their 'synthetic interpretation of current economic problems, including radical dissatisfaction and unrest of the labouring classes, economic instability and international economic disintegration', which was eagerly distributed by Lippmann among members of his circle and the Rockefeller Foundation. In a letter to the organiser of the Colloquium, Louis Rougier, Lippmann confided that he aimed 'to meet regularly and begin to develop a centre for the study of liberalism'.[1] Referred to as 'the Group', Lippmann and his like-minded colleagues decided to focus on 'the problem of organizing a federal union in Europe and the American relationship to such a union'.[2]

On the other side of the Atlantic, Rougier tried to keep alive the spirit of the Colloquium by organising two symposia, the first of which took place in July 1939 and dealt with the 'economic, political and spiritual status of tomorrow's Europe', a theme that was very much in vogue at the time. The second symposium was devoted to the topical issue of 'the economic conditions of a future federation of England and France',[3] a plan that was being actively explored in both countries. But the clear signs of impending war meant that Rougier was quickly losing leverage within pro-liberalism circles in Europe. Moreover, the window of opportunity within which neoliberalism could appeal to France's ruling elites as a reconciliatory force was rapidly shutting in the face of the grim reality of the geopolitical situation, which fragmented French liberals into different camps on a continuum that ran between the extremes of anti-German to pro-Nazi stances.

---

[1] Craufurd D. Goodwin, *Walter Lippmann. Public Economist* (Cambridge, MA: Harvard University Press, 2014), p. 258.
[2] Goodwin, *Walter Lippmann*, pp. 255–60.
[3] Rougier to Lippmann cited in Denord, 'French Neoliberalism', p. 47.

Around the time of the Munich Agreement of 30 September 1938 and the Phoney War that followed it, the revolutionary idea of a world federation – as actively promoted by Federal Union – began to develop in unforeseen directions. Although the trip to Paris in April 1940 by leading intellectual figureheads of Federal Union, including Barbara Wootton and Friedrich Hayek, had ended in disappointment due to the profound differences in opinion among the participants, the idea of federation was now being channelled into the more opportune Franco-British variant. In this context, the initiative shifted from the academics to those active in diplomacy, in particular the Frenchman Jean Monnet.

Monnet had been appointed by the French prime minister, Édouard Daladier, who was realistic and cynical about the Munich Agreement, to secretly arrange for France to acquire American aeroplanes directly via President Roosevelt. Daladier had been brought into contact with Monnet by the American ambassador to Paris, William Bullit, who was an intimate friend of Monnet and close to Roosevelt and Monnet's former League of Nations colleague Pierre Comert. Monnet's mission – which was shrouded in secrecy due to the restraints placed on Roosevelt because of the US Neutrality Act – was relatively successful. The real value of this undertaking, however, lay in the direct contact Monnet had established with the American president. On the day of France and Britain's declaration of war against Nazi Germany (3 September 1939), Monnet cabled to Daladier that it was no longer wise to continue his mission, as 'the programme to be put to the American President after the Neutrality Act has been repealed, but not before, ... must be achieved by Franco-British effort, as is plain from the conversations I had with Mr Roosevelt'. The last thing the American president needed at that moment was for European countries to openly compete for American support.[4] Monnet was exactly the right envoy to help piece together this 'Franco-British effort'.

By this point, Monnet could already boast of a long career in bringing about international cooperation. From 1919 to 1923, he had been deputy secretary-general of the League of Nations. His transatlantic network was unrivalled and was full of trustworthy and upcoming stars of American foreign policy like John Foster Dulles (with whom he also maintained a close business relationship), Dean Acheson, Douglas Dillon, George Ball, and McGeorge Bundy. He could count among his friends such influential people as the journalist Shepard Stone, who would become the director of the Ford Foundation in the 1950s,[5] and David Bruce, the

---

[4] Duchêne, *Jean Monnet*, pp. 64–71.
[5] Mathieu Segers (ed.), *Dagboeken van Max Kohnstamm, September 1957 – Februari 1963* (Amsterdam: Boom, 2011), entry 16 January 1961, pp. 164–5.

head of the European branch of the Office of Strategic Services during the war, who would become a key player in the administration of the Marshall Plan, as well as the American ambassador to France in the crucial years of 1949–52 (and also the man without whom, as Monnet would later write, 'I should never have succeeded in persuading the US Administration' to fund the French reconstruction with the sums they would allocate). Monnet's network, which further expanded during and after the Second World War, was crucial to enabling the decade-long, highly successful endeavour to build 'a unified community' in Western Europe, as Dulles put it in a personal note to Monnet in February 1953.[6]

Monnet led the committee to coordinate joint mobilisation of French–British forces, acting as liaison to President Roosevelt, from whom he received – but did not always follow – secret instructions directly. At the first Anglo-French Supreme War Council in Abbeville on the Somme in September 1939, Daladier had proposed that a 'Frenchman who is a friend of Roosevelt' take charge of joint Allied purchases abroad. Daladier was referring to Monnet, of course, who was immediately dispatched to London where he soon became 'the main fountainhead of the letters, the memoranda, the minutes of official meetings, and notes of informal discussions which from late September to early December marked the erection of a logical and genuinely combined structure of economic planning'. It was against this backdrop that the idea of an Anglo-French union was floated in London, with Prime Minister Chamberlain and Foreign Secretary Halifax alluding to an Anglo-French federation as a basis for a European federation in diplomat circles and in public in early 1940.[7]

On the other side of the Channel, however, the French were preoccupied with something completely different: their own survival as a nation. In the ominous months of the Phoney War, Frenchmen increasingly began to realise that even if France were spared the ordeal of a takeover by Germany, the country still needed 'to be saved from itself' – that is, 'we not only have to save France today; we shall have to rebuild her tomorrow', as the Catholic intellectual P.H. Simon put it. It was clear that France had to be reinvented, and one way to do this was economic planning. Hence, France began to plan its post-war economy already before the war had started. Before long, however, the country was invaded by Nazi Germany, leading to the definitive fall of France within six weeks.

Meanwhile, in London, Monnet was at the centre of a secret project aimed at winning over the British war cabinet to an Anglo-French union.

---

[6] Jean Monnet, *Memoirs* (New York: Doubleday, 1978), pp. 207, 379, and 464.
[7] Hancock and Gowing cited in Duchêne, *Jean Monnet*, pp. 71 and 76–7.

The idea was that since the current degree of Franco-British cooperation had failed to ward off the Nazis in France, the collaboration had to be taken to a more profound level. To do this, he closely collaborated with Sir Robert Vansittart, the senior British diplomat and cabinet attendee, and René Pleven, a prominent member of the Free French movement. The initial idea concentrated on a 'dramatic call for unity' that would lead to a joint war cabinet, mixed sessions of both countries' parliaments, and the promise of a common plan for reconstruction (in later versions, a customs union and common currency were added). On 16 June 1940, Prime Minister Churchill – who was clearly unenthusiastic about the whole idea – gave in to a majority of his cabinet (which included Neville Chamberlain, Clement Attlee, and Ernest Bevin) on the issue of the Anglo-French union, and the plan was redrafted as a declaration and proposed to the French government. This also had seemed to have the full backing of De Gaulle, who was at the time under secretary of state for national defence and war and was present in London that day to join a meeting between Churchill and Monnet on the Anglo-French union where he sided with Churchill in questioning whether the plan was compatible with the military realities on the ground.[8]

In France, the government's reaction to Britain's proposal for an Anglo-French union was one of disbelief: from his beleaguered position, Prime Minister Paul Reynaud simply could not believe the message that was coming from London that Sunday afternoon, particularly after repeated instances of help offered too little too late in the Anglo-French partnership. Reynaud wanted reassurance from Churchill in person, but this took time. The whole situation was illustrative of the poor communication between the two countries: under the chaotic circumstances of the war, the dramatic move from London had come too late to be of significance. Moreover, this 'epoch-making idea' and 'historic document', as John Colville described it in a detailed report of the episode in his diary,[9] became bogged down by the practicalities of military cooperation, in particular the French demand that the British air force be stationed in France and the British insistence on keeping their planes. In a special cabinet meeting convened in Bordeaux, an exhausted Reynaud failed to convince the 'armistice faction' within the cabinet to fight on. Led by Marshal Philippe Pétain, the First World War hero who ended up collaborating with Hitler's Germany, this faction characterised the offer from London as 'sleeping with a corpse'. After the cabinet meeting, Reynaud resigned as prime minister, allowing Pétain to take over the reins and arrange an armistice with Germany.[10]

[8] Duchêne, *Jean Monnet*, pp. 77–8.
[9] John Colville, *The Fringes of Power. Downing Street Diaries 1939–1955* (London: Hodder and Stoughton, 1985), entry Sunday, 16 June 1940, pp. 158–61; Bosco, *June 1940*.
[10] Duchêne, *Jean Monnet*, pp. 77–8.

3.1 Fighting the Ghosts of 'Après-Guerre'

In mid-June 1940, De Gaulle, who had fought the Germans in the weeks before and who categorically rejected compromise with Hitler, flew to London. On 18 June, he addressed his countrymen over the radio in what would become a historical broadcast. He took direct aim at Pétain and declared: 'The flame of French resistance must not be extinguished and will not be extinguished.' On 28 June, De Gaulle was publicly recognised by the British government as 'leader of all the Free French wherever they might be', an extraordinary move that Churchill himself insisted on.[11] In November 1942, the Allied forces landed in the French territories in Northern Africa governed by the Vichy regime (Operation Torch). The successful invasion took place under leadership of the American general, Dwight Eisenhower. Subsequently, President Roosevelt – ignoring De Gaulle and the Free French (also fighting the Nazis and Vichy in Northern Africa) – installed General Henri Giraud as the head of the French army in Africa based in Algiers and sent Monnet to the scene as a 'special envoy of the American President' to 'format' Giraud into 'the standards of democracy'. Soon after his arrival, however, Monnet sided with De Gaulle and became member of his Comité Français de Libération Nationale ('French Committee of National Liberation').[12] This would lead to a first successful cooperation between De Gaulle and Monnet (and paved the way for Monnet's role as head of the Commissariat Général du Plan de Modernisation, the powerful unit within the post-war French government apparatus charged with modernising the French economy, which was started by De Gaulle as first post-war prime minister of the French Fourth Republic).

The division of France into two rival camps – the Vichy regime versus the Free French – left French neoliberalism dead in the water, as the original group of French neoliberals broke off into a minority faction that teamed up with the Resistance (including Raymond Aron and Robert Marjolin) while a majority faction joined the Vichy government, sometimes in influential positions (note, however, that Louis Rougier remained hesitant for a while, because he tried to engineer a secret agreement between Pétain and Churchill; eventually, from a marginalised position at the New York School for Social

---

[11] Mark Mazower, 'The Man Who Was France', *New York Review of Books*, 16 January (2020), 45–8.
[12] Gérard Bossuat, 'Jean Monnet, 1943–1946, l'urgence et l'avenir', in Gérard Bossuat (ed.), *Jean Monnet et l'économie* (Brussels, etc.: Peter Lang, 2018), pp. 77–8.

Research, he sided with Vichy).[13] But there was another side to this story, too. The war also functioned as a catalyst for radical schemes of reform of the French economy. Such schemes came from both the 'Free French' camp and the Vichy regime.

In terms of thinking about the post-war order, the immediate consequence of France's defeat was the emergence of a 'political atmosphere highly conducive of the rhetoric of renewal' and radical reform, driven by a desire for a complete break with the pre-war status quo among members of the Resistance and Vichy supporters alike. Continuing the old ways of the French Third Republic of the inter-war years was not an option. This was simply drawing 'the lessons of the battles we have lost', as Pétain put it on 20 June 1940. At that point, Pétain was still preaching what was pronounced the Vichy regime's 'National Revolution' (which had also been accepted by the Catholic Church), but this endeavour soon turned sour also because it anticipated a German victory in the world war. Consequently, the centre of gravity in thinking and designing post-war France slowly and surely shifted beyond the borders of the country to the organisation of the Free French in exile located in London and Algiers. There, the anti-Vichy forces were determined not to repeat the failures of the first 'après-guerre' and feverishly engaged in the challenge to win the war without 'losing the peace once again'.[14]

Not losing the peace after the war was a transnational concern that preoccupied the Allied powers, members of the Resistance, anti-war forces, and all governments-in-exile of Europe.[15] As such, it also encapsulated a quest for a collective commitment to the rebuilding of Europe. Crucially, this quest for new national and international 'myths' to mobilise Europe's traumatised citizens in favour of a new and radical commitment to winning the peace cross-cut nation-states, political camps, and religions, and from 1942 concentrated on the American–British facilitated network of governments-in-exile.

The search for new myths was in tune with the assignment at the heart of the new endeavours of liberalism. To ensure public engagement and to rejuvenate democracy, it was deemed essential to shift the focus from politics (and ideology) to policies (and experiment): finding practical solutions to social problems and as such to organise democratic advocacy from below. If they were to be successful and sustainable, new approaches to societal order had to prioritise experiment over system. From this perspective, Roosevelt's New Deal was the ideal example, given that it

---

[13] Denord, 'French Neoliberalism', p. 51; Shennan, *Rethinking France*, pp. 4–5.
[14] Luc-André Brunet, *Forging Europe: Industrial Organisation in France, 1940–1952* (London: Palgrave Macmillan, 2017), p. 115; Shennan, *Rethinking France*, pp. 8–10.
[15] See Steehouder, 'Constructing Europe', p. 74.

was a societal experiment rather than an all-encompassing ideology. Or, as Walter Lippmann put it regarding the New Deal in 1935 (before he turned against the project's collectivism and interest politics): 'Clear doctrine and rigid purposes that apply to a whole nation have to be paid for; their price is the suppression of individuality and the regimentation of opinion ... It is better to move irresponsibly but with the minds of the people participating, than to impose grandiose logical patterns of conduct upon them and compel them to obey.'[16]

This lesson of the inter-war years, along with the emphasis on social justice, guided the creation of the post-war order in Europe. In post-war Western Europe, experimenting with capitalism and democracy became more important than grand schemes advocating systemic change, pushing the latter firmly into the background of contemporary history. Indeed, the great nineteenth-century ideologies of socialism and liberalism were mixed and blended and watered down in the social experiments of the welfare state, which focused on policies and their new 'myths' of feasibility and freedom. The backdrop of the emerging Cold War only solidified political and public support for this approach. The 'mixed economy' approach – which in many ways was the practical translation of the mixing of the ideologies of democracy and capitalism – united socialists, social democrats, Christian Democrats, liberals of all hues, and the church in a programme of international cooperation, free elections, the rule of law, human rights, capitalist economic growth, and social justice.

But there also is a deeper layer to this rather practical history of the emergence of the 'mixed economy' in France and Western Europe. The determination not to repeat the failures of the first 'après-guerre' not only energised a new creed of transnational policymakers in the Mitrany tradition, like Jean Monnet and Robert Marjolin, it also – via 'the minds of the people' – empowered transformative forces in the church. In France, this especially concerned the putting into action of 'ecclesial personalism' by the Catholic anti-fascist resistance against Nazism and the Vichy regime, which challenged the anti-individualist 'spiritual revolution' declared by Pétain.

In the context of harshening censorship, the leading voices of this (Jesuit) resistance assembled under the flag of the clandestine journal *Témoignage chrétien*, which informed the French people about the Nazi crimes in Europe and the 'Christian duty' to resist this. Crucially, *Témoignage chrétien* was 'an ecumenical as well as transnational enterprise'. As Sarah Shortall has shown: 'The editors compiled testimony

---

[16] Lippmann cited in Barry D. Riccio, *Walter Lippmann. Odyssey of a Liberal* (New Brunswick and London: Transaction, 1994), p. 105.

from popes and from Catholic bishops across Europe, but also from Protestant leaders, in order to counteract official propaganda and demonstrate that Nazism and Christianity were fundamentally irreconcilable.' The journal included statements by church leaders outside France, for instance from the German, Dutch, Polish, Greek, Norwegian, and Belgian churches. Protestant contributors to the journal included the influential Swiss theologian Karl Barth and Marc Boegner, the leader of the French Protestant community. Furthermore, the editors emphasised that their endeavour was a spiritual one, and thus not a political undertaking. Indeed, 'to combat Nazi and Vichy ideology, they deployed the "weapons of the spirit"', as Shortall has put it, quoting the journal.[17] Their writings reflected the ethics of their conscience and struggles in their soul.

A prominent intellectual inspiration of this 'personalism' was the French Thomist philosopher Jacques Maritain, the author of the influential book *Integral Humanism* (1936), who had invoked the 'distinction between the "person" and the "individual"' to distinguish his defence 'of personal freedom from the abstract individualism of liberal theory' – the former considered humans as 'both spiritual and social beings embedded in multiple overlapping communities (family, nation, church, etc.)', while the latter defined the individual as in essence 'interchangeable'. Stressing the Thomist principle of subsidiarity (which would become a key concept in the intellectual underpinning of European integration), Maritain promoted a vital civil society 'independent of the state', allowing for 'the greatest autonomy possible' for communities or 'societies of individuals' within a 'decentralised, pluralist polity'. His commitment to personal freedom, spontaneous social order, and pluralism led Maritain to call for a society and political model that would protect the human against 'both liberalism and totalitarian collectivism'. Moreover, this would inspire Maritain's intellectual shift towards democracy, human rights, and European unity in the 1940s (see chapter 2),[18] and as such would position him as the key intellectual leader in the build-up of post-war Christian Democracy.[19] Correspondingly, within the circles of *Témoignage chrétien* Nazism and communism were understood as ideological spin-offs of derailed liberalism – indeed, a conviction that would carry the highly popular conservatism of post-war Christian Democracy.

---

[17] Shortall, *Soldiers of God*, pp. 88–9 and 110–11.

[18] Walter Lipgens and Wilfried Loth (eds.), *Documents on the History of European Integration*, vol. III (Berlin: De Gruyter, 1988), pp. 445 and 471. I am grateful to Professor Madelena Meyer Resende for this reference: Madalena Meyer Resende, 'The Catholic Narrative of European Integration', in Mathieu Segers and Steven van Hecke, *The Cambridge History of the European Union*, vol. I (Cambridge: Cambridge University Press, 2023), ch. 25.

[19] Shortall, *Soldiers of God*, pp. 68–9 and 83–4.

3.2 'The Irrepressible Supremacy of Ideas'

In July 1940, the prominent Italian economist Luigi Einaudi published a remarkable article entitled 'The Nature of a World Peace' in the *Annals of the American Academy of Political and Social Science*. In this very short piece, Einaudi claimed that the war in Europe was 'not an economic or a political or a social war'. No, this new war was 'a religious war ... a clash of life ideals'. Hence, a durable peace would only be possible 'after the crushing defeat of one of the two opposing religious deals'. According to Einaudi, there would be 'two ways' open to the future 'victor': either to 'unify Europe' under 'one ruler, one law, one religion' or to 'unify Europe on a federal plan'. The first way left room for more liberal variations through voluntary limitations to 'absolute rule' by the victor if unification were pursued 'only in the political and economic fields ... leaving men free to believe, as in the old Roman Empire, in their respective national gods ... and to speak in their native languages ... and to follow their native traditions'. The latter – the federal Europe – was the 'ideal' preferred by Einaudi. However, this preferred option would also be 'a much more difficult enterprise', as it would require 'the unification of spirits without recourse to the suppression of unbelievers'. Consequently, the only way to realise this in practice was to let it flow from 'the belief of the victor in self-rule, his respect for dissentient opinions, and his confidence in the law-abiding conduct of dissentient minorities'. Einaudi was all too aware, however, that 'in the Europe of today these are more hopes than realities'. Yet what was also a certainty to him was that 'in our age of railways, sea and air navigation, telegraphs, telephones, and other communications, the anachronistic sovereign state must go'. According to Einaudi, the war was 'hastening the disappearance' of the state 'whose sovereignty is absolute and complete in itself', which represented 'a fiction'.[20]

When Einaudi published this piece, he was already in his mid-sixties and unchallenged in his status as a leading liberal Italian economist, economic historian, and political figure. He had taught public finance at the University of Turin for decades and had been the editor of the influential journal *La Riforma Sociale* during the inter-war years. In these capacities he had fought relentlessly against monopolies, protectionism, and the abuse of government power. When *La Riforma Sociale* was closed by the fascist regime in 1935, Einaudi had shifted his scholarly focus to the history of economics and economic policies, founding the

---

[20] Luigi Einaudi, 'The Nature of a World Peace', in Domenico da Empoli, Corrado Malandrino, and Valerio Zanone (eds.), *Luigi Einaudi. Selected Political Essays*, vol. III (Houndmills, Basingstoke: Palgrave Macmillan, 2014 [1940]), pp. 93–4.

Rivista di Storia Economica in 1936. Yet his academic work remained directly linked to the pressing practical economic problems of his time. Already a prominent voice in Italian politics and society after the First World War, Einaudi was nominated as senator of the Kingdom of Italy directly after the First World War in 1919. This partial move into politics had further strengthened the link between academia and the practical challenges of politics and policies in his work, even though as a liberal anti-fascist politician he had been gradually relegated to an isolated position from the mid-1920s during the Mussolini regime. Despite this, Einaudi was and remained a very productive writer and commentator for Italian newspapers such as *La Stampa* and *Il Corriere della Sera* during the inter-war and war years as well as a valued contributor to liberal international journals, most notably *The Economist* (from 1908 to 1946).

Together with the famous philosopher Benedetto Croce, who was nominated sixteen times for the Nobel Prize in Literature, Einaudi stood at the cradle of post-war Italian liberalism. Their long-running 'debate' on freedom between 1928 and 1941 – waged in academic publications – did much to shape post-war liberal thinking in Italy. For Einaudi's part, this debate reflected a constant quest to translate liberal political ideals and freedoms into practical policies for a functioning and just free market economy. Croce chose to highlight the eternal ethical and transcendent working of freedom, 'even in the darkest and grimmest period, vibrating in the lines of poets and breaking through the pages of thinkers, and glowing as a lone and proud flame in some men who cannot be coalesced into the world that surrounds them'. Indeed, 'if Croce's liberalism offered Italians a beam shining into the long night of negated and repressed freedom, Einaudi's liberalism showed them the way to the reconstruction of an Italy that was to regain freedom'. In his analysis of the endemic problems of capitalism and democracy, Einaudi consistently emphasised the urgent parallel need for a renewal of the state *and* alongside that the creation of supranational organisations (through which the state could be revitalised) to overcome the fatal problems of international anarchy. After the war, Einaudi served as governor of the Italian central bank (between 1945 and 1948) and, during the crucial years of 1947 and 1948, as deputy prime minister and minister of the budget – implementing the resolutely Austrian-School-inspired Einaudi Plan to stabilise the lira. In doing so, Einaudi took a typical Austrian-inspired austerity and staunchly anti-totalitarian approach in line with the 'Concluding Remarks' he had made in his capacity as governor of the Bank of Italy:

[The Italians] must not expect the lira to be saved by any Messiah or by any would-be thaumaturgus, even if he were in charge of the management of the money. They must not believe that salvation can come from anybody else but themselves... All that is needed is an act of willpower: the determination to waive all superfluous expenses... and the determination to bear all the necessary tax burdens.[21]

In 1948, Einaudi became president of Italy, a job he would continue to do until 1955.[22] When Einaudi addressed the Italian Constituent Assembly on 29 July 1947 as deputy prime minister in the fourth successive Italian government under the Christian Democrat Alcide de Gasperi, he elaborated upon his short American publication written seven years earlier. He stressed that 'the First World War was fought in vain, because it offered no solution to the European problem'. The 'deadly myth' of the 'absolute sovereignty of states', which was 'the true generator of wars', lay at the very basis of what Einaudi identified as 'the truth of the matter' in contemporary European history: that it was 'not true that the two great world wars arose from financial causes'. Instead, these wars had been 'civil wars, or indeed wars of religion'. But compared to 1940, Einaudi now put his analysis in a more philosophical, religious framework, stressing that the two wars only 'seemingly' had been 'wars between states and peoples'. On a deeper level, these two wars had 'displayed one fundamental characteristic that distinguishes them from the overwhelming majority of past conflicts': they had been 'fought within ourselves... Satan and God battled with each other in our souls, in our families, and our cities... on all sides, there were clashes between those who treasured freedom' – 'the Christian ideal of free individual improvement and the individual elevation of each man towards God' – 'and those ready to serve obsequiously'. Einaudi then concluded with a 'loud and clear' statement:

We will succeed in saving ourselves from the third world war only if we act in favour of the salvation and unification of Europe [by embracing] the undying idea of voluntary cooperation for the common good... Only by becoming flag-bearers, in the world-wide arena, of the need to replace the sword of Satan by the sword of God will we succeed in reconquering the lost primacy.

What he meant by 'the lost primacy' was not 'economic primacy' but spiritual primacy, because the former 'always follows on, as the humble

---

[21] Luigi Einaudi, 'The Concluding Remarks of the Governor of the Bank of Italy for the year 1946', in Luca Einaudi, Riccardo Faucci, and Roberto Marchionatti (eds.), *Luigi Einaudi. Selected Economic Essays*, vol. II (Houndmills, Basingstoke: Palgrave Macmillan, 2006 [1946]), p. 152.

[22] Luca Einaudi, Riccardo Faucci, and Roberto Marchionatti, 'Editors' Introduction', in Einaudi, Faucci, and Marchionatti (eds.), *Luigi Einaudi. Selected Economic Essays*, pp. 1–3, and Domenico da Empoli, Corrado Malandrino, and Valerio Zanone, 'Editors' Introduction', in Da Empoli, Malandrino, and Zanone (eds.), *Luigi Einaudi. Selected Political Essays*, pp. 1–27.

handmaiden' behind the latter. Einaudi's conclusion was that 'the European peoples' must become the advocate of 'a rich variety of lives, freely operating within the framework of a unified European life'.[23]

Einaudi was no liberal dogmatist or ideologue but a true libertarian who argued 'against the pursuit of perfection in economic policy' as well as against 'doctrinaire individuals who have a preconceived view and apply it to every situation'. Instead, he always stressed the need – both in general terms as in tangible issues of financial-economic policy – to combine economic thinking, planning, and modelling with social goals, institutional histories, and a constant awareness of 'the difficulty of change'.[24] In spite of all this nuance and the catastrophes he had lived through, Einaudi never became a cynic or abandoned his ideals. In the final phrases of his speech, Einaudi, in the spirit and style of Romain Rolland, called for action based on 'the irrepressible supremacy of ideas' (rather than force), for 'openly defending our ideals', 'those very ideals which are called the spiritual freedom of mankind, the elevation of every man towards the divine, cooperation among peoples, and the abandonment of useless pomp and circumstance – the very worst of the latter being the calamitous myth of absolute sovereignty'.[25]

3.3 Inventing European Christian Democracy

In 1951, Einaudi would join the Mont Pèlerin Society, along with his German counterpart Ludwig Erhard, who had formally accepted the position of economics minister in the first post-war West German government in September 1949 but had de facto been acting in this capacity already since 1948 (see chapter 7). However, Einaudi and Erhard, those two keybuilders of post-war Western Europe, by then were relatively late to the MPS party.

Alfred Müller-Armack, for example, who had made a name for himself in German academic circles shortly after the war, had been invited to the second general meeting of the MPS back in July 1949, as he was considered a kindred spirit by the leading men of the MPS and 'a personality' who could 'gain an impact among foreign scholars as we aim'.[26]

---

[23] 'The War and European Unity', Speech delivered to the Constituent Assembly in the session of 29 July 1947, in Da Empoli, Malandrino, and Zanone (eds.), *Luigi Einaudi. Selected Political Essays*, pp. 95–102.

[24] Alberto Alesina, 'Introduction to Luigi Einaudi', in Einaudi, Faucci, and Marchionatti (eds.), *Luigi Einaudi. Selected Economic Essays*, p. 18.

[25] Luigi Einaudi, 'The War and European Unity', pp. 95–102.

[26] Stefan Kolev, Nils Goldschmidt, and Jan-Otmar Hesse, 'Walter Eucken's role in the early history of the Mont Pèlerin Society', *Freiburger Diskussionspapiere zur Ordnungsökonomik*, 14, 02 (Freiburg: Institute for Economic Research, 2014), 6.

Müller-Armack was an economist and anthropologist from the University of Münster who became an influential advisor to Erhard at the West German Ministry of Economics. It had been this not very famous and rather modestly libertarian academic from Münsterland who had coined the term *soziale Marktwirtschaft*, 'social market economy',[27] which made his reputation. After publishing a book with this title in 1946, Müller-Armack's gripping tagline immediately became the 'verbal vehicle' that carried the transformation of West Germany into 'a liberal market society'.[28] Moreover, the term aptly and appealingly summarised the central mission of German ordoliberalism: the pursuit of 'economic humanism', which in the words of Wilhelm Röpke could bring about a 'civitas humana'. The goal of economic humanism would be reached via a 'third way' between socialism and liberalism. Indeed, as of 1946, the mission of German ordoliberalism would increasingly and persistently be condensed into the political catchword 'social market economy'.

Müller-Armack's model of a social market economy was based on Irenicism (from the Greek word for 'peace'), an ideology stemming from the Protestant Reformation that strove to resolve theological disagreements by way of consensus. The irenic nature of the social market economy enabled the German ordoliberals to bridge the more traditional, largely anti-capitalist, and religiously inspired ideas on the one hand and the future goals of the modern democratic-capitalist society on the other. This, almost perfectly, mirrored Müller-Armack's idealistic-religious outlook (shaped by a certain melancholy triggered by the phenomenon of secularisation),[29] bestowing it with a topical agenda of societal goals and policy action. Shortly after the war, Müller-Armack became a member of the Christian Democratic Union (CDU), which became the leading political party in post-war West Germany and thrived on ecumenical irenic practices that brought Catholics and Protestants together in a joint Christian political programme. In this way, Müller-Armack completed 'his transition from a fervent supporter of Italian fascism and Nazi Party membership in Germany during the 1930s to a proselytizer of (Protestant) Christianity as a key source for the post-war value orientation'.[30]

---

[27] Today, the concept of 'Social Market Economy' is still at the core of European integration. It figures prominently in the preamble of the 2007 Treaty of Lisbon (see Rutger Claassen, Anna Gerbrandy, Sebastiaan Princen, and Mathieu Segers (eds.), Special Issue: 'Rethinking the European Social Market Economy', *Journal of Common Market Studies*, 57, 1 (2019), 1–182).

[28] Kolev, Goldschmidt, and Hesse, 'Walter Eucken', 6.

[29] Müller-Armack's main scholarly work was a study in religious sociology published in 1948 under the title *Das Jahrhundert ohne God* ('The Century without God').

[30] Ptak, 'Neoliberalism in Germany', p. 116.

According to the history of ordoliberalism, the Protestant Müller-Armack hit upon the idea of a social market economy in the Catholic Herz-Jesu cloister in Vreden-Ellewick where he had taken shelter from the bombings of Münster in 1943. He subsequently wrote the book *Wirtschaftslenkung und Marktwirtschaft* (1946), in which he first developed the concept of social market economy.[31] The origins of this concept reveal its Christian roots as well as its deeply irenic and ecumenical inclination. This characteristic at the very core of its economic thought made 'the tradition of Christian culture ... the lowest common denominator of an ordoliberal system that insisted on a foundation in strong moral standards', as Christian values were deemed indispensable to efforts 'to resist the temptations of planning'. This 'new moral basis for economic action' was considered even more necessary 'both for ordoliberals and other people ... because of their entanglements in the Nazi-regime'.[32] Crucially, these characteristics set ordoliberalism apart from the Austrian School and made German ordoliberalism exceptionally fit for political translation in the sphere of liberal Christian Democratic governance. This explains its huge influence on the successive West German governments of Christian Democrats and Liberals throughout the 1940s, 1950s, and 1960s under the chancellorship of Konrad Adenauer (see chapter 7).

In summary, German ordoliberalism was indeed a policy-oriented economic approach, yet one embedded in a broader Western, ecumenical, societal agenda. However, Germany was just one region and German ordoliberalism merely one associated and applied branch of a globally oriented and Christian mission for the post-war world. For a substantial part, this Christian-driven political agenda had its modern origins in the closing years of the interbellum and the first years of the Second World War. Catholic social teaching – which in its modern form was based on the 'peerless' encyclical of Pope Leo XIII of 1891, entitled *Rerum Novarum* – was a central element in this agenda, as well as a key building block in a European bridge of Christian Democracy in the making that would conceptually connect the progressive forces in the Catholic Church to key German ordoliberals, like Rüstow and Röpke (see section 2.3), and fitted into the multilateral architecture that was emerging in the transatlantic world since the launch of Atlantic Charter and Roosevelt's 'Four Freedoms'.

---

[31] Michael Hochgeschwender and Bernhard Löffler (eds.), *Religion, Moral und Liberaler Markt. Politische Ökonomie und Ethikdebatten vom 18. Jahrhundert bis zur Gegenwart* (Bielefeld: Transcript, 2011), pp. 205n. 1, and 207–8.
[32] Ptak, 'Neoliberalism in Germany', p. 116.

When Roosevelt had outlined the 'Four Freedoms' in his State of the Union speech on 6 January 1941, Pope Pius XII had not much to say, as 'he was unprepared or unwilling to counter either the resurgence of American internationalism or the Nazi New Order'. While many Catholics in Germany and Italy saw this as a sign of his belated yet forthcoming support for Operation Barbarossa (the invasion of the Soviet Union by Nazi Germany in June 1941), the silence of the pope reflected something else: an overture to a re-positioning away from the back-seat role he had initially preferred in matters of international order (after Benedict XV had done the opposite after the First World War, by driving an activistic reactionary-conservative agenda). Things were about to change, albeit neither very soon nor very fast. Central to that change was what Pius XII explained to a flabbergasted Italian ambassador to the Holy See (in the context of the German invasion of the Soviet Union): until Operation Barbarossa Nazi Germany had been the Soviet Union's ally (through the Molotov–Ribbentrop Pact) – implying that the genuine conservative anti-communist force in Europe was the Vatican. This not only was key to the position of the Catholic Church in Europe, but it also signalled that the Vatican might side with the United States (in parallel American diplomacy towards the Holy See was intensified).[33]

During the early 1940s, new left-oriented movements, which had grown stronger after the Spanish Civil War, gained further momentum within the Catholic Church. They assembled on an outspoken agenda of anti-totalitarianism (against both Nazism and communism) that was carried by different staunchly anti-fascist individuals and groups, such as the People and Freedom group (founded by Luigi Sturzo, the Sicilian priest who after the First World War had founded the Italian Christian Democratic Party), the anti-fascist lecture series organised by Maritain – who already in 1940 had pleaded for 'a confederation of European nations' and the 'integration' of 'a federal Germany in a federal Europe'[34] – and other Catholics in New York, at Hunter College, and at the École Libre des Hautes Études, a 'university-in-exile' for French intellectuals – participants in these activities often were close to Catholics in the highest ranks of the Western European exile governments, for instance the Belgian, French, and Polish governments-in-exile in London. This created a branch of 'Catholic internationalists', as Giuliana Chamedes characterises this group, who increasingly dedicated themselves to creating a post-war order built on a threefold base of 'Democracy, regional cooperation, and the creation of a more effective

---

[33] Chamedes, *A Twentieth-Century Crusade*, pp. 215 and 219.
[34] Lipgens and Loth (eds.), *Documents*, vol. III, pp. 445 and 471.

League of Nations' – which, according to them, all went together, and 'all were essential for the creation of a new and peaceful Europe'. These left-leaning Catholic refugees 'were enthusiastic about the Atlantic Charter', including both the promise of the promotion of human rights through international cooperation, and the Anglo-American leadership, that the Charter entailed.[35] Key figures among them, like Maritain for instance, had participated in meetings with the CJDP (led by John Foster Dulles), in which they identified transatlantic common ground for the organisation of European (federal) unity as the international backbone of a post-war European order of peace[36] (note that it has long been assumed that Maritain attended a Protestant ecumenical network like the CJDP, but that this now has been confirmed by new archival findings by Van den Berg).

As of 1942, the pressure on the Vatican to break the policy of silence further increased; governments of countries like the United States, the United Kingdom, Brazil, Uruguay, Belgium, and Poland actively pushed for a clear condemnation of Nazi Germany. But nothing happened, as far as the position of the pope was concerned. In the summer of 1943, a group of prominent and activist Italian Catholics drafted a clandestine text under the title: 'Christian Democracy's Ideas for Reconstruction', co-authored by Alcide de Gasperi (the future leader of the Italian Christian Democratic Party and future prime minister of Italy). At the core of the text, which envisioned a trans-European democratic order, was the idea of a new international organisation that would have to replace the failed League of Nations. In the autumn of 1944, French Catholic activists followed the Italian example and founded their Christian Democratic Party, and within a year the Christian Democratic Union was founded in Germany – in all founding manifestos, the focus was on democracy, (Christian) human rights and social justice, and regional-international cooperation on a (partly) supranational basis.[37]

On Christmas eve 1944, the pope, finally, had something to say. In a radio address, Pius XII observed that in the context of war and horror 'people are at last awakening', as they were adopting 'a new attitude' towards the state and government: 'Taught by bitter experience' they turned against 'dictatorial, unaccountable, and untouchable monopolies of power, and they call for a system of government that is more compatible with the dignity and liberty of citizens'.[38] With the benefit of hindsight, this

[35] Chamedes, *A Twentieth-Century Crusade*, pp. 215–17.
[36] Van den Berg, 'European Believers', especially p. 105.
[37] Chamedes, *A Twentieth-Century Crusade*, pp. 229–31.
[38] Pius XII, 'Sur la démocratie: radio-message au monde', 24 December 1944 as translated in Emile Perreau-Saussine, *Catholicism and Democracy: An Essay in the History of Political*

was the opening move of the Catholic Church to truly reactivate itself internationally through a pro-democracy and human rights programme, seizing the opportunities offered by the booming of popular piety and the unprecedented popularity of the new Christian Democratic parties. The latter force would, rather surprisingly, steer post-war Western European politics towards the religiously inspired centre-right instead of to the left as many had anticipated (and as such would form an effective political bulwark against communism and the (extreme) left, even before the Cold War became a reality)[39] – at the heart of this Christian resurrection in Western Europe was the experiment of ecumene.

3.4 'Voices in the Night'

After the war, Visser 't Hooft, who had participated in both the Oxford and Edinburgh conferences and had facilitated inter-church cooperation from Switzerland during the war, became the linchpin in the post-war establishment of the World Council of Churches. Visser 't Hooft had managed the wartime inter-church cooperation via direct contact with Dulles (in his role as chair of the CJDP) and William Temple, the Anglican archbishop of York (1929–42) and later Canterbury (1942–4) who, in the words of Roosevelt, was 'an ardent advocate of international cooperation based on Christian principles' and as such had 'exerted a profound influence throughout the world'.[40]

In 1948, Visser 't Hooft was appointed the first secretary-general of the WCC, staying on until 1966 when he retired. The position landed him on the cover of *Time* magazine in 1961 under the heading 'World Churchman'. Visser 't Hooft's ecumenical activism found its inspiration in the prominent American theologian Reinhold Niebuhr and the German Lutheran theologian Dietrich Bonhoeffer who was a follower of the well-known Swiss–German theologian Karl Barth, a convinced social democrat and an early opponent of the Nazi regime. During the war, Bonhoeffer was an active member of the so-called 'Freiburg Circles' in which German ordoliberals met secretly in the private spheres of the academic community of the University of Freiburg to brainstorm on the post-Nazi societal order. Bonhoeffer had led one of these circles. He was

---

Thought (Princeton: Princeton University Press, 2012), p. 133. I am grateful to Professor Madelena Meyer Resende for this reference.

[39] Lanting and Palm, 'Change the Heart, and the Work Will Be Changed', 7ff; Chamedes, *A Twentieth-Century Crusade*, pp. 235–7.

[40] Roosevelt cited in A.E. Baker and George Bell, *William Temple and His Message* (London: Penguin, 1946); Willem Visser 't Hooft, *Memoires* (Amsterdam and Brussels: Elsevier, 1971), pp. 140ff.

also active in transatlantic inter-church networks to promote a liberal world order.[41] After having actively resisted the Nazi regime through the anti-Nazi *Bekennende Kirche* ('Confessing Church') and helping Jews to flee to Switzerland, Bonhoeffer was hung in the Flossenbürg concentration camp in the final month of the war. He was thirty-nine years old.

Reinhold Niebuhr, the other luminary guiding Visser 't Hooft, was from the late 1930s one of the most influential messengers of what he himself described as 'a tragic necessity': US involvement in the war in Europe. He established the journal *Christianity and Crisis* to fight the isolationist tendency in American politics and in American churches. In perhaps his most proselytising epigram in favour of the free world ambitions of the United States after the Second World War, Niebuhr wrote: 'Man's capacity for justice makes democracy possible, but man's inclination to injustice makes democracy necessary.' Niebuhr's so-called 'Biblical realism' sketched a path towards more societal harmony and the simultaneous strengthening of social order and individual liberty to be achieved through democracy and the constitutional state. Respect for human dignity and individual freedom was at the core of what he called 'an ethic of progressive justice', and he juxtaposed it with 'a conservatism which defends unjust privileges'.[42]

Niebuhr summarised his thoughts in a booklet titled *The Children of Light and the Children of Darkness. A Vindication of Democracy and a Critique of Its Traditional Defenders*, which was published in 1944 and became a lasting source of inspiration for internationalists and 'Europeans' alike particularly in the post-war decades but also today.[43] In it, Niebuhr managed to balance the nuanced neo-orthodox position of his theologian side and the conservative liberalism of his role as political advisor, which consistently factored in a sympathy for moderate socialism and an eye for the social dimension, most notably through a growing appreciation of the New Deal. Niebuhr was a prolific publicist and became one of the leading thinkers of his generation not only among theologians but among politicians and economists as well. He had been a keynote speaker at the above-mentioned Life and Work conference in Oxford and also spoke at the founding conference of the WCC in Amsterdam in 1948, remaining

---

[41] Visser 't Hooft, *Memoires*, pp. 106 and 150.
[42] Robert McAfee Brown, *The Essential Reinhold Niebuhr* (New Haven and London: Yale University Press, 1986), p. xii–xxii.
[43] Reinhold Niebuhr, *The Children of Light and the Children of Darkness. A Vindication of Democracy and a Critique of Its Traditional Defenders* (London: Nisbet & Co., 1944); Mathieu Segers (ed.), *De Europese dagboeken van Max Kohnstamm. Augustus 1953 – September 1957* (Amsterdam: Boom, 2008), pp. 27ff.

a supporter of the ecumenical cause. In Amsterdam, Niebuhr signalled the need for exploring a middle ground between laissez-faire, Austrian-inspired neoliberalism on the one hand and neo-Marxism on the other by posing the rhetorical question: 'Must we not say to the rich and secure classes of society that their vaunted devotion to the laws and structures of society which guarantees their privileges is tainted with self-interest?'[44]

The social dimension was also the main concern of the Freiburg Circles' secret work on 'a new liberal' (or 'neoliberal') order combining neoclassical economic theory with policies of state intervention. The Freiburg Circles originated from the *Freiburger Konzil*, which had been established at an informal meeting among academic staff of the University of Freiburg in reaction to the Nazi pogrom of *Kristallnacht* in 1938. This created 'an ordoliberal nucleus', which ensured the continuation of their work during the Nazi era (while left-wing oppositional economists had either fled the country or were eliminated by the regime).[45] Within the *Konzil* – which included historians, theologians, jurists, and both Protestant and Catholic Church ministers – ordoliberal economists and lawyers such as Walter Eucken and Franz Böhm played a key role. Within the Freiburg Circles, Protestants of various denominations had a stronger representation, but prominent Catholics such as Wendelin Rauch (who was appointed archbishop of Freiburg in 1948) were also included. The members of the *Konzil* were bound by Christian belief and often were active in two other 'religiously motivated working groups whose memberships overlapped': the *Bonhoeffer Kreis* (see further below) and the *Arbeitsgemeinschaft Erwin von Beckerath*, a Germany-wide group that originated from the *Arbeitsgemeinschaft Volkswirtschaftslehre* ('Working Committee Political Economy') within the (Nazi) *Akademie für Deutsches Recht* ('Academy for German Law') in Munich. All three working groups had ties to the Confessing Church, a resistance

---

[44] McAfee Brown, *The Essential*, p. xvi–xx.
[45] Ptak, 'Neoliberalism in Germany', p. 119. Ptak further notes that 'supporting the ordoliberals' effort in Germany were neoliberal exiles who had secured powerful academic positions in the UK (Hayek), the US (Karl Brandt, Gottfried Harberler) and Switzerland (Röpke). The involvement of prominent ordoliberals (such as Eucken) in the post-1942 oppositional activities of national conservative forces provided legitimacy for the cadres, despite their considerable roles in economic policymaking during the Nazi era (as they had as unambiguously opposed the Nazis before and after 1933 (when parliamentarian democracy and labour movement opposition were eliminated), and before and after 1938 (when the pogroms started), or even not at all). It was the Cold War constellation, however, that cleared the way for the prevailing one-sided representation of ordoliberal opposition to Nazi rulers: nearly everyone was welcome in the alliance against the widely perceived communist threat.' In this, the ordoliberal circle 'could also take advantage of the reputations of the "documented emigrants" Röpke and Rüstow' (Ptak, 'Neoliberalism in Germany', pp. 117–21).

movement within the Evangelical Church. Together, these Freiburg Circles would provide 'the platform for the renaissance of liberal political and economic thinking in post-war Germany'.[46] By rethinking the socio-economic order under the conditions of capitalism and democracy, both from a scholarly and a societal perspective, the Freiburg Circles were advocating a kind of 'mixed economy' *avant la lettre*.

In 1943, the *Bonhoeffer Kreis* issued a memorandum on 'Political Community Order'. At the heart of the memorandum was a condemnation of the authoritarian state, which had falsely claimed 'supreme authority' over God. Instead, the *Bonhoeffer Kreis* called for the rule of law (*Rechtsstaat*) and individual freedom guaranteed through democracy rooted in 'freedom of conscience and expression' instead of 'silent and blind submission'. In the economic domain, the state should protect its citizens against 'the demon of greed that perverts the moral relationship between people'. In order to deliver on these fundamental points, the future state should not only provide a legal framework that would safeguard the liberties of its citizens but also facilitate the interpersonal bonds of the family and the traditional local communities (*Volksgemeinschaft*), as the latter in many ways transcended the stratification of society along class lines and its fatal centrifugal tendencies. Crucially, the Bonhoeffer Circle's approach in this memorandum went beyond the strictly scientific approach to which the ordoliberal economists had explicitly adhered in their earlier 'Ordo Manifesto' of 1936 (prior to the establishment of the *Freiburger Konzil*).[47] The multidisciplinary nature of the Circle thus clearly opened new epistemological and methodological pathways that led to a more holistic approach. It also meant that theological, ethical, and moral considerations became an integral part of their scholarly approach towards the socio-economic challenges of post-war order. In the last section of the memorandum, the authors point the way to European cooperation, possibly in the form of a 'smaller federation of European nation-states' (which would guarantee a 'just peace' for Germany instead of the *Diktatfrieden* ('dictated peace') the country had to cope with after 1919).[48]

---

[46] Christian L. Glossner, *The Making of the German Post-War Economy. Political Communication and Public Reception of the Social Market Economy after World War Two* (London: I.B. Taurus, 2010), p. 32.

[47] Franz Böhm, Walter Eucken, and Hans Grossmann-Doerth, 'Our Task', reprinted as 'The Ordo Manifesto of 1936', in Alan Peacock and Hans Willgerodt (eds.), *Germany's Social Market Economy: Origins and Evolution* (Houndmills, Basingstoke: Palgrave Macmillan, 1989), pp. 15–26.

[48] 'Politische Gemeinschaftsordung: Ein Versuch des christlichen Gewissens in den politischen Nöten unserer Zeit' (Freiburg, 1943), in Walter Lipgens, *Europa-Föderationspläne der*

Re-conceptualising Capitalism and Democracy

Put in a European and transatlantic context, the Bonhoeffer Circle memorandum not only resembled the thinking of the Italian liberal Einaudi in a striking way, but it can also be seen as the precursor to the West German stance regarding the paradox identified by Reinhold Niebuhr in the wake of the Second World War. The paradox was that while the aversion to moral oversimplifications (because they were seen as drivers of the previous war) now induced the reflex to refrain from moral and ethical standpoints altogether, although what the situation of the moment required was exactly that, moral and ethical standpoints.[49] To overcome this paradox, the world needed prominent Christians courageous enough to speak up and to engage governments and churches alike in the battle against totalitarianism, violence, and suppression. The flame of this courage burned in the Christian resistance against the Nazis. Yet the flame also flickered and was almost snuffed out due to the choice that some made to remain silent rather than to speak up, giving in to the reflex to refrain from voicing one's standpoint. This silence also offered a comfort that many could not resist, also within the academic Freiburg communities (a prominent example is Ordo co-founder and prominent Freiburg School member, Hans Großmann-Doerth, who served in the Nazi regime and was expelled from the Freiburg School by Eucken in 1943 because of this).[50] This left almost nobody unmoved, certainly not Bonhoeffer.

In his cell in Flossenbürg concentration camp awaiting his execution, Bonhoeffer wrote poems. One of them was entitled 'Nächtliche Stimmen' ('Voices in the Night'), a description of the storm of feelings and sentiments he experienced within himself. The poem culminates in a sinister and haunting tale of guilt and penance, and ultimately in a confession of a man torn apart by the war. It is a gripping and apt description of the Second World War similar to the description used by Luigi Einaudi of a 'religious war'. This was a war between 'Satan and God [within] our souls', as Einaudi had put it (see section 3.2) – a war in which the 'voices in the night', whispering about the sins committed, would never be silenced again in Europe, certainly not in Germany. For his fellow Germans and his kindred spirits within the ecumenical movement alike,

---

Widerstandsbewegungen eingeleitet eingeleitet, 1940–1945. Eine Dokumentation (Munich: Oldenbourg, 1968); Jorrit Steehouder and Clemens van den Berg, 'A Wartime Narrative of Hope: The *Freiburger Bonhoeffer-Kreis's* 1943 Memorandum as a Blueprint for Europe', in Lennaert van Heumen and Mechtild Roos (eds.), *The Informal Construction of Europe* (New York: Routledge, 2019).

[49] The analysis of Niebuhr was wholeheartedly underwritten by Visser 't Hooft, who saw in it the most apt summary of the urgent trans-Christian mission he sought to promote (Visser 't Hooft, *Memoires*, p. 106).

[50] Glossner, *The Making*, p. 42.

Bonhoeffer's poem offered a guide on how to make possible the confession of German guilt after the war. After his death, Dietrich Bonhoeffer became an icon of the transnational Christian movement, embodying the translation of its lofty moral ambitions into practical policy goals. He was commemorated for his tireless efforts working and networking outside the box of his academic discipline and his religious profession to deliver on the promise underlying his mission: that 'Kirche müsse Kirche für andere sein' ('Church ought to be Church for others')[51] – and as such provided the (metaphysical) means to re-explore hope for a better future for Germany and Europe.

After the war, German ecumenists who had survived their imprisonment, like Martin Niemöller, were freed, and contacts between the WCC in the making and German Protestant church leaders were resumed. In his memoirs, Visser 't Hooft cites a letter he wrote to Otto Dibelius – then just re-established as bishop in Berlin Brandenburg – in those days. In this letter he called for a 'fraternal conversation', which 'would be greatly facilitated if the Confessing Church of Germany' were to speak out 'very frankly – not only about the crimes of the Nazis, but also especially about the sins of omission of the German people, including the church'. Subsequently, Visser 't Hooft referred explicitly to the poem by Bonhoeffer: 'The Christians of other countries do not want to take a pharisaic attitude. But they hope that it will be openly said – what is said so impressively in Bonhoeffer's poem – that the German people and also the church have not spoken out with sufficient clarity and with sufficient emphasis.'[52]

Against the majority within the German Protestant churches, Martin Niemöller – who had been the leader of the 'Pastors' Emergency League' (a schism in the *Reich* church) during its 1934 transformation into the 'Confessing Church' – inspired and instructed by the Swiss theologian Karl Barth would staunchly lobby for a recognition of guilt as a personal matter. Barth had captured this in the following formula: 'We Germans have erred – hence the chaos of today – and we Christians in Germany are also Germans!'[53] Following this line, however, implied the rejection of the 'two kingdoms doctrine' as traditionally upheld in Lutheranism. The reason for this rejection was clear to Barth and Niemöller. As highlighted by James Bentley and Van den Berg in their research into the matter, they both – Barth and Niemöller – concluded that this doctrine had led the German Protestants to think 'that we did not have any other responsibility

---

[51] 'Dietrich Bonhoeffer', *Brockhaus Enzyklopädie*.   [52] Visser 't Hooft, *Memoires*, p. 190.
[53] James Bentley, *Martin Niemöller, 1892–1984* (New York: The Free Press, 1984), p. 175; Van den Berg, 'European Believers', p. 138.

towards the state than to obey it', and that 'this attitude is wrong'.[54] Niemöller would prepare the ground for a meeting between a Europe-wide ecumenical delegation coordinated by Visser 't Hooft and George Bell and the leaders of the newly established *Evangelische Kirche in Deutschland* (EKD), which had been established in the city of Treysa on 31 August 1945.[55]

The month-long prepared meeting between a delegation of the ecumenical movement and the EKD took place in Stuttgart on 19 October 1945. The host of the meeting was Theophil Wurm, an active member of the Confessing Church who had – together with the Catholic bishop of Münster – led the opposition to the Nazi regime's murder of invalids, and who was now council chair of the EKD. Wurm formulated the overarching aim of the gathering as being the 're-Christianisation of the European world'. Crucially, however, he added a heartfelt German cry for help: 'Please help us!' This cry for help had confronted the ecumenical delegation with a dilemma: a confession of guilt by the German side was the sufficient precondition for restoring ecumenical cooperation with the Germans, but that confession could neither be forced by the delegation, nor accepted in incomplete form. The way out of this dilemma was found by Pierre Maury, a prominent French Protestant, and a translator of the works of Karl Bart. Visser 't Hooft, who spoke on behalf of the ecumenical delegation, was prepared along the lines of Maury's suggestion. He answered: 'We have come to ask you to help us to help you.' This was the breakthrough. The first meticulously orchestrated steps had been taken on what would be a thorny path of decisive text-drafting (as elaborately reconstructed by Van den Berg). The general outline for this endeavour was set now: the German question must be a European question, but only could be so after a confession of German guilt that would have to be credible from a European perspective. Eventually, Niemöller was the leading editor of the key passage in the 'Stuttgart Declaration of Guilt' (*Stuttgarter Schuldbekenntnis* or *Schulderklärung der evangelischen Christheit*

---

[54] The complete passage in German reads: 'Aus einem falsch verstandenen Luthertum heraus haben wir gemeint, dem Staat gegenüber keine andere Verantwortung zu tragen, als daß wir ihm gehorchen und die Christenheit zum Gehorsam ermahnen und erziehen, solange der Staat keine offenbare Sünde von uns fordert. Diese Haltung ist falsch, und wir haben uns hier neu auf unseren Auftrag zu besinnen' (Martin Greschat (ed.), *Die Schuld der Kirche: Dokumente und Reflexionen zur Stuttgarter Schulderklärung vom 18./19. Oktober 1945*, Studienbücher zur kirchlichen Zeitgeschichte (Munich: Chr. Kaiser, 1982), 4, p. 80; also cited and extensively commented upon in Van den Berg, 'European Believers', p. 134).

[55] It was at this meeting that the leaders of predominantly Lutheran churches (but also from the *Reformierte Kirchen* and the *Unierte Kirchen*) reconstituted themselves as a new post-war organisation, also to repair the schism among the churches that had been caused by the Nazi policy of *Gleichschaltung*.

Deutschlands) that declared the following: 'through us infinite wrong was brought over many peoples and countries ... we accuse ourselves for not standing to our beliefs more courageously, for not praying more faithfully, for not believing more joyously, and for not loving more ardently'.[56] Building on these words and their 'European embedding', the Protestant intellectual Karl Jaspers would prepare the ground for the reckoning with the war of the German Christian Democrats. His 1946 publication entitled *The German Guilt* stressed the 'collective responsibility' that the Germans had to shoulder because of the German crimes against humanity and would guide the European politics of Adenauer, FRG's first chancellor. Central to this then-controversial approach was that German repentance must steer Germany's definite break with the past in the form of its anchoring in the West and its democratic and constitutional order. In the practical (geo)political terms of the day, this meant the acceptance of the division of the country, a semi-sovereign status for the FRG, and a West German devotion to *Westbindung* ('binding to the West') and European cooperation and integration.[57]

The foreign press was pleasantly surprised by the Stuttgart Declaration of Guilt, but that was only the European side of the coin – many ordinary Germans abhorred this 'treason', while the pope and Italy's Christian Democrats acted in accordance with the statement the Christian Democratic Party had published on the day of Hitler's death: 'We have the strength to forget! Forget as soon as possible!'[58]

Moreover, the ecumenical and church-inspired confession as the beginning of an institutional way out of the horrors of the Second World War was only available to those Germans living in the West. The price that had to be paid for Hitler's war – and thus for the West German confession to be heard – was no *Diktatfrieden* but instead the segregation of Germany into West and East, the latter falling under yet another totalitarian government. In contrast, West Germany, in its provisional form of the Federal Republic of Germany, became the centre of what may be called an 'irenic exercise' extending from the world of the churches into the realms of society and politics. This exercise not only reconciled the Protestant church with the

---

[56] The complete passage reads as follows: 'Durch uns ist unendliches Leid über viele Völker und Länder gebracht worden. Was wir unseren Gemeinden oft bezeugt haben, das sprechen wir jetzt im Namen der ganzen Kirche aus: Wohl haben wir lange Jahre hindurch im Namen Jesu Christi gegen den Geist gekämpft, der im nationalsozialistischen Gewaltregiment seinen furchtbaren Ausdruck gefunden hat; aber wir klagen uns an, daß wir nicht mutiger bekannt, nicht treuer gebetet, nicht fröhlicher geglaubt und nicht brennender geliebt haben.'

[57] For this analysis of the meaning of the work of Jaspers for the German Christian Democracy, see: Meyer Resende, 'The Catholic Narrative'.

[58] Judt, *Postwar*, p. 61; Van den Berg, 'European Believers', pp. 134–5.

Catholic Church, but it also brought together liberalism and socialism, universalism and regionalism, Atlanticism and European integration, ordoliberalism and dirigisme, and – perhaps most crucially – emotion and planning. Indeed, the few blueprints for international cooperation that stood a chance of success were not only those that were feasible and practical under the circumstances of the Cold War and the growing degree of economic interdependence but also those that combined realpolitik with an appeal to the zeitgeist.

4 The Great Escape

In 1942, Joseph Schumpeter published his analysis of the situation in the Western world. In his book *Capitalism, Socialism and Democracy*, he outlined the decline of capitalism, bluntly stating in the first two sentences of the book's prologue: 'Can capitalism survive? No. I do not think it can.' Schumpeter was writing at a time when many saw the rise of Nazi Germany as a direct consequence of the Great Depression and thus an affirmation of capitalism's mortal crisis. What would replace capitalism was clear: 'I think we shall see, that socialism is a practical proposition that may become *immediately* practical in consequence of the present war.' Schumpeter defined socialism as an economic 'institutional pattern in which control over means of production and over production itself is vested with a central authority – or ... in which, as a matter of principle, the economic affairs of society belong to the public and not to the private sphere'.[1]

On 30 December 1949, Schumpeter delivered an address entitled 'The March into Socialism' before the American Economic Association in New York. He gave the speech from notes; the notes for this address were reproduced years later, in the 1976 version of *Capitalism, Socialism and Democracy* (used here). Schumpeter was planning to complete the paper on the basis of these notes on 8 January 1950, the day he died. In these notes, Schumpeter defines centralist socialism as follows:

> that organization of society in which the means of production are controlled, and the decisions on how and what to produce and on who is to get what, are made by a public authority instead of by privately owned and privately-managed firms. All that we mean by the March into Socialism is, therefore, the migration of people's economic affairs from the private into the public sphere.[2]

Socialism would offer the means to counter the social and psychological backlash that comes with the rationalising forces of competition 'that have made capitalism the most dynamic economic system in history' and that have brought unparalleled economic success but have simultaneously

---

[1] Schumpeter, *Capitalism*, pp. 413 and 410.   [2] Schumpeter, *Capitalism*, p. 421.

destroyed traditional non-economic forms of production. This led Schumpeter to the ironic conclusion that 'capitalism is being killed by its achievements [and] that childish ideal of enrichment through appropriation of existing wealth'. The latter may be 'politically attractive' but it remained 'nonsense' all the same and would eventually, through socialisation, paralyse economic life and destroy 'cultural private life'. This is because an unprecedented disciplining of the working classes would be necessary to balance a devastating regression of production.[3]

However, with the benefit of hindsight – and despite Schumpeter's superior sense of irony – we can conclude that his analysis rested ultimately on oversimplifications and excessive abstractions. As history would show, his prediction of the inevitable demise of capitalism turned out to be a flagrant underestimation not only of the societal legitimacy of the capitalist system but also of the ideas stemming from the intellectual countermovement against socialism. From the 1930s, this countermovement was situated in the so-called Austrian School of economics, of which Schumpeter himself was a prominent member. In post-war Western Europe, however, its main locus was to be found in the Freiburg School, the post-war intellectual nerve centre of the broader German tradition of ordoliberalism. Some of its leading figures – including Alexander Rüstow and Wilhelm Röpke – had participated in the Walter Lippmann Colloquium in 1938 and were present at the creation of the Mont Pèlerin Society in 1947 (see chapter 2).

Note, however, that the Freiburg School and ordoliberalism are not identical. The Freiburg School refers to the 'Freiburg School of Law and Economics' at the University of Freiburg am Breisgau, an academic community originally organised around Walter Eucken, Franz Böhm, and Hans Großmann-Doerth in the 1930s and 1940s. The Freiburg School was focused on what Eucken had described as 'Constitutional Economics' (*Ordnungsökonomie*). In their view (based on the work of Max Weber and Werner Sombart, and methodologically on the phenomenology of Edmund Husserl), the state should provide the legal institutional framework, within which healthy competition, through measures that follow market principles, could be guaranteed. This intimately liaised the Freiburg School with other currents in German liberal economics, most prominently represented by the 'ordoliberals' Rüstow and Röpke. From the ordoliberal perspective, however, competition was seen as the essential means to the ends of preventing monopoly and providing freedom and social justice. Indeed, according to the ordoliberals, competition must be

---

[3] Jerry Z. Muller, *The Mind and the Market. Capitalism in Western Thought* (New York: Anchor Books, 2003), pp. 288, 298, and 307; Schumpeter, *Capitalism*, p. 410.

considered a 'public good', which the state, through regulatory policies, should ensure and supply in such a 'social' form.[4] Analytically, ordoliberalism was closely associated with the Austrian School. But also here, there were crucial differences. Ordoliberalism tended to view interventionist economic policies with less rigid aversion than the Austrians, and it also emphasised the importance of 'social policy' as an integral part of any strong state.

Already before the war, Röpke was a leading figure in the ordoliberal school. He was a prolific contributor to the German-language press and had written a number of books on the economy, society, and the post-war order. In 1937, Röpke had accepted a professorship at the Institut Universitaire de Hautes Études Internationales in Geneva. Luigi Einaudi was one of his colleagues. The Institut was founded in 1927 and provided a refuge for an impressive list of leading liberal economists. Apart from Röpke, this list contained the names of Ludwig von Mises, Jacob Viner, and Einaudi (who fled from fascist Italy to Geneva in 1943).[5] After the war, Röpke became the unchallenged mouthpiece of ordoliberalism not only to the general public but also in the eyes of post-war West German politicians. The latter would make him hugely influential in West Germany's economic policymaking. In his new authoritative post-war role, Röpke summarised the mission of German ordoliberalism as pursuing the goal of 'economic humanism' via a 'third way' between socialism and liberalism.[6] For the record, the concept of a third way has a special historical meaning in Germany, when compared to other Western nations, which either practised 'freedom without regulation' (laissez-faire), or 'freedom through equality' (French Revolution) – German freedom, in contrast, was defined by Johann Gottlieb Fichte as 'freedom through the state'.[7]

In general, the mid- to late 1940s witnessed a renaissance in the Austrian School way of thinking on the post-war order which was most visible in the staggering list of influential books on this topic. These included Schumpeter's famous book, Friedrich Hayek's *Road to Serfdom* (1944), and Ludwig von Mises's *Bureaucracy* (1944). Somewhat on the fringes of the Austrian School but certainly associated with it intellectually and historically were Karl Polanyi's *The Great Transformation* (1944, see below) and Karl Popper's *The Open Society and Its Enemies* (1945).[8]

---

[4] Glossner, *The Making*, pp. 39–46.
[5] Mirowski and Plehwe (eds.), *The Road*, pp. 12–13.
[6] Röpke, *Civitas Humana*; Glossner, *The Making*, pp. 42 and 47.
[7] See Schlecht cited in Glossner, *The Making*, p. 48 n. 11.
[8] Stedman Jones, *Masters of the Universe*, pp. 30–73; Wasserman, *The Marginal Revolutionaries*, p. 176.

Of these influential works, Schumpeter's *Capitalism, Socialism and Democracy* would prove to be 'one of the greatest and subtlest apologia for capitalism and elitist liberalism ever written'. It was hugely and perennially influential in the post-war West through such conceptual ideas as 'creative destruction' (the continuous revolutionising of 'the economic structure' from within a capitalistic economy) and 'democracy as a means not an end'.[9]

The story of how Schumpeter's book was received and how he reacted to his critics in several later editions throughout the 1940s offers valuable insights into the mood of the times. When Schumpeter published his book in 1942, he had just reached his tenth year at Harvard, where he was to lecture until his death in 1950. He was considered a prominent but somewhat exotic outsider with a loyal group of followers and an academic and international cult image, yet he always stood in the shadow of the real star, Keynes. His audience of graduate students was 'supersaturated with Keynes, Marx, and Veblen'.[10] Schumpeter's true impact would be posthumous.

While lacking the fame of Keynes, Schumpeter could still make the claim that his books were being read by many. In the first years after the publication of *Capitalism*, it was translated into seven languages. Moreover, Schumpeter had provoked heated debate because of his forecast in the book that the Western world would 'march into socialism', with several accusing him of defeatism. This was a charge directed at many within the Austrian School diaspora – including Hayek, Mises, and now Schumpeter – largely as a result of their 'going to extremes', as critics claimed.[11] After the war, in the preface to the second edition of the book published in 1946, Schumpeter reacted to these critics. His confrontational diagnosis of them resulted in a mission statement loaded with urgency: 'Frank presentation of ominous facts was never more necessary than it is today because we seem to have developed escapism into a system of thought.' It prompted him to write a new chapter in which he presented 'facts and interferences' that were 'certainly not pleasant or comfortable' but also 'not defeatist'. For according to Schumpeter, 'defeatist is he who, while giving lip service to Christianity and all the other values of our civilization, yet refused to rise to their defence – no matter whether he accepts their defeat as a foregone conclusion or deludes himself with futile hopes against hope'. Schumpeter loathed 'these situations in which optimism is nothing but a form of defection'.[12]

---

[9] Wasserman, *The Marginal Revolutionaries*, pp. 178–9; cf. Mirowski and Plehwe (eds.), *The Road*, p. 7.
[10] Muller, *The Mind*, p. 307. [11] Burgin, *The Great Persuasion*, pp. 53–4.
[12] Schumpeter, *Capitalism*, pp. 413–14.

While *Capitalism* was all about economics, Schumpeter's criticism went far beyond economics. For instance, in his book Schumpeter also reports on his explorations into the mood of the times. What he had discovered was a clear shift towards a more interventionist if not activist governing mode. This had come about as a result of a new passion for realising – and not simply hoping for – a better world after the double disaster of the Great Depression and the fascist experiment. Schumpeter dubbed this new passion the 'radicalization of the public mind', a process that was caused by the fact that 'capitalism produces by its mere working a social atmosphere that is hostile to it [and] in turn produces policies which do not allow it to function'.[13] Crucially, the resulting anti-elitist strive for utopia went hand in hand with a shift in focus from the ideology of politics to the practicality of policy. This shift was the driving force for the radical change in public sentiment. To Schumpeter, however, it was precisely this new preference for a post-war order 'made' by government that was problematic. Why? It not only went at the cost of a more spontaneous order, (merely) facilitated by government (and leading to forms of liberal capitalism), it also was the root cause of the new belief in the manufacturability of society that went hand in hand with a naïve optimism that would turn out to be nothing more than defection. It was precisely the latter that he saw at work in the maddening neglect of facts that, according to him, was inherent to the Keynesian system built on excess consumption.

This new obsession with policy appealed to politicians and people alike, and would continue to do so – as Schumpeter realised all too well – precisely because of its utopian promise. In addition, this emphasis on policy was associated with rationalism, a problem-solving attitude and a progressive yet essentially apolitical approach. It was this last characteristic in particular that was both appealing and comforting, for the brute facts of recent history had dictated that politics should not be allowed to run wild again. To many in the post-war period, bureaucracy and state planning were seen as the only way to build a trustworthy fortress against the evil of a polarised politicisation of society. Indeed, the new approach seemed to offer a template for economic recovery and growth combined with political self-containment and a much-needed moderation of societal perturbations.[14]

4.1 Illusions and Experiments

That the reality inside the offices of planning was often not quite as rational as the image they portrayed to the outside world remained carefully hidden from the public eye. What made sense to the people in

[13] Muller, *The Mind*, p. 306. [14] See Maier, *In Search*, p. 130.

The Great Escape

the Western world was instead the hope that Schumpeter was referring to, a hope that became associated with clean interventionist rationalism as the basis for policymaking and which in many ways was at the heart of the American New Deal-inspired approach to issues of society and international cooperation. Moreover, the transnational intellectual and political leadership of this post-war planning revolution was aware of the need to continuously secure public support by referring to ethics and emotion. Although the single and most decisive attraction of planning was the expectation that it could relegate ideology to the background of politics, leading planners felt passionately that it was essential to connect with the moral zeitgeist, so as to mobilise support for their renewed emphasis on social cohesion and human rights. Obviously, this made planning far more than a purely rational affair. Post-war planning was also driven by emotions, just like its inter-war forerunner had been. There was a key difference, however, which lay in the apolitical, desperately post-ideological, and rather rigidly functionalist approach that was clearly the result of the horrific reality checks of unparalleled misery and violence during the inter-war period and the Second World War. In the confrontation between 'abstract ideas and material needs', the uncontested intellectual leader of twentieth-century functionalism, David Mitrany, 'diagnosed that materiality would prevail over ideology, and suggested adapting the former to the latter'.[15]

One notable example of this was the failure of a proposal by the British minister of foreign affairs, Ernest Bevin, for a Western Union in 1948 (see chapter 6). While one reason for this failure was the fact that British loyalty lay westward, as anchored in the Atlantic Charter of 1941, another just as important factor was the huge popularity of the Beveridge Report, which recommended a taxpayer-funded welfare state and the pursuit of full employment. Published in 1942 under the auspices of the Labour leader Clement Attlee (who had more or less a 'free hand to administer domestic policy' as the deputy prime minister in Churchill's wartime coalition government), this government report was seized upon as an opportunity to implement Keynesian policies and to establish a comprehensive nationalised system of social insurance and free health care under the National Health Service.[16] The spirit of the Atlantic Charter could not have been combined with the Beveridge Report without the outside spending of the Marshall Plan, which clearly outshone the outdated bickering between the US and the UK that Bevin's idea of a Western Union had tried to paper

---

[15] Rosenboim, *The Emergence*, pp. 29–34ff.
[16] William Beveridge, *Social Insurance and Allied Services* (Cmd. 6404, 1942), became known and highly influential as the 'Beveridge Report'. Wapshott, *Keynes–Hayek*, p. 227.

over. Yet in the end, as non-ideological as it would claim to be, planning was but politics with other means. Crudely put, in exploiting the apolitical appeal of planning, the proponents of planning were in effect using the powerful instrument of political persuasion.

Promoting and implementing planning essentially remained a deeply political and thus moral affair that took place behind the charade of policies, Schumpeter would have added. To him, all these new trends of government planning and public economics contributed to a general, tragic tendency of self-deception. As he put it in 1946: 'We always plan too much and think too little. We ... hate unfamiliar argument that does not tally with what we already believe or would like to believe. We walk into our future as we walked into the war, blindfolded.' In the end, Schumpeter's biting critique regarding the mood of the times was moral rather than economic, as was the case of the arguments used by his fellow Austrians, who had all been pushed into the defensive from the time of the Great Depression.

Nonetheless, three years after the release of the second edition of *Capitalism*, Schumpeter went to some lengths in the preface to the third edition to drive home his point that 'we seem to have developed escapism into a system of thought'. In an assessment of what he labelled the 'social situation in England', he argued that the United Kingdom in 1949 was characterised by an abnormal and untenable 'excess consumption' that was a sign of plain escapism. To substantiate his point, he sketched a breath-taking 'process of readjustment under the condition of suppressed inflation' that could best be described as 'socialist policy before the act'. The process of economic readjustment within the context of the transition from war to peace was being entangled with a domestic process of social transition. In Schumpeter's eyes, the serious economic responsibilities that should have been part and parcel of this major international transition – for instance monetary prudence and the price mechanism – were being dangerously neglected by an 'optimism [that was] nothing but a form of defection'. Hence the escapism he registered.

According to Schumpeter in the preface to the 1949 edition of *Capitalism*, 'the ethos of capitalism [was] gone'. His main criticism of the British example was focused on the 'many activities, entrepreneurial and other' that had been 'suppressed' by the post-war Labour government – including 'the "freedoms" with which the economist is concerned' such as the freedom of investment and consumer choice. The resulting obfuscation of economic choice had been the true cost at which Labour had 'avoided post-war readjustment' and had 'carried labour through the critical years without unemployment, on a rising level of real income'. Economically, that cost was a real wage bill plus the real cost of social services. As far as

Schumpeter was concerned, these real costs were 'incompatible with the other conditions of the English economy at its present level of productivity'. In other words, they represented the irresponsible, '*Après nous, le déluge*', free-spending attitude of the government.

This 'unpalatable' reality was constantly being swept under the carpet of the balance-of-payments crisis. For it was the British balance-of-payments position that was 'being made the one untenable feature' by the UK government. The reason for this was clear: the Labour government's goal was to use the aid received under the Marshall Plan to build an export surplus that would re-establish the UK's prominent position in the global economy and to thereby persuade the markets that the British pound was fully convertible with the dollar.[17] In Schumpeter's view, it was not wrong to focus on the balance-of-payments problem, but the 'error' consisted 'in believing that it spells out a [different] diagnosis'.

This brought Schumpeter to his main conclusion regarding the UK: to re-establish the UK's position in the global economy *and* 'to stay there without either foreign help or internal pressure, it is necessary to normalize England's domestic situation'. The economic recipe proffered by Schumpeter was aimed at preventing an addiction to loans and deficits by implementing austerity measures that would inevitably trigger structural reform. He started off gently by stating that 'something may indeed be gained by ... exploitation of the strong points in England's international position by regulative import and export policies', adding that a 'devaluation of the pound may help over the last steps'. That was the easy part. 'The fundamental condition for durable success' had to be sought in 'adjustment of [the British] economic process in such a way as to make it once more produce, along with the goods for her domestic consumption and the goods and services that are to pay for her imports, a genuine net surplus for investment at home and abroad'. According to Schumpeter, this goal would remain an illusion 'without a temporary decrease of consumption and a permanent increase of production'. These temporary and permanent preconditions, in turn, could not be 'brought about without an unpopular reduction in public expenditure and a still more unpopular shift of the burden of taxation'. Schumpeter – like Hayek – claimed that all this necessarily implied 'an uncompensated sacrifice of some vested interests of labour'.[18] This meant downgrading the battle against unemployment to a lower priority, which was not very realistic given the widely popular and fairly uncontested primacy of the goal of full employment and its Keynesian policies.[19]

---

[17] Schumpeter, *Capitalism*, pp. 415 and 418–19.
[18] Schumpeter, *Capitalism*, pp. 418–20.
[19] Wapshott, *Keynes–Hayek*, pp. 194–5 and 226–30.

Political support for these socialist policies could not be called anything but 'readjustment by catastrophe' according to Schumpeter, given that the situation would inexorably become untenable in the long run. This brought up the key question he was concerned with: 'how will the gradual elimination, within the period of Marshall Aid, of the untenable features of the situation affect' the future?[20] This was indeed the key question for the whole of free Western Europe. Answering it was the equivalent of untying the Gordian knot of how to handle 'readjustment' in a transition from war to peace and from external financial aid (i.e., the Marshall Plan) to internal socio-economic resilience. Schumpeter's own disconcerting answer to this pressing question was that the Keynesian charade would be continued due to popular support, and subsequently would drive the post-war democracies of the West into socialism at the cost of capitalism. Schumpeter also knew how this would happen: through the 'escapism' of excess consumption and public goods financed with deficits.[21]

The only way out of this fatal escapism that Schumpeter could identify was through what he very vaguely described as 'vicissitudes' in the last sentence of his 1949 foreword to *Capitalism*,[22] which can be interpreted as contingency, the unforeseen, or the force of history overpowering that of economics. This ultimate caveat about the vicissitudes of history turned out to be quite apt. Largely unforeseen, European integration soon came to the fore as the poster child of Schumpeter's vicissitudes.

Politically, this turn of history was driven by the mutually reinforcing twin forces of Europe's determination not to repeat the mistakes of the past on the one hand and the practical functionalist ideal of international cooperation on the other. This had the effect of pushing the policy approach *beyond policy*, so to say, into the realm of high politics. This was because the policy approach so deplored by Schumpeter offered a kind of purifying therapy that fulfilled a desperate need after the incomprehensible horror of the war, a need that was especially strong in Europe. The new approach, based on the American example, seemed to offer a template for economic recovery and growth coupled with much-needed political moderation.[23] Schumpeter's conviction that Europe had to choose between capitalism and socialism was largely inadequate to intellectually grasp what was going on in post-war Europe, as it turned out that capitalism did not have to give way to the goal of socialism. Instead, socialism could be encapsulated in the new phase of the great experiment with capitalism and democracy in the West.

[20] Schumpeter, *Capitalism*, p. 418.
[21] For an extensive summary of the comparable verdict on untenable 'economics of abundance' resulting from Keynesian policies by Hayek, see Wapshott, *Keynes–Hayek*, pp. 184ff.
[22] Schumpeter, *Capitalism*, p. 420.   [23] See Maier, *In Search*, p. 130.

4.2 Two-Step Move in Multilateralism

The far-fetched possibility of a way out of the 'untenable' situation – a possibility that Schumpeter had explicitly factored into the last sentence of his 1949 preface to *Capitalism, Socialism and Democracy* – was to become reality. This largely unimaginable reality crystallised in the process of building what would later be called a 'mixed economy'. As it turned out, the pre-war warning that gradual collectivism could turn into aggressive collectivism – which had, incidentally, inspired the Walter Lippmann Colloquium (see section 2.3) – was offset not by an old-school laissez-faire approach nor by a new-style collectivism but by an innovative form of institution building situated somewhere in between the two extremes of the spectrum. The new institutions that emerged on this 'third road' seized on the concept of integration as a counterforce against the 'disintegrating' tendencies in societies of the free world.[24] This approach received traction in the aftermath of the Second World War, and it was this evolution that was at the heart of the construction and re-construction of post-war Western Europe. Its essence was twofold: planning and multilateralism, with the latter being the truly new element.

But what was it that was driving this revolution in transnational institution building in Western Europe? Beginning in the first years of the Second World War, three developments took place that set the stage for an institutional re-design of the Western world – and Western Europe in particular. First, the Second World War had raised the institutions of the Anglo-American partnership to the status of a lodestar for the post-war West while simultaneously giving rise to a transatlantic world of policy planning as the new main 'space' for transnational cooperation and coordination efforts for the wider world. Secondly, in the context of the beginning of the Cold War, this 'new space' of policymaking was turned into a controlled laboratory – transnational yet not global – for the relatively safe testing of modes of international planning and cooperation in the West. Thirdly, and in parallel, key Anglo-American projects of institution building were put on a multilateral footing from their very inception. In combination, these three developments determined the institutional framework for post-war Western Europe and in so doing foreshadowed thinking on the post-war European order.

Somewhat counterintuitively in the context of the start of the Cold War, these developments occurred within a post-ideological, transatlantic

---

[24] Philip Plickert, *Wandlungen des Neoliberalismus. Eine Studie zur Entwicklung und Ausstrahlung der 'Mont Pèlerin Society'* (Stuttgart: Lucius & Lucius, 2008), pp. 87, 100, and 102.

process of policy exploration. In that process, the ideology of non-ideology was tested in the form of new, more effective, and above all practical policy solutions to the deep-seated problems of social inequality and poverty. It was within this process of exploration that the impassioned proponents of practical planning prevailed, serving as an inspiration. Moreover, there was a sense of urgency because the general feeling was that there was no time to waste in building a new Western order based on effective transnational cooperation. It was time to draw the lessons of the failed experiments with international organisation during the inter-war period – most notably the League of Nations – and to move on.

From this perspective, the war worked as a catalyst that channelled the efforts of international cooperation into the institutional structures of the Anglo-American wartime partnership. The Western world revolving around the Anglo-American axis provided the emerging 'space' for policy engineering with a rock-solid political basis, which was further hardened and strengthened by the Cold War. It was in this transnational space that the American and Western European approaches towards post-war society and international organisation converged and where the achievements of planning and international cooperation were codified in a special form of 'constitutional ethos'.[25] It was this space that allowed the Western world to enter into a new and stunningly prosperous phase of the 'experiment with capitalism and democracy', which had been steering the 'free world' since the French and American Revolutions (see chapter 2).

With the origins of this historic advancement in international cooperation largely in the Anglo-American partnership, it was inevitable that many of the first post-war initiatives aimed at international cooperation were based on the lessons and best practices derived from the national experiences of the US and the UK. The introduction of these best practices in Western Europe fell on fertile ground. Not surprisingly, it was a relatively small but coherent group of transatlantic 'policy therapists' who played a key role in the construction of post-war multilateralism within the Western world. Their influence was considerable, as they offered precisely what was required at the time: political-ideological modesty mixed with convincing rationalism and a strong dose of idealism. They provided something new to believe in after the disasters of nationalism.

These men also largely succeeded in fundamentally revising the old regime 'of the financial, industrial, political, and journalistic establishments', thereby becoming true 'miracle-makers' in the eyes of the public.

---

[25] Van Zon, 'Assembly', p. 49; Lindseth, *Power*, pp. 85–8.

They included John Maynard Keynes, James Meade, Lionel Robbins, Dean Acheson, Henry Morgenthau, and Will Clayton[26] as well as the economic policymakers and post-war 'reconstructers' Averell Harriman, David Bruce, Milton Katz, Paul Hoffman, and Richard M. Bissell; the Belgians Robert Triffin and Paul Henri Spaak; and the Frenchmen Jean Monnet and Robert Marjolin (the latter four were all well connected within the US government from before or during the Second World War).[27] Their greatest achievement was that they facilitated a move towards multilateralism never seen before in the history of international relations. It was this that offered the post-war Western world, and Western Europe in particular, the great escape out of the stalemate and shackles of the interwar period and into a future of international cooperation and integration.

The grand designs for post-war multilateralism drawn up during the 1940s and engineered within the largely Anglo-American policy community shared four main characteristics. First, these plans – however far-reaching their goals might have been – remained nestled within institutional forms of capitalism and constitutional democracy. This meant that a radical overthrow of the existing system was never on the cards. In the end, it was all about readjustment, not revolution. Secondly, the policy engineers involved were strongly committed to promoting transborder cooperation and ensuring that the boundaries of identity would not harden again. It became a goal in itself to 'multilateralise'. In this sense, multilateralisation became a substitute for ideology in what would become the beginning of post-ideological times in the Western world. A third characteristic of Western efforts to achieve international cooperation was its focus on technical policy domains that were seemingly apolitical such as trade, finance, and monetary governance. And fourthly, all the designing and planning of the post-war capitalist order shared one primary and all-encompassing goal: stability.[28]

Together, these four characteristics enabled the transatlantic world to free itself of the dogmatism of that false and ultimately destructive 'utopia'

---

[26] Gardner, 'Sterling-Dollar', 22–3; Michael Daunton, 'From Bretton Woods to Havana: Multilateral Deadlocks in Historical Perspective', in Amrita Narlikar (ed.), *Deadlocks in Multilateral Negotiations* (Cambridge: Cambridge University Press, 2010), p. 49. The original list of Gardner is limited to a group of British and American economic policymakers and economists also including Dennis Robertson, Richard Hopkins, Sir Percivale Liesching, Richard Law, Sir Kingsley Wood, Sir John Anderson, Cordell Hull, Edward Bernstein, Ansel Luxford, Harry Hawkins, Winthorp Brown, and Willard Thorp.

[27] See Historical Archives of the EU (HAEU), Florence, Jean Monnet American Sources, Interview Paul Hoffman, 25 October 1964, p. 19.

[28] See John Ruggie, 'International Regimes, Transactions, and Change: Embedded Liberalism in the Post-War Economic Order', *International Organization*, 36, 2 (1982), 394; Gardner, 'Sterling-Dollar', 22; Maier, *In Search*, pp. 5 nn. 8 and 9, and 128; Segers, 'Eclipsing', 61–4; Wapshott, *Keynes-Hayek*, pp. 225ff.

of the 'self-regulating market', as Karl Polanyi described it in his timely and lastingly influential book *The Great Transformation* (1944). This was the first step in the move towards multilateralism: the stripping away of the utopia of free markets from liberalism. The second step was the incorporation of 'socialism' in a new and softened version of capitalism,[29] mainly in the form of prioritising the goals of full employment and eradicating poverty through Keynesian social policies. This second step meant entering the new realm of 'mixed economies', a new habitat for the free nation-states of post-war Western Europe that would prove to be essential for their 'rescue', as Alan Milward has described their post-war existence.[30]

How Europe got to this moment in history is worth examining briefly. From the early nineteenth century, efforts to act on pressing domestic issues were constantly being impeded by a destructive cocktail consisting of increasingly complex societal problems, a growing number of conflicting interests, and a multiplication of actors and institutions. In the first half of the twentieth century, this increasingly boiled down to a dilemma between the growing belief in the manipulability of society as the way to correct inequality on the one hand, and the devastating centrifugal forces this had been triggering in societies on the other. The former was the work of passionate policy engineers and planners, while the latter was fuelled by the fierce competition between their ideas and action plans. In terms of solutions to the problem of inequality, this dilemma led to an inability to take credible action.[31] It was only after two world wars that the circumstances in Western Europe were ripe for a reconciliation between the varieties of socialism and laissez-faire liberalism in a practical, durable, and international manner – outside the sphere of totalitarianism. Driven by a passionate desire for a more stable and apolitical society, a middle ground was created to allow for more moderate, less ideological experiments with capitalism and democracy – mixing various watered-down elements of both utopias – that could count on broad public support in Western Europe's still fragile democracies. And because this remained in large part a Western European affair,[32] it led to a very specific, European form of integration from the late 1940s and early 1950s onwards. During

---

[29] Or, as Schumpeter noted in 1946: 'Socialism has ceased to be resisted with moral passion. It has become a matter to be discussed in terms of utilitarian arguments ... this is ... proof that the ethos of capitalism [individualism and free enterprise] is gone' (Schumpeter, *Capitalism*, p. 416).

[30] Milward, *The European Rescue*; Wapshott, *Keynes–Hayek*, p. 225; Patel, *The New Deal*, pp. 272–4.

[31] Hochgeschwender and Löffler (eds.), *Religion*, p. 87.

[32] See Peter A. Hall and David Soskice (eds.), *Varieties of Capitalism. The Institutional Foundations of Comparative Advantage* (Oxford: Oxford University Press, 2001), for instance 'Introduction' and pp. 220–3.

that period, the initially dominant Anglo-Saxon blueprints for post-war European order were steadily abandoned.

The integration of the ideologies of socialism and liberalism and its translation into practical socio-economic policies in industrialised societies eventually took root in post-war Western Europe and subsequently transformed into a process of 'Europeanisation' facilitated by the process of European integration (see chapter 8). This transformation did not occur by accident, as it was consistently and actively supported at the grassroots level in Western Europe. Western Europe's societies – all characterised in their own way by decentralisation and/or the protection of regional and local diversity and social cohesion – leaned heavily on Christian Democratic principles (such as subsidiarity), Christian Democratic political parties and their extended trans-European political network,[33] and regionally based associated corporatist and civil society organisations. In addition, the churches – in particular the Catholic Church under the influence of intellectuals such as Maritain and faced with the realities of the Cold War – played a binding and supporting role in favour of European cooperation particularly in the 1940s and 1950s, given that they were located in the ideological middle ground and followed a third way. Alongside the changes in the attitude of religious forces in these matters, there was a parallel process of reconciliation among Christian churches through the ecumenical movement that won influence after the war, most notably in matters of European cooperation.[34] Inherent in this broader societal base for change towards the moderate and practical were two alleviating societal-psychological forces that helped to crystallise post-war Western European institutions.

The first force was the political re-empowerment of religion. The war years and the immediate post-war period was a period of 'general religious revival', especially in Western Europe. Within the context of the unfolding Cold War, the 'free world' and 'Christian civilisation' were increasingly perceived as 'synonymous'.[35] To be sure, religion 'highlighted' the deep-seated 'ideological differences between East and West'.[36] This surge in the political-ideological status of Christianity as a force for the good in the

---

[33] Sergei A. Mudrov, 'Religion and the European Union: Attitudes of Catholic and Protestant Churches toward European Integration', *Journal of Church and State*, 57, 3 (2014), 509–10; Lucian N. Leustean and John T.S. Madeley, 'Religion, Politics and Law in the European Union: An Introduction', *Religion, State & Society*, 37, 1–2 (2009), 4; Kaiser, *Christian Democracy*.

[34] Lucian N. Leustean, 'What Is the European Union? Religion between Neofunctionalism and Intergovernmentalism', *International Journal for the Study of the Christian Church*, 9, 3 (2009), 166; Mudrov, 'Religion', 509–10.

[35] Casanova cited in Leustean and Madeley, 'Religion', 4.

[36] Leustean, 'What Is the European Union?', 165.

post-war world was also rooted in an American wartime campaign to prepare and motivate American soldiers for the war in Europe. By formulating a compelling and overarching goal of the war – which had to go beyond 'making the world safe for democracy', the slogan under which the United States had entered the First World War – the US army leadership in effect addressed the centrifugal forces in society that clearly threatened to weaken morale within the army. Eventually, this resulted in a religiously charged answer to the question 'Why We Fight': because God and Nazi rule are irreconcilable. This was a war of 'God versus Satan', in the words of Luigi Einaudi. From this perspective, the Second World War had been a war to save Judeo-Christian civilisation, a story of 'Interfaith in Action', but above all an invention of the US army to motivate its troops in a society of destabilising centrifugal forces, rampant social injustices, and virulent antisemitism and racism.[37] All in all, it was an example of superior marketing that had a deep and lasting influence on the post-war West, not least in the form of the consistent moral and political Christian and Christian Democratic sponsorship of experiments in European cooperation and integration in post-war Western Europe.

The second force that helped to crystallise post-war Western European institutions was the casting off of the American example and the American way of thinking. The first half of the twentieth century had made Europeans sadder but also wiser. Utopias, while elegant and appealing to the imagination, had lost their spell. Consequently, as described above, a preference took hold in Western Europe for adapting ideology to practical policies. In terms of institution building, this had a direct consequence in terms of a turn away from the 'utopia' of a European federation, at least in the short to medium term. Naïvely optimistic American ideas for European federation did not land on fertile ground in post-war Western Europe, even if they came from influential figures like John Foster Dulles.[38] Europe's leading thinkers of functionalism remained unconvinced, and history would prove them right. In the sadder, wiser, and forthright words of David Mitrany, who in the 1960s used the benefit of hindsight to assess all the attempts of federation: 'As for the grander federal designs, offering prefabricated Cities of God for the Atlantic World or even for the world at large, one can only deplore the loss they have certainly caused to constructive international action by turning popular good will . . .

---

[37] Deborah Dash Moore, *GI Jews. How World War II Changed a Generation* (Cambridge, MA: Harvard University Press, 2006); Pieter van Os, *Liever dier dan mens. Een overlevingsverhaal* (Amsterdam: Prometheus, 2009), pp. 204–8, and 'Hoezo eeuwenoude traditie? De eerste dagen van de joods-christelijke beschaving', *De Groene Amsterdammer*, 3 October 2019, 40–1.

[38] Berghahn, *Europe*, p. 136; see also Heyde, 'Amerika', 134.

in the vital post-war years into idealistic blind alleys with no effect on public action at all.'[39] Europe would do it differently. Western Europe would transform into a provisional building site for constructive international and public action. Grounded in realism, the business of planning changed in a fundamental way. It became less academic and intellectual and more hands-on and practical, less ambitious in terms of geographical and societal span and more regional and tailor-made in its policy elaborations and implementations. Plans were now carried out in a learning-by-doing kind of way – not juridical but practical, and less centralised.[40] These were the values at the core of the ideology of the non-ideological, in which the implementation of policy was fundamental. The latter harked back to the example of Roosevelt's New Deal but also to the British Fabian tradition of democratic socialism, gradual reform, and the organisation of knowledge and ideas across borders. Last but not least, these plans were also attractive to liberals, especially those who promoted the 'strong state'.[41]

Post-war planning fitted well in the moderate political programmes of the political centre, especially those of the Christian Democrats, and as such got connected to the actual religious sphere of the Christian church. Early adapters to this interlinkage gained significant influence in designing post-war Europe's institutions. The realistic pragmatism and conservatism ingrained in their approaches even kept the door open for cooperation with the more confrontational branches within neoliberalism, including those who displayed outright cynicism in reaction to general calls for social justice and the struggle for 'freedom from want' (one of Roosevelt's Four Freedoms from his 1941 State of the Union address). Hayek labelled the demand for social justice a 'dishonest insinuation': the most 'dangerous and seductive enunciation of tyranny that is intrinsic to the expression of "freedom from want"';[42] Schumpeter called it 'this childish ideal of enrichment'. The emerging Western world between Roosevelt's 'freedom from want' and Hayek's and Schumpeter's serious concerns about the survival of capitalism significantly narrowed down, and moderated, the ideological battle between collectivist socialism and clinical laissez-faire. It was against this backdrop that the Western world, and Western Europe in particular, made its two-step move during the 1940s: first away from laissez-faire and then towards a more social version of capitalism that prioritised goals such as full employment and battling poverty. What made this two-step move feasible was next-level multilateralism.

---

[39] Mitrany, *A Working*, pp. 16–17.
[40] Steehouder, 'Constructing Europe', p. 381; Van Zon, 'Assembly', pp. 51 and 56.
[41] Mirowski and Plehwe (eds.), *The Road*, p. 7; Steel, *Walter Lippmann*, pp. 67–72ff; Judt, *Postwar*, p. 67.
[42] Bonefeld, 'Freedom', 645.

How did this two-step move come about in practice? Its root causes lay in the 1930s and were insightfully and coherently presented by Polanyi in *The Great Transformation*. According to Polanyi, the inevitable decline of the gold standard represented the 'proximate cause of the catastrophe' the world had been thrown into from the interbellum onwards. During this episode of international history, governments had been on a futile quest for stability in the inherently unstable realm of international trade. In the first decades of the twentieth century, this had ushered in a series of hopeless endeavours to stabilise world trade by stabilising the exchange rates, based on the fiction of self-regulating markets – a 'preoccupation which spanned the Atlantic'. What this non-system brought about, according to Polanyi, was exactly the opposite of what it was designed for. It set off the Great Depression and subsequently drove the United States to go off the gold standard in 1933, leaving it in shambles – it was an irony of history that this happened after the gold standard had been grandiosely restored in the 1920s as 'the symbol of world solidarity'.

Writing in 1944, Polanyi highlighted a general trend that was recognised also among fellow academics as well as among policy elites: 'we are witnessing a development under which the economic system ceases to lay down the law to society and the primacy of society over that system is secured ... The market system will no longer be self-regulating, even in principle.' From the perspective of political economy, Polanyi concluded that this 'situation may well make two apparently incompatible demands on foreign policy: it will require closer co-operation between friendly countries than could even be contemplated under nineteenth century sovereignty, while at the same time the existence of regulated markets will make national governments more jealous of outside interference than ever before'. Hence, the world Polanyi saw emerging was a place where 'economic collaboration of governments and the liberty to organize national life at will' would co-exist as integral parts of a new system.[43]

Furthermore, within this new system envisioned by Polanyi, the idea of a federation – 'an idea ... deemed a nightmare of centralization and uniformity under market economy and the gold standard' – might in fact be one of the 'great varieties of ways' to reconcile 'effective co-operation with domestic freedom'.[44] It was indeed the concept of federation in which the avenues for the great escape of post-war capitalism were sought. Moreover, most 'miracle-makers' were exactly on the same page as Polanyi was regarding the engineering of post-war capitalist societies and

---

[43] Karl Polanyi, *The Great Transformation* (Boston: Beacon, 1957 [1944]), pp. 3, 26, and 231).
[44] Polanyi, *The Great Transformation*, pp. 251–4.

multilateral cooperation.[45] For the immediate post-war reality, however, these conclusions were too forward-looking. In the year in which his book was published, it became unmistakably clear that Polanyi had been plainly wrong about one key element in his sweeping analysis, for the fixation on stabilising currencies appeared to have outlived the war.

This unwavering policy fixation on the stabilisation of exchange rates had everything to do with the overwhelming desire for stability. In fact, when it came to actual policies to satisfy the desire for stability, post-war planning was not very innovative after all. In the eyes of many, stable currencies were simply 'the touchstones of rationality in politics'.[46] As a result, the multilateral discussions on financial-economic affairs focused almost exclusively on exchange rate stabilisation, which was perceived to be the *sine qua non* for any sustainable order. The single most important event that defined that order in institutional terms was the Bretton Woods Conference in 1944, a major undertaking aimed at promoting stable exchange rates.

How was this possible? What about the generally accepted movement towards coordinated welfare state policies? What happened to the multilateral mission to prevent a repetition of the money-gold logic that had governed the disastrous interbellum? Why this preoccupation with monetary policy? It was in this emerging sphere of policy paradoxes that the distinct worlds of Keynes, Schumpeter, and Polanyi merged, in a way, into an unfathomable amalgam of economic facts, historical (Cold War) circumstances, and high-flown policy ambitions that would set the boundaries of the multilateral efforts to build institutions. Crucially, this put economic and monetary governance at the core of international cooperation.

4.3   Grand Engineering: Banking without Banks

Undoubtedly, the building of the post-war West during most of the 1940s, and much of the societal planning inherent in it, was guided by the American government (the Treasury and State Departments in particular) and the established practices that had been created as part of the wartime Anglo-American partnership.[47] The primary goal was to achieve sustainable

---

[45] See Ruggie, 'International Regimes'.
[46] Polanyi cited in Mark Blyth, *Great Transformations: The Rise and Decline of Embedded Liberalism* (Cambridge: Cambridge University Press, 2002), p. 3; see also Dyson, *States*, p. 578.
[47] John Ikenberry, 'Creating Yesterday's New World Order: Keynesian "New Thinking" and the Anglo-American Postwar Settlement', in Judith Goldstein and Robert Keohane (eds.), *Ideas and Foreign Policy* (Cambridge: Cambridge University Press, 1993), pp. 58ff; Maier, *In Search*, pp. 121–2; Gardner, 'Sterling-Dollar', 21–2; Ben Steil, *The Battle of Bretton Woods. John Maynard Keynes, Harry Dexter White and the Making of a New World Order* (Princeton and Oxford: Princeton University Press, 2013).

economic stability, and the means to achieve it was through state control of the economy on the basis of multilateral agreements. Stability, however, was a multifaceted concept that was far from easy to come to grips with. The most intractable of all the problems attached to economic stability was its Janus-faced nature, for while a country could achieve domestic socio-economic stability (which in those days meant full employment), doing so threatened the external stability of the international economy in the form of a balance-of-payments disequilibrium. The dilemma of internal versus external stability rekindled fears of a repetition of the beggar-thy-neighbour policies of competitive currency devaluations and deflation that had amplified the negative effects of the Great Depression. There were those who argued that countries had to be prevented by any means necessary from resorting once again to these devastating nationalist economic policies. The challenge policymakers faced was to achieve domestic socio-economic justice, international balance-of-payments stability, and monetary and financial soundness all at the same time.

Initially, post-war thinking focused on rather unrestrained attacks on the old system of the gold standard – in which defending the exchange rate overrode the pursuit of domestic full employment – even if it was not quite clear what the alternative should be.[48] However, when policymakers faced the reality of drafting actual plans and negotiating international agreements, the reforms they ended up with were less radical a departure from the old system than might have been expected based on their initial zeal for change.

One of the leading innovators with his hand on the steering wheel of the international economy was Harry Dexter White. White was assistant to the US Treasury secretary and was also the man who had masterminded the Bretton Woods Conference. The international monetary system that sprang from that conference was his 'creation'.[49] White was a child of his time. He believed a sustainable post-war order required 'state interference with trade and with capital movements'. In practice, this meant that international investment, capital movements, exchange rates, and commodity prices had to be seen from a completely new perspective: they were now legitimate instruments of active policy engineering in the hands of technocrats operating in state bureaucracies.[50] To think of state intervention as 'harmful' to the working of the economy was nonsense to White.[51]

---

[48] See, for instance, Donald Moggridge (ed.), *The Collected Writings of John Maynard Keynes*, vol. XXV, *Activities 1940–1944, Shaping the Post-War World: The Clearing Union* (Cambridge: Cambridge University Press, 2013 [1980]), pp. 2ff.
[49] Steil, *The Battle*, p. 334.
[50] Harold James, *International Monetary Cooperation since Bretton Woods* (New York and Oxford: Oxford University Press, 1996), pp. 19, 23, and 26; Ruggie, 'International Regimes', 388ff.
[51] Ikenberry, 'Creating', p. 70; James, *International*, p. 39.

During the first half of the 1940s, the search for stability rapidly developed into something close to an obsession with new possibilities for state control of the economy based on multilateral agreements. State control was seen as the key to any successful future order. It was thought that the state should intervene in at least three broad policy fields: employment, growth, and trade. After Keynes, the objective of full employment was increasingly considered a historical task, for this was seen as necessary to ensure a sufficient degree of social cohesion and to preclude violent social upheaval. Indeed, there were those who argued that full employment had to be guaranteed no matter what the short-term costs were. And persistent growth had to be realised to enable governments to alleviate the booms and busts of the business cycle. International trade had to be curbed or regulated to prevent a balance-of-payments disequilibrium. Already in 1942, the liberal American economist Jacob Viner had summed up the multilateral post-war assignment for the West:

> There is a wide agreement today that major depressions, mass unemployment, are social evils, and that it is the obligation of governments to prevent them ... [and there is] wide agreement also that it is extraordinary difficult, if not outright impossible, for any country to cope alone with the problem of cyclical booms and depressions ... while there is good prospect that with international cooperation ... the problem of the business cycle and of mass unemployment can be largely solved.[52]

Viner was not alone in believing that international cooperation was the answer to the problem of the business cycle. There was a collective mood throughout the West in support of state action and Keynesianism which fuelled the plans for establishing post-war multilateral institutions. As described above, Keynes's plea was for active state intervention – not to socialise the entire economy[53] but to stabilise the demand for money (rather than its supply) in order to stabilise prices. In this sense, Keynesian economics was a clean break with the status quo and with classical thinking on monetary management.[54]

Thus, when it came to the general issue of state control of the economy (based on multilateral agreements), White and Keynes were in the same camp: that of the innovators. The gold standard and its pre-war laissez-faire system represented the corrupted and 'lunatic' Old World they wanted to move away from.[55] Closely connected to these aims was the

---

[52] Jacob Viner, 'Objectives of Post-War International Economic Reconstruction', in W. McKee and L.J. Wiesen (eds.), *American Economic Objectives* (New Wilmington: Economic and Business Foundation, 1942), p. 168; Ikenberry, 'Creating', p. 72.
[53] Muller, *The Mind*, p. 321.
[54] For the origins of Keynes's stance in this matter, see, for instance, Moggridge (ed.), *The Collected Writings of John Maynard Keynes*.
[55] Keynes cited in Ikenberry, 'Creating', p. 76.

conviction that money and capital movements should not be allowed to rule the world as they had done during the era of the gold standard via a largely automatic mechanism devised to react to cross-border movements in gold stocks. Keynes and White felt strongly that it should be the other way around: the world ought to rule money and use it as an instrument to engineer more stable and just societies.[56]

White's boss, Treasury Secretary Henry Morgenthau, was quite explicit when he addressed this issue at the final session of the Bretton Woods Conference on 22 July 1944. He argued that statesmen should aim to 'drive ... the usurious money lenders from the temple of international finance', for this temple belonged to the 'instrumentalities of sovereign governments and not of private financial interests'.[57] Thus, it was envisioned that in any future international system, capital movements had to be controlled. This implied that freedom from exchange controls – a hard precondition for any functioning international system based on free trade – would be limited to current account transactions. Short-term capital and speculative 'hot money' were diagnosed as disruptive movements that had to be reined in by state control. Indeed, 'a case could be made for capital controls as contributing to economic stability'. The argument ran as follows: while changes in the exchange rate did indeed destabilise the domestic economy, they might become unnecessary if the balance of payments could be buttressed – even if only temporarily – by capital controls.[58] Capital controls were also deemed necessary because of a shortage of international reserves after the devastation of the war.[59]

All in all, it was quite clear that international banking in its old, unfettered form would not be part of the multilateral Western world of the future. Yet ironically, this new world order that Keynes and White were laying the foundations of was based on borrowing and lending (i.e., banking). The two men put forward a path to future stability that relied on international monetary cooperation, which in turn inevitably included banking as an integral part. The key novelty of the new system was that essential elements of banking would now become the responsibility of the state – or more precisely a group of states cooperating and coordinating among each other. In other words: the stability the innovators were striving to achieve lay in banking without the banks. The linchpin of the

---

[56] Steil, *The Battle*, pp. 125–55.
[57] Morgenthau cited in James, *International*, p. 39; Gardner, 'Sterling-Dollar', 26.
[58] Frances Cairncross (ed.), *Changing Perceptions of Economic Policy. Essays in the Honour of the Seventieth Birthday of Sir Alec Cairncross* (London and New York: Methuen, 1981), pp. 82 and 86.
[59] Michael D. Brodo and Barry Eichengreen, *A Retrospective on the Bretton Woods System* (Chicago and London: University of Chicago Press, 1993), p. 38.

first post-war constructions of Western multilateralism was the mechanism of capital controls and not free trade, as is often supposed.[60] Partly as a result, the level of capital mobility in the early post-war period reached a historical low.[61]

Nonetheless, the principle of free trade – however elusive it might have been at the time – had not been completely abandoned in the post-war reconstruction of the West, if only because it was firmly anchored in the few established practices that functioned to some extent in the early 1940s, such as the Atlantic Charter and the Lend Lease agreement. Nonetheless, free trade would soon become a relic of the past, maybe not in rhetoric but certainly in practice. Leading policy innovators such as White and Keynes had embarked on an experimental course that gradually and steadily downgraded free trade – and trade as such – to a matter of secondary importance for the multilateral organisation of the post-war West. For a substantial part this was a matter of pragmatism, as the issue of free trade confronted planners with an unsolvable problem. If free trade were considered a prerequisite for stabilisation (as laid down in the Atlantic Charter and the infamous Article VII of the Lend Lease Act),[62] then lending and borrowing to adjust countries' balance of payments would have to be subordinated to that overarching aim rather than to the pursuit of domestic social policies. But the uncontrollable divergence of national economic developments in the West because of the devastating effects of the war in Europe made free trade an utterly impossible priority in practice.

Keynes's fear was that this divergence in national economies, which led to balance-of-payments difficulties, might prompt deficit countries trying

---

[60] See James, *International*, p. 58.
[61] In addition to capital controls, the expansion of international banking was significantly slowed as a result of the limited amount of international reserves, the dollar gap, and the lack of convertibility of the European currencies and the Japanese yen.
[62] Article VII of Lend Lease referred to the Atlantic Charter and stated the following: 'In the final determination of the benefits to be provided to the United States of America by the Government of the United Kingdom in return for aid furnished under the Act of Congress of March 11, 1941, the terms and conditions thereof shall be such as not to burden commerce between the two countries, but to promote mutually advantageous economic relations between them and the betterment of world-wide economic relations. To that end, they shall include provision for agreed action by the United States of America and the United Kingdom, open to participation by all other countries of like mind, directed to the expansion, by appropriate international and domestic measures, of production, employment, and the exchange and consumption of goods, which are the material foundations of the liberty and welfare of all peoples; to the elimination of all forms of discriminatory treatment in international commerce, and to the reduction of tariffs and other trade barriers; and, in general, to the attainment of all the economic objectives set forth in the Joint Declaration made on August 14, 1941 by the President of the United States of America and the Prime Minister of the United Kingdom.'

to attain full employment to deflate demand. If such a scenario were not matched by an offsetting expansion in demand in surplus countries, this would give rise to global deflation. The solution to this conundrum lay according to Keynes in multilateral coordination. Already during the early 1940s, Keynes had become preoccupied with schemes for an international organisation that could manage the thorny balance-of-payments issue. At the core of his thinking was the idea that a country's balance of payments could be managed by using the lever of monetary policy.[63] This was the Copernican revolution in economic thinking that brought about 'a shift from contentious trade issues to monetary issues' to tackle the persistent problems of international cooperation. Keynes surmised that what was most urgently needed to manage the balance-of-payments crisis – and thus to curb the risk of disarray in Europe – was loans and investment, not free trade. What Europe needed was capital! It was clear to Keynesians that the only way to generate reconstruction and stimulate some productivity and growth in Western Europe was for the United States to inject money into the region, hence the Marshall Plan.

Thus, solving the balance-of-payments crisis became the priority and monetary management the instrument. Keynes's innovative ideas created 'an emerging middle ground', as John Ikenberry has pointed out, between national sovereignty and international cooperation. This middle ground also constituted the realm in which the British and American views (the former represented by Keynes and the latter by White) were able to meet halfway and where the goal of full employment (pursued by Keynes) could be reconciled with the costs associated with it (which was White's concern). And it was on this middle ground that discussions and negotiations among the Western nations on the post-war order were able to take place in a more or less orderly manner.[64] This new middle ground was full of opportunities for progressive policies, but it was above all the manifestation of the new hope culminating in the Bretton Woods agreements signed in the summer of 1944, which represented 'a new beginning ... a belief that there was a future and a promise'.[65]

Keynes's trick, which set in motion the decisive dynamics behind the two-step move in post-war multilateralism, was to broaden the horizon of international economics. What Keynes did in essence was to redefine the material world of inter-state trade by coupling it to the

---

[63] See D. Vines, 'James Meade', *Discussion Paper Series*, 330 (Department of Economics, Oxford University, 2007).
[64] Ikenberry, 'Creating', pp. 58, 61–2, and 76.   [65] James, *International*, pp. 56–8.

The Great Escape

more virtual world of money in a system of multilateral coordination.[66] These liberated countries from the maddening structural strains on their balance of payments that had been indissolubly linked to the old system. The monetary sphere, in other words, offered possibilities – up to then largely unexplored – for redefining the hard problems of the inherently unstable socio-economic situation, both within countries and internationally.

It was inevitable, however, that these possibilities would eventually come face to face with reality. For Bretton Woods merely enabled the states involved to buy time in their struggle with the unsolvable entanglements of capitalism, democracy, and socialist ambitions; it did not actually solve them (hence Schumpeter's pessimism). While Keynes's multilateral solution to the existing trade imbalance allowed countries to pursue their domestic social policies without fear of a balance-of-payments crisis, it inevitably led to a point – decades later – at which the Western world once again had to confront the trade-off between domestic and international stability. During the 1940s, most policymakers viewed the risk of an international economic crisis as rather far-fetched, preferring to leave any pondering over contingencies to academics such as Schumpeter. Moreover, immediate policy problems took precedence. Accordingly, the focus of post-war planning was on the monetary sphere, and the theoretical underpinnings of that planning came from Keynesianism. What Keynesian thinking offered was a world in which the budget no longer had to be balanced but could instead be transformed into an instrument in the hands of policy engineers and planners. This represented a quantum leap in the realm of planning, a seismic shift away from politics towards policy – and precisely the kind of escapism that Schumpeter so abhorred but that was so in tune with the longing for social justice characteristic of this period in history.

Keynesianism came to dominate thinking from the mid-1940s. The generally accepted opinion among the transatlantic builders of the post-war Western order was that the national budget must be made available to policymakers to enable them to smoothen the business cycle, which remained part and parcel of the imperfect markets that came with any capitalist order. From now on, the fluctuations in the economic cycle would be counteracted by policy measures in the new experiment with capitalism and democracy in the post-war Western world and Western Europe in particular.[67]

---

[66] See the next section of this chapter for the elaboration of this approach in the form of multilateral policies.
[67] Kathleen McNamara, *The Currency of Ideas. Monetary Politics in the European Union* (Ithaca and London: Cornell University Press, 1998), p. 85; Ikenberry, 'Creating', p. 77.

4.4 The Vicissitudes of Multilateralism

While Keynes was the one to provide the intellectual framework for the Bretton Woods system, the practicalities of the system drew heavily on the American counter-plan, which had been drafted to a large extent by White. As mentioned above, White fully shared Keynes's goal to 'multilateralise' the post-war world, as this was seen as the only way to realise the twofold aim of getting rid of national exchange controls and their associated restrictive financial measures while protecting domestic economies from the harsh repercussions of unfettered capital mobility. However, the plan White proposed was far more modest than Keynes's ideas both in ambition and in form. What White suggested was merely to establish a fund of rather limited size, created by pooled contributions of the member states, that members with balance-of-payments difficulties could draw on to offset exchange rate adjustments. Moreover, member states could only rely on the fund up to a certain limit and under strict rules of conditionality.[68]

What started off as an ambition to set up a supranational institution overlooking a system of fixed exchange rates – deemed to be a precondition for stabilising the international economy and trade in particular – ended in a multilateral experiment with three distinct characteristics: far-reaching state control (over trade), international funding (to compensate for economic blows in national situations), and capital controls for an unlimited period of time.[69] While not all that innovative when assessed in isolation, when combined, these ingredients marked the beginning of a new phase of capitalism in the Western world. Paradoxically, this infrastructure of multilateral coordination based on domestic state control, international funding, and capital controls gave rise to a system that had a built-in tendency towards self-destruction (through multilateral 'decontrol'). Two specific features of the system devised in Bretton Woods were responsible for this.

The first of these features is the explicit guarantee of national sovereignty and the corresponding lack of any form of supranational supervision.[70] The intellectual inspiration for the Bretton Woods system largely came from Keynes's famous plan for an international clearing union.[71] A key element of this plan was a multilateral (originally supranational) overdraft facility to create and manage tens of billions of a new international currency to settle balance-of-payments disequilibria. In addition, this future union would have had the authority to set conditions for both debtor and creditor countries to correct the imbalance (through governance guidance, for instance, or a tax on excessive reserves).

---

[68] Ikenberry, 'Creating', pp. 77–8; McNamara, *The Currency*, pp. 73–5.
[69] See Daunton, 'From Bretton Woods', pp. 52–9.   [70] Gardner, 'Sterling-Dollar', 27.
[71] Moggridge (ed.), *The Collected Writings of John Maynard Keynes*.

The distribution of the new international currency would have allowed members to remove restrictions on all capital movements yet maintain stable exchange rates at the same time and pursue domestic welfare state policies without the threat of a devastating external payments crisis.

At Bretton Woods, however, this fancy theoretical scheme did not survive the harsh test of political reality. National sovereignty was a *sine qua non* for any global monetary system, which made any supranational institution a no go and reduced the system to not much more than a gentlemen's agreement among the cooperating nation-states. And right from the start, this intergovernmental agreement became vulnerable to undermining by member states' short-term political calculations.

The second feature responsible for the built-in tendency towards self-destruction in the Bretton Woods system was the goal of future convertibility, which was seen as a fundamental requirement for the durability of the system. The non-convertibility of European currencies, which prevented their free flow across borders even when required for international trade payments, was deemed only acceptable for a transition period during which countries would work to overcome their severe balance-of-payments instabilities of the first post-war years. To that end, Article VI of the rules and regulations agreed at Bretton Woods allowed members to place capital controls on currency transactions if such capital flows threatened to overwhelm a member's balance of payments or exchange rate stability.[72] This provision, however, was inherently temporary in the light of the goal of convertibility. In turn, this implied that future convertibility unavoidably resulted in pressure on the temporary regime of capital controls.

These two built-in features of the new system led in the long run to something quite remote from the stable system envisaged at Bretton Woods. Given that the Western economies were becoming increasingly financially integrated, the combination of full currency convertibility and the primacy of national short-term goals over multilateral coordination ultimately resulted in the formation of trade blocs. Largely uncontrollable capital flows together with the return of international banking in turn re-empowered financial markets, allowing them to put pressure on countries' currencies and thereby limit their room for manoeuvre in terms of domestic social policy. This was a more than realistic scenario, especially because allowing one of the built-in features to take its course would mean augmenting the effects of the other feature. In concrete terms, this meant that countries' focus on cost-benefit calculations stimulated bloc formation, which in turn would lead to regional convertibility and regional

---

[72] McNamara, *The Currency*, p. 65.

market integration. More regionalisation would then increase calls for the free movement of capital to prop the emerging regional market. This mutually reinforcing process inevitably led to countries decontrolling their foreign exchange markets regionally. After all, the free movement of capital in a world of welfare states was sure to provoke protectionist reflexes, either nationally or regionally.

All in all, this meant that over time, both built-in features served to undermine the safe haven provided by the Bretton Woods system. This resulted in growing pressure to choose between either free-floating exchange rates or monetary union, a dilemma that the most far-sighted economist at that time, Robert Triffin, had pinpointed already in the earliest days of Bretton Woods.[73]

What is important to note here is that the post-war Western world had in essence but two backstops – and rather shaky ones at that – to ward off the ominous choice between all-out union, regional bloc formation, or a re-entry of laissez-faire thinking through the backdoor of multilateral coordination. These two backstops were American hegemony and capital controls, and their 'shelf life', so to say, amid the vicissitudes of multilateralism was of decisive importance for the future of Western Europe.

Already by early 1947, many illusions of planning had been smashed. The sterling crisis of that year had thwarted ambitious schemes to extend the transatlantic arrangement of financial-economic management beyond the Bretton Woods agreement.[74] Moreover, an extremely harsh winter had resulted in a severe shortage of coal in Europe and a disastrous harvest, which in turn had exacerbated already existing food shortages. Against this bleak backdrop, the main conclusion among the policy engineers of the West was that more rather than less planning was needed. This was not naïve, for there was reason to hope that things could be changed for the better. After all, and in spite of all the setbacks, a multilateral structure had been erected: the 'system' of Bretton Woods existed. What was needed now was to further work out this new transnational framework to prepare it for the ultimate litmus test: to put theory into practice, to translate ambitious concepts into durable and credible policies that would foster stability. This was the only way to weather the international storms of the late 1940s. But the increasing emphasis on being practical also meant being more specific and more regional.

[73] See The National Archives (TNA), Kew, Surrey, T230/156, 'Points for discussion on the problem of currency transferability in Europe, prepared by R. Triffin', December 1949; HAEU, Etienne Hirsch, 5, 'UDIT: Le Renouveau de la France', May–June–July 1943, pp. 2–8; Ivo Maes (with Ilaria Pasotti), *Robert Triffin. A Life* (Oxford: Oxford University Press, 2021), pp. 71ff.
[74] Milward, *The Reconstruction*, pp. 43–55.

In the wake of the crisis of 1947, the planners shifted their focus from grand designs to practical governance and concrete problem-solving. At the same time, as the emerging Cold War increasingly came to determine the global setting, it became clear that Europe's destiny was dependent on decisions being made by the two superpowers, the United States and the Soviet Union. Two speeches in the first half of 1947 portended a crucial turning point for the post-war development of Western Europe. The first speech was by President Harry S. Truman on 12 March, in which he argued to Congress that 'it must be the policy of the United States to support free peoples who are resisting attempted subjugation by armed minorities or by outside pressures'. He thereby pledged support to the Greek and Turkish governments which were both dealing with communist uprisings. More importantly, the speech established what would come to be known as the Truman Doctrine, the US foreign policy of containing the Soviet Union and the spread of communism by coming to the aid of anti-communist governments. The Truman Doctrine was a defining feature of the Cold War that effectively side-lined that other bastion of multilateralism – the United Nations (UN).

The second speech was specifically about the future of Europe. On 5 June, Secretary of State George Marshall not only announced that the US was launching a revolutionary recovery plan for Europe to 'save the free community of Europe',[75] he also made US aid to Europe conditional on European cooperation. Marshall left the 'how' of the European Recovery Programme up to the Europeans, allowing them to come up with a common reconstruction plan to allocate the dollars of the Marshall Plan and to run the organisation themselves. Nonetheless, there was one thing that was intentionally left out of Marshall's speech that gave a clue to how the United States felt that Europe should proceed. To the surprise of many planners both within and outside of Washington, the secretary of state 'purposefully did not mention the UN or the UN Economic Commission for Europe' (ECE)[76] which had been set up just a few weeks earlier in Geneva and was the only existing organisation focused on general economic cooperation in Europe. In fact, the ECE had replaced all inter-Allied humanitarian and emergency organisations that had been active in the final war years and the immediate aftermath of the war (the United Nations Relief and Rehabilitation Administration, the

---

[75] Leffler, 'The Emergence', p. 78.
[76] Daniel Stinsky, 'Western Europe vs. All-European Cooperation? The OEEC, the European Recovery Program, and the United Nations Economic Commission for Europe, 1947–1952', in Matthieu Leimgruber and Matthias Schmelzer (eds.), *The OECD and the International Political Economy since 1948* (Cham: Springer Nature/Palgrave Macmillan, 2017), p. 69.

European Coal Committee, the European Central Inland Transport Organization, and the Emergency Economic Committee for Europe). Although in line with the emerging Truman Doctrine, the fact that Marshall neglected to mention the ECE was nonetheless a game-changer for post-war Europe. It was clear to the entire world that the wartime collaboration between the Allies and the prevention of a division in Europe – of which the UN was the institutional embodiment – was now a thing of the past.

Part 2

The Making of European Integration
(1947–1951)

5 The Marshall Plan: Western Europe as a Unit

After a trip to devastated Europe during the spring of 1947 which followed the harshest winter in a century, the American under secretary of state for economic affairs, William Clayton, drew up an urgent memorandum that was to become the catalyst for a radical change in US policy towards Europe. In the memorandum, Clayton outlined the economic and political rationale for a more regional approach to Europe's acute structural problems. This included an innovative institutional strategy that opened up new possibilities for tackling the economic and political problems in Europe, where the situation in Italy and Germany in particular bordered on despair.

During his visit to Europe, Clayton had attended the first session of the United Nations Economic Commission for Europe. Based on that experience, he had concluded that US foreign policy in Europe had thus far been ineffective. He stated that 'we grossly underestimated the destruction to the European economy by the war ... Europe is steadily deteriorating. The political position reflects the economic ... Millions of people in the cities are slowly starving. More consumer's goods and restored confidence in the local currency are absolutely essential.' The memorandum then reported Europe's annual balance-of-payments deficits: 'UK #2.25 billion, France #1.75 billion, Italy #1.5 billion, US–UK Zone Germany #1.5 billion, not to mention the smaller countries'. Clayton's concluding words delivered a stark warning: these figures 'represent[s] an absolute minimum standard of living. If it should be lowered, there will be revolution. *Only until the end of this year* [emphasis in original] can England and France meet the above deficits out of their fast-dwindling reserves of gold and dollars. Italy can't go that long.'[1]

The inability of European countries to pay for imports due to their huge balance-of-payments deficits was the all-consuming problem, resulting in

---

[1] Department of State, *Foreign Relations of the United States* (FRUS), 1947, vol. III, *The British Commonwealth; Europe* (Washington: US Printing Office, 1972), 'Memorandum by the Under Secretary of State for Economic Affairs (Clayton)', 27 May 1947, pp. 230–2; see also Leffler, 'The Emergence', p. 75.

raging inflation particularly in France and Italy. This made the need for dollars to combat hunger, to enable the industry to increase production, and to boost agriculture even more desperate. The only way to solve Europe's balance-of-payments crisis was via real money, and the only viable option to pump such money into Europe was for the US to provide grants and loans while stimulating and facilitating international trade in parallel.[2] This would serve American interests, as it would revive European export markets for American trade. The conclusion to Clayton's memorandum was unambiguous: 'Without further prompt and substantial aid from the United States, economic, social and political disintegration will overwhelm Europe ... the immediate effects on our domestic economy would be disastrous: markets for our surplus production gone, unemployment, depression, heavily unbalanced budget on the background of a mountainous war debt. *These things must not happen* [emphasis in original].'[3]

Action was needed. Clayton believed it was 'wholly unnecessary' to conduct a further investigation into US national assets and liabilities to determine the country's ability to assist Europe – as proposed by some prominent advisors to the government – as 'the facts' were 'well known' by now: 'Our resources and our productive capacity are ample to provide all the help necessary.' Nonetheless, Clayton was fully aware that his proposed approach would be an arduous task, since it required organising 'our fiscal policy and our consumption so that sufficient surpluses of the necessary goods are made available out of our enormous production, and so that these surpluses are paid for out of taxation and not by addition to debt'. Essentially, this required the US government to make an audacious appeal to American citizens: 'This problem can be met only if the American people are taken into the complete confidence of the Administration and told all the facts and only if a sound and workable plan is presented.' Furthermore, Clayton stressed that this obliged 'the President and the Secretary of State to make a strong spiritual appeal to the American people to sacrifice a little themselves ... to save Europe from starvation and chaos (*not* [emphasis in original] from the Russians), and, at the same time, to preserve ourselves and our children the glorious heritage of a free America'. This would legitimise '6 or 7 billion dollars' worth of goods a year for three years' provided to Europe 'as a grant', which 'should be based on a European

---

[2] Luigi Einaudi, 'Why We Need a European Economic Federation' (1943 and 1948) and 'The Economic Tasks of the Federation' (1944 and 1948) in in Einaudi, Faucci, and Marchionatti (eds.), *Luigi Einaudi. Selected Economic Essays*, pp. 248 and 256–7; Hervé Alphand, *L'étonnement d'être. Journal 1939–1973* (Paris: Fayard, 1977), pp. 199–200.
[3] FRUS, 1947, vol. III, pp. 230–2.

plan' modelled on 'the Belgium–Netherlands–Luxembourg Customs Union'. Clayton ended his memorandum with a clear piece of advice on the practicalities of the ground-breaking plan he proposed: 'We must avoid getting into another UNRRA [the United Nations Relief and Rehabilitation Administration]. *The United States must run this show* [emphasis in original].'[4]

Two days later, in a follow-up meeting with State Department officials in the midst of drafting Secretary of State George Marshall's Harvard speech, Clayton furthermore 'stated his conviction that the ECE [the UN's Economic Commission for Europe] is completely unusable as a forum, even to make a beginning, since the paralyzing fear of the USSR by the small countries would permit her to carry out her undoubted intention to block all constructive action'.[5] He suggested orienting US action towards Western Europe instead, a suggestion that did not fall on deaf ears. Between the first and second sessions of the ECE, Marshall launched the European Recovery Plan, which soon replaced the ECE in the practical planning of American aid to Western Europe.

5.1   Marshall's Message and the Failure of the ITO

On 5 June 1947, one week after the meeting on the Clayton memorandum in the State Department, Marshall gave his speech at Harvard announcing an extensive American plan for reconstruction in Europe. The plan implied a radical overhaul of the mission of the World Bank, which had been established at the 1944 Bretton Woods Conference to financially support European reconstruction. The new US approach to engaging with Europe made these World Bank loans meaningless, as the total sum of these loans to Europe was less than half a million dollars while the Marshall Plan proposed pumping four *billion* dollars into the reconstruction of Europe. As a result, the World Bank switched to focusing on its second mission – promoting the development of backward member countries – much earlier than expected.[6]

Marshall's message was unmistakably clear: the US was offering a massive aid programme, but the Europeans had to take responsibility for implementing it themselves – which implied doing so even outside the

---

[4] FRUS, 1947, vol. III, pp. 230–2; Stinsky, 'Western Europe', p. 70.
[5] FRUS, 1947, vol. III, 'Summary of Discussion on Problems of Relief, Rehabilitation and Reconstruction of Europe', 29 May 1947, p. 236; Werner Bührer, *Westdeutschland in der OEEC. Eingliederung, Krise, Bewährung 1947–1961* (Munich: Oldenburg, 1997), p. 39.
[6] Michele Alacevich, 'The World Bank's Early Reflections on Development: A Development Institution or a Bank', *Centro Studi Luca D'Agliano Development Studies Working Papers*, 122 (2007), 1–2.

structure of the UN institutions if need be. As Marshall himself put it, reconstruction was 'the business of the Europeans'.

Around the same time, the renowned Swedish economist Gunnar Myrdal was touring Europe in his capacity as the first ECE executive secretary. During his visit to Moscow, Myrdal warned the Soviet Minister of Foreign Affairs Vyacheslav Molotov that 'a lack of positive Soviet response to the Marshall declaration [would] show green light to the advocates of [an] ad hoc West Bloc organization for European construction'. And indeed, it was soon thereafter that Myrdal heard, much to his dismay, about Franco-British exploratory talks to bypass the ECE and invite only a few European countries (including Poland but not the USSR) to discuss the Marshall Plan. It was clear that Marshall's speech had sparked a competition between rival organisations for the European management of US aid dollars. Myrdal was convinced that the way to prevent an 'ad hoc West Bloc organization' was for all European countries to opt for the ECE route to channel and manage the Marshall dollars. He therefore lobbied for an 'ad hoc European planning committee' nestled within the ECE. However, during the crucial first European talks on the Marshall Plan, organised in Paris in June/July on the initiative of the British and French ministers of foreign affairs, Molotov flatly rejected the Marshall Plan. The Russian minister also took the Polish and Czechoslovakian delegations with him and subsequently pressured Hungary, Romania, Bulgaria, Yugoslavia, and Finland into declining the invitation to the September conference organised by the British and French governments.[7] One day before the start of the Paris talks with his French and Russian counterparts Bidault and Molotov, British Foreign Minister Ernest Bevin had acquired the crucial American confirmation (in a meeting with Clayton in London) that the US would also back a joint European effort, were the USSR not participating in it.[8]

The eventual decision of the Soviet Union not to participate in the Marshall Plan meant that the European Recovery Plan could no longer be a UN project. Thus, actions taken by both superpowers were clearly nudging the European continent towards bloc formation.[9] The ERP became a Western European affair, and a newly formed Organisation for European Economic Cooperation was put in charge of implementing the plan.[10]

---

[7] Benn Steil, *The Marshall Plan. Dawn of the Cold War* (Oxford: Oxford University Press, 2018), pp. 127–33.

[8] Allan Bullock, *Ernest Bevin. Foreign Secretary* (Oxford: Oxford University Press, 1983), p. 417.

[9] Stinsky, 'Western Europe', p. 71.

[10] The original members of the OEEC were Austria, Belgium, Denmark, France, Greece, Iceland, Ireland, Luxembourg, the Netherlands, Norway, Portugal, Spain, Sweden, Switzerland, Turkey, the United Kingdom, West Germany, and Italy (joining in 1949).

Meanwhile, the US continued to put pressure on the Europeans to move swiftly towards a 'European economic federation' as Clayton made clear during a dinner with French government officials on 10 July.[11] He outlined how he felt Europe should achieve this goal: it required a plan to create a customs union within a fixed timeframe – that is, as soon as possible. Clayton's plan was fully in line with the ideas and political agendas of influential protagonists of supranational economic cooperation such as Jean Monnet and Luigi Einaudi, the well-connected liberal economist who was part of the activist pro-European Italian government of the Christian Democrat Alcide de Gasperi (Einaudi was to join the Mont Pèlerin Society in 1951 with, among others, the West German economics minister, Ludwig Erhard). Indeed, back in 1943, Einaudi had published a plan for a European economic federation which included the idea of using a customs union as a steppingstone.[12]

Developments in the policy realm of international trade also conspired to push Western Europe towards bloc formation. The single most important flaw in the post-war multilateralist system sculpted at Bretton Woods was the failure to create a true 'trade counterpart' to the International Monetary Fund (IMF). Although the United States had envisioned the establishment of an International Trade Organisation (ITO), the bringing into being of this organisation ultimately failed. This was another setback for the international planners of multilateralism who were active supporters of Bretton Woods and its global free trade outlook. By 1947, it was getting clearer and clearer that it would become very difficult to avoid the failure of the ITO. Harold Wilson, president of the Board of Trade in the UK, summed it up neatly in November of that year: 'the multilateral, all-convertible trading world envisaged in 1945 crashed in the summer'.[13] The final blow was delivered by the very country that had proposed the idea of an international trade organisation: the US. Under pressure from public opinion, President Truman eventually decided not to submit the Havana Charter providing for the establishment of the ITO to Congress for ratification. The result was that the multilateral system was left with only the General Agreement on Tariffs and Trade (GATT), originally conceived as a preparatory step towards the ITO.

The failure of the Havana Charter had a profound impact on Western European and transatlantic cooperation. Moreover, the fact that it was the United States that had pulled the plug on the ITO could be seen as the writing on the wall. Through its actions, the US government had effectively

---

[11] Steehouder, 'Constructing Europe', p. 197.
[12] Einaudi, 'Why We Need a European Economic Federation', pp. 245–9.
[13] Richard Toje, 'The Attlee Government, the Imperial Preference System and the Creation of the GATT', *English Historical Review*, 118, 478 (2003), 930.

shown that it had given up the pursuit of a transatlantic community encompassing multilateralism and convertibility. The dream of a transatlantic community in which the United States would work together with Western European countries based on equality proved to be just that – a dream.

5.2 An Island in the West

Another consequence of the failure to establish the ITO was that the goal of currency convertibility had been pushed into the future. This in turn made obsolete many of the blueprints for post-war society put forward by the British. The British economist James Meade had emphasised 'the need for flexible exchange rates' to adjust a country's balance of payments in a world in which internal wage levels were not easily reduced, as flexible exchange rates would prevent countries from resorting to import controls in times of balance-of-payments crises. To facilitate the political acceptance of this type of adjustment, an international agreement to lower trade barriers was needed, since free trade would soften the blow resulting from exchange rate movements. Meade was convinced that state involvement at the macroeconomic level could be combined with liberalism at the microeconomic level. It was clear to him that the emerging circumstances of inconvertibility required debate on a fundamental question: whether the pursuit of multilateralism, which he supported in theory, should be 'on the same terms as Labour's earlier thinking on free trade – namely, on the condition that it was firmly linked with domestic redistribution and employment?'[14] The Attlee government's answer to this question was a reflex: an unsurprising and resounding 'yes'. This popular and easy going approach of this thorny issue maddened liberal economists such as Meade and Schumpeter. More importantly, however, it led to serious tensions with Washington and presented the movement towards multilateralism with new problems.[15]

The United Kingdom was, of course, not the only European country suffering from persistent balance-of-payments problems, but its situation was worsened by a sharp decline in British trade with its colonies, its high military expenditures overseas, and the heavy financial burden of the British zone in occupied Germany. And as long as the UK failed to offer a credible solution to this balance-of-payments problem, it was difficult for the other Europeans to take seriously British pleas for 'free competition' through 'the abolition of quantitative restrictions'. By focusing on freeing up intra-European trade before dealing with the intra-European payments problem, the British approach was effectively putting the cart before the

[14] Vines, 'James Meade'.   [15] Daunton, 'From Bretton Woods', p. 55.

horse.[16] This meant that the UK was slowly but surely being outmanoeuvred in the practical plan-making for post-war Western Europe within the context of the Bretton Woods system.

In the diplomatic wings, the United Kingdom's most loyal friends in Western Europe, the Dutch, continued to search feverishly until the very last moment for ways to prevent the British from being cut off from the organisation of post-war Western Europe. As late as the summer of 1949, the Dutch minister of foreign affairs, Dirk Stikker, was lobbying in and around the OEEC for what he described as a 'global solution', linking up with 'constructive ideas to this effect' in the United Kingdom, in spite of the fact that the trend was unmistakably in the opposite direction: continental integration, or 'bloc formation' *within* the West. Stikker stressed that the Netherlands must not go along with this, if only because it was unclear 'what form this bloc formation would take', but especially because to him it was still unclear 'which bloc the Netherlands should join'.[17] The Dutch actions and doubts were to no avail. After two years of struggling with this frustrating reality, London eventually ended up outside of the emerging regional bloc formation in Western Europe and its embryonic common market. This was the political price the British government had to pay for insisting on a 'special position' for the pound sterling within the newly erected European Payments Union. This was not an outcome that landed well in Washington, where the British empire was essentially perceived as a discriminatory trade bloc standing in the way of more important priorities related to Europe and the Cold War.

From the British perspective, the mere act of accepting Marshall Aid represented an agonising 'conflict between poverty and pride', especially since the US was insisting that the United Kingdom be an equal partner of the other Western European countries – who had been the losers, collaborators, or aggressors during the war – instead of the preferred equal partner of the United States. The result of this attitude was that Britain was excluded from joint European programmes throughout the course of 1948 – in a certain way, already a very early announcement of 'Brexit'. The British position was characterised by paradoxes bordering on contradiction. On the one hand, the Attlee–Bevin approach distinguished itself by resisting the continuous American pressure towards more unbridled forms of capitalism, which was at odds with the Labour government's ambitious Keynesian social programme. On the other hand, the British

---

[16] TNA, T230/155 (Intra-European Trade and Payments), OEEC, 'Present Positions on the Principles of the Payments Scheme for the 1949–50 Financial Year', Paris, 27 June 1949; see also FO 371/87108, Cabinet Office, 'EPU and Trade Rules: Note by Mr. Fleming on the Dangers of Gold Losses by the UK', 6 March 1950.
[17] DNA, 2.0205.02, 371, REA, 17 August 1949, p. 5.

government steered away from any truly impactful initiative of European cooperation – the most realistic way to resist the American pressure in the longer run – that implied a certain degree of supranational integration. While the UK played an instrumental role and was often even actively leading efforts to set up the ERP and the OEEC in 1947–9, the country remained unwilling to commit to any joint European programme, persistently seeking reassurance from the Americans that the ERP would remain an essentially intergovernmental and bilateral affair. The British insisted that any European recovery scheme should guarantee national veto power and avoid 'European pooling', as pooling would relegate the UK to the status of 'merely another European country', something that was utterly unthinkable to the British. After all, had it not been their own Bevin who 'never hesitated to "stand up to the Americans" in a way that no other political figure in Western Europe in these years ever did'? (Bevin biographer Allan Bullock notes that when Attlee was asked what Bevin's greatest contribution as foreign secretary had been, he replied: 'standing up to the Americans'.)[18]

Consequently, the UK remained an island in the West when it came to deeper European cooperation. From a broader perspective, these realities were also interlinked to two other developments that were co-shaping the emerging post-war Western Europe. The first development concerned the gradual Americanisation of the ecumenical movement and the World Council of Churches after the Second World War. This Americanisation reflected the realities of the earthly and geopolitical power relations within the post-war West. Moreover, as of 1946, this Americanisation got paired to a growing obsession with the upgrowth of the American–Soviet rivalry. Superpower antagonism became the dominant lens through which Christian goals and ambitions could be translated into political and societal action. Indeed, as the Cold War dawned upon the world, bipolarity often became a substitute for thought, not in the least (ironically) in the Western sphere of Christian-unity ambitions embodied by the WCC (see next chapter). The second development entailed the process of the regionalisation or 'Europeanisation' of Western Europe (at the cost of broader Western or Atlantic schemes for international cooperation and the One World approach).

The effect of Marshall's speech was felt directly in Western Europe, albeit initially mostly in the realm of diplomacy and foreign policy. Before Marshall's speech, an essentially reactive British foreign policy had set the tone in Western Europe, but had not exactly created new realities. After Marshall's speech, things changed rapidly and profoundly. Soon, the

---

[18] Bullock, *Ernest Bevin*, pp. 415–16.

British approach was branded as not merely too little too late, but also as an utter illusion in practical political terms. As such, Marshall's speech enhanced an Anglo-American divergence in post-war European affairs, in which practical problems of (geo)politics and (geo)economics would outstrip global-inspired grand designing and suppress Atlantic imagination. The suffocation of the Anglo-American wartime partnership and the fading of Atlantic imagination, however, would create a unique breeding ground for feasible modes of Western European integration that soon would represent more credible and tangible forms of new and old, Christian-inspired, transatlantic dreams. Seen from this angle, it might have been no coincidence that Ernest Bevin, the British minister of foreign affairs, in January 1948 christened the edifice 'Western Union' to package the British European policy of the moment – a last futile attempt to keep the UK at the centre of the making of post-war Western Europe (see chapter 6).

It was against the backdrop of the American shift towards 'building (Western) Europe' – and including West Germany as an integral and vital part of that construction project – that 'the whole question of sovereignty and integration', the elephant in the room of the emerging Western Europe, 'was raised actively', in terms of practical solutions for pressing (economic) problems, 'for the first time'.[19] Eventually, continental Europe went on without the British to form the European Payments Union, which regulated intra-European payments in a way that facilitated intra-European trade. This was only possible thanks to the institutional structures that were set up for the administration of the Marshall Plan. And thus, the problem of how to revive the European economy was solved not within the framework of the Bretton Woods system nor through the institutional structures of the UN but via the institutional set up connected to the Marshall Plan, in particular the OEEC – the institution in which Europeans implemented their ideas for monetary regionalism that had their roots in the inter-war period and the period of exile in London.[20]

In sum, the possibility of pooling the sovereignty was increasingly seen as a means to the end of liberating Western Europe from the shackles of bilateralism and tackle the problem of inflation; the rough sketch of an action plan for pooling that in the following years would be promoted tirelessly by Hervé Alphand, as head of the French delegation to the Committee of European Economic Cooperation (CEEC)/OEEC, Monnet, as the transatlantic linchpin (outside the OEEC in the making),

---

[19] Duchêne, *Jean Monnet*, p. 168.
[20] Jorrit Steehouder, 'In the Name of Social Stability: The European Payments Union', in Mathieu Segers and Steven van Hecke (eds.), *The Cambridge History of the European Union*, vol. II (Cambridge: Cambridge University Press, 2023), ch. 7.

and by Robert Marjolin, who had been appointed Monnet's deputy at the French Planning Commission in Paris – and would be OEEC's future secretary-general (appointed in April 1948) – from the multilateral bureau-political inside of the CEEC/OEEC.[21] Crucially, it was also this European institutional framework that allowed the Europeans and Americans to devise new solutions to the so-called 'German problem' – that is, the problem of how to deal with a Germany that was divided.

5.3   Dealing with the German Problem

The Potsdam Conference in the summer of 1945 made it clear that it was impossible to conclude a peace treaty with Germany for the time being. The obstacle to a peace treaty was not Germany itself but rather the schism among the victors: the differences of opinion between the Soviet Union and the Western Allies proved too fundamental to overcome. As a result, the division of Germany into four occupation zones, decided by the Allies at the Yalta Conference in February 1945, remained in place. The same applied to the agreement that each occupying power represented the highest authority in its own zone, which boiled down to a right of veto on all matters of policy concerning the whole of Germany. This situation prevented the development of a policy for Germany as a whole. Thus, the failure of Potsdam to bring about a definitive end to the war with Germany meant that, by default, the provisional 'Yalta order' remained in effect. This effectively divided Germany and Europe in two.[22] By 1947, this de facto division became official as the American and British occupation zones merged to form the Bizone on 1 January. They were joined in 1948 by the French zone (after which it was renamed the Trizone). For the United States, this situation meant that cooperation with the Soviet Union, initially considered possible by Washington, became increasingly unlikely. The American position towards Europe clearly had to be reviewed, as an 'overall strategy' for the new situation was lacking.[23]

Opinions in Washington were now rapidly moving in new directions. One of the prevailing insights was that a customs union in Western Europe was urgently needed to ensure that free trade could continue to

---

[21] Kenneth Dyson and Lucia Quaglia (eds.), *European Economic Governance & Policies. Commentary on Key Historical & Institutional Documents*, vol. I (Oxford: Oxford University Press, 2010), p. 32; Duchêne, *Jean Monnet*, pp. 168–9.

[22] *Dokumente zur Deutschlandpolitik*, II. Series, vol. I, *Die Konferenz von Potsdam* (Neuwied and Frankfurt: Albert Metzner, 1992), pp. 2289–96 and 2312–13; William Smyser, *From Yalta to Berlin: The Cold War Struggle over Germany* (New York: St Martin's Griffin, 1999), pp. 10–17.

[23] See Gillingham, 'From Morgenthau', pp. 111ff.

be promoted. Such a customs union soon came to be seen as the only way to stimulate production and growth, eradicate the acute dollar shortages, and promote cooperation and unity against the communist danger and the threat from the Soviet Union – all at the same time. Realising these three goals was the United States' overriding objective of the Marshall Plan. But all this still failed to address the most glaring problem in Europe: how to deal with the question of Germany and its provisional status in the Yalta agreement?

It was Charles Bohlen, one of Marshall's chief advisors, who proposed a radical new take on 'the German problem' that eventually came to shape American policies regarding European affairs. Bohlen argued that the 'question of Germany' should be treated as a European matter rather than as an issue of occupation. Ultimately, this implied that 'the three Western zones should be regarded not as part of Germany but as part of Western Europe'. Bohlen proposed that the three Western occupation zones be considered an integral part of Western Europe instead of simply a part of Germany, which offered a better chance of realising the main aims of the US policy towards Europe. To begin with, the German threat could be neutralised by containing it within a larger Western European context. In addition, incorporating the West German economy and its vast potential within Western Europe would make it significantly easier to revive the other European economies. Indeed, finding a way to reconnect the West German economy to the rest of Western Europe was of vital importance for the survival of Western Europe as such.

The change of approach suggested by Bohlen cast the situation in Europe in an altogether new light. Europe could be viewed not as a continent with a divided Germany in its midst but rather as a unified Western Europe, or Western Europe as a unit. Following this new line of analysis, the main priority of American foreign policy was to establish a West German state that would forge unity in Western Europe by creating institutional structures through which the US government could support Western Europe economically. It was this change in approach that made 'building Europe' the new American mission, with West Germany at the heart of an emerging Western Europe.[24]

From a broader historical perspective, this change in the US approach to Europe represented nothing less than a revolutionary shift in American foreign policy. It established a break with both isolationism and globalism

---

[24] Marc Trachtenberg, *A Constructed Peace: The Making of the European Settlement 1945–1963* (Princeton: Princeton University Press, 1999), pp. 63–5; FRUS, 1947, vol. I, *General* (Washington: US Printing Office, 1973), 'Interdepartmental meeting, August 30, 1947', pp. 762–3.

in favour of a new strategy of engagement with Europe.[25] Such a fundamental change does not come about without a struggle, particularly since this new approach was at odds with the traditional maxim of American foreign policy of staying out of 'foreign entanglements' – something the founding fathers had been so insistent about.[26] The US policy towards Europe pieced together following the launch of the Marshall Plan led to severe tensions within the US government, for instance between Bohlen and the more traditional hardliner George Kennan.[27] Yet in spite of these internal turf battles, it was clear that the die had already been cast by Marshall's speech at Harvard (in June 1947), which marked a turning point in US foreign policy and clearly empowered revisionists like Clayton and Bohlen at the expense of the traditionalists.

This shift in US foreign policy matched the mood of the time, a peculiar mixture of budding optimism in Western Europe – rooted in the post-war economic growth fuelled by the multilaterally coordinated liberalisations of trade and the American 'politics of productivity'[28] – and the fast-growing urgency around an American-inspired 'crusade' against communism and the Soviet Union. The latter had culminated already in the speech by President Truman on 12 March 1947, in which he had pledged the support of Congress to the Greek and Turkish governments which were struggling with communist uprisings, and in doing so had launched the Truman Doctrine (see chapter 4). The Truman Doctrine, however, not only was a defining feature of the Cold War – and as such a defining feature of a Western context in which a unified Western Europe made all the more sense as the best way to deal with the German question (through a division of the country in East and West). Through the Truman Doctrine, this American president also, and explicitly, made religion an 'integral part' of the US Cold War campaign to convince the Americans to embrace the ambition of 'world leadership'. The crucial means to this end of world leadership was an active roll-back policy towards communism 'infused with religious imagery' aimed at 'the formation of an international religious front against the Soviet Union', which he consistently pushed for personally.[29]

---

[25] Heyde, 'Amerika', 119.
[26] Stanley Hoffmann, 'US–European Relations: Past and Future', *International Affairs*, 79, 5 (2003), 1029–30.
[27] Weisbrode, *The Atlantic Century*, pp. 94–7.
[28] Charles Maier, 'The Politics of Productivity: Foundations of American International Economic Policy after World War II', *International Organization*, 31, 4 (1977), 607–33.
[29] Dianne Kirby, 'Harry Truman's Religious Legacy: The Holy Alliance, Containment and the Cold War', in Dianne Kirby (ed.), *Religion and the Cold War* (Houndmills, Basingstoke: Palgrave Macmillan, 2003), pp. 77–102.

These changes in atmosphere of the West were also registered in the Vatican. In the course of 1948, after he had already steered the Catholic Church away from its associations with nationalist movements and had aligned the church to humanist values and human rights in 1946, Pope Pius XII would join Truman in his 'crusade' against the Soviet Union. Against this backdrop, he called for a swift build-up of West Germany and a state-led unification in Western Europe, which included the further strengthening of the free world of liberalism under the Pax Americana – this all, according to the pope, was essential to 'the Christian necessity of defence' (by which the Vatican was de facto supporting a military Cold War).[30]

The teaming up of Pope Pius XII with the US government in the matter of the Cold War further boosted the political rise of the Christian Democrats in Western Europe and West Germany, where the 'Stuttgart Declaration of Guilt' (see chapter 3) had been a decisive first Christian ecumenical-inspired step in West Germany's reincorporation into Western Europe as an integral part of a more stable and secure post-war order and even as a constructive partner in the effort to build a better world of international cooperation, peace, and social justice. Taking place in October 1945, just six months after Germany's unconditional surrender, the Stuttgart meeting had been a harbinger of the processes in which Germany dealt with truth, guilt, and reconciliation (such as the Nuremberg trials). It is important to note that these processes preceded the restoration of West Germany as a provisional state within the framework of transatlantic *Westbindung*. The Stuttgart Declaration of Guilt had led to a swift inclusion of the German churches into the transnational Christian fellowship via precursors of the WCC, binding the German churches not only to each other but also to Christian partners abroad at a crucial moment in German history. A similar reconciliation process took place in the realm of international politics and diplomacy, but it was clear that the Christian leaders were one step ahead in this regard – also the overture of the Catholic Church towards the US in the early Cold War years had been meticulously prepared.

In the subsequent years, the political course of the Catholic Church in European matters consisted of a combination of pro-US, pro-West Germany, and pro-European integration standpoints, which backed up the Vatican's anti-communist crusade, but certainly also the incorporation of the *Evangelische Kirche von Westfalen* (EKW) into the WCC, came to be seen as an example of how to handle the geopolitics of the post-war

---

[30] Chamedes, *A Twentieth-Century Crusade*, pp. 246–7; see also Anonymous, *Correspondence between President Truman and Pope Pius XII* (Truman Library, Independence), pp. 9–21.

Western order in such a way as to allow the realpolitik of the Cold War – that is, the American leadership of the West – to prevail and the German question to be brought under control at the same time.

5.4   'Coined Freedom'

The task that Marshall had set for Europe – reconstruction being 'the business of the Europeans' – had been rather vague and lacking in detail. When Clayton met with Bevin at the end of June 1947, it was clear that 'most of [Clayton's] views came out of his own head as he had only one talk with Marshall ... he had no well-thought-out plan or scheme to lay out'.[31] Clayton was merely in Europe to facilitate the discussion among Europeans and to judge the feasibility of European ideas. The Paris Conference in the summer of 1947 was where the Europeans would flesh out the details of the European Recovery Plan.

It was not a surprise that it was the Benelux countries that presented the first detailed plans for the reconstruction of Europe, given that the Benelux customs union represented the only working example of what Clayton was envisioning. A proposal for the convertibility of European currencies was presented on behalf of the Benelux countries by Hubert Ansiaux, the Belgian deputy administrator of the Bank for International Settlements and administrator of the International Bank for Reconstruction and Development. In post-war Western Europe, the absence of currency convertibility compelled countries to set up bilateral payment agreements and to restrict trade to mitigate their dollar shortages. This meant that trade was being conducted on a bilateral basis, with countries trying to keep imports and exports in balance to prevent the net loss of currency through trade deficits. To encourage European countries to ease their restrictions on imports from the rest of Europe, the Benelux plan proposed that multilateral arrangements be established via a clearing house that would ensure that export surpluses were equalised with import surpluses in other sectors. This would enable transnational payments based on a categorisation of Western European countries as net debtors and net creditors. The creditors would receive payments from their debtors, who in turn could rely on Marshall Aid dollars. In short, the plan was to create a dollar pool to reinvigorate intra-European trade in a more integrated way within the framework and timeframe of Marshall Aid. Moreover, it was envisioned that this could presage a genuine common market in Western Europe. As becomes clear from a detailed reconstruction by Jorrit Steehouder,

---

[31] Clayton paraphrased in Bullock, *Ernest Bevin*, p. 417.

the Benelux proposal offered the promise of liberalisation embedded in the Bretton Woods system, which meant that 'the Bretton Woods [institutions] would be able to play the role they have been created for'.[32]

It was at the Paris Conference that 'the whole question of sovereignty and integration', which had been the elephant in the room, 'was raised actively' – that is to say in terms of practical solutions to pressing economic problems – 'for the first time'. The possibility of pooling sovereignty was increasingly seen as a means of liberating Western Europe from the shackles of bilateralism and of tackling the problem of inflation. This was the rough sketch of an action plan for pooling that in the ensuing months and years was promoted tirelessly by Alphand (as head of the French delegation to the CEEC/OEEC), by Monnet, and by Marjolin (whose appointment as OEEC's first secretary-general was suggested by Monnet, who himself consistently refused to take on any official leadership position in the intergovernmental OEEC/CEEC when offered the opportunity to do so by the Americans). Jean Monnet indicated that France might be willing to include West Germany in their plans for a European customs union, thereby opening up a new diplomatic path.[33] This allowed France to displace the UK in its leadership role in planning the post-war European order, as the British were wary of any plans for a European customs union. Importantly, this French move also matched recent developments in thinking in the Benelux, mainly the Netherlands.[34]

Eventually, the Paris Conference managed to agree on an approach that was acceptable to the Americans. The final report introduced four main objectives for Europe's economic recovery: (1) a 'strong production effort by each of the participating countries', (2) the 'creation and maintenance of internal financial stability', (3) increasing and developing 'economic co-operation', and (4) a solution to the 'deficit with the American Continent' while explicitly acknowledging that 'instability' in one country impacted the participating countries 'as a whole'.[35]

While the Paris Conference was reaching conclusions, in Washington, more detailed information was coming in from Europe, in particular via the so-called Harriman Committee, which reported on its travels throughout Europe and offered its advice to the US president on the restrictions within which the US should plan

---

[32] Steehouder, 'Constructing Europe', p. 208.   [33] Duchêne, *Jean Monnet*, pp. 168–9.
[34] See Steehouder, 'Constructing Europe', pp. 209–10.
[35] Committee of European Economic Co-Operation, *General Report* (Paris, 1947) cited in Steehouder, 'Constructing Europe', p. 215; see: www.marshallfoundation.org/wp-content/uploads/2014/04/Committee_of_European_Economic_Co-operation_General_Report_1947.pdf, p. 26.

and budget the ERP.[36] This new information from Europe unquestionably reconfirmed two things: communism was winning ground in Western Europe and clearly had the potential of being seriously disruptive, and there was a pressing need for food. The latter was not simply a humanitarian matter, as it was also causing a decline in production – in Germany, for example – and therefore it was clear that it had to be addressed.

In an unforeseen way, the developments in Paris and Washington mirrored the central conclusions drawn by a group of liberal intellectuals who were gathering high in the Swiss Alps that same spring. At the founding meeting of the Mont Pèlerin Society in early April, well before the launch of the Marshall Plan, the prominent German ordoliberal Wilhelm Röpke argued that the German people were suffering and needed additional international aid. Yet Röpke felt this aid should not come in the form of grants but instead as direct investments in the German economy. For this approach to work, what was needed was 'drastic money reform', as Röpke tirelessly stressed. This implied nothing less than 'drastic deflation' in order to re-establish the proper working of the price mechanism, which Röpke argued was the only way to once again bind individual citizens to society: through money in their pockets. Money flowing through the pockets of citizens would allow them to become 'small capitalist[s]', as long as the value of that money was credible and trustworthy. According to Röpke, sound money was the be-all and end-all of true freedom in the ongoing experiment with capitalism and democracy in the Western world – it was, in his words, 'coined freedom'. In Röpke's view, it was essential that a properly functioning price mechanism be the central pillar of any capitalist-democratic future order.[37]

From Röpke's perspective, the Marshall Plan was too centralised, overly bureaucratic, unnecessarily redistributive, and too heavily oriented towards grants. He therefore argued forcefully against the establishment of the ERP. Nonetheless, in the later stages of the implementation of the Marshall Plan, Röpke found himself in the position of being able to steer the European recovery effort more in the direction he felt was desirable. In his capacity as advisor to the provisional West German government and Economics Minister Ludwig Erhard in particular, Röpke ensured that the West German and Western European policies of recovery remained focused on the realisation of 'coined freedom'.[38]

---

[36] W. Averell Harriman, 'Recalling the Work of the Harriman Committee', in Stanley Hoffmann and Charles Maier (eds.), *The Marshall Plan. A Retrospective* (Boulder: Westview Press, 1984), pp. 15–19; Maes, *Triffin*, pp. 80–1; Steehouder, 'Constructing Europe', p. 217.
[37] Bonefeld, 'Freedom', 645.   [38] Plickert, *Wandlungen des Neoliberalismus*, p. 144.

But in 1947, it remained far from clear how the CEEC (OEEC as of 1948) would go about achieving its stated aims, even if the consensus in Europe was already moving in the direction of regional market integration. Moreover, the main players in transatlantic planning such as Will Clayton and Jean Monnet were preoccupied with thinking beyond the Marshall Plan and were not really interested in the details or problems of policy implementation. They were instead focused on the longer-term project of a more supranational form of economic cooperation in Western Europe. In the meantime, when speaking frankly in confidential meetings, they admitted they were convinced that Western Europe in 1947 was still 'too weak' economically and politically 'to accept conditions of regional free trade'. According to Clayton, the whole region 'had to get a good deal more flesh on its bones before' it could be expected to set up 'a common market'.[39] How to go about strengthening the European economy became the main issue that occupied the OEEC from 1948 to 1950, eventually creating such division among its member states as to render the organisation effectively impotent. Monnet quickly lost confidence in the OEEC and carefully kept his distance from the whole undertaking in Paris.[40] But in 1948, the initiative to build the emerging Western European bloc still lay in London, and thus the British-oriented OEEC was still the main player. But this, too, was about to change.

---

[39] William L. Clayton, 'GATT, the Marshall Plan, and OECD', *Political Science Quarterly*, 78, 4 (1963), 501.
[40] Duchêne, *Jean Monnet*, p. 169.

6 British Preoccupations and Ecumenical Politics

In early 1948, Ernest Bevin, the British minister of foreign affairs, embarked upon a quest to create what he called a 'Western Union', an ambitious project of 'economic', 'political', and 'cultural' cooperation between the nation-states of Western Europe. Greater cooperation was deemed an urgent task now that it was unmistakably clear that communism and the Soviet Union posed a direct threat to peace and stability in Western Europe – a fact cruelly underlined by the Prague coup of February 1948. The 'precarious unity' of the 'Big Three' – maintained until the end of the war and reconfirmed during the conferences in Tehran in November 1943 and Yalta in February 1945 – had not led to the triumph of the One World approach in post-war world politics, an approach that had been consistently pursued by the American government during the war[1] and was exemplified by the signing of the United Nations Charter in San Francisco in June 1945. Yet just before the signing of the UN Charter, Soviet authorities had arrested 16 leaders of the Polish underground state, bringing them to Moscow for what came to be known as the Trial of the Sixteen and giving the Western world its first taste of the Soviet Union's peacetime intentions and practices. The trial sent a shock wave throughout the Western world during the conference in San Francisco, soon followed by the repeated use of the veto by the Soviet Union, which bogged down the UN machinery and demonstrated that the UN 'would be as helpless as the League of Nations if a war ... were threatened'.[2]

6.1 Bevin's Grand Design

When Ernest Bevin entered the Foreign Office in July 1945, the Potsdam Conference was underway – a conference that failed to resolve the differences between the Big Three that were so evident at Yalta. If there was one thing evident from Potsdam, it was that the sun of bipolarity was

---

[1] Heyde, 'Amerika', 116 and 136.
[2] Chatham House Archives, London, 9/43a–b, 'Notes on Western European Cooperation: Historical Review' (Matthews), May 1948, pp. 3–4 and 11.

rising over the horizon of world politics. This new phenomenon in world politics would be caught in words during the famous Stuttgart Speech of US Secretary of State James Byrnes on 6 September 1946 (based on the preparatory work of General Lucius Clay). In this speech, Byrnes publicly justified the American decision to 'go it alone' in its governance of its occupation zone in Germany, blaming the Soviets for the failure of Potsdam (and therefore for the division of Germany), while giving the Western Germans some hope that they could eventually regain some control over their destiny, by coupling this prospect to a future which lay in partnership with the West.[3]

Nevertheless, the rays of the sun of bipolarity were so unfamiliar that much of this early sunrise went unnoticed. While the emerging bipolar world could be discerned on the horizon of international politics, this new reality was still far from obvious in the day-to-day world of politics, certainly to the more globally oriented Churchill government. But more discerning civil servants within the Foreign Office placed 'Western bloc policy' at the top of the agenda for Bevin in the light of the Allied deadlock at Potsdam. The ministry left little doubt about the 'urgency' of the matter, given the danger that recent developments posed to the UK's two-pronged strategy in Europe – containing possible French claims on German territories (especially in the Ruhr and Westphalia) while at the same time preventing a Franco-Russian entente.[4]

Bevin readily heeded this call to action and stressed that he especially wanted 'to build up our trade relations with France' and improve the UK's relations with France in general. This would enable a 'long-term policy' directed at establishing 'close relations' between the United Kingdom and 'the countries on the Mediterranean' (Greece, Italy) and on the 'Atlantic fringes of Europe' (Belgium, the Netherlands, Scandinavia, Poland). To transform this vision into feasible goals of foreign policy – that is, 'workable understandings with a group of friendly countries around Germany' – 'it was necessary to make a start with France'. Finally, Bevin 'did not wish to talk in terms of a Western bloc' publicly because this 'would upset the Russians'. This indicated that the UK essentially still was undecided how to manoeuvre in the crystallising Cold War reality. For the time being, the key objective of Bevin's overture to France and continental Europe was twofold: to keep options open and achieve more economic independence from the US.[5]

---

[3] Gillingham, 'From Morgenthau', p. 117; Trachtenberg, *A Constructed Peace*, pp. 53 and 41–55.
[4] Sean Greenwood, 'The Third Force Policy of Ernest Bevin', in Michel Dumoulin (ed.), *Plans des Temps de Guerre pour l'Europe d'Après-Guerre, 1940–1947* (Brussels, etc.: Bruylant, etc., 1995), pp. 422–3.
[5] Segers, 'Eclipsing', 65.

In keeping with what had become the leading line of thought in the Labour Party, Bevin considered his main priority in foreign policy to be the battle against poverty and inequality throughout Western Europe, but in the UK in the first place. The UK had to lead by example in this by creating a credible political-economic counterweight to American-style capitalism. Tellingly, Jim Tomlinson points to a memorandum drawn up in early 1947 by James Meade (then head of the Economic Section at Whitehall), in which Meade elaborates upon the differences between French and British planning (Meade, above all, points to the focus of the French 'on growth and industrial development rather than employment as primary goals', and subsequently notes 'that French planning took place "outside the normal administrative machinery" and explains the benefits that stemmed from this').[6] Moreover, Bevin was convinced that 'the spiritual forces of the Nation ... [were] on [his] side', as evidenced by the overwhelmingly positive reception of the Beveridge Report published in 1942.[7] This new line of thought came to override the Anglo-American commitment to a mutual reduction of tariffs enshrined in the Atlantic Charter, a commitment that Bevin considered vulnerable to a panicked reaction on the part of the United States that would trigger a new round of trade wars.

In summary, two overarching priorities dictated Bevin's thinking on post-war Europe: the battle against unemployment and – related to this – more independence from the US. Bevin believed that the means to this end was Western European cooperation based on a Franco-British partnership, and he was convinced that the success of this endeavour depended on the Big Three powers continuing their collaboration. It was this imagined precondition that tied Bevin's hands and made it impossible for him to take any proactive British stance in the matter of Western European cooperation. And this was what was to be the undoing of Bevin's grand design.[8]

Although Bevin's grand design was to come to nothing, there were two elements in his plan that did prove to be useful to the efforts to build Western Europe. First, Bevin's 'long-term objective was to make the Ruhr industries a central pivot in the economy of an eventual "Western Union"'. In this way, the German steel and chemical industries could be

---

[6] Bodleian Special Collections, Oxford, Attlee Papers, 50: 137–66, [1438] 12 March 1947; Greenwood, 'The Third Force', p. 427; Jim Tomlinson, *Democratic Socialism and Economic Policy. The Attlee Years, 1945–1951* (Cambridge: Cambridge University Press, 1997), p. 294.
[7] Peter Hennessy, *Never Again. Britain 1945–1951* (London: Penguin Books, 2006 [1992]), p. 75.
[8] Greenwood, 'The Third Force', pp. 423–6.

incorporated into the Western Union.[9] This foreshadowed the radical change in US foreign policy that was to take place two years later, when the focus shifted towards establishing a West German state to allow the US to approach Western Europe as a unit and to economically support this unit.[10] Secondly, Bevin's proposal for a Western Union answered the British *and* trans-European call for an imaginative post-war policy towards Western Europe, one that offered a European 'middle way' between Soviet communism and American capitalism.

Bevin was 'tapping a reservoir of thoughts', ideas, and emotions concerning the essential relation between peace and 'the necessity for regional economic groupings' to cherish and nourish that peace.[11] Bevin had certainly not been the only one championing such approaches in the 1920s and 1930s, nor had he been alone in sensing a deeper spiritual basis for some sort of European cooperation. Indeed, the promotion of Europe – and more generally the West – as a Christian community had been essential in the rhetoric against Nazi Germany and totalitarianism in general.[12] In addition, the shame with which Europeans now looked back on the 1930s played into the post-war activism that strove for peace and social justice. A recurrence of the 'devil's decade' was deemed 'unacceptable',[13] and the fact that the pacifist cause had been cynically shrugged off was readily recalled. All in all, Bevin was tapping into a well of emotions and trauma.

This emotionally charged context formed the backdrop to the signing of the Treaty of Brussels – more commonly referred to as the 'Brussels Pact' – in March 1948 by the United Kingdom, France, the Netherlands, Belgium, and Luxembourg. The treaty expanded upon the Treaty of Dunkirk signed by the UK and France a year earlier (on 4 March 1947, the UK and France had signed a fifty-year treaty of Alliance and Mutual Aid at Dunkirk; drawn up in accordance with the UN Charter, which stressed the importance of regional agreements). In Bevin's view, this was the essential Western European building block. The treaty was specifically designed to protect against any form of future German aggression and

---

[9] TNA, FO/371/UE3689/3683/53 (Bevin-Dalton, 17 August 1945).
[10] Bevin thus developed these ideas already when the US government had only just embarked on the long policy journey from the notorious Morgenthau Plan – 'to raze the Ruhr industry, flood the region's mines, and return Germany to the economic conditions of circa 1850' – drawn up in the aftermath of the Teheran Conference of 1943 and its follow-ups which coloured American policymaking on the matter as of August 1944 (Gillingham, 'From Morgenthau', pp. 112–13).
[11] Greenwood, 'The Third Force', pp. 426–7.
[12] Coupland, 'Western Union', 368; see also Dash Moore, *GI Jews*.
[13] Geoff Eley, 'Corporatism and the Social Democratic Moment: The Postwar Settlement, 1945–1973', in Dan Stone (ed.), *The Oxford Handbook of Postwar European History* (Oxford: Oxford University Press, 2014), p. 41.

provided for continuous consultations on economic matters concerning the two nation-states. It committed the signatories to collectively defend themselves against possible aggression from Germany. However, given the circumstances unfolding in 1947, the treaty also – and perhaps primarily – encapsulated Western Europe's hopes for a transatlantic alliance, hopes that were fulfilled in April 1949 with the foundation of the North Atlantic Treaty Organization.[14] Although the Brussels Pact was viewed as simply an expansion of the anti-German Dunkirk Treaty, in the reality of post-war Western Europe, it turned out in retrospect to be a crucial steppingstone towards Western security cooperation shouldered by the US.

6.2 The Delusion of 'Western Union'

It was in the run-up to the signing of the Treaty of Brussels that Bevin had called for the creation of a Western Union based on common values and policies. That such a union would be under British leadership was beyond doubt, also because no one in or around the British government in the 1940s considered the United Kingdom 'in terms of long-run economic decline' – a notion that only became common towards the end of the 1950s.[15] What Bevin wanted to achieve with his plan for a Western Union was to move beyond the immediate problems in post-war Western European politics and to stabilise British foreign policy following the government's volte-face on its stance on bloc formation. Back in November 1946, the UK government had declared its commitment to a One World approach in a foreign policy speech given by Prime Minister Clement Attlee in which he said: 'Let me state emphatically that the Government do not believe in the forming of groups and opposes groups – East, West or centre.' But the shift in thinking among European and American policymakers regarding the desirability of a Western bloc forced the British to retreat from this stance and effect a 'complete change in government policy'.[16]

On 22 January 1948, Bevin gave a lengthy speech in the House of Commons to explain his plan for a Western Union. He opened the speech

---

[14] FRUS, 1948, vol. III, *Western Europe* (Washington: US Printing Office, 1974), p. 35; Elisabeth du Réau, 'Integration or Co-operation? Europe and the Future of the Nation-State in France, 1945–1955', in Dominik Geppert (ed.), *The Postwar Challenge: Cultural, Social, and Political Change in Western Europe, 1945–1958* (Oxford: Oxford University Press, 2003), pp. 241–57, here pp. 243–7.

[15] Tomlinson, *Democratic Socialism*, p. 285; Anne Deighton, 'Don and Diplomat: Isaiah Berlin and Britain's Early Cold War', *Cold War History*, 13, 4 (2013), 525–40.

[16] Chatham House Archives, London, 9/43a–b, 'Notes on Western European Cooperation: Historical Review' (Matthews), May 1948, p. 18 n. 1. For an overview of the historiography on the 'Bevin Plan' for Western Union, see Coupland, 'Western Union', 366–7.

with a sense of urgency: 'We are, indeed, at a critical moment in the organisation of the post-war world, and decisions we now take, I realise, will be vital to the future peace of the world.' Detailing the most important developments in international relations since the end of the war and in particular the emerging bipolarity in world affairs, Bevin concluded that the Marshall Plan had 'brought out what must have been there before' – that is, the division of Europe into East and West. According to Bevin, the reality of the unfolding Cold War and its bipolar logic made it imperative for the Western world to understand that the unity of Europe would have to be limited to Western Europe. He described the moment he himself had come to this conclusion. At the London Conference in November 1947, Bevin had 'felt very often like the boy who was asked what he would do if he were hit on the one cheek by his schoolteacher. He said he would turn the other. His schoolteacher said: "That is a good boy, Tommy, but supposing you were hit on the other cheek, what then?" The boy replied, "Then heaven help him."' Bevin confessed that he had felt like that schoolboy in his dealings with the Russian delegation. This experience had brought him to the following assessment regarding the situation in Western Europe:

It is easy enough to draw up a blueprint for a united Western Europe and to construct neat-looking plans on paper ... it is a much slower and harder job to carry out a practical programme which takes into account the realities which face us ... But surely all these developments ... point to the conclusion that the free nations of Western Europe must now draw closely together. How much these countries have in common! Our sacrifices in the war, our hatred of injustice and oppression, our parliamentary democracy, our striving for economic rights and our conception of love and liberty are common among us all. Our British approach ... is based on principles which also appeal deeply to the overwhelming mass of the peoples of Western Europe. I believe time is ripe for a consolidation of Western Europe ... We are thinking now of Western Europe as a unit.

Although himself not a religious man per se, Bevin envisioned that 'if we are to have an organism in the West it must be a spiritual union ... It must be on terms of equality and it must contain all the elements of freedom for which we all stand.' This was no easy goal, however, because 'there had never been a war like this before ... it is not a question of sitting down together, as it was at Versailles, and then at the end signing a treaty'. The situation was fundamentally different: 'this time it is systems, conceptions and ideologies which are in conflict'. This was why Bevin felt it was necessary to think out of the box, beyond the Old Europe of global empires, beyond the One World approach, beyond the Allied powers, and beyond splendid isolation and staying out of continental entanglements. This represented a significant leap in British thinking about international affairs, post-war Europe, and the role of the United Kingdom.

It was, however, the phrase 'Western Europe as a unit' that represented the true leap in thinking of the UK government. This policy shift raised tricky questions. Who exactly belonged to 'Western Europe'? And which countries should take the lead in shaping this 'unit'? Bevin made it clear in his speech that the UK was well placed to play a leading role in the consolidation of Western Europe, also because of its special relationship with the United States and its ability to act as a transatlantic bridge. In addition to France, with which the United Kingdom was already firmly allied through the Treaty of Dunkirk, Bevin envisioned enlisting the Benelux countries and possibly 'other historic members of European civilisation, including the new Italy'.[17] There was, apparently, no place for Germany in the British-led endeavour towards a Western Union. Even though at that moment the Western Allied powers merely had Bizone in place (and not yet Trizone, which would include France) and the feasibility or form of a future (West) German state was still unclear, the exclusion of (West) Germany was the most blatant indication of how soon the Bevin scheme would be outdated. But there was more.

There were two other aspects that revealed how far the British were trailing the rest of Europe in their thinking. To begin with, the shift towards a 'regional' approach in international affairs was not new, as Bevin seemed to imply in his speech, but had already been going on for months, if not years. The Marshall Plan was in fact a milestone in this development, not its beginning. It had been Winston Churchill himself who in a speech in September 1946 called for 'a United States of Europe' led by France and in partnership with a future Germany.[18] Plans for the organisation of a grouping of Western European states could even be traced back to the war years when the idea circulated among European governments in exile in London. One of the more developed plans was the customs union that Belgium, the Netherlands, and Luxembourg agreed to form after the war. The Benelux, as the union came to be called, was fleshed out in April 1946, and came into effect on 1 January 1948. Originally, the Benelux had been focused on levelling out balance-of-payments imbalances and joint strengthening of economic recovery, essentially based on Belgian–Dutch economic rapprochement and aimed at establishing a common external tariff (Belgium and Luxembourg had already been in an economic union since 1922). As such, however, and despite the numerous difficulties in its implementation, it also set an example for how the post-war Western

[17] Hansard, Foreign Affairs, HC Deb., 22 January 1948, vol. 446 cc383–517: https://api.parliament.uk/historic-hansard/commons/1948/jan/22/foreign-affairs.
[18] Winston Churchill, Speech at Zurich University, 19 September 1946, in Anjo G. Harryvan and Jan van der Harst (eds.), *Documents on European Union* (Houndmills, Basingstoke: MacMillan, 1997), pp. 38–42.

European economies could speed up their recovery and thereby multiply their political weight in international relations. The customs union eventually transformed into a full-fledged economic union on 3 February 1958.[19] At the time of Bevin's speech, the Benelux was a showcase for regional cooperation.

Another way in which Bevin's plan for a Western Union was outdated was the claim it made to British leadership in Western Europe, which was rapidly becoming an illusion. This was made starkly clear by the sterling crisis of 1947, which also put the Anglo-American partnership under severe stress and undermined the privileged position of the British government in Washington.[20] Moreover, within the context of the US–Soviet rivalry, the vision that Churchill had outlined in his 1946 Zurich speech – which had the UK excluding itself from a united Europe given its ties to the British Commonwealth, the US 'and, I trust, Soviet Russia, for then indeed all would be well' – was changing from unrealistic to outright delusionary. The misconception not only pertained to Churchill's assessment of the situation in Russia, it also revealed in a rather painful way how removed from reality the UK's self-image was: as one of the victorious Big Three powers, a confident and independent country heading an empire and naturally assuming a global role for itself, one that also matched its Commonwealth interests. Bevin's initiative was a belated attempt to make a clean break with the Churchillian vision of British aloofness in Europe by putting the UK at the centre of cooperative endeavours in Europe,[21] but this turned out to be too little, too late.

While Ernest Bevin was still designing his grand schemes, the UK's key partners in the West – France and the US – were already adapting to the new reality of a bipolar world. Earlier than Bevin, they had acknowledged that the emerging Western hemisphere would form an essential part of the new world. The main challenge in this new world was to find a political-economic modus operandi for post-war Western Europe as an integral part of a Western world built upon democracies and capitalist economies, but above all as a secure and protected unit of free states. The key task in this challenge was to find ways to reconcile the ideals of freedom and human rights with the pressing goals and desires of individual and collective security. The credibility of the American claim to leadership of the 'free world' hinged on the ideals, while the need for security

---

[19] Skander Nasra and Mathieu Segers, 'Between Charlemagne and Atlantis: Belgium and the Netherlands during the First Stages of European Integration', *Journal of European Integration History*, 18, 2 (2012), 183.
[20] Milward, *The Reconstruction*, pp. 55ff; Greenwood, 'The Third Force', p. 429; Segers, *The Netherlands*, pp. 45–55.
[21] Greenwood, 'The Third Force', p. 433.

transfixed Europe's traumatised nations. Crucially, this reconciliation of Western ideals and European needs had to be achieved *within the unit* of Western Europe. Moreover, it was increasingly becoming an undisputed view that the means to this end had to be sought in international cooperation on practical problems of economics and finance, as this was the only short-term feasible way to facilitate recovery and growth within a framework built on international capitalism and national democracies.

Already in the years preceding the launch of the Marshall Plan, many had concluded that the creation of a stable and promising Western Europe depended on the active involvement of two powers in particular: the US and a future Germany. This was exactly what the Marshall Plan was all about: the active engagement of the US *and* Germany in Western Europe. In this context, Bevin's Western Union initiative was a throwback to wartime thinking in terms of coalitions and keeping options open at a time when the practical policy implementation of the Marshall Plan already prefigured a Western European 'unit'. Moreover, the unit that the Marshall Plan ended up creating was far more integrated than Bevin had imagined, given his aversion to federalist schemes.[22]

6.3   The Spiritual Dimension

Ernest Bevin had been, however, right on another matter. The whole undertaking of building this Western European 'unit' was impossible without some sort of spiritual unity. Moreover, given the 'systems in conflict' stressed by Bevin, there was a clear and pressing political and societal demand for some kind of spiritual community or community feeling. This demand was a trans-European phenomenon that could be observed in all free nations of Western Europe. Indeed, the longing for renewed hope – something to believe in, something to counter the fear bred by war – may even have been the dominant emotion of the time. In this atmosphere, Christianity united under one church was for many Europeans 'a model for the future too'. In the same month that Bevin launched his Western Union plan, the prominent Anglo-Catholic poet T.S. Eliot delivered a series of radio talks on the theme of the uniting potential of Christianity in Europe. It was one of many initiatives of cultural diplomacy that re-created 'a space in public and political discourse' in which the churches engaged in discussions on reconstruction and the post-war order. This phenomenon was matched by the steady growth of

---

[22] Bodleian Special Collections, Oxford, Attlee Papers, 70: 56–63, Federal Western Union, 4 May 1948; Greenwood, 'The Third Force', pp. 426ff; Coupland, 'Western Union', 373.

the ecumenical movement, which led to the founding of the WCC in Amsterdam in 1948, just three months after the Congress of Europe held in The Hague.[23]

The Congress was a non-governmental conference organised by the International Committee of the Movements for European Unity, which included the umbrella organisations Federal Union and the Union of European Federalists and assembled some 800 activists, politicians, businessmen, trade unionists, etc. This was not a one-off affair. As of 1946, multiple efforts had been made to create more coherence and unity among the numerous 'federal movements' and loosely associated entourages focused on inter-European reconciliation – sometimes explicitly Christian-inspired – ranging from intellectual and academic gatherings (like the Rencontres International de Genève (as of 1946), in which intellectuals like Denis de Rougement, Julien Benda, and Karl Jaspers participated) and the Moral Re-Armament Movement in Caux to emerging political movements like the Christian Democratic Nouvelles Équipes Internationales and the French Mouvement pour les États-Unis Socialistes d'Europe. In September 1946, activist federalists from 14 countries had met in Hertenstein (Switzerland), and had adopted a declaration on the basis of which Union of European Federalists was founded later that year. The Federal Union, however, had remained a separate organisation. Because of this state of affairs, the federalists that met in The Hague were still divided among themselves.

Despite the wariness of the national governments, the Congress of Europe had been a political event of substantial political impact that marked the changes in the mood of time. As Stella Ghervas has pointed out, the event not only included key intellectuals and political movers and shakers of post-war Western Europe – like Salavador de Madariaga, De Rougemont, the Belgian social-democrat Paul-Henri Spaak, Robert Schuman, Konrad Adenauer, and Walter Hallstein (who would become the year-long state secretary for European affairs in the successive Adenauer governments) – it also 'revived the legacy of the peace congresses of the nineteenth and early twentieth century' and produced 'an

---

[23] American Theological Library Association Serials, 'Secular Press Reactions to Amsterdam in the U.S.A.', October 1948; Coupland, 'Western Union', 371–2. From the British perspective, Coupland, referring to Zeilstra, adds: 'When British Christians published their statement on "The Future of Europe" of March 1944, it emerged from the Peace Aims Group formed under the auspices chaired by William Temple, archbishop of Canterbury and one of the pioneers of the WCC. The statement favoured common social, economic, and political institutions for Europe and spoke of Britain as "bound to Europe by ties of history, culture and economic interdependence"' (Zeilstra, *European Unity*).

audacious "Political Resolution"'.[24] This resolution called upon the European nations to 'transfer and merge some portion of their sovereign rights so as to secure common political and economic action for the integration and proper development of their common resources'.[25] Moreover, within this context of sovereignty transfer, the resolution had confirmed the way out of the German problem, which was already crystallising (see chapter 5): Germany's 'integration in a United or Federated Europe alone provides a solution to both the economic and political aspects of the German project'[26] – foreshadowing European integration as the political double-edged sword as it would reappear in Monnet's 1950 plan for Schuman to pool the coal and steel sectors of Western Europe in a functionalist-supranational organisation (see chapter 7).

On the Anglo-American side of the Atlantic, the church had already tried to seize the opportunity to use this 'space for discourse on European unity' in the late 1930s and early 1940s. In the US, John Foster Dulles had been one of the prominent drivers of this movement. Dulles had argued publicly in favour of European unity back in 1940, when he was president of the Federal Council of Churches. In 1948, at the first session of the WCC in Amsterdam, he was seen as the uncontested and 'experienced lay leader' of the American Protestants. His call to them to 'join themselves with the Roman and Anglican churches in a great crusade for God and civilization' did not go unheard.[27] There were some crucial differences with Dulles's earlier call for unity, however. For one thing, Dulles was expected to be appointed secretary of state after the presidential elections that were to take place later that year, as he was the chief foreign policy advisor to the Republic presidential candidate Thomas E. Dewey, who was widely expected to win the 1948 elections. In one of the greatest election upsets in US history, however, incumbent Harry S. Truman would defeat Dewey, and Dulles was forced to see his dreams of becoming secretary of state go up in smoke. Most importantly, however, the Dulles of 1948 was a cold warrior. This coloured his message at the WCC on the future of Europe considerably, for it meant that the 'great crusade' was to be deployed for America's Cold War aims. It was indeed enticing to utilise the unifying potential of Christianity for diplomatic or geopolitical purposes, especially following events such as the

---

[24] Ghervas, *Conquering Peace*, pp. 246–7.
[25] 'Résolution Politique', Congrès de l'Europe, 10 May 1948. cited in Ghervas, *Conquering Peace*, p. 246.
[26] 'Résolution Politique', Congrès de l'Europe, 10 May 1948 cited in Ghervas, *Conquering Peace*, pp. 246–7.
[27] American Theological Library Association Serials, 'The Amsterdam Reports: Secular Press Reactions to Amsterdam in the U.S.A.', October 1944; Heyde, 'Amerika', 134.

Prague coup (in February 1948), the monopolisation of power by the communists in Poland, and the Berlin Blockade which began in June 1948. These shocking incidents came in the months following Bevin's speech and highlighted the difficulty of striving for Christian spiritual union in the midst of increasing geopolitical tension.

As with so many leading politicians of his generation, Bevin was confident that common ground did exist in Europe at the spiritual level. There was, however, one problem: it turned out to be painstakingly difficult to navigate this common territory. It was no coincidence that Bevin had remained rather vague and superficial in that part of his speech that dealt with spiritual union. And it was precisely this part that had been picked up by the press, filled as it was with big ideas like 'freedom', 'democracy', 'rights', and 'love and liberty' that appealed to the imagination. Captivating as they were, however, these ideas proved to be nearly impossible to translate into an actual plan or programme for action.

Bevin himself was aware of this weakness in his plan, and so he set up working groups in the Foreign Office to turn his 'spiritual union' into something tangible. It soon became clear, however, that coming up with a description of a coherent and consistent set of European values, let alone a European identity that constituted the heart of the spiritual union, was an impossible task. It was simply unfeasible for Bevin's advisors to define what it was that united Europeans or what it was that made Europeans European. Bevin and his staff therefore turned to the Oxford philosophy professor Isaiah Berlin, who reluctantly accepted the assignment. His final advice to the minister was clear: the minister was in search of something that did not exist.[28] In the meantime, international developments were making it clear that it would be virtually impossible to establish a Western Union as envisaged by Bevin.

While the Soviet Union's rejection of Marshall Aid was anticipated by Washington and other Western capitals, what had been disappointing and even shocking to Bevin was that all Central and Eastern European countries seemed to follow suit. From that moment on, 'Europe' for the Americans meant Western Europe. In return for Marshall Aid, the Europeans were expected to move towards a type of cooperation that went beyond classical intergovernmentalism, since the latter had proven to be ineffective in preventing a repetition of the violence seen in recent European history. It was only in the second half of 1948, however, that it became clear that the quid pro quo for the Marshall Plan was horizontal trade liberalisation with an eye on 'European integration'.[29] And indeed, this notion of European integration rather than Bevin's idea of a Western

---

[28] Deighton, 'Don and diplomat'.   [29] Lundestad, *'Empire'*, p. 6.

Union was what had been foreshadowed in the transatlantic network of churches directly after the war. The conclusion that was forced upon Bevin by international circumstances in the course of 1948 had already been drawn by prominent figures in the ecumenical movement in 1946 and 1947, even before the launch of the Marshall Plan. Whereas Bevin was playing catch-up regarding the Marshall Plan, the ecumenical movement was one step ahead of policymakers on both sides of the Atlantic.

In early 1946, the ecumenical movement appeared to be very much in tune with the zeitgeist. The grand ambitions that ecumenical groups like the CJDP had proselytised during the war now seemed to be bearing fruit in the arena of international politics: in the summer of 1945, the United Nations Declaration had been signed by 47 nations in San Francisco, while the process of reconciliation between churches and their parishioners in former aggressor nations had been initiated in Stuttgart. Amidst these pro-ecumenical winds of change, the WCC's Provisional Council met for the first time since 1939 to prepare for the official establishment of the WCC planned for 1948.[30] The ecumenical movement held high ambitions of becoming involved in international political affairs. The Provisional Council asked the CJDP, of which Dulles was the chair, to organise a 'conference of Christian leaders' in close collaboration with the British members of the former Peace Aims Group.[31]

On 4 August 1946, this all-male meeting took place at the all-female Girton College in Cambridge. The conference roughly followed the format of the first meeting of this type in Oxford in 1937, albeit with one crucial difference: this time the representatives were predominantly from the United States and the United Kingdom and the Commonwealth. And it was clear that the Americans, who had requested that a foreign affairs chapter be established within the movement, were now dominant. During the war, the Americans had worked hard to bring the focus within the ecumenical movement to international relations and foreign affairs, and now they were eager to capitalise on their preparatory work. Dulles was keen on the success of this enterprise. This came at a price, however, as the emerging Cold War started to discredit the ecumenical movement's aspirations of international Christian unity.

At the Cambridge Conference of Church Leaders on International Affairs, the influential American theologian Reinhold Niebuhr shared his thoughts on the future directions the church might take and their

---

[30] Matti Peiponen, *Ecumenical Action in World Politics: The Creation of the Commission of the Churches on International Affairs (CCIA), 1945–1949*, Schriften Der Luther-Agricola-Gesellschaft 66 (Helsinki: Luther-Agricola-Gesellschaft, 2012), pp. 104–5; Van den Berg, 'European Believers'.
[31] Visser 't Hooft, *Memoires*, p. 195.

pitfalls. With the task of building spiritual bridges between the Germans and other Europeans underway, Niebuhr called on the German Protestant churches to keep their efforts directed towards more unity in Europe. Niebuhr recognised, however, that there was a clear Russian threat to stability in Europe. The conclusion he drew from this brute reality echoed the pure realpolitik approach of a Cold War superpower: 'If Russia established herself fully in Western Europe, there would be war ... There would be no possibility to better contacts with Russia if we allowed Western Europe to fall into complete political and economic decay. Therefore, Western Europe must be helped.' These clear-cut words put Niebuhr squarely in the camp of those who believed that Eastern Europe was lost, at least for the moment. Niebuhr preached patience in dealing with the question of Eastern Europe, as the alternative in his opinion was atomic warfare. He believed Eastern Europe had to be given up for some time until the Russians' new empire collapsed from within. In this respect, he was on the same page as Dulles in claiming that it was better to focus on the countries that could be made safe for democracy – and, by extension, capitalism.[32] This line of reasoning won overwhelming credibility during the Cold War build-up that followed and became the guiding principle of the first governments of West Germany under the Christian Democrat Konrad Adenauer.[33] Last but not least, Niebuhr's contribution to the Cambridge Conference implied a clean break with socialism as a system, which, to be sure, did not imply a break in his support for political forces which stood at the left of American liberal thought.

6.4   The Emergence of a Continental West

After the Cambridge Conference, Niebuhr visited Germany and wrote an article for *Life* magazine titled 'The Fight for Germany' based on his experiences there. In this piece, Niebuhr outlined his vision of Western European reconstruction and the role of the United States in it. The starting point of Niebuhr's analysis was the speech given by US Secretary of State James Byrnes on 6 September in Stuttgart announcing a US policy of containment in reaction to the Soviet threat – which effectively meant the end of the One World approach in US foreign policy. The re-emerging threats of violence and totalitarianism in Europe caused Niebuhr to lament 'the confusion in American liberalism', which resulted in a lack of political action and will, and according to him 'must be regarded as catastrophic in the light of the European realities'.

---

[32] Van den Berg, 'European Believers', p. 160.   [33] Segers, *Deutschlands Ringen*, ch. 2.

In this new geopolitical landscape, Niebuhr felt that the economy was the key area in which US foreign policy could have a decisive impact.

He found it unsettling that the US military government in Germany had refused requests by Socialists and Christian Democrats in Bavaria to create a planning commission for economic reconstruction – a new political experiment that Niebuhr had praised – on the grounds that this was incompatible with the American interpretation of 'democracy' (which was considered synonymous with 'capitalism'). Niebuhr fumed: 'Amidst the awful shambles of the German cities, such notions of "free enterprise" are as irrelevant as Communism is noxious.' He understood that it was precisely in the enormous economic challenge of battling hunger and poverty that the responsibilities and opportunities lay for the US and that some sort of economic planning had to be pursued through a 'clear-cut and creative economic policy' that entailed most importantly the opening up of trade between the Bizone and the other Western countries. This would yield two concrete positive results: it would stimulate productivity and growth both in Germany and in its neighbouring countries, and it would prevent the 'unnecessarily provocative step' of a European federation, an idea that Churchill had proposed in Zurich. But workers in Germany were hungry, and this meant that food had to be imported immediately from America 'on a charitable basis', since doing nothing would lead to severe malnutrition among children, thereby impacting the workforce of the next generation. Anticipating strong opposition by 'misguided liberals' at home who would criticise the gigantic costs of such an undertaking, Niebuhr stressed that 'a little more justice now would obviate the necessity of charity later'. For Niebuhr, it was clear that there was 'no possibility of saving freedom in Europe except by the support of political forces which stand to the left of American liberal thought'.[34]

All in all, Niebuhr's advice was as unorthodox as it was consistent with the key aim of the newly emerging US foreign policy. To prevent the Soviet Union from easily winning over an impoverished European population to the communist cause, the US had to step into the European game more actively and practically, using its formidable arsenal of commercial economic power. This was a conclusion that Niebuhr had come to in the summer of 1946, well before the term 'Cold War' was coined by veteran policy advisor Bernard Baruch.[35] While many of his ecumenical partners were at that moment still searching for ways to relax the tension

---

[34] Reinhold Niebuhr, 'The Fight for Germany', *Life Magazine*, 21 October 1946, 65.
[35] Andrew Preston, *Sword of the Spirit, Shield of Faith: Religion in American War and Diplomacy* (Toronto: CNIB, 2014), ch. 24; Van den Berg, 'European Believers', ch. 4.

with the Soviets, Niebuhr had already outlined his plan for the political and economic containment of the totalitarian Soviet threat. Significantly, his approach was focused on Western Europe – or more precisely, a Western Europe built around the Western zones of occupied Germany. Implicit in Niebuhr's approach was a shift from a UN-focused American foreign policy to an American foreign policy focused on the formation of a Western bloc with Western Europe as a crucial partner, and as such this approach was in tune with an already developing new post-war era, that of the Cold War.

Niebuhr's views on the Soviet threat were shared by the diplomat George Kennan, who had argued in a well-crafted and emotionally charged telegram sent from Moscow that 'while cooperation with the Kremlin was impossible and war was unnecessary, a policy of "containing" Soviet expansion was feasible'.[36] Moreover, he added that such an American foreign policy of containment of the Soviet Union could eventually trigger a collapse of the communist regime. His telegram of more than 5,000 words – later published anonymously, as the infamous 'X-article', in the journal *Foreign Affairs* – was powerfully argued and became the trigger for what came to be known as the Truman Doctrine announced in a speech given by President Truman to the US Congress on 12 March 1947. To secure public and bipartisan support for this policy, Truman repeatedly referred to the presumed 'atheistic' and godless nature of the Soviet Union that forced 'human beings into spiritual straitjackets' due to the regime's 'materialistic view of man'.[37] He often spoke of the 'crusade' the Western world had to wage to nip the communist threat in the bud.[38] This anti-atheistic campaign against the Soviet Union crossed party boundaries, as exemplified by the Republican Dulles who was a key supporter of the Truman Doctrine.

Paradoxically, it was in this emerging context of superpower rivalry and the Cold War that the increasingly American-oriented WCC steadily began to communicate a growing disconnect from the political developments on the ground in Western Europe. The post-war changes in the WCC's missionary scope, which were also guided by Cold War

---

[36] Frank Costagliola (ed.), *The Kennan Diaries* (New York and London: Norton, 2014), p. xxviii.
[37] Dulles, cited in Van den Berg, 'European Believers', p. 169.
[38] Dianne Kirby, 'Divinely Sanctioned: The Anglo-American Cold War Alliance and the Defence of Western Civilization and Christianity, 1945–48', *Journal of Contemporary History*, 35, 3, (2000), 385–412, and 'The Impact of the Cold War on the Formation of the World Council of Churches', in Joachim Garstecki (ed.), *Die Ökumene und der Widerstand Gegen Diktaturen: Nationalsozialismus und Kommunismus als Herausforderung an die Kirchen*, Konfession und Gesellschaft, 39 (Stuttgart: W. Kohlhammer Verlag, 2007), pp. 135–58.

preoccupations, led the ecumenical movement away from a primary focus on European matters. While the political realities in Western Europe created by the unfolding Cold War led to the institutionalisation of a Western European bloc centred around West Germany, the WCC turned its attention to more global aims. As Van den Berg shows in 'European Believers', WCC General Secretary Willem Visser 't Hooft had done everything within his power to keep alive the One World approach within the WCC, during the preparations of the founding assembly of the WCC in 1948 in Amsterdam. He did so by including representatives from Central and Eastern Europe such as the Czech theologian Josef Hromàdka and Bishop Alfred Bereczky of the Reformed Church in Hungary, by welcoming representatives from India and China (who would hold leadership positions in the WCC) and even by trying to get the Russian Orthodox Church on board despite stiff opposition from within, notably from the ranks of the Commission of the Churches on International Affairs. This last effort failed, as at the assembly in Amsterdam and in the meetings that followed, Dulles was in full-fledged cold warrior mode, preaching the pressing binary logic of the politics of containment.[39]

Nevertheless, the ecumenical movement had been instrumental in fleshing out the possibilities for both deeper international cooperation in Western Europe and for reconciliation with Germany, and yet it found itself outmanoeuvred when the building of post-war Western Europe really began. Its success in the immediate post-war years was rooted in the Christian fundament of the One World approach, an approach that at the time was the uncontested light of hope for many of those in the Western world who were occupied with international politics, especially in matters of transnational rapprochement and reconciliation. But this approach, which had guided the establishment of the United Nations in 1945 and was preserved in the Universal Declaration of Human Rights of 1948, soon foundered under the pressure of the unambiguous beginnings of the Cold War and state-centred thinking in Western Europe in particular.

In summary, the gradual shift towards a continental European approach to a revival of Western Europe, already apparent in and around Washington in 1946, had wide-ranging implications for the way international politics were perceived in the Western world. Most importantly, more regional approaches toppled the One World approach.[40] Among those regional approaches, increasingly sophisticated and tailor-made Western European models pushed all-European or all-Atlantic schemes

---

[39] Toulouse, 'Working', 406–7; Van den Berg, 'European Believers', pp. 167–81.
[40] See Steel, *Walter Lippmann*, p. 404.

into the background. This development was driven by a combination of mutually reinforcing factors: the institutional tendencies inherent in the Bretton Woods system, practical policy challenges in Western Europe, and the crystallisation of a new bipolar world order. As becomes clear through the research of Van den Berg in the WCC archives, this shift towards regionalisation was largely overlooked by the WCC,[41] even though the organisation had been useful in setting this change in motion and even if prominent participants – most notably Niebuhr – had already foreseen what was to come in international politics.

Ultimately, this change in approach towards regionalism set the stage for the launch of the Schuman Plan in May 1950 and the establishment of the European Coal and Steel Community in 1951. This laid the foundations for European market integration based on socio-economic planning. It all started with the Marshall Plan, which triggered the shift in power away from the UN's Economic Commission for Europe to the Committee of European Economic Cooperation – which became the Organisation for European Economic Cooperation in 1948 – and subsequently from the OEEC to the European Payments Union in September 1950 (by the eighteen members of the OEEC, including the UK). The process continued in 1952 with the institutional shift from the EPU to the ECSC, which definitively cut off the UK from continental Europe. The linchpin in this series of shifts was the OEEC, the regional Western European body set up to administer the Marshall Plan for Western Europe.

[41] Van den Berg, 'European Believers', p. 176.

7   Reality Check: The OEEC and 'Integration'

During a crucial three-year period from 1948 to 1950, the OEEC played a unique role in shaping the contours of post-war Europe. At a decisive moment in European history, it was the OEEC that channelled ideas into concrete proposals, functioning as a sort of transmission belt for those ideas. Until then, supranational schemes and plans for economic federation had been floating around without leading to concrete results, fuelling endless rounds of discussions that kept the Western world under their spell. With the establishment of the OEEC, this storm of ideas was finally translated into truly feasible projects and programmes within the framework of the ERP. Eventually, this produced a winning alternative that, despite appearing technocratic, was deeply political, tailored to meet specific national European interests. It was precisely this combination of practical projects, feasibility, and realpolitik that made the regional continental European approach the winning alternative, allowing Europe to circumvent the more independent and apolitical UN bodies.[1]

But this is an analysis we can make with the benefit of hindsight. At the time, the OEEC was generally thought of as a cumbersome structure bogged down by intergovernmental hesitance. As Jean Monnet put it: 'the OEEC is nothing; it's only a watered-down British approach to Europe – talk, consultation, action only by unanimity. That's no way to make Europe.'[2] While this might have been a correct assessment from Monnet's perspective, it overlooked the crucial role the OEEC played in creating momentum during the first five years following the end of the war as well as the subtle 'process of creative adaptation'[3] it fostered, without which Monnet's ambitions would probably have remained pipe dreams. As it was, the OEEC never managed to move beyond its role as generator of blueprints for European cooperation and recovery. After initiating the exercises of planning that led to the translation of ideas

---

[1] Stinsky, 'Western Europe', pp. 75–6.
[2] Monnet cited in Leimgruber and Schmelzer (eds.), *The OECD*, pp. 1–10 and 28.
[3] Matthias Schmelzer, *The Hegemony of Growth. The OECD and the Making of the Economic Growth Paradigm* (Cambridge: Cambridge University Press, 2016), p. 38.

into concrete programmes, it was effectively made redundant. Its very structure made it impossible to fulfil its objective of setting up institutional structures for deeper and resilient European cooperation, and it was therefore swept aside to make way for the boldly revolutionary move towards supranational European integration. In 1949, the OEEC even downgraded its ambitions substantially, adopting an apolitical mission statement that gradually reduced it to a de facto statistics bureau or think tank.

The culprit responsible for the inefficacy of the OEEC was clear enough. As Monnet rightly observed, the UK had from the very beginning been watering down all proposals and putting the brakes on moves to implement far-reaching economic and financial integration. There was a reason the British were dragging their feet: if there was one country that feared trade liberalisation, it was – ironically enough – the United Kingdom, because it knew that liberalisation would place pressure on the pound as an international currency.[4]

7.1 Transatlantic Action on Intra-European Trade

The institutional counterpart to the OEEC in Paris was the Economic Cooperation Administration (ECA) in Washington, established in 1948 to oversee the Marshall Plan. The ECA was headed by the well-known businessman Paul Hoffman, the socially engaged president of Studebaker Cars who had already served on the Harriman Committee as one of its prominent members. A child of his time, Hoffman was convinced of the need to search for a balance between free enterprise and individual and social security as well as the vital role the state should play in achieving that balance and placing 'moral restraints' on the workings of capitalism to prevent social chaos.[5] The ECA's main task consisted of coordinating the hundreds of American diplomats in Paris and elsewhere through the Office of the Special Representative in Paris, the de facto US permanent representation to the OEEC run by Averell Harriman and linked to a team of like-minded confidants, including the trained economists Milton Katz and Richard Bissell (who had been the administrator of the Marshall Plan in Germany).

In early 1949, a group of international finance experts was created within the ECA to develop feasible financial-economic policies for Western European cooperation. The group, which included economists like Robert Triffin, was steered by the young Richard Bissell and therefore

[4] Walter Salzmann, *Herstel, wederopbouw en Europese samenwerking* (The Hague: Sdu, 1999), pp. 162–3.
[5] Alan R. Raucher, *Paul G. Hoffman: Architect of Foreign Aid* (Lexington: Kentucky University Press, 1986), p. 55; Steehouder, 'Constructing Europe', pp. 219–21.

dubbed the Bissell Group.[6] Bissell had been executive secretary of the Harriman Committee and like Harriman and Hoffman was from a well-to-do business family. After obtaining a degree in history at Yale, he had gone to London where he was educated in economic theory by none other than Friedrich Hayek. It was in London that he became acquainted with the work of other 'Austrian economists', most notably Gottfried Haberler and his research on international trade. Bissell then returned to Yale as a professor and promotor of liberalism and 'activist good government' in the Lippmann spirit.[7] With his appointment to the ECA, Bissell was challenged to put his academic training into practice. All in all, the ideas emanating from the ECA laid the groundwork for making convertibility and the liberalisation of intra-European trade a feasible option, eventually allowing for the creation of the European Payments Union.

As mentioned earlier, trade was the one area in which no agreement had been reached at the 1944 Bretton Woods conference establishing the post-war international economic order. After the war, therefore, intra-European trade became mired in a tangle of quantitative restrictions on imports and high import tariffs. Many European countries felt compelled to implement these restrictions due to the post-war currency shortages they were experiencing, but this only hampered economic growth and exacerbated their dollar shortages. A system of bilateral drawing rights emerged in which countries with a balance-of-payments surplus provided financial support to countries with a balance-of-payments deficit by offering credits on the condition that the money be used to buy imports from the donor country. Despite serious efforts to move towards trade liberalisation and full currency convertibility, intra-European trade and payments remained trapped in 'the shackles of bilateralism'.

This was one reason the American government insisted on dismantling these quantitative restrictions – also referred to as horizontal (across-the-board) trade liberalisation – as a *sine qua non* for the provision of Marshall Aid. But by doing so, the Americans ended up slowing down and complicating the negotiations within the OEEC. Even those countries which backed the liberal American approach had serious problems with the proposals being tabled. The Benelux countries, for instance, maintained low import tariffs among themselves in contrast to most other European countries, which meant that horizontal trade liberalisation could have placed them at a disadvantage to countries with higher import tariffs. To counter this threat, the Netherlands even put forth plans

---

[6] Milward, *The Reconstruction*, pp. 282–5.
[7] Richard M. Bissell, *Reflections of a Cold Warrior: From Yalta to the Bay of Pigs* (New Haven: Yale University Press, 1996).

for far-reaching vertical liberalisation (per sector) within the framework of the OEEC,[8] but this move yielded few results. Given the recent radical shift in US policy towards Europe, the movement towards regionalisation could no longer be stopped, nor could the testing and fine-tuning of blueprints within the framework of the OEEC, which was inherent to this shift of focus (away from the UN's ECE) to the OEEC. Because of this, the onus of responsibility for enabling durable European cooperation was increasingly put on the *regional* assignment to enhance valuta convertibility in Western Europe to facilitate (and cushion) the horizontal trade liberalisation programme pushed for by the Americans. Eventually, this resulted in the coming about of the EPU.

The first decisive step towards the establishment of the EPU was taken in October 1948, when the Intra-European Payments Scheme (IEPS) was signed by all OEEC countries. The IEPS was a system of drawing rights and monetary compensation that built on the Benelux approach proposed earlier by Hubert Ansiaux. As Harriman described it: '[this is] the piece in which the various countries say that the creditor countries are going to be good to the countries who have drawing rights and see that there is no question about their getting the goods they want'.[9] As foreseen in the Ansiaux proposal, these drawing rights used Marshall Aid dollars to create an extra – and extra-binding – relationship between creditor and debtor countries in Western Europe by redistributing the dollars from countries with surpluses to countries with deficits. In this way, the IEPS helped to alleviate the distortions in bilateral economic relations caused by balance-of-payment difficulties. Indeed, although the IEPS was set up as a temporary mechanism and was full of uncertainties in terms of how it would work in practice – especially due to its intergovernmental character – the new scheme functioned like a 'little Marshall Plan' within Western Europe.[10] More importantly, however, the IEPS opened new avenues for the OEEC, as becomes clear in the meticulously researched thesis by Steehouder. Emboldened by this first real stimulus for intra-European economic dynamism, the Executive Committee of the OEEC felt that the time was ripe to take on the task of trade liberalisation. At the OEEC ministerial gathering on 17 February 1949, the Executive Committee argued that the focus

---

[8] Segers, *The Netherlands*, pp. 68 and 81.
[9] Harriman cited in Steehouder, 'Constructing Europe', p. 294; Christoph Buchheim, *Die Wiedereingliederung Westdeutschlands in die Weltwirtschaft 1945–1958* (Munich: Oldenbourg, 1990), pp. 46–8.
[10] James Ransom, '"A Little Marshall Plan": Britain and the Formation of the European Payments Union, 1948–50', *International History Review*, 3 (2010), 438.

of the OEEC should now shift to a 'speedy increase of exports' and the 'transferability' of European currencies.[11]

Harriman could not have agreed more with the OEEC's new focus. In a direct dispatch to OEEC Secretary-General Robert Marjolin, Harriman threw his considerable political weight behind a fresh plan for multilateral payments, which in practice implied a more automatic clearing system. His views were strongly backed by the ECA in Washington, which was pushing for a 'multilateralisation' of the 'drawing rights', in the first instance for payments foreseen for the years 1949–50. This would allow countries to use their drawing rights not only in the creditor country that had granted the drawing right but in any of the OEEC countries, creating a system of transferable multilateral drawing rights that would have the effect of boosting intra-European trade. By February 1949, only 42.6 per cent of the total of drawing rights had been used. Estimates clearly signalled that this number could have been much higher, had the drawing rights been transferable in a multilateral way.

Opposition to this plan came from key creditor countries like the United Kingdom and Belgium, which were concerned about a possible dollar drain as well as the intensified competition inherent in convertibility. Nonetheless, relentless American pressure led to European talks on a mixed model of bilateral and multilateral drawing rights in the spring of 1949. Echoing the views of the ECA, Marjolin stressed that bilateralism could not be countered by multilateralism in a series of gradual steps. Instead, audacious decisions were necessary to break the existing system, which was suppressing a recovery of the European economy. The final version of the new payments agreements was to be coupled to a proposal adopted by the OEEC Council to liberalise trade by calling upon all OEEC members to 'abolish ... restrictions unilaterally as fully as their economic and financial position would permit'.[12] But although momentum for a 'bold and simple' European move towards convertibility was building up within the policy realm, it was far from clear that such a move could be made acceptable to the people of Western Europe. But there were other headwinds rising too.

This whole European undertaking was far from a given, nor very clear, to leading German ordoliberals, such as the highly influential Wilhelm Röpke, who occupied himself with the unfolding process of Europeanisation that had been triggered by the Marshall Plan, from 1948 onwards. Röpke had a rather different take on the matters that

---

[11] HAEU, OECD-9, Council Minutes for 1949, and OEEC-113.007, Executive Committee Minutes for 1949, CE/A(49)007; Steehouder, 'Constructing Europe', p. 294.
[12] HAEU, OECD-116.018, Executive Committee Minutes for 1949, CE(49)088; Steehouder, 'Constructing Europe', pp. 310–14.

were at the top of the international agenda of the Western world. His main concern was the balance-of-payments problem, which he felt was a symptom of the inner disorder of the country concerned. This meant that a true restoration of the economy concerned was only possible by allowing prices to reflect true costs (*Preiswahrheit*). It made him an ardent supporter of currency convertibility, which Röpke saw as a necessary precondition for any sensible programme of European cooperation. He was, however, less than sanguine about the prospects for European countries achieving convertibility. The powerlessness of the OEEC framework made it obvious that Western Europe was still far from ready to allow their currencies to be convertible. What was emerging, according to Röpke, was a 'fake multilateralism': The multilateral system as it was being set up within the framework of the Bretton Woods agreements implied the subordination of intra-European trade to a system of financial settlements (through the IMF), which, moreover, was largely undemocratic in Röpke's view. This shadow system of loans was ultimately aimed at enabling European governments to implement their ambitious social policies aimed at full employment (which they in essence could not afford).

According to Röpke, roughly the same could be said of the EPU efforts. And indeed, they were a perfect reflection of the rather uncrystallised state of affairs in financial-economic management in the Western world at that moment. On the one hand, they were regionally oriented European efforts for organisation, and on the other hand, they remained located within the framework of the Atlantic-oriented OEEC. To introduce even more unclarity into the situation, the increasing prioritisation of balance-of-payments issues gave impetus to French-inspired plans for even further regionalisation in the form of a free trade association between France, Belgium, Luxembourg, the Netherlands, and Italy based on floating currencies and possibly leading to some sort of 'union'.[13] Indeed, EPU remained a counterproductive European project in the vision and outlook of Wilhelm Röpke.[14] As it turned out, this did not diminish his influence on the process of Western multilateralisation in Western Europe. On the contrary, Röpke became more and more influential as West Germany in the form of the Federal Republic of Germany began to contribute to the shaping of Western European multilateralism as an economic force to be reckoned with.

---

[13] DNA, 2.08.50, 15.50, 'Commentaar bij Nota van President DNB terzake van Multilateralisatie van het Europese Handelsverkeer', 15 November 1949; Dyson and Quaglia (eds.) *European Economic Governance*, p. 29.

[14] See Nachlass Wilhelm Röpke (NWR), Institut für Wirtschaftspolitik, Cologne, 'Lose Blattsammlung', 'Europäische Wirtschaftsintegration: Illusionen und Möglichkeiten', June 1953.

From the FRG's founding, the German economics minister Ludwig Erhard would not only preach but also implement Röpke's ordoliberal ideas, fighting hard to have convertible currencies and trade liberalisation enshrined as the main principles of post-war European integration. This meant that the FRG stood for a form of functional integration that was firmly grounded in free markets and in *national* framework treaties that guaranteed respect for property and contracts, protected free competition, and honoured monetary prudence. It was the national element of this approach in particular that put these German ordoliberals at odds with the more politicised *European* institution building *à la* Monnet.[15] Röpke felt strongly that national governments – and not international organisations – ought to hold the responsibility for setting the framework for their own national order. Out of these national orders, an 'international order' would 'emerge as a by-product'. Röpke fervently hoped and believed that a cleansed and reformed German nation could provide a beacon of light that 'other governments would follow through competitive emulation'.[16]

Given that Germany had lost the war and had been split in two as a result of the Cold War, it was surprising that the FRG and its ordoliberal orientation managed to set the boundaries within which the planners of European integration realised their supranational ambitions. The boundaries within which ordoliberals themselves operated in West Germany shaped the way in which they proceeded in matters of European integration. From its first day in office, the West German government and its chancellor, Konrad Adenauer, had made it clear that supranational European integration based on Franco-German reconciliation was viewed as vital to securing the future of the FRG politically and geopolitically. Indeed, it was considered taboo within the Adenauer government to openly question this political priority.[17] Consequently, the key question regarding European integration for the FRG government was not *if* but *how*: how should integration be developed and organised? This forced the ordoliberals, advisors, government officials, and academics alike to be practical in their pro-European constructive ideas. In 1949, however, this was far from clear yet.

[15] NWR, Korresp. II 60–6, 'Der Schumanplan – ein europäisches Experiment', 1950, and Bundesarchiv, Koblenz, N1254/84, Etzel to Erhard, 31 May, 1954; see also Hans Jörg Hennecke, *Wilhelm Röpke. Ein Leben in der Brandung* (Stuttgart: Schäffer-Poeschel, 2005), pp. 175–8 and 184; Ludwig Erhard, *Deutschlands Rückkehr zum Weltmarkt* (Düsseldorf: Econ, 1953); Mathieu Segers, 'The FRG and the Common Market', in Carole Fink et al. (eds.), *1956. European and Global Perspectives* (Leipzig: Leipziger Universitätsverlag, 2006), p. 170.
[16] John Gillingham, *European Integration 1950–2003. Superstate or Market Economy?* (Cambridge: Cambridge University Press, 2003), p. 13.
[17] Segers, *Deutschlands Ringen*, pp. 30–41.

7.2 The Challenges of Convertibility

In September 1949, the painstaking preparations for a move to convertibility were derailed when the UK abruptly devalued its currency by 30 per cent. The American recession of 1949 had plunged the UK into a balance-of-payments crisis: the dollar drain put sterling under heavy pressure, and reserves in the sterling zone were at risk. Shortly before stunning the world with its announcement of a devaluation, the UK had threatened to withdraw completely into its own sterling zone. This was a nightmare scenario for the US, for if the British were to carry through on their threat, it would have split the West in two, leaving a hard currency zone led by the US and a soft currency zone led by the UK. This would have severely undermined the US position in the Cold War. The message the British were sending out was unmistakable: British foreign policy was focused on the world and not on Europe. As Bevin rather bluntly told the US ambassador to the UK: 'perhaps Washington did not fully comprehend that Great Britain could not accept integration in western Europe on a scale which would impair its other responsibilities', as the country 'was a world power and not merely a European power'.[18] In more concrete terms, London was not afraid to go against America's European initiatives. From an American perspective, this had two far-reaching implications. First, Washington had to give up all hope of the UK being the driver of European integration. Secondly, the abrupt and drastic devaluation of the pound forced the US to arrange a rescue package for the British pound in the form of special dollar guarantees. The US had to give the British pound and the British economy special treatment now, ultimately implicating that the UK could no longer be made to fit within the Western European economic system.

The British move came as a complete shock to the continental European countries: only the United States and Canada had been informed prior to the move, while the UK's Western European partners had been left in the dark. This threw a spanner in the negotiations within the OEEC and its regional sub-branches. Countries with a natural affinity with the UK such as the Netherlands became reluctant to commit to any kind of continental European customs union, which would have excluded them from the Anglo-Saxon world and bound them to the pooling of trade revenues within continental Europe. Italy became similarly disinclined to consider schemes such as the French-inspired plan to create a free trade association with France, Italy, and the Benelux

---

[18] FRUS, 1949, vol. IV, *Western Europe* (Washington: US Printing Office, 1974), 'The Ambassador in the UK (Douglas) to the Secretary of State', 26 October 1949, pp. 435–7; Segers, 'Eclipsing', 69.

(dubbed Fritalux and later Finebel),[19] given that it was a creditor country to the UK.

The pre-coordinated American–Canadian–British response to the United Kingdom's acute financial problems caused by the dollar drain – which came in the form of a rescue package within the framework of the Anglo-American 'special economic relationship' – also aroused suspicions, particularly in France, about the sincerity of US efforts to stimulate European integration. In discussions within the Bureau of European Affairs, Bohlen remarked that 'the French ... feel that while we are still giving lip-service to ... the general unification of Europe, in reality, we are as a matter of basic policy envisaging future developments more along the line of Anglo-American partnership'. Given this situation, Bohlen aired his 'strong conviction that if it becomes evident that we are creating an Anglo-American-Canadian bloc as a political reality in our European policy, we will not be able to hold on to the nations of Western Europe very long'. Kennan disagreed, asking rhetorically 'would the French prefer to have the British dollar drain progress *more* rapidly than it is progressing? Do they think that the continent has something to gain from the blows which are going to fall on the entire non-communist world within the coming months from the disintegration of the British financial system?' Contemplating such a scenario left him 'with a feeling of hopelessness'.[20]

Having acted unilaterally, the British made it clear that they were willing and ready to 'go it alone'. This only reinforced the extant centrifugal forces within Europe. To be sure, the French position also did not engender trust among the other continental European countries. According to the economist Miriam Camps, a key figure at the State Departments Policy Staff (led by Kennan) and in the Bureau of European Affairs, 'the French had proposed various things ... [but] they had never done them'; for example, with regard to 'the trade liberalisation programme of the OEEC, they were the worst at ever liberalising anything, and the first always to reimpose restrictions'.[21] Moreover, the

---

[19] In addition to Finebel and Fritalux, a number of other initiatives for regional trade blocs and/or customs unions were the subject of discussion within the OEEC, most notably within the European Customs Union Study Group. These ideas ranged from a Scandinavian customs union and Atlantic schemes including the UK to Fritalux and the Benelux, which was still largely in its set-up phase. In the end, almost all these initiatives were primarily a means to secure a bigger piece of the Marshall Aid pie. Yet they all failed to include West Germany, and (thus) remained non-starters.

[20] Weisbrode, *The Atlantic Century*, pp. 94–7 and 114–16. Trachtenberg, *A Constructed Peace*, pp. 99–103.

[21] HAEU, *Oral History Collections*, Interview Miriam Camps (by F. Duchêne), 30 August 1988, p. 15.

French government was still carefully avoiding making any high-level political commitment to further steps in deepening European cooperation within the framework of the OEEC, deliberately keeping discussions at the level of experts and technocrats while accommodating American wishes without fully committing to them politically.

In this rather disconcerting context of an increasingly dysfunctional OEEC, it was the US that gave new impetus to endeavours to move towards convertibility and trade liberalisation. The head of the ECA, Paul Hoffman, was set to address the OEEC Executive Council in what was to become a key speech outlining the US position on Europe. During preparatory meetings on the speech, Miriam Camps suggested: 'let us use the word "integration" instead of "unification", because unification to Congress means the United States of Europe, and Europeans aren't going to do that, and it won't go down well. "Integration", nobody knows what it means. That's a far less loaded word.'[22] This seemingly negligible change in wording was to be key in reviving the momentum behind greater European cooperation.[23]

In his speech on 31 October 1949, Hoffman called upon the European delegations to create a 'single large market within which quantitative restrictions on the movement of goods, monetary barriers to the flow of payments, and, eventually, all tariffs are permanently swept away'. Hoffman carefully tied the creation of an economically unified Western Europe to the principles of freedom, peace, and justice which guided the 'free world'. What lay beyond the immediate goal of deeper economic integration in Western Europe was 'the hope of all men of good will ... an enduring peace founded on justice and freedom' which could be realised 'if we, the people of the free world, continue to work together and stick together'.

Hoffman further outlined that the two central pillars of the 'Atlantic Community' were to be economic cooperation in Western Europe and transatlantic cooperation in the security realm through NATO. He emphasised that the pillar of transatlantic security cooperation rested on the achievement of Western European economic cooperation, for if Western Europe could not integrate its economies, it was almost certain that the 'vicious cycle of economic nationalism would again be set in motion'. If Western European governments 'would each separately try to protect their dollar reserves', this would lead to 'the cumulative narrowing of markets, the further growth of high cost protected industries, the

[22] HAEU, Interview Miriam Camps, pp. 15–16; Stinsky, 'Western Europe', p. 77.
[23] Camps said of herself that 'there were many fathers of the OEEC, but there was only one mother' (Stanley Hoffmann and Charles Maier (eds.), *The Marshall Plan. A Retrospective* (Boulder: Westview Press, 1984), p. 71).

mushrooming of restrictive controls, and the shrinkage of trade into the primitive pattern of bilateral barter' – a course that would spell 'disaster for nations and poverty for people'.[24]

And then came the punchline: 'This is why *integration* is not just an ideal, it is a practical necessity. [And] it is your job to devise and put into effect your own programme to accomplish this purpose – just as it was your responsibility ... to take Secretary Marshall's original suggestion and give it life and breath' (italics added).[25] This new focus on practical and pragmatic steps towards the new ideal of 'European integration' began with convertibility and a common market.

Hoffman's speech made it clear to Europeans that the US was at last giving up on the model of the United Kingdom driving Western European cooperation. Indeed, with the sterling devaluation derailing OEEC efforts to move forward with new forms of European cooperation, many European governments were themselves concluding that 'Europe' would have to do without the British. This created space for potentially bold new leadership. There was still, however, the issue of West Germany, whose delegates were present for the first time at the OEEC Council meeting in an observer capacity. Hoffman's speech made it clear that the US would consider any Western European country able to unite Europe behind convertibility and a common market *and* include West Germany as a partner in this effort to be in the best position to claim leadership of Western Europe. After all, the US was now in search of ways to transform its mission of 'building Europe' into 'building Europe from within'.

The first step taken towards this new ideal of European integration was the European Payments Union. This scheme not only left the idea of a Finebel dead in the water, it also brought West Germany into the game of Western European economic cooperation. The increasingly practical and realistic efforts to pull off some kind of durable European cooperation – or even integration – took the geographical form of 'the Six': France, Belgium, the Netherlands, Luxembourg, the Federal Republic of Germany, and Italy. And so it was that through policy channels that reached the highest political levels of the successive CDU–Freie Demokratische Partei governments under Chancellor Konrad Adenauer, German ordoliberal ideas were injected into the 'European experiment', as Röpke called it.[26] With the United Kingdom retreating economically, intellectually, and

---

[24] Dyson and Quaglia (eds.), *European Economic Governance*, Doc. 1/23, pp. 84–5; see also FRUS, 1949, vol. IV, 'Editorial Note', pp. 438–40.
[25] Steehouder, 'Constructing Europe', p. 317.
[26] NWR, Korresp. II 60–6, 'Der Schumanplan – ein europäisches Experiment', 1950, and Bundesarchiv, Koblenz, N1254/84, Etzel to Erhard, 31 May 1954.

politically from initiatives of Western European integration and the United States promoting forms of practical 'Europeanisation' with the FRG as its linchpin, German ordoliberals were thrust into the position of helping to shape the post-war order in Western Europe. The gap left by the numerous failed Anglo-Saxon plans to set up a new multilateral order was huge and urgently waiting to be filled by more feasible and credible ideas for European integration, as it was now called.

7.3   The German Re-entry

Despite all the initiatives inside and outside the OEEC, old patterns of economic politics and policymaking remained leading in the late 1940s. Moreover, the fate of Western Europe, especially the smaller countries, remained in the hands of outside forces as had traditionally been the case. Three of these forces, which were intimately interconnected, are worth mentioning here. In the first place, Marshall Aid and its multilateral institutions built a crucial lifeline for Western Europe. The UK's erratic 'European policy' formed the second outside force that steered Western Europe – especially the north-western part of Europe – at decisive moments. The UK's devaluation of sterling left the Scandinavian countries and the Netherlands with little choice but to follow suit (this move substantially improved the competitive position of the Netherlands, boosted exports, and made the country more attractive for foreign investors, especially from the United States).

The third outside force determining Western Europe's future was undisputedly the most important, and that was the United States. The country that had helped defeat the dark forces of fascism in Europe now proved willing and able to impose watershed decisions. The often-overlooked decision of the US to completely liberalise imports into West Germany in September 1949 was a key example of this. Although the step was a decisive one, it did not come about in a pre-planned or calculated way. The practical decision that guided Western Europe in the direction of a future of stability and prosperity through integration was taken while US foreign policy towards Europe was in utter disarray. This was symbolised by the state of affairs in the OEEC, where member states were entangled in a fierce struggle over the organisation's raison d'être.

The US government may have embraced the ERP and the OEEC after their establishment and assessed them as adequate instruments with which to promote peace, stability, and prosperity in Europe, but that was about as far as clarity of thinking went in Washington. And especially now that the sterling devaluation had highlighted the severe cracks under the surface, the OEEC was on such thin ice that the situation was getting perilous. When it became abundantly clear in 1949 that the OEEC was unable to 'itself recommend the allocation of ERP funds' – which Clayton, Harriman, Hoffman, and others had energetically tried to bring about – the ECA decided to work around the 'political machinery' of the OEEC by dealing more directly on an ad hoc basis with the more practical policy channels of the ECA itself (as well as with the emerging institutional structures of the EPU-in-the-making).[27] Apart from the fact that this did not happen smoothly at all, the situation created fault lines within the State Department, where the leading Europe experts increasingly disagreed with each other. Sometimes these differences were only about details but more often than not they were based on fundamental differences of understanding and insight, most notably centred around the uncertainties related to the departure of the United Kingdom from the cockpit of European integration.[28]

Yet another omen of the impending end of the OEEC as the main forum for Western European cooperation was the fact that continental Western Europe, unlike the UK, experienced no serious fallout from the US recession of 1949. Intra-European trade had made the continent less vulnerable to external turbulence than the UK and its waning empire and global exposure. Crucially, the economies in continental Western Europe were already hooked up to the West German motor, which was now being revived in the Rhineland, the heart of European industry. An impressive economic recovery in West Germany led to a rise in German imports, giving an enormous boost to neighbouring economies, often at the expense of the UK.[29] These were the centrifugal forces Bohlen had been so concerned about – forces that were at work on both sides of the Channel and that were ironically strengthened by the increasingly politicised OEEC.

Meanwhile, the centre of gravity of the Western European economic recovery was shifting from Paris to Bonn. The London Six-Power Conference in the spring of 1948, which brought together the three Western occupation forces in Germany (the US, the UK, and France) and the Benelux countries, confirmed that the Western occupation zones would fall completely under the Marshall Plan and that a provisional federal government would be established for the joint Western occupation zones. On hearing of this, the Soviet Union stopped attending the meetings of the Allied Control Council, the body in which the Allies held

---

[27] Milward, *The Reconstruction*, pp. 275–81 and 469.
[28] Weisbrode, *The Atlantic Century*, pp. 94–7.
[29] Milward, *The Reconstruction*, pp. 473–4 and 488.

meetings to agree on a common policy for Germany. The agreements reached at the London Conference formed the foundation for the *Frankfurter Dokumente* – the first blueprints submitted for the foundation of West Germany as a state – which were presented on 1 July 1948. Two months later, the West German Parliamentary Council started drafting the *Grundgesetz*, the constitutional basis for the provisional state of West Germany, as it was becoming clear that a peace treaty regarding Germany would not be signed in the near future. It was adopted in May 1949 by the *Länder* (regions) and the Western occupying powers. In September, the first free elections were held in West Germany. More than anything else, the so-called *Weststaatsgründung* of West Germany formed the foundation underlying the process of European integration, which was to take an unprecedented leap forward a few months later.

Within this context, the decisive momentum for forward action in line with American goals in Europe came from an extraordinary, self-convinced, non-partisan academic from the Rhineland, trained and tenured in the Austrian and ordoliberal schools of economic thought and policies, who singlehandedly saved US policies on Europe by translating them into bold and practical action: Ludwig Erhard.

In the wake of the first German elections, Ludwig Erhard positioned himself at the helm of economic policymaking in West Germany. Erhard had been director of the Administration for Economics in the Bizonal Economic Council. He was called in by the CDU to strengthen its election campaign with a leading economic programme, which was subsequently modelled on his ideas and summarised in the election catch-phrase 'Market or Planned Economy?' used by the CDU to differentiate itself from the Social Democratic Party. Although he was not a member of the CDU, Erhard was invited to the CDU conference in Königswinter on 24 February 1949, where he stated: 'for my part, you can deploy me in your campaign twice or three times a day ... Then we will not only win the elections, and thus make the history of Germany, but also shape the vision of Europe.'[30] And in his new capacity as the CDU's *Wahl-Lokomotive* (election locomotive) under Konrad Adenauer, he ensured that the party adopted the 'Social Market Economy' in its main manifesto – the *Düsseldorfer Leitsätze* – in July 1949.

This was how Erhard transplanted German ordoliberal thinking from the ivory towers of academia to the more public political realm. In doing so, Erhard was the decisive force. Crucially, the (Protestant) ordoliberal Erhard counterbalanced the influence of Catholic social thought within the German Christian Democratic political family (also helped by the fact

---

[30] Glossner, *The Making*, p. 58.

that so many left-wing academic economists had fled from Nazi Germany after 1933 and did not return after the war). In general, as Kenneth Dyson has remarked, ordoliberalism, through the politics of Erhard, 'nudged post-war German identity-shaping in an historically new and distinctive direction', as 'it helped to establish new standards of legitimacy for a stability-based market order and to mobilise support for new modes of governance' (including, for instance, central bank independence).[31] 'What really happened in the years 1945 to 1948' in West Germany, according to Müller-Armack, was an ideational shift, driven by a small group of ordoliberal-inspired economists and intellectuals, an 'academic elite which had the real influence on the decisive decisions'.[32] Ludwig Erhard was their political mouthpiece.

Like Röpke, Erhard had been a student of Franz Oppenheimer and had a relevant track record studying the problems of war debt and economic policy in defeated countries. Before entering active politics in 1949, Erhard had carried out scholarly market research into long-term economic problems in the city of Nuremberg and had also been director of the Nuremberg Institute for Economic Studies. After briefly serving as economics minister in Bavaria under American sponsorship, he returned to academia as a professor at the University of Munich. Through the Economic Working Committee for Bavaria (*Volkswirtschaftliche Arbeitsgemeinschaft für Bayern*), Erhard had in 1945 provided the military government in the US occupation zone with an advisory report on the reorganisation of German finance that recommended major currency reform. Erhard's Economic Working Committee in Bavaria had close ties to an entourage of academics working on a new liberal – or neoliberal – economic order at the University of Freiburg, which combined classical economic theory with policies of state intervention.

It was from these circles of academics that the famous Freiburg School emerged.[33] They had been secretly formed during the war as an underground movement of 'resolute opponents of National Socialism' and included the *Bonhoeffer Kreis*, a religiously motivated working group whose members were also active in the Freiburg Circles. Erhard nourished the close ties he had with his fellow economists in the Rhineland, and in the meantime the US military government in Germany continued to push the political career of the economics professor, appointing him as director of economics on the Bizonal Economic Council in 1948. From that moment on, Erhard proved to be of paramount importance to the

---

[31] Dyson, *Conservative Liberalism*, p. 353.
[32] Müller-Armack cited in Dyson, *Conservative Liberalism*, p. 353.
[33] The journal *ORDO*, the main and influential outlet of the Freiburger School, was founded in 1948.

implementation of the American goal of liberalisation. Regarding the latter, the transformations in the European politics of the Netherlands during this period are telling.

For the Netherlands, Erhard's implementation of the economic policy goals determined by the United States was the single most important factor contributing to its economic recovery. On 7 September 1949, the governments of the Netherlands and West Germany signed a new trade agreement lifting the embargo between the two countries that had been imposed when the occupying powers in the Bizone insisted that German products be paid for in hard currency, which meant dollars.[34] The Netherlands had been fighting against this measure for years, and now it had been knocked down in one fell swoop. The agreement obliged the Dutch to purchase non-essentials from West Germany up to a value of 32 million dollars, but beyond that, German trade remained fully subject to import quotas while Dutch exports were liberalised. It was a golden deal that gave the Dutch economy a spectacular boost (within only a few months, West Germany was the largest importer of Dutch exports, the long-standing deficit on the balance of payments became a surplus of hundreds of millions of guilders and transit trade – through the Netherlands to Germany – grew explosively). This was how the system of 'embedded liberalism', as described by John Ruggie in 1982, worked – the promotion of free trade and multilateral coordination was 'embedded' in a large measure of autonomy for the participating states, whose governments within their own borders were free to create a welfare state as they saw fit and shape the social policy most appropriate to it, in line with the views of their national, domestic democracy.[35] In practice, this system of 'embedded liberalism' could exist through a mix of multilaterally coordinated policies and bilateral deals tailor-made to suit the different needs of the various countries of Western Europe.

For the Dutch government, this sudden change in fortune was a very welcome 'surprise' it had 'never dared to dream of'. At the same time, it hit a sensitive nerve among the Dutch.[36] For no matter how necessary and desirable it may have been for the Dutch to couple their trade to that of West Germany, it had a very serious implication. Back in 1946, *The Economist* had emphasised how important the reconstruction of

---

[34] Richard Griffiths (ed.), *The Netherlands and the Integration of Europe* (Amsterdam: NEHA, 1990), pp. 9–17; Friso Wielenga, *West-Duitsland: partner uit noodzaak. Nederland en de Bondsrepubliek 1949–1955* (Utrecht: Spectrum, 1989), pp. 235–6; Milward, *The Reconstruction*, pp. 469–70, 474, and 489. Exceptions were made for fish, vegetables, and products manufactured by the Dutch company Philips.
[35] Ruggie, 'International Regimes', 379–415.
[36] Wielenga, *West-Duitsland*, pp. 235–7; Salzmann, *Herstel*, pp. 186–8.

Germany was for the future of Europe: 'The truth is that nothing can finally compensate continental Europe for the loss of its largest market.'[37] In 1949, the 'lost market' of Germany was reactivated, which boosted economic recovery throughout Western Europe and attacked the problem of scarcity. This led to surprising political consequences. In December 1949, the Dutch government resolutely rejected a British proposal for the Netherlands to join the sterling zone. Finance Minister Pieter Lieftinck explained that the 'centre of gravity' of Dutch trade relations may have traditionally been 'focused on the English' but the German–Dutch trade agreement had shifted it towards Germany, which mean that the FRG had 'taken over England's role'.[38] This was an extraordinary statement for a Dutch minister to make, and it was evidence of a silent revolution made possible by the new means of multilaterally organised trade under the Pax Americana.

Earlier that year, Max Kohnstamm, head of the German Bureau within the Foreign Affairs Office, had presented a 'Memorandum on the Allied and Dutch policies on West Germany'.[39] The main argument Kohnstamm made in his memorandum was that the German economy was indispensable to the recovery of the Dutch as well as the European economy. The 'Germany memorandum', as it came to be called, contained far-reaching and controversial recommendations for the policy of the Netherlands towards Europe, including the advice that the Dutch government should focus strongly on West Germany, actively promoting the German economy's production potential and helping to open up the German market. This could only be achieved by working closely with West Germany within the framework of Western European multilateralism.

The document caused quite a stir within civil service circles in The Hague, especially at the Ministry of Foreign Affairs. But however fierce the criticism expressed by prominent figures in the *corps diplomatique* was,[40] it lost its urgency as soon as the Dutch–German trade agreement was signed in September. And, conversely, the trade agreement gave the Germany memorandum the allure of foresight. After all, what was more logical than to focus on West Germany and on advancing Western

---

[37] William Mallinson, *From Neutrality to Commitment: Dutch Foreign Policy, NATO and European Integration* (London and New York: Tauris, 2010), pp. 12 and 16.

[38] Pieter Lieftinck, *Lieftinck 1902–1989: Herinneringen opgetekend door A. Bakker and M.M.P. van Lent* (Utrecht and Antwerp: Veen, 1989), pp. 172–3.

[39] The memorandum elaborated on ideas that Hirschfeld had formulated earlier (in 1946) in a memorandum on Germany and which had since then been lying on a shelf in The Hague (Meindert Fennema and John Rhijnsburger, *Dr. Hans Max Hirschfeld: Man van het grote geld* (Amsterdam: Bert Bakker, 2007), p. 160).

[40] DNA, 2.05.117, 22481-2, Van Kleffens to the ministry, 21 June 1949; De Booy to the ministry, 9 May and 6 June 1949.

European economic cooperation, even if it meant abandoning customs that had dominated Dutch foreign policy for at least the past century?

The Germany memorandum was an analysis of the state of affairs in Western European politics at that moment. Outlining the 'historical development' in Europe since the American intervention in the Second World War, the memorandum highlighted two shifts in attitude. To begin with, the US view on how to deal with the German economy – which had been the engine of two world wars – 'changed completely'. While initially insisting on restricting any form of economic development that went beyond relieving immediate hunger, the Americans were now calling for the German economy to be stimulated. The bipolar 'Yalta order' began to impact the situation on the ground in Germany, as 'the exchange of food from the East and industrial products from the West that had always occurred within Germany came almost to a standstill'. This forced the United States and the United Kingdom to make 'significant financial sacrifices' to prevent serious starvation in the country, which 'forcefully contributed to a growing awareness of the importance of productivity in Germany'. Secondly, the devastation and impoverishment throughout Europe led to 'a dire need for goods of all kinds'. In short, 'the termination of production in Germany proved to have serious consequences for Europe as a whole'. The Americans and the British therefore decided to increase maximum production levels substantially in Germany. That change in thinking had opened the way for the establishment of the Bizone and the provisional West German state.

The memorandum's main conclusion from this historical overview was that the circumstances concerning Germany were now completely different from those following the end of the First World War. The US was now actively and constructively involved in the future of Western Europe and West Germany. An Atlantic Treaty establishing NATO had even recently been signed. Moreover, the 'fact' of the Cold War made 'a powerful and united Western Europe ... [indispensable]' and meant that 'a politically and economically weak Germany on this side of the Iron Curtain ... was a dangerous weak point for Western Europe'. There could be 'no other conclusion' than that 'West-German territory would have to be integrated in the defence of Western Europe'. And there was an additional factor: due to the changing circumstances, 'an independent threat to the West from Germany' had become 'very unlikely'. That had been replaced by the threat from the Soviet Union, which called for 'a positive policy focused on incorporating Germany into Western Europe' – not least to avoid 'the great danger ... of a newly strong Germany, with its political, military and economic power, allying with Russia'.

From an economic perspective, too, there were good arguments to be made for a lasting reconciliation between West Germany and the rest of Western Europe. The Dutch situation was a good example. The memorandum noted that between 1930 and 1938, around 25 per cent of Dutch imports came from Germany (not including trade with Dutch overseas territories), while some 19 per cent of Dutch exports went in the other direction, around half of which constituted agricultural products. Furthermore, the memorandum pointed out that the disappearance of Germany as a producer and market after the Second World War was causing serious problems for the Dutch economy. At the time Kohnstamm was writing, it was not at all clear when the German market would be opened up to the Dutch, which meant that Dutch needs had to be fulfilled elsewhere. This had led to an increase in imports from the dollar zone from 189 million guilders in 1938 to 1,410 million guilders in 1947 and from England from 180 million to 452 million guilders over the same period. In addition to exacerbating the country's dollar deficit, the Netherlands' traditional trade surplus with England was transformed into a deficit of 233 million guilders. Furthermore, agricultural production, which was an important component of the Netherlands' export package, could only be partially absorbed by the English market, while exporting these products to the dollar zone was considered to be 'completely out of the question'.

In economic terms, therefore, there appeared to be only one possible conclusion: it was of vital importance to the Dutch economy that Germany be restored as quickly as possible as a dynamic economy in Western Europe as both producer and market. And this in fact held for all of the Western European economies. This analysis pointed towards the 'only solution' to the German problem:

A future for Western Europe without West Germany [is] unthinkable. The danger of a Germany that turns against Western Europe – if not on its own, then as an ally of Russia – remains. If this were to materialise, Western Europe would no longer have a future. The only policy that offers any future prospects for Western Europe is one aimed at making Germany stronger and, at the same time, absorbing it into Western Europe. Thus is our objective clear.

The memorandum thus concluded with a passionate plea for the integration of West Germany into Western Europe, which was seen as essential for a stable system. It was 'extremely necessary [to avoid] a "too little and too late" approach in tackling the German question', even though people were 'rightly afraid of making the international game once again a stage for German arrogance'. Normalising relations was the best choice, as 'incorporating Germany in Western Europe by force' was 'impossible'. Security could only be achieved by establishing 'European organisations'. The memorandum warned that time was of the essence, as 'the stronger Germany is, the more difficult the integration of Western Europe will be'.[41] In other words, the time was ripe for European integration. This simply was (geopolitical) realism.

7.4 Launching European Integration

While the newly formed West German state tended to prevail in matters of a financial-economic nature, international diplomacy was an altogether different game. And here, the French were more adept at guiding the US in Western Europe. In mid-September 1949 – before Hoffman's speech at the OEEC and while desperate efforts were being made to save the British pound – US Secretary of State Dean Acheson met with his French counterpart Robert Schuman and urged him to finally show some French leadership in the question of embedding West Germany within Western Europe. Acheson made it clear that the French government could count on support from Washington for any serious initiative to achieve that objective. In Schuman's eyes, this meant that the US government had given him a 'mandate' to take action in Europe. He understood the growing American impatience but was at a loss as to how to make the rehabilitation of Germany palatable to his fellow politicians in France–and more importantly to the French people. For that reason, he had initially decided to do nothing and wait.[42]

Acheson was convinced that Europe could no longer waste time by taking into account the doubts and problems of the United Kingdom. In an internal memorandum, he remarked: 'Recent trends suggest that the most likely tight grouping of the character we have in mind would be a continental union including France, Italy, Belgium, West Germany and possibly the Netherlands ... We must insist that the UK not interfere with developments on the continent nor impede any other country's joining a continental union or unions.'[43] This was the defining moment that the idea of 'Atlantis' – that imaginary notion of an Atlantic Community – was scuttled and bloc formation within continental Western Europe was given unambiguous political priority in American foreign policy. A couple of weeks later, Acheson stepped up his pressure on Schuman: it was imperative that France come up with a plan – and now.

---

[41] DNA, 2.05.117, 22481–2, Nota betreffende de geerde en de Nederlandse politiek ten aanzien van West-Duitsland, 28 April 1949.
[42] Segers, *The Netherlands*, pp. 75–8.
[43] Acheson cited in Klaus Schwabe, *Die Anfänge des Schuman-Plans 1950/51* (Baden-Baden: Nomos, 1988), p. 218 n. 23.

The day before Hoffman's speech, Acheson wrote personally to Schuman, imploring: 'Now is the time for French initiative and leadership of the type required to integrate the German Federal Republic promptly and decisively into Western Europe. Delay will seriously weaken the possibilities of success.' In an instruction to the US embassy in France, he added: 'this does represent our analysis of what is needed if Russian or German, or perhaps Russian–German domination, is to be avoided'.[44]

Under increasing pressure from Washington, Schuman went outside of the Quai d'Orsay to consult the quintessential European, Jean Monnet (then still heading the government staff responsible for the Plan de Modernisation, see chapter 3). To break the vicious circle of a West German economic recovery posing a future German threat to the rest of Western Europe, Monnet put forward a plan to bring the French and German coal and steel industries together under a joint organisation in which France and Germany would be represented equally. This would not only hide geopolitical considerations behind the technocratic arrangements of a supranational form of cooperation, it would also bring the former German war industry under control. Already in the summer of 1945 Jean Monnet, while on a mission for the provisional French government to the United States, had put a plan to create a European coal community to increase production in Germany to US Assistant Secretary of State Clayton. Furthermore, the Commissariat Général du Plan de Modernisation headed by Monnet was behind plans for an autonomous New Deal-type international organisation of the Rhine, Elbe, Danube, and Oder valleys.[45]

All in all, this was how Monnet proposed to tie West Germany and its enormous economic potential to France and to Western Europe for the long term. But there was more to Monnet's plan. The great mission Monnet had established for himself in those years, went far beyond planning France's economic modernisation. He wanted to change Europe through European integration (see chapter 1). In his view, that had to be done one step at a time and, above all, functionally: through economic cooperation between Western European states per sector. At first glance, this might give an impression of modesty and continuity, but Monnet's plan was revolutionary in a key way: the limited functional cooperation he proposed had to be anchored in *supranational* institutions. This was how Monnet envisioned the realisation of Mitrany's goal 'to

---

[44] FRUS, 1949, vol. IV, Acheson to the ambassador in France, 19 October 1949, pp. 469–72; Schwabe, *Die Anfänge*, p. 219.
[45] I am grateful to Professor Gérard Bossuat for this information.

complete the state': not by launching all-encompassing schemes for federalisation, but by small sector steps of functional yet supranational integration (of European economies and societies).

Schuman immediately signed on to the plan convinced that it fulfilled the mandate the Americans had given him (and matched his own 'European thinking' on the future of the industry of the Saar and the Ruhr)[46]. He then took the necessary steps to bring it to fruition. Through Bernard Clappier, who headed his cabinet and who was a close acquaintance of Monnet, he bypassed his own ministry. He presented the plan in rather vague terms at a cabinet meeting on 3 May 1950, which proved enough to obtain the cabinet's approval. Six days later, on 9 May, he announced the plan to the outside world in a press conference. The exact details of the plan, which Schuman had not revealed at the cabinet meeting, were there for everyone to read. The Schuman Plan envisaged bringing French and German coal and steel production under the umbrella of a supranational 'European' institution in which other Western European countries could also participate. What made the Schuman Plan radical was that the proposed European Coal and Steel Community, as it was called, would be supranational rather than intergovernmental as was customary in multilateral organisations such as the OEEC. Except for those at the highest levels in Washington, Paris, and Bonn, nobody had taken part in the preparations for what the Belgian newspaper *La Relève* described as '*la bombe Schuman*': a fait accompli for the rest of Western Europe.[47]

Schuman had pulled off a masterpiece of tactical manoeuvring to sidestep the widespread scepticism in his country and to ensure that Monnet's proposal was given the most forceful possible introduction. Parallel to his machinations at home, Schuman made one other move to prepare for the launch of his plan. On 7 May, two days before the presentation, he sent details of the plan to West German Chancellor Konrad Adenauer, a fellow Christian Democrat. Schuman's message to Adenauer was accompanied by a personal letter in which Schuman emphasised the political aspects relating to the practical character of the plan. 'Europe' could only be achieved if concrete steps were first taken to create 'de facto solidarity'. That meant 'eliminating' the age-old tensions

---

[46] Summarised as follows by Stella Ghervas: 'if it cannot be mine and it cannot be yours, then it should be ours to share' (Ghervas, *Conquering Peace*, p. 253).

[47] '*La bombe Schuman*', *La Relève*, 20 May 1950; Robert H. Lieshout, *The Struggle for the Organization of Europe. The Foundations of the European Union* (Cheltenham: Edward Elgar, 1999), ch. 6; Andreas Wilkens, 'Jean Monnet, Konrad Adenauer und die deutsche Europapolitik: Konvergenz und Dissonanzen (1950–1957)', in Andreas Wilkens (ed.), *Interessen Verbinden. Jean Monnet und die europäische Integration der Bundesrepublik Deutschland* (Bonn: Bouvier, 1999), pp. 76–9.

between France and Germany. In this letter, Schuman emphasised that the system he proposed would change economic relations between France and Germany 'completely' and 'focus them definitively on peaceful cooperation'. At the same time, it would lay 'a concrete basis' for 'an economic European organism, accessible to all countries in favour of a regime of liberty and aware of their solidarity'.[48]

Adenauer sent a reply a day later. Without wasting words, he welcomed Schuman's plan as 'a decisive step towards a partnership between Germany and France and therefore to a new order in Europe, based on peaceful cooperation'. In a personal note, he thanked Schuman sincerely for his 'gute Nachricht' – his good news. Adenauer also assured him that he was convinced that West German public opinion would give the plan a positive reception.[49] He was to be proved right.

Schuman and Adenauer found common ground in the core principles of what the latter referred to as the 'Wesen des Abendländische Christentums' (values of Western Christianity): individual freedom, democracy, and social cohesion. Both were Roman Catholics, and they believed that the individual should be put at the centre of the post-war future of Europe, something that could only be achieved through democracy. They also shared the conviction that this had to be Christian Democracy so that the state and the market would serve the individual and not vice versa, as had happened all too often in the inter-war years. Human rights were, after all, a Christian concept, as Schuman once said.[50] Adenauer agreed completely. He also agreed with Schuman that Christian values had to form the basis of a new Europe, a Europe that could also offer the stability required for the future of West Germany. The essential first step was, in Adenauer's words, 'eine deutsch-französische Zusammenarbeit und Solidarität' (German–French cooperation and solidarity).

Back in 1923, when he was mayor of Cologne, Adenauer had proposed the establishment of a French–Belgian–German Rhine–Ruhr state. The plan proved to be ahead of its time, however, as many saw it as obscure Rhineland separatism. Shortly after the war, he had tried to revive this old plan but was met once again with resistance. For the British authorities who were occupying the region at the time, it was reason enough to dismiss this 'born intriguer' from his position as mayor, as they saw him as 'dangerous'.[51] But his views remained unchanged when he received

---

[48] Politisches Archiv Auswärtiges Amt, Berlin, B20, vol. XX, Schuman to Adenauer, 7 May 1950.
[49] Konrad Adenauer, *Briefe 1949–1951* (Berlin: Siedler, 1985), pp. 208–9.
[50] Milward, *The European Rescue*, p. 328.
[51] Charles Williams, *Adenauer: The Father of the New Germany* (London: Little Brown, 2000), p. 294; Henning Köhler, *Adenauer: Eine politische Biografie* (Frankfurt: Propyläen,

Schuman's 'good news' a few years later. Adenauer was still convinced that a regional grouping in continental Western Europe, which he called the 'Vereinigten Staaten von Europa' – the United States of Europe – was the best guarantee of security and stability in the continent and 'die große Hoffnung' (the great hope) for Germany *and* for Europe.[52]

For the other countries of Western Europe, the Schuman Plan offered a new and hopeful solution to the persistent German question. For France, it marked a radical turnaround in its European policy which had, until then, been mainly focused on dismantling Germany's potential, especially in the Ruhr and Rhineland. In the first years of the post-war era, however, this traditional French policy had proved largely futile and ill-suited to the needs of an exhausted Western Europe. More importantly, it also clashed with the American vision of the future of Europe. For the US government, the launch of the Schuman Plan was a relief: after the frustrating experiences in the OEEC, the Europeans were finally making progress on cooperation and bloc formation. And they were at last on the path leading to West Germany's rehabilitation, which was essential for the country's much-needed rearmament in the light of the Cold War. In the years that followed, the Schuman Plan proved to be the game-changer that Western Europe needed. It was also the lever that elevated Christian Democratic political parties to positions of leadership in the process of European integration.

This all unfolded within the context of the British retreat from the centre stage of European politics. During the closing years of the 1940s, the British government watered down the Bevin Plan for a Western European customs union. The arguments to do this were familiar (and opportunistic): Anglo-Saxon sincerity, British independence, Commonwealth interests, and the display of condescending characterisations of France's economy. In the end, however, it appeared that it was the United Kingdom's own 'lack of economic muscle'. As the latter turned out to be a structural rather than a temporary phenomenon, it slowly but surely would manoeuvre the United Kingdom to the wings of financial-economic planning in Western Europe (and relegate the OEEC to the status of think tank and statistics bureau).[53]

In general, the growing aloofness of London in European matters created political room and momentum for bolder Franco-German (supranational) initiatives of European integration. Animated by Jean Monnet, an influential group of policymakers and politicians on key

---

1994), p. 15; Herbert Blankenhorn, *Verständnis und Verständigung* (Frankfurt: Propyläen, 1980), p. 43.
[52] Adenauer, *Erinnerungen*.   [53] Greenwood, 'The Third Force', pp. 428–36.

positions within the French governmental organisation, as well as in the bureaucracy of the Marshall Plan, was keen to rise to this European occasion par excellence. At the same time, the force of American planning was counterbalanced by home-grown European ideas, tailored to the regional situation of Western Europe. This situation crystallised ever more clearly as the United Kingdom retreated from the leader's position in Europe. Nonetheless, the Monnet-inspired pro-European vision that would prevail in France met with deep scepticism in circles of German economists.

In fact, German ordoliberals abhorred this regionally oriented institutional route. These defenders of the free enterprise anchored in framework treaties (guaranteeing respect for property and contract, protecting free competition, and honouring monetary prudence) were, however, strongly on the defensive just like their kindred spirits on the other side of the Atlantic.[54] Yet unlike the latter, the German ordoliberals would uniquely qualify to directly influence the history of European institution building. This happened in the closing years of the 1940s, via the first governments of the new FRG. The ordoliberal representative with the deepest impact on policymaking in Bonn was Wilhelm Röpke, Professor of Economics in Geneva, dedicated to the Freiburg School and prominent member of the MPS.[55]

Röpke was a fervent opponent of Keynesian planning in general. He had not been a fan of the Marshall Plan, which he characterised as an opportunistic blood transfusion, and he was on the same page as Schumpeter when it came to the policies of the Labour government in the UK. In Röpke's view, the Attlee government's projects proved how Keynesian planning, government debt, and centralised government could demolish an economy and a currency in no time. He argued that it was only through a free market and price correction via deflation that a more spontaneous and therefore more vital economic and social order could arise. In short, what Röpke stood for was exactly the opposite of the cocktail of interventionist Keynesian policies, dirigisme, and international lending and price fixing that were in vogue at that moment. And the way in which these ill-conceived policies were extended to the international sphere via multilateral organisations was an affront to Röpke. He even went so far as to argue that it was in Germany's interest to eliminate its tariffs regardless of what other Western European countries did, also to create a countermovement against the multilateral trend towards regulation.[56]

[54] Burgin, *The Great Persuasion*, pp. 87–122.   [55] Stedman Jones, *Masters*, p. 123.
[56] NWR, 'Lose Blattsammlung', 'Europäische Wirtschaftsintegration: Illusionen und Möglichkeiten', June 1953; Hennecke, *Wilhelm Röpke*, pp. 171–3; Plickert, *Wandlungen des Neoliberalismus*, p. 144; Gillingham, *European Integration*, p. 13.

In direct messages to Chancellor Adenauer, he warned not 'to put the European economy under the leadership of an all-encapsulating planning' (through a process of spill-over from one economic sector to the other) – not planning but the market should lead the European economy of the future, according to Röpke.[57]

But politics superseded economics in the West Germany of Adenauer that aligned its foreign policy to the American Cold War desires. Moreover, Schuman had stressed that 'the solidarity in production thus established will make it plain that any war between France and Germany becomes not merely unthinkable, but materially impossible'. In addition, the economics of the ECSC indeed matched key interests of the to-be-members of the ECSC: it gave France more control over the coal and steel markets of the Saar and the Ruhr and muzzled the German *Konzerne* (which had been a powerful industrial engine for Nazi Germany), it respectively substantiated and unleashed economic growth in Belgium and the Netherlands,[58] and it provided Italy not only with a huge future market for raw materials and Italian products, but also with a way out of its pressing problem of unemployment, for which the De Gasperi government saw 'emigration as the only solution' (the ECSC offered Italy 'easier movement of the Italian unemployed throughout Europe').[59]

Under Monnet's impassioned leadership, the complex negotiations on the ECSC treaty regularly proceeded in a rather unorthodox fashion. But they continued to make progress, and the atmosphere was often one of solidarity and a feeling of joint responsibility for the success of this revolutionary project. On 18 April 1951, the participating countries signed the treaty establishing the European Coal and Steel Community. A little over a year later, this first 'European Community' started operating. Its objectives focused particularly on two areas. It aimed to establish a common market for coal and steel and to harmonise and improve the working conditions and living standards of coal and steel workers. The ECSC granted credit to coal and steel producers to invest and guaranteed supply by regulating prices (by establishing maximum and minimum prices on the common market). The community also introduced a flanking social policy for miners and steel workers, including retraining programmes and allowances relating to benefits and pre-pensions. High Authority decisions on these matters had to be applied directly in the coal and steel sectors in the member states. Indeed, the ECSC was concerned with more than just the economy – at least, that was the intention.

[57] Wilkens, 'Jean Monnet', p. 81. [58] Segers, *The Netherlands*, ch. 2.
[59] Linda Risso, 'Cracks in a Façade of Unity: The French and Italian Christian Democrats and the Launch of the European Integration Process, 1945–1957', *Religion, State & Society*, 37, 1–2 (2009), 102.

In theory, the common market (in which there was a ban on discrimination enforced by the High Authority) was an instrument to achieve an optimal division of production and maximum productivity. At the same time, employment had to be safeguarded and disruptions in the national economies of the member states had to be avoided. This soon proved far from simple, and much of the ECSC's concrete policy had yet to be formulated. In addition, sensitive issues – such as price-setting within the common market and the decartelisation of the West German *Gemeinschaftsorganisation Ruhrkohle*, an institution for the buying and selling of coal from the Ruhr area – would lead to fierce clashes of interest between the member states. This made it more difficult for the community to function, and it regularly became bogged down in laborious decision-making and bureaucracy.

The core of the matter was however that the ECSC was anchored in supranational institutions. This is where it was revolutionary. Moreover, the ECSC was to be seen as the first crucial step towards a supranational community, through which Europe could wrest itself free from its tragic history. New supranational institutions would be the embodiment of that promise. The collective memory of peaceful and profitable cooperation that could be built up in these alternative constitutional institutions would then work as an antidote to the nationalism that predominated in those other institutions – the nation-states – and that repeatedly manifested itself in mutual mistrust, protectionism, and cynical power politics. In that respect, the history of the OEEC spoke volumes. According to Monnet, and politicians like Schuman, Adenauer, Spaak, and De Gasperi, the ECSC therefore had to be the start of a process of far-reaching integration that would change Europe permanently and lead to reconciliation between its people and nations, in tune with the popular Christian-inspired goal of international reconciliation. As such, the political gamble of the ECSC was in tune with the mood of the post-war times in Western Europe and tapped into a new reservoir of hope for the old continent. Crucially, this process was to be founded on mutual benefit in the sense of prosperity and stability – and to such an extent that could be attained only by community policies. The ECSC was to be the start of an institutional countermovement to state sovereignty because, as Monnet himself said, 'nothing is possible without men, and nothing is lasting without institutions'.[60]

It was exactly for this reason that the institutions of the new Europe had to be supranational. Only then could the mutual mistrust deeply embedded in European relations through the absolutism of state sovereignty be

---

[60] Monnet, *Mémoires*, p. 447.

sufficiently held in check. Monnet's goal may have been ambitious and compelling, but the practical, step-by-step technocracy into which he succeeded in translating that vision and which formed the core of the Schuman Plan was lacking neither political realism, nor economic realism, and matched both the intellectual and spiritual mood of the times, both from a pragmatical and principled point of view.

Conclusion

8   Eclipsing Atlantis

After it became clear that there was insufficient (domestic) support to establish an International Trade Organisation, American policymakers gave up on their pursuit of a transatlantic trade area characterised by multilateralism and convertibility. As a result, grand designs and blueprints for an Atlantic Community were put aside, allowing room for institutional pragmatism to develop. The Western world subsequently entered 'an intermediate phase of widening trade between countries, in conjunction with the regionally focused European Payments Union'.[1] The General Agreement on Tariffs and Trade – 'this supposedly interim agreement, which was meant to provide a framework for tariff reductions in advance of the creation of the ITO' – ended up becoming the basis on which world trade was regulated, an ad hoc solution that ended up continuing for decades.[2] Institutionally, however, GATT remained an empty shell in comparison with the Bretton Woods institutions – the World Bank and the International Monetary Fund – which implied that GATT could not function as the multilateral framework for European integration. This task was therefore left to the more regionally focused European Payments Union, in the void left by the UK's abdication of leadership in Europe.

The EPU created a temporary system to overcome the difficulties of non-convertibility and acted as a clearing house for intra-European settlements of surpluses and deficits. But once implemented, the EPU became much more than a system to clear payments. In many ways, the launch of the EPU marked the beginning of an eclipse of Atlanticism. The EPU represented an alternative, a second 'halfway house' next to 'Bretton Woods', a safe place for the nation-states of Western Europe to complete their difficult 'transition from bilateralism to currency convertibility'. This was something that the Bretton Woods system had tried to create but had failed to deliver.[3] With promises of transatlantic multilateralism

[1] Daunton, 'From Bretton Woods', p. 75; see also Maier, *In Search*, pp. 144–9.
[2] Toye, 'The Attlee Government', 912.
[3] Jacob J. Kaplan and Günther Schleiminger, *The European Payments Union. Financial Diplomacy in the 1950s* (Oxford: Clarendon Press, 1989), p. 1.

waning, the EPU evolved into 'an instrument of Europe's integration'. It not only it enabled the freeing of intra-European trade, but it also became a central 'forum for multilateral negotiations about European financial policies'. More importantly, the EPU allowed Western Europe to start weaving its own regional 'web of financial and commercial relations', which was urgently needed to allow intra-European trade to grow even after the end of the Marshall Plan.[4] The previous years had proven how difficult it was to overcome old-fashioned bilateralism and how strong the temptation was for nations to strive to maintain a current account surplus and to be paid for it in dollars, even if this was utterly self-defeating and poisonous to intra-European trade.[5] Moreover, it was precisely the threat of a stagnation in intra-European trade that had made European balance-of-payments issues 'the central policy problem of international economic cooperation'.[6] Now, at the end of this crazy decade, the EPU had unexpectedly created the institutional context in which economic welfare could be promoted in concert in Western Europe.

8.1 The Narrowing of Community

The regional approach inherent in the EPU matched the mission of building Europe that gradually came to prevail among influential policymaking circles in the US – the State Department in particular – from the summer of 1947, and harked back to regional European plans that had already been advanced in exile circles in London during the Second World War (a history meticulously fleshed out by Steehouder).[7] Two tenets characterised this American mission. First, the American government would take on this challenge from the outside, leading from the wings. And secondly, the mission was built around the German economy's re-entry into the post-war economy of Western Europe. This gave the FRG a central role as an integral part of Western Europe. By approaching Western Europe as a unit instead of separate states, the US was able to stimulate economic integration in Western Europe, mainly through its dollars, leaving the politics to the Europeans themselves. It was believed that this would in turn strengthen the Western world's position vis-à-vis the Soviet Union.[8] This line of reasoning was also easier to sell to the American public. With the US Congress increasingly wary of unlocking more funds

---

[4] Diebold cited in Kaplan and Schleiminger, *The EPU*, p. 24.
[5] Kaplan and Schleiminger, *The EPU*, pp. 22–4.
[6] Dyson and Quaglia (eds.), *European Economic Governance*, p. 28.
[7] Steehouder, 'Constructing Europe'.
[8] Weisbrode, *The Atlantic Century*, pp. 94–7 and 114–16; Trachtenberg, *A Constructed Peace*, pp. 99–103.

for Europe and yet at the same time 'attracted by the idea of a united Europe' due to enlightened self-interest, 'building Europe' became more appealing to Americans than 'building Atlantis'. The Americans considered the EPU to be the best way to bridge the gap between their 'missionary' goals and the 'practical' aspects of rebuilding Western Europe.

As it turned out, the defining framework for European cooperation was based not on Anglo-Saxon market liberalism with its global focus nor on Keynesianism with its policy interventions, but on German ordoliberalism and its emphasis on decentralisation (gradually worked out as 'subsidiarity' within the context of European integration, a typically (Catholic) Christian Democratic management principle for administering community),[9] the price mechanism, and the 'strong state'. Initially however – during the late 1940s – this was far from a given, nor very clear to the leading German ordoliberals, such as the highly influential Wilhelm Röpke, who warned that a 'fake multilateralism' based on a shadow system of loans was ultimately intended to enable European governments to implement their ambitious social policies aimed at full employment, which they in essence could not afford.

According to Röpke, who was a prominent member of the Mont Pelèrin Society – an influential international ideas-incubator-hub for the post-war liberal order of the West, including many leading ordoliberals and prominent economists, like Hayek – roughly the same could be said of the EPU (see chapter 7). Eventually, however – and pace Röpke – it was precisely the EPU that succeeded in creating a temporary system to overcome the difficulties of non-convertibility, as it acted as a clearing house for intra-European settlements of surpluses and deficits, and West Germany, in its new form of the Federal Republic of Germany, was at its very core: a shaping force of Western European multilateralism and an economic power to be reckoned with.

Given that Germany had lost the war and had been split in two, it was surprising that the FRG and its ordoliberal orientation managed to set the boundaries within which the planners of European integration realised their supranational ambitions. The boundaries within which ordoliberals themselves operated in West Germany shaped the way in which they proceeded in matters of European integration. From its first day in office, the West German government and its chancellor, Konrad Adenauer, had made it clear that supranational European integration based on Franco-German reconciliation was viewed as vital to securing the future of the FRG politically and geopolitically.[10] The key question for the FRG government was not *if* but *how*: how should European integration be developed and organised?

[9] Ghervas, *Conquering Peace*, p. 257.   [10] Segers, *Deutschlands Ringen*, pp. 30–41.

202 Conclusion

This forced the ordoliberals to be practical in their pro-European constructive ideas.

European integration in fact became the key issue over which ministries and planning staffs in the West German government wrangled. This was reinforced by the fact that the FRG essentially had no say in its own foreign affairs – until the mid-1950s, the 'semi-sovereign' status of the FRG implied that the responsibility of its foreign policy lay with the Western occupation powers – apart from its foreign policy adventures in European cooperation. The ordoliberal-inspired Adenauer governments considered financial-economic governance a key aspect of FRG's contribution to European integration. Indeed, during the 1950s it became increasingly clear that it was through modes of financial-economic governance that the conditio sine qua non of European integration, which was forced upon the FRG's policy of *Westbindung* by recent history and the FRG's Western partners (and the FRG itself) could be influenced and controlled.[11] In other words, financial-economic governance within the framework of European integration also was an instrument for the FRG to take back control over its own future. This made financial-economic governance within the process of European integration essential not only for the democratic legitimisation and domestic political ratification of the whole European experiment but also more generally for the durability and inner strength of the integration process.

All in all, the EPU's success can be attributed to the fact that it encompassed four elements of vital importance to the future of Western Europe. First, the EPU enhanced the modernisation and industrialisation of the Western European economies. Secondly, it freed international trade and payments, which resulted in 'an enormous increase in economic efficiency'. Thirdly, the EPU prompted 'the adjustment of economic policies to control foreign exchange imbalances'. And perhaps most importantly, the EPU paved the way for the integration of the economies of Western Europe into a common market.[12]

8.2   Europeanisation

The main casualty of the EPU was the Anglo-American partnership. Although the EPU had originally been the idea of the ECA – a product of ambitious American planning under the energetic aegis of Paul

---

[11] See Dyson, *States*, p. 579.
[12] See Kaplan and Schleiminger, *The EPU*, pp. 1–8, 15, and 21; Trachtenberg, *A Constructed Peace*, pp. 63–5.

Hoffman, Averell Harriman, and Richard Bissell – it marked a shift in initiative away from Washington and London towards Paris and Bonn.

The Europeans proceeded to pave their own path, abandoning several American plans that proved to be too far-fetched or idealistic for the harsh realities shaped by the heavy hand of history. For example, the ECA had envisaged the EPU to be a steppingstone towards monetary union,[13] but it soon became clear that it was unfit for this role. The institution remained a multilateral payments system that did what it was meant to do: provide a solid basis for gradual trade liberalisation in Western Europe by allowing member states to manage bilateral trade deficits with credit margins and providing ad hoc loans to countries with balance-of-payments problems.[14] It was essentially as a bank that the EPU exerted its power to force compliance. Yet as an institution it was ill equipped to handle the political prerequisites for monetary union. The experience of the EPU nonetheless did elevate discussions about the longer-term future of European integration to the next level, and it enhanced 'the credibility of the Marshall Plan liberalisation policy' both within *and* outside the regional sphere of EPU.

In an unforeseen way, the EPU served the multilateral ambitions of the Western world, as it allowed the Bretton Woods system to work quite adequately after all, despite the absence of a formal multilateral institution regulating trade. In addition, as the *Deutsche Mark* moved towards convertibility in the first half of the 1950s, the EPU evolved into a 'bilateral affair' between France and West Germany, which was pivotal to maintaining the drive towards further European integration. The Franco-German reconciliation remained the basis for this drive, as was acknowledged by the Adenauer government which allowed 'accumulating German surpluses [to cover] deficits in much of the remaining union and especially in France'.[15] More than anything else, these continental European policy realities – both Franco-German reconciliation and the fact that the EPU filled in what the Bretton Woods system had failed to provide – became the practical fruits of the bloc formation and subsequent European regionalism that had been taking root gradually since 1947.

Despite its centrality in the earliest days of European integration, the history of international monetary and trade cooperation remains a research

---

[13] See DNA, 2.08.50 (Directie Buitenlands Betalingsverkeer, FIN), 15.50, 'Multilateralisatie van het Europese Betalingsverkeer', 10 November 1949.
[14] Dyson and Quaglia (eds.), *European Economic Governance*, p. 29; Milward, *The Reconstruction*, pp. 208–11; see also *Agreement on the Establishment of a European Payments Union*, Paris, 19 September 1950, in Dyson and Quaglia (eds.), *European Economic Governance*, Document 1/26.
[15] Gillingham, *European integration*, pp. 20, 40, and 42.

domain that is distinctly separate from that of the history of European integration, even though the EPU was established before the ECSC was even launched. This is regrettable, also because from a perspective of (international) planning, the core struggles of the post-war West were focused on the paradoxes of capitalism in the free world: domestic versus international stability, market-led growth versus state control, and welfare and social cohesion versus economic competitiveness. Indeed, these endemic paradoxes still play a key role in the Western world in its ongoing search for stability, growth, prosperity, and welfare. Seen from this perspective, the Bretton Woods system, the failed ITO, the GATT, and European integration were, at their root, all multilateral endeavours to build institutions designed to help countries come to grips with the challenges of market economies and open societies after the Great Depression and the Second World War. In essence, they were all part of the same feverish pursuit of a resilient form of capitalism and democracy, a quest for 'a historical compromise ... based on a system of market stabilization in economics and constitutional democracy in politics'.[16] As from the 1930s, this quest was taken up by a new elite of experts in the transatlantic world. This new elite found itself and formed itself into what could be called a European Republic of Planning, a contemporary and policy-focused version of the old *Respublica literaria*.

The ideational context in which European integration was set in motion must be traced back to before the war. It was only in the second half of the 1940s, however, that a steady erosion took place in the 'belief that an ITO-type multilateral world trading regime would help avert a recurrence of the economic errors of the interwar years'. This was, moreover, 'matched by a simultaneous desire to undertake socialist planning at the domestic level'. The inevitable conclusion was that 'multilateralism abroad was inconsistent with a high level of planning at home'.[17] It was simply not realistic to suppose that a world trading regime could handle immediate problems of financial-economic governance and rapidly changing circumstances in the societies of the western nation-states involved. This also implied that an ITO-type multilateral organisation could never have become the instrument to hold together the transatlantic world of financial-economic governance in the medium to long term. Instead, a process of regionalisation (and regional bloc building) became dominant. Or more precisely, what kicked in was a process of Europeanisation. This was a process in which the nation-states of

---

[16] Peter Gourevitch, *Politics in Hard Times. Comparative Responses to International Economic Crises* (Ithaca and London: Cornell University Press, 1986), p. 167.
[17] Toye, 'The Attlee Government', 914.

Western Europe were forced to gradually develop and acquire common European values and practices in the above-mentioned quest for a stable and resilient form of capitalism and democracy. In Western Europe, this initially took the institutional form of the EPU, which gave further impetus to the 'continentalisation' of European integration. Given the institutional dynamics connected to these developments, the FRG emerged not only as the vital motor of Western European economic recovery and growth,[18] but also as a decisive force in combining progressive trade liberalisation, currency convertibility, and monetary management in Western Europe.

As the Franco-German alternative of continental European cooperation – devised to cope with the pressing problems of Western European security and stability – began to eclipse the transatlantic model of multilateral governance, this ironically brought about the market integration originally envisaged in the ITO scheme. This winning alternative evolved only very slowly and vaguely, and remained very limited in geographical scope (as it excluded the United Kingdom, Scandinavia, and the Iberian Peninsula). But it nonetheless created a financial-economic framework that induced the Franco-German gamble of the ECSC in May 1950 and the durable form of European integration that took root since that historic take-off. Essentially, the key steps to that turning point in 1950 were taken in the preceding years, when policy pragmatism and the ad hoc management of events triggered feasible economic blueprints that both inspired and 'made' the engineers of the take-off of European integration. Therefore, the history of international monetary and trade cooperation should be an integral part of the study of the origins of European integration.

8.3 Political and Spiritual Shifts

The emerging centrality of the Federal Republic of Germany in this process of Europeanisation was the final development phase in a threefold narrowing of geographical scope: first, from a One World approach to a transatlantic approach; secondly, from a transatlantic to a Western European orientation; and, thirdly, from an Anglo-Saxon-inspired to a Franco-German-inspired outlook. With every narrowing in scope came the rise and fall of ideas and practical schemes. These blueprints have left traces of their institutional path dependencies, about which we still know far too little. More multidisciplinary, multiarchival research is needed to better understand this unique experiment in institution building – and to question our common understanding of the history of European integration. And there is more to this history than policy plans and designs alone.

[18] Milward, *The Reconstruction*.

Soon after the Second World War, it crystallised that building a Western European 'unit' would be impossible without some sort of spiritual unity. The pressing political and societal demand for the latter reflected a trans-European phenomenon. Maybe, the longing for renewed hope – a hope that could counter the fears bred by war and radical politics on the right and left – was the dominant collective emotion of those years. In the atmosphere of collective longing, the uniting potential of Christianity in Europe was an increasingly prominent force, carried by the churches, involving themselves more and more actively in societal and political debates on the post-war order. The steady growth and influence of the ecumenical movement, which led to the founding of the World Council of Churches in Amsterdam in 1948, was a case in point. In addition, towards the end of the war, the Catholic Church had reactivated itself internationally promoting a democracy and human rights agenda, but also anticipating political exploitation of Christian religion.

On the Anglo-American side of the Atlantic, the church had already anticipated this 'space for discourse on European unity' as of the late 1930s. John Foster Dulles had been one of the early adapters and a prominent driver of this political-activist Christian agenda. But by 1948, Dulles had transformed into a cold warrior. This twisted his message at the WCC on the future of Europe: now the 'great crusade' was to be deployed for America's Cold War aims: the unifying potential of Christianity was now used for (geo)political Cold War purposes. The locus of action for the Christian agenda promoting European unity as a goal in itself now shifted.

At around the same time, the British minister of foreign affairs, Ernest Bevin, called for a 'Western Union' based on 'spiritual union'. That plan would fail but Bevin's call resonated in the press, loaded as it was with the big ideational concepts of those times, like 'freedom', 'democracy', 'rights', and 'love and liberty'. Slogans that appealed to the imagination and were broadly adhered to as the means to 'win the peace' – propped as they were by the mores of Roosevelt's 'Four Freedoms' (1941), the Universal Declaration of Human Rights, but also by leading Christian intellectuals openly associated with the WCC, like Reinhold Niebuhr, or explicitly linked to the Catholic Church, like Jacques Maritain. This all went hand in hand with a narrowing of political focus on the countries of the West and Western Europe in particular. Indeed, those countries of which it was realistic to expect that they could be made safe for democracy – and, by extension, capitalism.

This was not without consequences in the ideational realm of the emerging West and the crystallising Western Europe. The new line of (often-Christian-inspired) reasoning implied a clean break with socialism 'as a system'. Politically, this proved a winner's move. During the Cold War build-up and in the context of the Christian-inspired Truman Doctrine, stressing this new agenda that combined democracy and human rights with Christian values acquired political credibility in overwhelming portions. Tellingly, this new doctrine of the West became the guiding principle of the first governments of West Germany under the Christian Democrat Konrad Adenauer.[19] Moreover, this Europeanisation (or de-Americanisation) of the ideal of European unity effectively meant the end of the One World approach in US foreign policy, and a further reorientation towards practical and regionally (US-led) coordinated economic liberalism in Europe with a keen eye for the social question. Crucially, this development in Europe, which diverged from the original US agenda for Western Europe, nonetheless remained bolstered by US charity. An important argument for this persistent American support came from leading intellectual voices like Niebuhr's, who were advocating concentration on the economy as the key area in which US foreign policy could have a decisive impact in the world affairs of the Cold War era.

The ecumenical movement had been instrumental in fleshing out the possibilities for both reconciliation with Germany and for deeper cooperation in Western Europe.[20] Concerning the former, the ecumenical movement had played a decisive role in the coming about of the historic Stuttgart Declaration of Guilt (see chapter 3), and as such had a profound and lasting influence on the collective emotions (notwithstanding the fact that this influence initially worked via the intellectual, ecclesiastical, and political elites linked to and associated with these exercises of reconciliation). And yet the WCC, the ecumenical movement's transnational organisation, would find itself outmanoeuvred when the building of post-war Western Europe really began. Why?

The WCC's success in the immediate post-war years was rooted in the Christian fundament of the One World approach, an approach that at the time was the uncontested light of hope for many of those in the Western world who were occupied with international politics. But this approach, which guided the establishment of the United Nations in 1945 and was preserved in the UDHR of 1948, soon foundered under the pressure of the Cold War. Linked to that emerging new reality, post-war international circumstances re-energised state-centred thinking in Western

---

[19] Segers, *Deutschlands Ringen*, ch. 2.
[20] For a detailed description and analysis of this process under the co-coordination of the WCC in the making, see the Ph.D. thesis of Clemens van den Berg: Van den Berg, 'European Believers', especially ch. 4.

Europe. Moreover, it was in the ideological context of a world of two superpowers that the WCC steadily began to communicate a growing disconnect from the political developments on the ground in Western Europe. Its missionary scope was increasingly guided by Cold War preoccupations, also in line with Churchill's famous Iron Curtain speech in Fulton in 1946 (in which the prime minister diagnosed 'Christian civilisation' endangered),[21] and led the ecumenical movement away from European matters. While the political realities in Western Europe stimulated the institutionalisation of a Western European bloc centred around West Germany, the WCC turned its attention to ideology on a global (Cold War) level.

8.4 Arsenal of the Free World

While the One World approach lost out to more regional approaches, increasingly sophisticated and tailor-made Western European models pushed Atlantic schemes into the background. This development thrived on a combination of mutually reinforcing factors: the institutional tendencies inherent in the Bretton Woods system, practical (domestic) policy challenges in Western Europe, and the crystallisation of a new bipolar world order. Ultimately, the drive towards regionalism set the stage for the launch of the Schuman Plan in May 1950 and the establishment of the ECSC in 1951. This laid the foundations for European market integration based on socio-economic planning. It also heralded the dominance of a new political family in Western Europe: Christian Democracy. This political force bent post-war Western European politics towards the religiously inspired centre-right instead of to the left, as many had anticipated. Christian Democracy was in tune with the mood of the new time. It had managed to form an effective political bulwark against communism even before the Cold War was a reality.

At the heart of this Christian resurrection in European politics was the experiment and experience of ecumene that harked back to the voices of the practitioners of trans-European resistance. Those who had deployed the 'weapons of the spirit' against the evil of the Nazis, but also had inspired more 'personalist' views on the human condition in the modern democratic, capitalist, and anti-totalitarian societies of the West. During the post-war *and* post-Cold War decades, the Western European undertaking that had been so shaky and US-dependent at the outset evolved into a pre-reflection of what could become a truly

---

[21] Leffler, 'The Emergence', p. 72.

European alternative that, against the odds of the history of the twentieth century, became a co-carrier of the so-called free world alongside the United States. The free world – again – has to deploy its complete 'arsenal of democracy' (Roosevelt), both abroad and at home, in order to survive. The European Republic of Planning remains at the epicentre of the struggle for survival of the free world, as a powerhouse of peace in European history and a source of learning.

Epilogue

George Kennan was a master strategist in the US government in the 1940s. In those years, 'his career seemed unlimited'.[1] Kennan was a prolific writer, producing a vast, almost unparalleled quantity of memos, policy recommendations, opinion pieces, and books. His feeling for the nuance and contingency of history could be called European, but his opinions were decidedly American in a realist and staunchly Western, anti-communist, and anti-totalitarian way. This was a compelling combination. During crucial periods in the 1940s, Kennan's voice was influential in the State Department, but its impact beyond Foggy Bottom[2] remained limited. Within the hierarchy of the US administration, the State Department was rather weak and powerless. As a result, Kennan's arguments were not decisive in the pre-war and wartime governments of President Franklin Delano Roosevelt, who tended to listen to others.[3] But after the end of the Second World War, Kennan's writings and analyses steadily gained influence and soon became instrumental in shaping the Western narrative of the Cold War.[4] Indeed, the post-war Western world largely crystallised into the world that Kennan had envisaged, which became his claim to fame.

Within the Truman administration, Kennan first gained praise with the circulation of his 'long telegram', a cable of more than 5,000 words sent from Moscow in February 1946. The American public learned about him when he was revealed as the author of the 'Mr. X' article, published anonymously in the journal *Foreign Affairs* in July 1947. The two pieces stated that 'while cooperation with the Kremlin was impossible and war was unnecessary, a policy of "containing" Soviet expansion was feasible'. Moreover, Kennan added that such an American foreign policy of containment vis-à-vis the Soviet Union could eventually trigger a collapse of the regime. According to the historian Frank Costagliola, 'Kennan's writing in the long telegram and in the Mr. X article was so skillfully

---

[1] Costagliola (ed.), *The Kennan Diaries*, p. xxviii.
[2] Foggy Bottom is where the Department of State is headquartered.
[3] Heyde, 'Amerika', 134.
[4] Costagliola (ed.), *The Kennan Diaries*, especially pp. xxxii–xxxiii.

crafted that his emotionally charged, exaggerated depictions of the Soviet Union as an existential threat were accepted as being what he claimed they were: hard-headed descriptions of unavoidable reality.'[5]

Behind the superiority of his professional American writings and the veneer of his American patriotism, Kennan was at heart a European. The European element in his personal background formed the breeding ground for his doubt, his melancholy – that European disease – and his romantic longing for the mystique of Scandinavia and the Baltic, his 'mother-countries'.[6] In order to keep these ghosts in check, Kennan wrote letters. In the years of the unfolding of the Cold War, some of his more soul-searching letters were addressed to the prominent philosopher Isaiah Berlin, the famous Oxford professor who had come to the UK as a refugee from Riga, Latvia. Kennan and Berlin knew each other from the Anglo-American policy elite of the American East Coast, where Berlin had spent some time working for the British Foreign Office in the final years of the war.[7] After this brief excursion to the world of diplomacy, Berlin had returned to academic life in Oxford. From the side-line, Berlin quickly became the conscience of the West during the Cold War. It was in this capacity that he became the recipient of Kennan's letters.[8]

One such letter was a reaction to an article written by Berlin for the spring 1950 issue of *Foreign Affairs*. What unnerved Kennan the most about the article was the somewhat laconic way Berlin approached the phenomenon of totalitarianism.[9] He was particularly disturbed by Berlin's failure to spell out that communism was an intolerable system that ran counter to human nature. In Kennan's view, what the implementers of totalitarianism were doing was nothing less than committing 'original sin' by taking advantage of human vulnerability to manipulation. In totalitarian regimes such as the Soviet Union, rulers acted as though 'problems have been caused to disappear in order that they may not have to be solved'. This was trickery and deceit. In the end, this could easily result in 'another form of taking human life arbitrarily and in cold blood, because of calculation'. There was no fundamental difference between this and Nazi practices. According to Kennan, the success of a civilisation depended 'on the readiness to refrain from doing so; and on their sticking

---

[5] Costagliola (ed.), *The Kennan Diaries*, p. xxviii; Leffler, 'The Emergence', pp. 72–3.
[6] John Lamberton Harper, *American Visions of Europe* (Cambridge: Cambridge University Press, 1996), pp. 149ff; George F. Kennan, *Sketches from a Life* (New York: Pantheon, 1989), p. 274.
[7] Deighton, 'Don and Diplomat', 525–40.
[8] For the Kennan–Berlin correspondence quoted below, see Isaiah Berlin, *Enlightening. Letters 1946–1960* (London: Pimlico, 2011), pp. 212–13 and 218–19.
[9] Isaiah Berlin, 'Political Ideas in the Twentieth Century', *Foreign Affairs*, April 1950, 351–85.

to the rational appeal which assumes ... that in the long run each man can be taught to rise above himself'. He was prepared to concede that 'perhaps this is the supreme make-believe', a fairy tale. Ultimately, however, this did not trouble him, since this was 'the inexorable price of human progress' and *the* argument 'for clinging to the belief that questions are important, are susceptible of solution by rational processes, and should be so approached and solved'.

Kennan's written outburst was an apt summary of the delusion of his era. It covered the whole programme of action for a new and improved post-war Western world – manufacturability (of a better society), elevation (of the masses), and progress (of humankind through a Western (American) programme of civilisation for the free world) – all without once mentioning the word 'politics' or 'ideology'. Kennan deliberately avoided these terms because he considered ideology to be the cause of a wild and misguided form of politics based on emotions, a throwback to the sinister Europe of the 1930s and early 1940s. The American leadership of the free world embodied something rather different, something that represented the next step in human progress: a radically rational approach that would definitively subdue the old seductions of emotions in politics and their inevitable tendency towards totalitarianism.

It may have been that Kennan felt stung by Berlin's article because he sensed that his friend from Oxford had laid bare a glaring inconsistency in the ambitious American-led programme for the post-war Western world: the incongruence between the image of a supremely rational US foreign policy and its ideational hard core. When stripped of the rhetoric of the American Enlightenment, the core of US foreign policy was based not so much on reason as on a belief in the infallibility of the rational method in its modern American varieties, most notably the 'politics of productivity' and the activist American agenda to 'multilateralise' this best practice.[10]

Berlin had clearly touched a nerve because he had demonstrated that beliefs based on emotions rather than pre-calculated solutions to problems were the driving force of America's post-war leadership of the West. What was even worse in Kennan's opinion was that Berlin had gone public with this analysis amid what was widely perceived to be a make-or-break period for American foreign policy in which it would be revealed whether or not the United States could carry the free world as it had claimed. It was imperative that the United States succeed in building a lasting cooperative relationship with its European partners to ward off

---

[10] Romero, *The United States*, ch. 1, section 1. The concept of the 'politics of productivity' was introduced by the American historian Charles S. Maier in the 1970s (Maier, 'The Politics of Productivity').

the dangers of communism and Soviet expansion. Openly discussing the intellectual weaknesses at the heart of this programme at this critical moment, as Berlin had done, was the equivalent of dealing a fatal blow to the credibility of this whole endeavour and to the entire programme of American foreign policy. It was an act that Kennan perceived as utterly irresponsible both politically and morally in the unstable world of escalating superpower rivalry.

Isaiah Berlin, the historian of ideas, was greatly affected by his American friend's heartfelt cry. Almost a year went by before he could bring himself to communicate this to Kennan with a lengthy line of argumentation. According to Berlin, the world of 'good cops and bad cops' described by Kennan was simplistic and a denial of the tragedy of human nature. The European thus gave the wannabee European a lesson on Europe: ambiguity and darkness were fundamental to the continent; what is more, they swirled at the core of human affairs and the course of events. As far as Berlin was concerned, though, this lesson did not have to be learned per se; perhaps, for practical politics in the age of the Cold War, it was better if it were not. Nevertheless, in his reply, Berlin did his best to explain clearly where he stood. He agreed with Kennan that it was wrong to treat people as though one were '"moulding" them like pieces of clay'. Berlin completed the argumentation as follows:

> our answer has to be that certainly all 'moulding' is evil, and that if human beings at birth had the power of choice and the means of understanding the world, it would be criminal; since they have not, we temporarily enslave them, for fear that, otherwise, they will suffer worse misfortunes from nature and from men, and this 'temporary enslavement' is a necessary evil until such time as they are able to choose for themselves – the 'enslavement' having its purpose not an inculcation of obedience but its contrary, the development of power of free judgement and choice; still evil it remains even if necessary.

What Kennan branded as 'Soviet evil', however, was ultimately 'an extreme and distorted but only too typical form of some general attitude of mind from which our own countries are not exempt'. And he warned: 'we must avoid being inverted Marxists'. He moreover suggested that his friend was engaged in a battle above all with himself. After all, Kennan's letter had shown that his fiery plea for a 'solution by rational processes' was built upon make-believe and that it was, in fact, a pretence maintained against one's better judgement.

Kennan wanted to unconditionally choose rationality, to harness passion to do good, but such things did not convince Berlin. In this, he was not alone. Staunchly pro-Western defenders of liberalism also warned against holding too firm a belief in rationality and the tendency towards excessive policy planning that this belief fuelled. Their predictions of how a society built on rampant planning would culminate in a totalitarian horror were best articulated in Friedrich Hayek's 1944 bestseller, *The Road to Serfdom*.

To be sure, Kennan, Berlin, and Hayek all became prominent Anglo-Saxon stars of the post-war era. They emerged as the scholarly and intellectual lights of the Western world during the Cold War alongside already more established guides of the twentieth century like John Maynard Keynes – the opposite of Hayek in the stylised world of post-war economics – and the politically savvy, socially engaged, internationalist American theologian Reinhold Niebuhr, or the post-war Western splendour of Eleanor Roosevelt, the driving force behind the Universal Declaration of Human Rights. Albeit these stars figured, and still figure, prominently in the histories of post-war Western Europe, they were not, however, the main protagonists of this narrative, as they were not the builders or real architects of the post-war West or of European integration. As stars, they shone their guiding lights of rationalism, realism, and idealism on others, but it was the policymakers, economists, jurists, politicians, and pastors in their shadow who did the tedious day-to-day work of designing and assembling institutions. They were the ones who created the post-war West, in particular Western Europe. These policy engineers were on a constant and feverish quest to reconcile lofty ambitions with the brute facts of geopolitics and economics and to translate the Western agenda of capitalism and democracy into feasible and emotionally compelling policies. In their work, American examples of societal organisation set a new and often inspiring standard.

This was also the beginning of 'Americanisation' taken to the next level. America was not only a dominant and victorious power in geopolitics, it was also 'the suggestive image of a rich and democratic society, and ideal for many to emulate ... a force of attraction'.[11] In spite of the repulsion inherent in any fatal attraction, for Europe, the pull of the American lifestyle time and again overpowered the push. As the twentieth century progressed, Western Europe in a certain way became part of America and the American world, however much it essentially remained non-American. A crucial element in this trajectory was the tragic hope aroused in Europe by Woodrow Wilson during the First World War that resurfaced in the Second World War in another form, and unmistakably signalled how radically new, at last, the times would be in post-war Europe. In this emerging new reality, it was the American president who spoke most compellingly of European civilisation and ideals, and it

---

[11] Romero, *The United States*, preface.

was the truncated Western segment of Europe that slowly but surely became a bastion of solace and hope. It was an extremely shaky bastion but a bastion all the same, complete with the clear-cut division between those on the outside and those on the inside, following the leading maxim of any common identity: we are one world, they another.

In 1983, Milan Kundera described the callous reality of Western Europe in his essay, 'The Tragedy of Central Europe'. Kundera began the piece by citing the battle cry of the director of the Hungarian Press Bureau in November 1956. The last telex that he sent ended with the sentence: 'We are going to die for Hungary and Europe.' The pan-European contact that this invoked proved to be a phantom. Shortly thereafter, the futility of his act of resistance was written in blood by the Red Army into the annals of European history. Reflecting on the telex of 1956, Kundera asked himself many years later: 'When Solzhenitsyn denounces communist oppression, does he invoke Europe as a fundamental value worth dying for?' Kundera's answer was: 'No.' And he explained this further: '"To die for one's country and for Europe" – that is a phrase that could not be thought in Moscow or Leningrad; it is precisely the phrase that could be thought in Budapest or Warsaw', where 'the word "Europe" does represent a spiritual notion synonymous with the word "West"'; their regions lie 'culturally in the West', rooted in 'Roman Christianity'.[12] The present times confront this Europe with the test of inclusiveness, the promise that is at the very heart of the ideas and programme on which the Europe of European integration has been built.

---

[12] Milan Kundera, 'The Tragedy of Central Europe', *New York Review of Books*, 31, 7 (1984 [1983]).

Bibliography

Archives Referred to in the Text

Bodleian Special Collections, Oxford
Bundesarchiv, Koblenz
Chatham House Archives, London
Europe Archive Maastricht, Maastricht
Historical Archives of the EU (HAEU), Florence
——— *Oral History Collections*
Nachlass Wilhelm Röpke (NWR), Institut für Wirtschaftspolitik, Cologne
Nationaal Archief, Dutch National Archives (DNA), The Hague
Politisches Archiv Auswärtiges Amt, Berlin
The National Archives (TNA), Kew, Surrey

Published Primary Sources and Media Sources

American Theological Library Association Serials, 'Secular Press Reactions to Amsterdam in the U.S.A.', October 1948

Anonymous, *Correspondence between President Truman and Pope Pius XII* (Truman Library, Independence)

Beveridge, William, *Social Insurance and Allied Services* (Cmd. 6404, 1942), 'Beveridge Report'

Churchill, Winston, Speech at Zurich University, 19 September 1946, in Anjo G. Harryvan and Jan van der Harst (eds.), *Documents on European Union* (Houndmills, Basingstoke: MacMillan, 1997)

Committee of European Economic Co-Operation, *General Report* (Paris, 1947)

Department of State, *Foreign Relations of the United States* (FRUS), 1947 (vol. I, *General*, vol. III, *The British Commonwealth; Europe*), 1948 (vol. III, *Western Europe*), 1949 (vol. IV, *Western Europe*) (Washington: US Printing Office, 1972–4)

Dokumente zur Deutschlandpolitik, II. Series, vol. I, *Die Konferenz von Potsdam* (Neuwied and Frankfurt: Albert Metzner, 1992)

Hansard, Foreign Affairs, HC Deb., 22 January 1948, vol. 446 cc383–517: https://api.parliament.uk/historic-hansard/commons/1948/jan/22/foreign-affairs

'La bombe Schuman', *La Relève*, 20 May 1950

Moggridge, Donald (ed.), *The Collected Writings of John Maynard Keynes*, vol. XXV, *Activities 1940–1944, Shaping the Post-War World: The Clearing Union* (Cambridge: Cambridge University Press, 2013 [1980])

Pius XII, 'Sur la démocratie: radio-message au monde', 24 December 1944, as translated in Emile Perreau-Saussine, *Catholicism and Democracy: An Essay in the History of Political Thought* (Princeton: Princeton University Press, 2012)

'Politische Gemeinschaftsordung: Ein Versuch des christlichen Gewissens in den politischen Nöten unserer Zeit' (Freiburg, 1943), in Walter Lipgens, *Europa-Föderationspläne der Widerstandsbewegungen, 1940–1945. Eine Dokumentation* (Munich: Oldenbourg, 1968)

Quadragesimo Anno, 'On Reconstruction of the Social Order' (1931)

Roosevelt, Franklin D., (6 January) 1941, 'The Four Freedoms', in Andrew J. Bacevich (ed.), *Ideas and American Foreign Policy* (Oxford: Oxford University Press, 2018)

References

Adenauer, Konrad, *Briefe 1949–1951* (Berlin: Siedler, 1985)
  Erinnerungen 1945–1953 (Stuttgart: DVA, 1963)
  'Rede in der Aula der Universität zu Köln', 24 March 1946 (Konrad Adenauer Stiftung), reprinted in English in Mathieu Segers and Yoeri Albrecht (eds.), *Re: Thinking Europe. Thoughts on Europe: Past, Present and Future* (Amsterdam: Amsterdam University Press, 2016)
Alacevich, Michele, 'The World Bank's Early Reflections on Development: A Development Institution or a Bank', *Centro Studi Luca D'Agliano Development Studies Working Papers*, 122 (2007)
Alphand, Hervé, *L'étonnement d'être. Journal 1939–1973* (Paris: Fayard, 1977)
Anderson, Perry, *The New Old World* (London and New York: Verso, 2009)
Assmann, Aleida, *Der europäische Traum. Vier Lehren aus der Geschichte* (Munich: C.H. Beck, 2018)
Baker, A.E. and George Bell, *William Temple and His Message* (London: Penguin, 1946)
Bauman, Zygmunt, *In Search of Politics* (Cambridge: Polity Press, 1999)
Bentley, James, *Martin Niemöller, 1892–1984* (New York: The Free Press, 1984)
Berghahn, Volker R., *Europe in the Era of Two World Wars. From Militarism and Genocide to Civil Society, 1900–1945* (Princeton and Oxford: Princeton University Press, 2006)
Berlin, Isaiah, 'The Bent Twig: On the Rise of Nationalism', *Foreign Affairs*, 51 (1972), 11–30
  Enlightening. Letters 1946–1960 (London: Pimlico, 2011)
  'European Unity and Its Vicissitudes', in *The Crooked Timber of Humanity. Chapters in the History of Ideas* (London: John Murray, 1990 [1959])
  Flourishing. Letters 1928–1946 (London: Chatto & Windus, 2004)
  'Political Ideas in the Twentieth Century', *Foreign Affairs*, April 1950, 351–85
Bissell, Richard M., *Reflections of a Cold Warrior: From Yalta to the Bay of Pigs* (New Haven: Yale University Press, 1996)

Bitsch, Marie-Thérèse, and Gérard Bossuat (eds.), *L'Europe Unie et l'Afrique* (Brussels: Bruylant, 2006)
Blankenhorn, Herbert, *Verständnis und Verständigung* (Frankfurt: Propyläen, 1980)
Blower, Brooke L., *Becoming Americans in Paris. Transatlantic Politics and Culture between the World Wars* (Oxford and New York: Oxford University Press, 2013)
Blyth, Mark M., '"Any More Bright Ideas?" The Ideational Turn of Comparative Political Economy', *Comparative Politics*, 29, 2 (1997), 229–50
  Great Transformations: The Rise and Decline of Embedded Liberalism (Cambridge: Cambridge University Press, 2002)
  'Powering, Puzzling, or Persuading? The Mechanisms of Building Institutional Orders', *International Studies Quarterly*, 51 (2007), 761–77
Boerger-De Smedt, Anne, 'Negotiating the Foundations of European Law, 1950–57: The Legal History of the Treaties of Paris and Rome', *Contemporary European History*, 21, 3 (2012), 339–56
Böhm, Franz, Walter Eucken, and Hans Grossmann-Doerth, 'Our Task', reprinted as 'The Ordo Manifesto of 1936', in Alan Peacock and Hans Willgerodt (eds.), *Germany's Social Market Economy: Origins and Evolution* (Houndmills, Basingstoke: Palgrave Macmillan, 1989)
Bonefeld, Werner, 'Freedom and the Strong State: On German Ordoliberalism', *New Political Economy*, 17, 5 (2012), 633–45
Bosco, Andrea, *June 1940, Great Britain and the First Attempt to Build a European Union* (Newcastle upon Tyne: Cambridge Scholars Publishing, 2016)
Bossuat, Gérard, 'Jean Monnet, 1943–1946, l'urgence et l'avenir', in Gérard Bossuat (ed.), *Jean Monnet et l'économie* (Brussels, etc.: Peter Lang, 2018)
Brodo, Michael D., and Barry Eichengreen, *A Retrospective on the Bretton Woods System* (Chicago and London: University of Chicago Press, 1993)
Brunet, Luc-André, *Forging Europe: Industrial Organisation in France, 1940–1952* (London: Palgrave Macmillan, 2017)
Buchheim, Christoph, *Die Wiedereingliederung Westdeutschlands in die Weltwirtschaft 1945–1958* (Munich: Oldenbourg, 1990)
Bührer, Werner, *Westdeutschland in der OEEC. Eingliederung, Krise, Bewährung 1947–1961* (Munich: Oldenburg, 1997)
Bullock, Allan, *Ernest Bevin. Foreign Secretary* (Oxford: Oxford University Press, 1983)
Burgin, Angus, *The Great Persuasion. Reinventing Free Markets since the Depression* (Cambridge, MA: Harvard University Press, 2012)
Cairncross, Frances (ed.), *Changing Perceptions of Economic Policy. Essays in the Honour of the Seventieth Birthday of Sir Alec Cairncross* (London and New York: Methuen, 1981)
Chamedes, Giuliana, *A Twentieth-Century Crusade. The Vatican's Battle to Remake Christian Europe* (Cambridge, MA: Harvard University Press, 2019)
Claassen, Rutger, Anna Gerbrandy, Sebastiaan Princen, and Mathieu Segers (eds.), Special Issue: 'Rethinking the European Social Market Economy', *Journal of Common Market Studies*, 57, 1 (2019), 1–182

Clavin, Patricia, *Securing the World Economy: The Reinvention of the League of Nations, 1920–1947* (Oxford: Oxford University Press, 2013)

Clayton, William L., 'GATT, the Marshall Plan, and OECD', *Political Science Quarterly*, 78, 4 (1963), 493–503

Colville, John, *The Fringes of Power. Downing Street Diaries 1939–1955* (London: Hodder and Stoughton, 1985)

Conway, Martin, 2020, 'Legacies of Exile: The Exile Governments in London during the Second World War and the Politics of Post-War Europe', in Martin Conway and José Gotovitch (eds.), *Europe in Exile. European Exile Communities in Britain 1940–45* (New York and Oxford: Berhahn, 2001)

   Western Europe's Democratic Age, 1945–1968 (Princeton: Princeton University Press)

Costagliola, Frank (ed.), *The Kennan Diaries* (New York and London: Norton, 2014)

Coupland, Philip M., 'Western Union, "Spiritual Union", and European Integration, 1948–1951', *Journal of British Studies*, 43 (July 2004), 366–94

Croce, Benedetto, *History as the Story of Liberty* (Indianapolis: Liberty Fund, 2000 [1941])

Da Empoli, Domenico, Corrado Malandrino, and Valerio Zanone (eds.), *Luigi Einaudi. Selected Political Essays*, vol. III (Houndmills, Basingstoke: Palgrave Macmillan, 2014 [1940])

Dash Moore, Deborah, *GI Jews. How World War II Changed a Generation* (Cambridge, MA: Harvard University Press, 2006)

Daunton, Michael, 'From Bretton Woods to Havana: Multilateral Deadlocks in Historical Perspective', in Amrita Narlikar (ed.), *Deadlocks in Multilateral Negotiations* (Cambridge: Cambridge University Press, 2010)

Davies, Norman, *Europe. A History* (London: Pimlico, 1997)

De Bellefroid, Diane, 'The Commission pour l'Étude des Problèmes d'Après-Guerre (CEPAG), 1941–1944', in Martin Conway and José Gotovitch (eds.), *Europe in Exile. European Exile Communities in Britain 1940–45* (New York and Oxford: Berhahn, 2001)

De Graaf, Beatrice, 'Bringing Sense and Sensibility to the Continent: Vienna 1815 Revisited', *Journal of Modern European History*, 13, 4 (2015), 447–57

   Fighting Terror after Napoleon. How Europe Became Secure after 1815 (Cambridge: Cambridge University Press, 2020)

   'A New Perspective on the European Security Culture after 1815', *Confronti* (Bologna: Società editrice il Mulino, 2019), 627–34

   Über die Mauer. Die Kirchen, die Friedensbewegung und die DDR (Münster: Agenda Verlag, 2007)

De Graaf, Beatrice, Ido de Haan, and Brian Vick (eds.), *Securing Europe after Napoleon. 1815 and the New European Security Culture* (Cambridge: Cambridge University Press, 2019)

De Grazia, Victoria, *Irresistible Empire: America's Advance through Twentieth-Century Europe* (Cambridge, MA: Belknap Press and Harvard University Press, 2005)

De Haan, Ido, 'The Western European Welfare State beyond Christian and Social Democratic Ideology', in Dan Stone (ed.), *The Oxford Handbook of Postwar European History* (Oxford: Oxford University Press, 2014)

Deighton, Anne, 'Brave New World? Brave Old World?', *Contemporary European History*, 28, 1 (2019)31–4

'Don and Diplomat: Isaiah Berlin and Britain's Early Cold War', *Cold War History*, 13, 4 (2013), 525–40

Denord, François, 'French Neoliberalism and Its Divisions. From the Colloque Walter Lippmann to the Fifth Republic', in Philip Mirowski and Dieter Plehwe (eds.), *The Road from Mont Pèlerin. The Making of the Neoliberal Thought Collective* (Cambridge, MA: Harvard University Press, 2015)

Duchêne, François, *Jean Monnet. The First Statesman of Interdependence* (New York and London: Norton, 1994)

Dulles, John Foster, 'The Problem of Peace in a Dynamic World', in *The Universal Church and the World of Nations*, The Official Oxford Conference Books, vol. VII (Chicago: Willet, Clark & Company, 1938)

Du Réau, Elisabeth, 'Integration or Co-operation? Europe and the Future of the Nation-State in France, 1945–1955', in Dominik Geppert (ed.), *The Postwar Challenge: Cultural, Social, and Political Change in Western Europe, 1945–1958* (Oxford: Oxford University Press, 2003)

Dyson, Kenneth, *Conservative Liberalism, Ordo-Liberalism, and the State. Disciplining Democracy and the Market* (Oxford: Oxford University Press, 2021)

States, Debt and Power: 'Saints' and 'Sinners' in European History and Integration (Oxford: Oxford University Press, 2014)

Dyson, Kenneth, and Lucia Quaglia (eds.), *European Economic Governance & Policies. Commentary on Key Historical & Institutional Documents*, vol. I (Oxford: Oxford University Press, 2010)

Einaudi, Luigi, 'The Concluding Remarks of the Governor of the Bank of Italy for the Year 1946', in Luca Einaudi, Riccardo Faucci, and Roberto Marchiontti (eds.), *Luigi Einaudi. Selected Economic Essays*, vol. II (Houndmills, Basingstoke: Palgrave Macmillan, 2006 [1946])

'The Nature of a World Peace', in Domenico da Empoli, Corrado Malandrino, and Valerio Zanone (eds.), *Luigi Einaudi. Selected Political Essays*, vol. III (Houndmills, Basingstoke: Palgrave Macmillan, 2014 [1940])

Einaudi, Luca, Riccardo Faucci, and Roberto Marchiontti (eds.), *Luigi Einaudi. Selected Economic Essays*, vol. II (Houndmills, Basingstoke: Palgrave Macmillan, 2006 [1946])

Eley, Geoff, 'Corporatism and the Social Democratic Moment: The Postwar Settlement, 1945–1973', in Dan Stone (ed.), *The Oxford Handbook of Postwar European History* (Oxford: Oxford University Press, 2014)

Ellwood, David W., *The Shock of America. Europe and the Challenge of the Century* (Oxford: Oxford University Press, 2016)

Enzensberger, Hans Magnus, *Hammerstein oder der Eigensinn. Eine deutsche Geschichte* (Frankfurt: Suhrkamp, 2008)

Erhard, Ludwig, *Deutschlands Rückkehr zum Weltmarkt* (Düsseldorf: Econ, 1953)

Fennema, Meindert, and John Rhijnsburger, *Dr. Hans Max Hirschfeld: Man van het grote geld* (Amsterdam: Bert Bakker, 2007)
Fioretos, Orfeo, *Creative Reconstructions. Multilateralism and European Varieties of Capitalism after 1950* (Ithaca: Cornell University Press, 2011)
Friis, Lykke, '"The End of the Beginning" of Eastern Enlargement – Luxembourg Summit and Agenda-Setting', *European Integration Online Papers*, 2, 7 (1998)
Gardner, Richard N., 'Sterling-Dollar Diplomacy in Current Perspective', *International Affairs*, 62, 1 (1986), 21–33
Gassert, Philip, 'The Spectre of Americanization: Western Europe in the American Century', in Dan Stone (ed.), *The Oxford Handbook of Postwar European History* (Oxford: Oxford University Press, 2014)
Ghervas, Stella, *Conquering Peace, from the Enlightenment to the European Union* (Cambridge, MA: Harvard University Press, 2021)
Gillingham, John, *European Integration 1950–2003. Superstate or Market Economy?* (Cambridge: Cambridge University Press, 2003)
  'From Morgenthau Plan to Schuman Plan', in Jeffry M. Diefendorf, Axel Frohn, and Hermann-Josef Rupieper (eds.), *American Policy and the Reconstruction of West Germany, 1945–1955* (Cambridge: Cambridge University Press, 2004)
Glendon, Mary Ann, *A World Made New. Eleanor Roosevelt and the Universal Declaration of Human Rights* (New York: Random House, 2002)
Glossner, Christian L., *The Making of the German Post-War Economy. Political Communication and Public Reception of the Social Market Economy after World War Two* (London: I.B. Taurus, 2010)
Goldstein, Judith, and Robert O. Keohane (eds.), *Ideas and Foreign Policy: Beliefs, Institutions, and Political Change* (Ithaca: Cornell University Press, 1993)
Goodwin, Craufurd D., *Walter Lippmann. Public Economist* (Cambridge, MA: Harvard University Press, 2014)
Gourevitch, Peter, *Politics in Hard Times. Comparative Responses to International Economic Crises* (Ithaca and London: Cornell University Press, 1986)
Greenwood, Sean, 'The Third Force Policy of Ernest Bevin', in Michel Dumoulin (ed.), *Plans des Temps de Guerre pour l'Europe d'Après-Guerre, 1940–1947* (Brussels, etc.: Bruylant, etc., 1995)
Greschat, Martin (ed.), *Die Schuld der Kirche: Dokumente und Reflexionen zur Stuttgarter Schulderklärung vom 18./19. Oktober 1945*, Studienbücher zur kirchlichen Zeitgeschichte (Munich: Chr. Kaiser, 1982)
Griffiths, Richard (ed.), *The Netherlands and the Integration of Europe* (Amsterdam: NEHA, 1990)
Haas, Ernst B., 'The Challenge of Regionalism', *International Organization*, 12, 4 (1958), 440–58
  The Uniting of Europe: Political, Social and Economical Forces 1950–1957 (Notre Dame: University of Notre Dame Press, 1958)
Hall, Peter A., and David Soskice (eds.), *Varieties of Capitalism. The Institutional Foundations of Comparative Advantage* (Oxford: Oxford University Press, 2001)
Hansen, Peo, and Stefan Jonsson, *Eurafrica. The Untold History of European Integration and Colonialism* (London: Bloomsbury Academic, 2014)

Harriman, W. Averell, 'Recalling the Work of the Harriman Committee', in Stanley Hoffmann and Charles Maier (eds.), *The Marshall Plan. A Retrospective* (Boulder: Westview Press, 1984)

Hemingway, Ernest, *A Moveable Feast* (London: Arrow Books, 2011 [1964])

Hennecke, Hans Jörg, *Wilhelm Röpke. Ein Leben in der Brandung* (Stuttgart: Schäffer-Poeschel, 2005)

Hennessy, Peter, *Never Again. Britain 1945–1951* (London: Penguin Books, 2006 [1992])

Hewitson, Mark, and Matthew D'Auria (eds.), *Europe in Crisis. Intellectuals and the European Idea, 1917–1957* (New York and Oxford: Berghahn, 2012)

Heyde, Veronika, 'Amerika und die Neuordnung Europas vor dem Marshallplan (1940–1944)', *Vierteljahreshefte für Zeitgeschichte* (Munich: Oldenbourg), 58, 1 (2010), 115–39

Hirsch Ballin, Ernst, Emina Cerimovic, Huub Dijstelbloem, and Mathieu Segers, *European Variations as a Key to Cooperation* (Cham: Springer, 2020)

Hochgeschwender, Michael, and Bernhard Löffler (eds.), *Religion, Moral und Liberaler Markt. Politische Ökonomie und Ethikdebatten vom 18. Jahrhundert bis zur Gegenwart* (Bielefeld: Transcript, 2011)

Hoffmann, Ross, 'Europe and the Atlantic Community', *Thought*, 20 (1945), 25–34

Hoffmann, Stanley, 'US–European Relations: Past and Future', *International Affairs*, 79, 5 (2003), 1029–36

Hoffmann, Stanley, and Charles Maier (eds.), *The Marshall Plan. A Retrospective* (Boulder: Westview Press, 1984)

Hooghe, Liesbet, and Gary Marks, 'Is Liberal Intergovernmentalism Regressive? A Comment on Moravcsik, *Journal of European Public Policy*, 27, 4 (2020), 501–8

Howson, Susan, and Donald Moggridge (eds.), *The Wartime Diaries of Lionel Robbins & James Meade 1943–45* (New York: St Martin's Press, 1990)

Ikenberry, John, 'Creating Yesterday's New World Order: Keynesian "New Thinking" and the Anglo-American Postwar Settlement', in Judith Goldstein and Robert Keohane (eds.), *Ideas and Foreign Policy* (Cambridge: Cambridge University Press, 1993)

James, Harold, *International Monetary Cooperation since Bretton Woods* (New York and Oxford: Oxford University Press, 1996)

Jones, Michael, Mark McBeth, and Elizabeth Shanahan (eds.), *The Science of Stories* (New York: Palgrave Macmillan, 2014)

Judt, Tony, *Postwar. A History of Europe since 1945* (London: Pimlico, 2007)

Kaiser, Wolfram, *Christian Democracy and the Origins of the European Union* (Cambridge: Cambridge University Press, 2007)

Kaiser, Wolfram, and Brigitte Leucht, 'Informal Politics of Integration: Christian Democratic and Transatlantic Networks in the Creation of ECSC Core Europe', *Journal of European Integration History*, 14, 1 (2008), 35–49

'Transatlantic Policy Networks in the Creation of the First European Anti-Trust Law: Mediating between American Anti-Trust and German Ordo-Liberalism', in Wolfram Kaiser, Brigitte Leucht, and Morton Rasmussen (eds.), *The History of the European Union: Origins of a Trans- and Supranational Polity 1950–72* (Abingdon: Routledge, 2009)

Kaiser, Wolfram, Brigitte Leucht, and Michael Gehler (eds.), *Transnational Networks in Regional Integration: Governing Europe 1945–83*, Studies in EU Politics Series (Houndmills, Basingstoke: Palgrave Macmillan, 2010)

Kaiser, Wolfram, Brigitte Leucht, and Morton Rasmussen (eds.), *The History of the European Union: Origins of a Trans- and Supranational Polity 1950–72* (Abingdon: Routledge, 2009)

Kaplan, Jacob J., and Günther Schleiminger, *The European Payments Union. Financial Diplomacy in the 1950s* (Oxford: Clarendon Press, 1989)

Kennan, George F., *Sketches from a Life* (New York: Pantheon, 1989)

Kirby, Dianne, 'Divinely Sanctioned: The Anglo-American Cold War Alliance and the Defence of Western Civilization and Christianity, 1945–48', *Journal of Contemporary History*, 35, 3 (2000), 385–412

'Harry Truman's Religious Legacy: The Holy Alliance, Containment and the Cold War', in Dianne Kirby (ed.), *Religion and the Cold War* (Houndmills, Basingstoke: Palgrave Macmillan, 2003)

'The Impact of the Cold War on the Formation of the World Council of Churches', in Joachim Garstecki (ed.), *Die Ökumene und der Widerstand gegen Diktaturen: Nationalsozialismus und Kommunismus als Herausforderung an die Kirchen*, Konfession und Gesellschaft, 39 (Stuttgart: W. Kohlhammer Verlag, 2007)

Kissinger, Henri, *Diplomacy* (New York: Simon & Schuster, 1994)

Kjaer, Poul F., 'The Transnational Constitution of Europe's Social Market Economies: A Question of Constitutional Imbalances?', *Journal of Common Market Studies*, 57, 1 (2019), 143–58

Kleine, Mareike, and Mark Pollack (eds.), Special Issue: 'Liberal Intergovernmentalism and Its Critics', *Journal of Common Market Studies*, 56, 7 (2018), 1491–696

Köhler, Henning, *Adenauer: Eine politische Biografie* (Frankfurt: Propyläen, 1994)

Kolev, Stefan, Nils Goldschmidt, and Jan-Otmar Hesse, 'Walter Eucken's role in the Early History of the Mont Pèlerin Society', *Freiburger Diskussionspapiere zur Ordnungsökonomik*, 14, 02 (Freiburg: Institute for Economic Research, 2014), 6

Kool, Martijn, and Trineke Palm, 'Crafting Emotions: The Valence of Time in Narratives about the Future of Europe in the Council of Europe (1949)', *Journal of Contemporary European Research*, 17, 4 (2021), 463–81

Koschut, Simon, 'Speaking from the Heart: Emotion Discourse Analysis in International Relations', in Maéva Clément and Eric Sanger (eds.), *Researching Emotions in International Relations* (New York: Palgrave Macmillan, 2018)

Kosseleck, Reinhart, *Vergangene Zukunft: Zur Semantik geschichtlicher Zeiten* (Frankfurt: Suhrkamp, 1988)

Kundera, Milan, 'The Tragedy of Central Europe', *New York Review of Books*, 31, 7 (1984 [1983])

Kunter, Katharina, '"Zurück nach Europa". Kirchen und Christen als politische und gesellschaftliche Faktoren im demokratischen Transformationsprozess Tschechiens', *Kirchliche Zeitgeschichte*, 19, 1 (2006), 145–58

Küsters, Hanns-Jürgen, 'West Germany's Foreign Policy in Western Europe 1949–58', in Clemens Wurm, ed., *Western Europe and Germany* (Oxford and Washington, DC: Berg, 1995)

Lamberton Harper, John, *American Visions of Europe* (Cambridge: Cambridge University Press, 1996)
Lankford, Nelson D., *The Last American Aristocrat. The Biography of Ambassador David K.E. Bruce* (Boston: Little, Brown and Company, 1996)
Lanting, Dorien, and Trineke Palm , '"Change the Heart, and the Work Will Be Changed": Pius XII's Papal Blueprints for Europe', *Contemporary European History*, 31, 1 (2021), 1–13
Leffler, Melvyn P., 'The Emergence of an American Grand Strategy, 1945–1952', in Melvyn Leffler and Odd Arne Westad (eds.), *The Cambridge History of the Cold War*, vol. I (Cambridge: Cambridge University Press, 2010)
Leucht, Brigitte, and Katja Seidel, 'Du Traité de Paris au règlement 17/1962: ruptures et continuités dans la politique européenne de concurrence, 1950–1962', *Histoire, économie et société*, 27, 1 (2008), 35–46
Leustean, Lucian N., *The Ecumenical Movement and the Making of the European Community* (Oxford: Oxford University Press, 2014)
  'What Is the European Union? Religion between Neofunctionalism and Intergovernmentalism', *International Journal for the Study of the Christian Church*, 9, 3 (2009), 165–76
Leustean, Lucian N., and John T.S. Madeley, 'Religion, Politics and Law in the European Union: An Introduction', *Religion, State & Society*, 37, 1–2 (2009), 3–18
Lieftinck, Pieter, *Lieftinck 1902–1989: Herinneringen opgetekend door A. Bakker and M.M.P. van Lent* (Utrecht and Antwerp: Veen, 1989)
Lieshout, Robert H., *The Struggle for the Organization of Europe. The Foundations of the European Union* (Cheltenham: Edward Elgar, 1999)
Lieshout, Robert, Mathieu Segers, and Anna van der Vleuten, 'De Gaulle, Moravcsik, and *The Choice for Europe*. Soft Sources, Weak Evidence', *Journal of Cold War Studies*, 6, 4 (2004), 89–139
Lindseth, Peter, 'Equilibrium, Demoi-cracy, and Delegation in the Crisis of European Integration', *German Law Journal*, 15, 4 (2014), 529–67
  Power and Legitimacy: Reconciling Europe and the Nation-State (Oxford: Oxford University Press, 2010)
Lingen, Markus, 'Müller-Armack, Alfred' (Konrad Adenauer Stiftung: www.kas.de)
Lipgens, Walter and Wilfried Loth (eds.), *Documents on the History of European Integration* (Berlin: De Gruyter, 1988)
Lippmann, Walter, *The Political Scene. An Essay on the Victory of 1918* (New York: Henry Holt and Company, 1919)
Luce, Henry, 'The American Century', in Andrew J. Bacevich (ed.), *Ideas and American Foreign Policy* (Oxford: Oxford University Press, 2018)
Lundestad, Geir, *'Empire' by Integration. The United States and European Integration, 1945–1997* (Oxford: Oxford University Press, 1998)
McAfee Brown, Robert, *The Essential Reinhold Niebuhr* (New Haven and London: Yale University Press, 1986)
McBeth, Mark, and Elizabeth Shanahan, 'Introducing the Narrative Policy Framework', in Michael Jones, Mark McBeth, and Elizabeth Shanahan (eds.), *The Science of Stories* (New York: Palgrave Macmillan, 2014)

MacMillan, Margaret, *The War that Ended Peace: The Road to 1914* (New York: Random House, 2013)
McNamara, Kathleen, *The Currency of Ideas. Monetary Politics in the European Union* (Ithaca and London: Cornell University Press, 1998)
Maes, Ivo (with Ilaria Pasotti), 2021, *Robert Triffin. A Life* (Oxford: Oxford University Press, 2021)
Maier, Charles, 'The Politics of Productivity: Foundations of American International Economic Policy after World War II', *International Organization*, 31, 4 (1977), 607–33
 In Search of Stability (Cambridge: Cambridge University Press, 1987)
Malaparte, Curzio, *The Skin [La Pelle]* (n.p: Pickle Partners Publishing, 2015 [1949])
Mallinson, William, *From Neutrality to Commitment: Dutch Foreign Policy, NATO and European Integration* (London and New York: Tauris, 2010)
Mazower, Mark, 'The Man Who Was France', *New York Review of Books*, 16 January (2020), 45–8
Melandri, Pierre, *Les États-Unis face à l'unification de l'Europe 1945–1954* (Paris: Pedone, 1980)
Mercer, Jonathan, 'Emotional Beliefs', *International Organization*, 64 (2010), 1–31
 'Rationality and Psychology in International Politics', *International Organization*, 59 (2005), 77–106
Meyer Resende, Madalena, 'The Catholic Narrative of European Integration', in Mathieu Segers and Steven van Hecke (eds.), *The Cambridge History of the European Union*, vol. I (Cambridge: Cambridge University Press, 2023)
Migani, Guia, 'Europe, Decolonization and the Challenge of Developing Countries', in Mathieu Segers and Steven van Hecke (eds.), *The Cambridge History of the European Union*, vol. I (Cambridge: Cambridge University Press, 2023)
Milward, Alan S., *The European Rescue of the Nation-State* (London: Routledge, 1994)
 The Reconstruction of Western Europe 1945–51 (London: Methuen & Co., 1984)
Mirowski, Philip, and Dieter Plehwe (eds.), *The Road from Mont Pèlerin. The Making of the Neoliberal Thought Collective* (Cambridge, MA: Harvard University Press, 2015)
Mitrany, David, *A Working Peace System* (Chicago: Quadrangle Books, 1966 [1943])
Monnet, Jean, *Memoirs* (New York: Doubleday, 1978)
Montarsolo, Yves, *L'Eurafrique: contrepoint de l'idée d'Europe. Le cas français de la fin de la deuxième guerre mondiale aux négociations des traités de Rome* (Aix en Provence: Publications de l'Université de Provence, 2010)
Moravcsik, Andrew, *The Choice for Europe. Social Purpose and State Power from Messina to Maastricht* (London: UCL Press, 1995)
 'De Gaulle between Grain and Grandeur' (part 1), *Journal of Cold War Studies*, 2 (2000), 3–43
 'De Gaulle between Grain and Grandeur' (part 2), *Journal of Cold War Studies*, 3 (2000), 4–68

'Liberal Intergovernmentalism and Integration: A Rejoinder', *Journal of Common Market Studies*, 33, 4 (1995), 611–28
'Preference, Power and Institutions in 21st Century Europe', *Journal of Common Market Studies*, 56, 7 (2018), 1648–74
Morgenthau, Hans J., *Politics among Nations* (New York: McGraw Hill, 1993 [1948])
Mudrov, Sergei A., 'European Integration and the Churches', in Mathieu Segers and Steven van Hecke, *The Cambridge History of the European Union*, vol. I (Cambridge: Cambridge University Press, 2023)
  'Religion and the European Union: Attitudes of Catholic and Protestant Churches toward European Integration', *Journal of Church and State*, 57, 3 (2014), 507–28
Muller, Jerry Z., *The Mind and the Market. Capitalism in Western Thought* (New York: Anchor Books, 2003)
Nasra, Skander, and Mathieu Segers, 'Between Charlemagne and Atlantis: Belgium and the Netherlands during the First Stages of European Integration', *Journal of European Integration History*, 18, 2 (2012), 183–206
Niebuhr, Reinhold, *The Children of Light and the Children of Darkness. A Vindication of Democracy and a Critique of Its Traditional Defenders* (London: Nisbet & Co., 1944)
  'The Fight for Germany', *Life Magazine*, 21 October 1946, 65–72
Niemann, Arne, *Explaining Decisions in the European Union* (Cambridge: Cambridge University Press, 2006)
O'Reilly, William, 'Genealogies of Atlantic History', *Atlantic Studies*, 1, 1 (2004), 66–84
Palm, Trineke, 'Interwar Blueprints of Europe: Emotions, Experience and Expectation', *Politics and Governance*, 6, 4 (2018), 135–43
Parmar, Inderjeet, *Foundations of the American Century. The Ford, Carnegie, and Rockefeller Foundations in the Rise of American Power* (New York: Columbia University Press, 2014)
Parsons, Craig, *A Certain Idea of Europe* (Ithaca and London: Cornell University Press, 2003)
Patel, Kiran Klaus, *The New Deal. A Global History* (Princeton and Oxford: Princeton University Press, 2016)
  Project Europe: Myths and Realities of European Integration (Cambridge and New York: Cambridge University Press, 2020)
  'Widening and Deepening? Recent Advances in European Integration History', *Neue Politische Literatur*, 64 (2019), 327–57
Patel, Kiran Klaus, and Wolfram Kaiser, 'Continuity and Change in European Cooperation during the Twentieth Century', *Contemporary European History*, 27, 2 (2018), 165–82
Peiponen, Matti, *Ecumenical Action in World Politics: The Creation of the Commission of the Churches on International Affairs (CCIA), 1945–1949*, Schriften Der Luther-Agricola-Gesellschaft 66 (Helsinki: Luther-Agricola-Gesellschaft, 2012)
Pierson, Paul, 'The Path to European Integration: A Historical Institutionalist Analysis', *Comparative Political Studies*, 29, 2 (1996), 123–63

Piketty, Thomas, *Capital in the Twenty-First Century* (Cambridge, MA, and London: Harvard University Press, 2014)
Plickert, Philip, *Wandlungen des Neoliberalismus. Eine Studie zur Entwicklung und Ausstrahlung der 'Mont Pèlerin Society'* (Stuttgart: Lucius & Lucius, 2008)
Polanyi, Karl, *The Great Transformation* (Boston: Beacon, 1957 [1944])
Preston, Andrew, *Sword of the Spirit, Shield of Faith: Religion in American War and Diplomacy* (Toronto: CNIB, 2014)
Preston, Andrew, and Doug Rossinow (eds.), *Outside In. The Transnational Circuitry of US History* (New York: Oxford University Press, 2017)
Ptak, Ralf, 'Neoliberalism in Germany. Revisiting the Ordoliberal Foundation of the Social Market Economy', in Philip Mirowski and Dieter Plehwe (eds.), *The Road from Mont Pèlerin. The Making of the Neoliberal Thought Collective* (Cambridge, MA: Harvard University Press, 2015)
Ransom, James, '"A Little Marshall Plan": Britain and the Formation of the European Payments Union, 1948–50', *International History Review*, 3 (2010), 437–54
Raucher, Alan R., *Paul G. Hoffman: Architect of Foreign Aid* (Lexington: Kentucky University Press, 1986)
Reuter, Hans-Ulrich, 'Die Europäische Ökumenische Kommission für Kirche und Gesellschaft (EECCS) als Beispiel für das Engagement des Protestantismus auf europäischer Ebene', dissertation Universität Hannover, Stuttgart/Hannover, 2002
Riccio, Barry D., *Walter Lippmann. Odyssey of a Liberal* (New Brunswick and London: Transaction, 1994)
Richard, Anne-Isabelle, 'The Limits of Solidarity: Europeanism, Anti-Colonialism and Socialism at the Congress of the Peoples of Europe, Asia and Africa in Puteaux, 1948', *European Review of History*, 21, 4 (2015), 519–37
Risso, Linda, 'Cracks in a Façade of Unity: The French and Italian Christian Democrats and the Launch of the European Integration Process, 1945–1957', *Religion, State & Society*, 37, 1–2 (2009)
Romero, Federico, *The United States and the European Trade Union Movement, 1944–1951* (Chapel Hill and London: University of North Carolina Press, 1992)
Röpke, Wilhelm, *Briefe. Der innere Kompass, 1934–1966* (Erlenbach and Zurich: Rentsch, 1976)
  Civitas humana. Grundfragen der Gesellschafts- und Wirtschaftsreform (Bern and Stuttgart: Paul Haupt, 1979 [1944])
Rosenboim, Or, 'Barbara Wootton, Friedrich Hayek and the Debate on Democratic Federalism in the 1940s', *International History Review*, 36, 5 (2014), 894–900
  The Emergence of Globalism. Visions of World Order in Britain and the United States, 1939–1950 (Princeton and Oxford: Princeton University Press, 2017)
Roussel, Eric, *Jean Monnet* (Paris: Fayard, 1996)
Ruggie, John, 'International Regimes, Transactions, and Change: Embedded Liberalism in the Post-War Economic Order', *International Organization*, 36, 2 (1982), 379–415

Salzmann, Walter, *Herstel, wederopbouw en Europese samenwerking* (The Hague: Sdu, 1999)
Sandholtz, Wayne, and Alec Stone Sweet (eds.), *European Integration and Supranational Governance* (Oxford: Oxford University Press, 1997)
Schmelzer, Matthias, *The Hegemony of Growth. The OECD and the Making of the Economic Growth Paradigm* (Cambridge: Cambridge University Press, 2016)
Schmidt, Vivien, 'Discursive Institutionalism: The Explanatory Power of Ideas and Discourse', *Annual Review of Political Science*, 11, 1 (2008), 303–26
Schroeder, Paul, *The Transformation of European Politics, 1763–1848* (Oxford: Clarendon Press, 1994)
Schumpeter, Joseph, *Capitalism, Socialism and Democracy* (London: Allen and Unwin, 1981 [1942])
Schwabe, Klaus, *Die Anfänge des Schuman-Plans 1950/51* (Baden-Baden: Nomos, 1988)
Shennan, Andrew, *Rethinking France. Plans for Renewal, 1940–1946* (Oxford: Oxford University Press, 2001 [1989])
Shortall, Sarah, *Soldiers of God in a Secular World. Catholic Theology and Twentieth-Century French Politics* (Cambridge, MA: Harvard University Press, 2021)
Segers, Mathieu, *Deutschlands Ringen mit der Relance. Die Europapolitik der BRD während der Beratungen und Verhandlungen über die Römischen Verträge* (Frankfurt etc.: Peter Lang, 2008)
  'Eclipsing Atlantis: Trans-Atlantic Multilateralism in Trade and Monetary Affairs as a Pre-History to the Genesis of Social Market Europe (1942–1950)', *Journal of Common Market Studies*, 57, 1 (2019), 60–76
  'European Integration and Its Vicissitudes', Inaugural Lecture, 7 December 2018 (Maastricht: UM)
  'Flags and Bones. The Europe of Malaparte', *European Review of Books*, 2 (2022), 76–91
  'The FRG and the Common Market', in Carole Fink et al. (eds.), *1956. European and Global Perspectives* (Leipzig: Leipziger Universitätsverlag, 2006)
  The Netherlands and European Integration, 1950 to Present (Amsterdam: Amsterdam University Press, 2020)
  'Preparing Europe for the Unforeseen, 1958–63. De Gaulle, Monnet and European Integration beyond the Cold War: From Cooperation to Discord in the Matter of the Future of the EEC', *International History Review*, 24, 2 (2012), 347–70
Segers, Mathieu (ed.), *Dagboeken van Max Kohnstamm, September 1957 – Februari 1963* (Amsterdam: Boom, 2011)
  (ed.), *De Europese dagboeken van Max Kohnstamm. Augustus 1953 – September 1957* (Amsterdam: Boom, 2008)
Slobodian, Quinn, *Globalists. The End of Empire and the Birth of Neoliberalism* (Cambridge, MA: Harvard University Press, 2018)
Smyser, William, *From Yalta to Berlin: The Cold War Struggle over Germany* (New York: St Martin's Griffin, 1999)
Stedman Jones, Daniel, *Masters of the Universe. Hayek, Friedman, and the Birth of Neoliberal Politics* (Princeton and Oxford: Princeton University Press, 2012)

Steehouder, Jorrit, 'Constructing Europe. Blueprints for a New Monetary Order 1919–1950', Ph.D. thesis, Utrecht University (NWO 360-52-190), 2022
  'In the Name of Social Stability: The European Payments Union', in Mathieu Segers and Steven van Hecke (eds.), *The Cambridge History of the European Union*, vol. II (Cambridge: Cambridge University Press, 2023)
Steehouder, Jorrit, and Clemens van den Berg, 'A Wartime Narrative of Hope: The *Freiburger Bonhoeffer-Kreis's* 1943 Memorandum as a Blueprint for Europe', in Lennaert van Heumen and Mechtild Roos (eds.), *The Informal Construction of Europe* (New York: Routledge, 2019)
Steel, Ronald, *Walter Lippmann and the American Century* (New York: Vintage, 1981)
Steil, Ben, *The Battle of Bretton Woods. John Maynard Keynes, Harry Dexter White and the Making of a New World Order* (Princeton and Oxford: Princeton University Press, 2013)
  The Marshall Plan. Dawn of the Cold War (Oxford: Oxford University Press, 2018)
Stinsky, Daniel, 'Western Europe vs. All-European Cooperation? The OEEC, the European Recovery Program, and the United Nations Economic Commission for Europe, 1947–1952', in Matthieu Leimgruber and Matthias Schmelzer (eds.), *The OECD and the International Political Economy since 1948* (Cham: Springer Nature/Palgrave Macmillan, 2017)
Tischner, Wolfgang, 'Wilhelm Röpke' (Konrad Adenauer Stiftung: www.kas.de)
Toje, Richard, 'The Attlee Government, the Imperial Preference System and the Creation of the GATT', *English Historical Review*, 118, 478 (2003)
Tomlinson, Jim, *Democratic Socialism and Economic Policy. The Attlee Years, 1945–1951* (Cambridge: Cambridge University Press, 1997)
Toulouse, Mark G., 'Working toward Meaningful Peace: John Foster Dulles and the F.C.C., 1937–1945', *Journal of Prebysterian History*, 61, 4 (1983), 393–410
Trachtenberg, Marc, *A Constructed Peace: The Making of the European Settlement 1945–1963* (Princeton: Princeton University Press, 1999)
Tribe, Keith, *Strategies of Economic Order. German Economic Discourse 1750–1950* (Cambridge: Cambridge University Press, 1995)
Van den Berg, Clemens, 'European Believers. Ecumenical Networks and Their Blueprints as Drivers of Early European Integration, 1933–1954', Ph.D. thesis, Utrecht University (NWO 360-52-190), 2022
Van Os, Pieter, 'Hoezo eeuwenoude traditie? De eerste dagen van de joods-christelijke beschaving', *De Groene Amsterdammer*, 3 October 2019, 40–1
  Liever dier dan mens. Een overlevingsverhaal (Amsterdam: Prometheus, 2009)
Van Zon, Koen, 'Assembly Required. Institutionalising Representation in the European Communities', Ph.D. thesis Radboud University, Nijmegen, 2019
Viner, Jacob, 'Objectives of Post-War International Economic Reconstruction', in W. McKee and L.J. Wiesen (eds.), *American Economic Objectives* (New Wilmington: Economic and Business Foundation, 1942)
Vines, D., 'James Meade', *Discussion Paper Series*, 330 (Department of Economics, Oxford University, 2007)
Visser 't Hooft, Willem, *Memoires* (Amsterdam and Brussels: Elsevier, 1971)

Wapshott, Nicolas, *Keynes–Hayek. The Clash that Defined Modern Economics* (New York and London: Norton, 2011)
Warneke, Sara, *Die euroäische Wirtschaftsintegration aus der Perspektive Wilhelm Röpkes* (Stuttgart: Lucius & Lucius, 2013)
Wasserman, Janek, *The Marginal Revolutionaries. How Austrian Economists Fought the War of Ideas* (New Haven and London: Yale University Press, 2019)
Weisbrode, Kenneth, *The Atlantic Century. Four Generations of Extraordinary Diplomats Who Forged America's Vital Alliance with Europe* (Cambridge, MA: Da Capo, 2009)
Welles, Sumner, 'Blueprint for Peace', in *Prefaces to Peace* (New York: Simon & Schuster/ Doubleday, etc./Columbia University Press, 1943)
Wells, H.G., *The War That Will End War* (London: Frank & Cecil Palmer, 1914)
Wielenga, Friso, *West-Duitsland: partner uit noodzaak. Nederland en de Bondsrepubliek 1949–1955* (Utrecht: Spectrum, 1989)
Wilkens, Andreas, 'Jean Monnet, Konrad Adenauer und die deutsche Europapolitik: Konvergenz und Dissonanzen (1950–1957)', in Andreas Wilkens (ed.), *Interessen Verbinden. Jean Monnet und die europäische Integration der Bundesrepublik Deutschland* (Bonn: Bouvier, 1999)
Williams, Andrew, *Failed Imagination? The Anglo-American New World Order from Wilson to Bush* (Manchester: Manchester University Press, 2007)
Williams, Charles, *Adenauer: The Father of the New Germany* (London: Little Brown, 2000)
Willkie, Wendell L., 'One World', in *Prefaces to Peace* (New York: Simon and Schuster/ Doubleday, etc./Columbia University Press, 1943)
Winter, Jay, *Dreams of Peace and Freedom. Utopian Moments in the Twentieth Century* (New Haven and London: Yale University Press, 2006)
Winter, Jay, and Antoine Prost, *René Cassin and Human Rights. From the Great War to the Universal Declaration* (Cambridge: Cambridge University Press, 2013)
Wootton, Barbara, *Freedom under Planning* (Chapel Hill: University of North Carolina Press, 1945)
Zeilstra, Jurjen A., *European Unity in Ecumenical Thinking, 1937–1948* (Zoetermeer: Boekencentrum, 1995)

Index

Acheson, Dean, 187
Adenauer, Konrad
   adopted the social market economy, 181
   Christian unity inspired, 207
   collective responsibility guided leadership of, 100
   at the Congress of Europe, 159
   the ECSC and, 194
   guiding principle of leadership of, 163
   on the importance of Franco-German reconciliation, 201
   influence of ordoliberalism on, 178
   proposed a French-Belgian-German Rhine-Ruhr state, 190
   on reasons for the fall of Germany, 40
   success of West German governments under, 90
   supported the values of Western Christianity, 190
Akademie für Deutsches Recht, 95
Algiers, 81, 82
Allied Control Council (ACC), 180
Alphand, Hervé, 40, 134, 141, 147
America. *See* United States
American Century, 58
American Enlightenment, the, 212
American power, 30
American Revolution, the, 20, 112
Americanisation, 6, 8, 30, 44, 47, 140, 214
Amsterdam, 206
Anglo-American partnership, 7, 49, 111, 112, 119, 157, 176, 202
Ansiaux, Hubert, 146, 171
Anti-Comintern Pact, 65
anti-Keynesianism, 52
antisemitism, 116
anti-socialism, 52
anti-totalitarianism, 91
Arbeitsgemeinschaft Erwin von Beckerath, 95
Arbeitsgemeinschaft Volkswirtschaftslehre, 95
Aron, Raymond, 67
Atlantic Century, 13, 26, 34, 59, 176

Atlantic Charter, the, 123
   the Beveridge Report and, 107
   Catholic internationalists were enthusiastic about, 92
   declarations of, 58
   failure of the Western Union and, 107
   free markets in, 60
   free trade and, 123
   the Marshall Plan and, 107
   multilateralism emerging after, 90
   reduction of tariffs in, 152
   significance of, 58
   signing of, 17, 59
Atlantic civilization, 28
Atlantic imagination, 1, 29, 141
Atlanticism, 101, 199
atomic bomb, the, 49
atomic warfare, 163
Attlee, Clement, 107
Austria, 66, 136
Austrian School of economics, 50, 51, 52, 67, 71, 74, 76, 90, 103, 104, 105

balance of power, 53
balance-of-payments, 120, 121, 123, 170, 173, 183
balance-of-payments crisis, 109, 124, 125, 134, 175
bancor, 73
Bank for International Settlements (BIS), 146
banking, 122, 127
Banque d'Indochine, 66
Barth, Karl, 84, 93, 98
Baruch, Bernard, 164
battle of the blueprints, 18
Baudouin, Paul, 66
Bauman, Zygmunt, 1
Belgium, 36, 92, 136, 151, 153, 156, 172, 173, 178, 187, 193
Belgium-Netherlands-Luxembourg Customs Union, 135

232 Index

Bell, George, 63, 99
Benda, Julien, 159
Benelux countries, 146, 156, 170, 175, 180
Benelux customs union, 146
Bereczky, Alfred, 166
Berlin Blockade, 161
Berlin Wall, the, 4
Berlin, Isaiah, 8, 161, 211
Beveridge Report, the, 72, 107, 152
Beveridge, William, 57, 72
Bevin, Ernest, 136, 140, 141, 175
  1947 meeting with Clayton, 146
  calls for a 'Western Union', 150, 206
  failure of Western Union proposal, 107
  fight against unemployment of, 152
  grand design of, 150
  relevance to Western Europe of, 152
  sought to break from Churchill's vision, 157
  on spiritual unity, 158, 161
  struggle against poverty and inequality of, 152
  undoing of grand design of, 152
  visions about inclusion in Western Union, 156
Biblical realism, 94
bilateralism, 141, 147, 170, 172, 199
bipolarity, 140, 150, 151, 155
Bissell Group, the, 170
Bissell, Richard, 169, 203
Bizone, 142, 156, 164, 183, 185
blueprints, 7, 16, 43
  abandoning Anglo-Saxon versions of, 115
  for an Atlantic community, 199
  battles over competing versions of, 19
  in Cold War politics, 28
  as a conceptual key, 18
  discussions about Europe's future created, 26
  for Europe's future, 37
  false elegance of, 15
  for foundation of West Germany, 181
  hides the drama of European history, 17
  impacts of regionalisation on, 171
  imperfections of, 19
  inspired the engineers of European integration, 205
  for international cooperation, 101
  made obsolete by failure of the ITO, 138
  of multilateralism, 53
  Niebuhr on, 42
  OEEC as generator of, 168
  of early post-war Western Europe, 40
  as an omen of hope, 9, 27
  of ordoliberalism, 51, 74
  people of inter-war Europe not interested in, 5
  of phases of integration, 205
Blum, Léon, 65
Boegner, Marc, 63, 84
Bohlen, Charles, 143, 144, 176, 180
Böhm, Franz, 95, 103
Bonhoeffer Kreis, 95, 96, 182
Bonhoeffer, Dietrich, 40, 62, 63, 93, 94, 97, 98
Bonn, 180, 192, 203
Bordeaux, 80
Brazil, 92
Brent, Charles, 62
Bretton Woods Conference, 125
  British influence on, 73
  culminated a new hope among Western nations, 124
  defined order of exchange rate stabilisation, 119
  establishment of the World Bank at, 135
  ideas developed in, 44
  Morgenthau's address at, 122
  no agreement on trade at, 170
  vicissitudes of multilateralism and, 126–8
  White masterminded, 120
Bretton Woods system, 139
  Benelux proposal supported the liberal promises of, 147
  the EPU and, 199, 203
  facilitated failure of the 'One World' approach, 167
  failed to create currency convertibility, 199
  fake multilateralism of, 173
  flaws in, 137
  GATT in comparison with, 199
  the Marshall Plan and, 141
  the paradoxes of capitalism and, 204
  vicissitudes of multilateralism and, 126–8
  the WCC and, 208
Briand, Aristide, 23
Britain, 78, 80, 139, 159, 175, *See also* England, United Kingdom
British Commonwealth, the, 36, 133, 157
British foreign policy, 140, 154, 175
British Labour Party, 72
(Hancock and Gowing), 79
Bruce, David, 78
Brunner, Emile, 63
Brussels Pact. *See* Treaty of Brussels
Budapest, 215
Bullit, William, 78
Bullock, Allan, 140

Index

bureaucracy, 106, 192, 194
Bureaucracy (von Mises), 104
business cycles, 121, 125
Byrnes, James, 151, 163

Camps, Miriam, 176, 177
Canada, 175
capital controls, 122, 123, 126, 127, 128
capital movements, 120, 122, 127
capitalism, 41, 125, 214
   after the Bretton Woods Conference, 125
   American democracy synonymous with, 164
   American focus on, 163
   as a beacon of freedom, 14
   Bevin's ideas between communism and, 153
   Bretton Woods system a new phase of, 126
   British opposition to, 139
   the Catholic church and, 22
   choice between socialism and, 110
   economic planning for, 29
   Einaudi's views on, 86
   establishment of NATO and, 27
   ethos of, 108
   Europeanisation and, 205
   federation and, 118
   focus on the paradoxes of, 204
   Freiburg Circles on, 96
   had to promote universal ideals, 53
   Hoffman on, 169
   multilateralism and, 113, 114
   neoliberal concerns about survival of, 117
   non-ideological experiments with, 114
   ordoliberal views of, 75
   in post-war Europe, 26
   pursuit of a resilient form of, 204
   readjustment of Western Europe leads away from, 110
   reconciliation of ideals and needs with, 158
   Schumpeter on, 102, 105, 106, 108
   socialism as a counter to, 102
   sound money as aim of, 148
   triggered obsession with planning, 60
   United Kingdom's counterweight to, 152
   in the Walter Lippmann Colloquium, 61, 66
   Western European experimentation with, 83
   Western experimentation with, 112
   'Western Union' and, 206
Capitalism, Socialism and Democracy (Schumpeter), 102, 105, 111

Cassin, René, 39, 54, 56
Catholic Church, the, 82, 115, 145, 206
Catholic internationalists, 91
Catholic social thought, 181
Central Europe, 166
Centre International d'Études pour la Rénovation du Libéralisme, 66
Chamberlain, Neville, 79
Chamedes, Giuliana, 38, 91
charity, 22, 164, 207
China, 166
Choice for Europe, The (Moravcsik), 31
Christendom, 28
Christian Democracy
   became a vital political force, 37
   Catholic Church boosted the rise of, 145
   Catholic social teaching was key for, 90
   growth of, 44
   influence in Western Europe of, 45
   invention of, 88–93
   liberalism and, 84
   ordoliberalism and, 71
   planning fit well with, 117
   regionalism set the stage for, 208
   rise of, 28
   Schuman and Adenauer united over, 190
'Christian Democracy's Ideas for Reconstruction' (de Gasperi), 92
Christian Democratic Union, 92
Christianity
   defeatism and, 105
   Dulles on the role of, 206
   is irreconcilable with Nazism, 84
   Müller-Armack became a proselytizer of, 89
   need for spiritual community and, 158
   post-war ideological status of, 115
   Schuman and Adenauer united over, 190
   Söderblom on, 62
   state power and, 41
   trans-Atlantic community rooted in, 14
   uniting potential of, 21, 206
   use for diplomatic purposes of, 160
Christianity and Crisis, 94
Churchill, Winston, 36, 80
   on Anglo-French cooperation, 80
   the Atlantic Charter and, 58, 59
   Attlee and, 107
   calls for a 'United States of Europe', 156
   failed secret agreement between Pétain and, 81
   Iron Curtain speech of, 208
   proposed a European federation, 164
   relationship with de Gaulle of, 81
   relationship with Reynaud, 80

Churchill, Winston (cont.)
  on UK exclusion from a united Europe, 157
  was oblivious to post-war bipolarity, 151
Clappier, Bernard, 189
class conflict, 74
Clay, Lucius, 151
Clayton, William, 133–5, 144, 146, 149
coal, 128, 160, 188, 189, 193
coalitions, 16, 18, 37, 158
coined freedom, 148
Cold War, the, 38, 44
  Adenauer aligned his foreign policy to, 193
  American attitude in, 28
  Berlin as Western conscience during, 211
  bipolar logic of, 155
  British diplomacy and, 139
  Catholic involvement in, 22, 145
  chances for international cooperation during, 101
  Christian Democracy and, 208
  Christian unity during the build-up of, 207
  Christianity through the lens of, 140
  churches faced with the realities of, 115
  coining of term, 164
  defined post-war politics and geopolitics, 53
  as a determinant of Europe's destiny, 129
  devaluation of UK currency and, 175
  discredited aspirations for Christian unity, 162
  either-or American politics during, 28
  end of, 4
  as the 'great crusade', 206
  growth of Western Europe during, 30
  ideas and policies generated because of, 2
  impact on WCC of, 160, 165
  importance of Christian unity for, 206
  Kennan shaped the narrative of, 210
  led to institutionalisation of a Western bloc, 166
  made a united Western Europe indispensable, 185
  need for West German rearmament during, 191
  as a new post-war era, 165
  'One World' approach foundered during, 166, 207
  planning culminated in triumph in, 4
  policymaking experiments during, 111
  practical thinking during, 213
  Realpolitik of, 146, 163
  religion an integral part of American effort during, 144
  religious revival during, 115
  reunification of Germany and the end of, 36
  role of the WCC in, 165
  significance of the Marshall Plan for, 27
  solidified experimental approach to politics, 83
  split of Germany as a result of, 174
  strengthened Anglo-American partnership, 112
  the Truman Doctrine and, 129
  Truman Doctrine as a defining feature of, 144
  United Kingdom's indecision about, 151
  US charity and, 207
  was higher order problem than Western Europe, 28
  weakening of WCC during, 208
  West German re-entry during, 45
  Western European cooperation during, 52
  Western intellectuals during, 214
collective memory, 17, 194
collective responsibility, 100
collectivism, 83, 84, 111
Colville, John, 80
Comert, Pierre, 78
Comité Français de Libération Nationale (CFNL), 81
Commissariat Général du Plan de Modernisation, 81, 188
Commissariat Général de Plan de Modernisation, 42
Commission of the Churches on International Affairs (CCIA), 166, 226
Commission to Study the Bases of a Just and Durable Peace (CJDP), 63, 92, 93, 162
Committee of European Economic Cooperation (CEEC), 141, 142, 147, 149, 167
commodity prices, 120
communism, 36, 56, 69
  American crusade against, 144
  Bevin's ideas between capitalism and, 153
  Christian Democracy as a bulwark against, 93, 208
  Kennan and Berlin on, 211
  leftist opposition to, 91
  as an offspring of liberalism, 84
  religious opposition to, 144
  Rougier's opposition to, 65

Index

as a threat to Western Europe, 150
the Truman Doctrine and, 129
US sought to ward off dangers of, 213
in Western Europe, 148
competition, 172
  the Austrian school on, 50
  British pleas for, 138
  Freiburg School's views on, 103
  in the FRG, 174
  human dignity of the worker and, 70
  ordoliberal framework-treaties protected, 192
  ordoliberal views of, 74, 103
  in *Quadragesimo Anno*, 71
  required dedicated institutions, 68
  socialism as a counter to, 102
Confédération Génerale du Travail (CGT), 66
Confessing Church, 40, 62, 94, 96, 98, 99
Congress of Europe, 21, 159
conservatism, 76, 84, 94, 117
containment, 106, 163, 165, 166, 210
continentalisation, 205
corporatism, 5, 71
Costagliola, Frank, 210
creative destruction, 105
Croce, Benedetto, 16, 86
cultural diplomacy, 158
cultural pessimism, 60
currency convertibility, 127, 138, 146, 170, 173, 175–9, 199, 205
customs union, 80, 137, 142, 147, 156, 175, 176, 191

Daladier, Édouard, 78, 79
Davies, Norman, 4
de Gasperi, Alcide, 87, 92, 194
de Gaulle, Charles, 42, 55, 80, 81
de Graaf, Beatrice, ix, 9
de Madariaga, Salvador, 159
de Rougemont, Denis, 159
Declaration of the International Rights of Man, 56
Decline of the West, The (Spengler), 60
decolonization, 35
defeatism, 105
deflation, 74, 120, 124, 148, 192
democracy, 41, 81, 125, 214
  after the Bretton Woods Conference, 125
  American focus on, 163
  as a beacon of freedom, 14
  Bevin on, 161
  Bonhoeffer Kreis called for, 96
  the Catholic church and, 22
  challenge of totalitarianism to, 65
  Christian Democracy on, 92
  Christian unity and, 207
  Einaudi's views on, 86
  embedded liberalism and, 183
  establishment of NATO and, 27
  Europeanisation and, 205
  Freiburg Circles on, 96
  functionalism and, 57
  German reconstruction attempts incompatible with, 164
  as a goal of World Wars, 116
  had to promote universal ideals, 53
  Maritain's shift towards, 84
  as a means, 105
  multilateralism and, 113
  neoliberals devalued, 60
  Niebuhr on, 94
  non-ideological experiments with, 114
  ordoliberal views of, 75
  planning for success of, 29
  political victories of, 4
  in post-war Europe, 26
  in post-war Western Europe, 110
  pursuit of a resilient form of, 204
  role of Christendom in, 28
  search for new myths of, 82
  sound money as aim of, 148
  Spanish Civil War and, 65
  the Treaty of Versailles and, 23
  as a value of Western Christianity, 190
  in the Walter Lippmann Colloquium, 61
  Western European experimentation with, 83
  Western experimentation with, 112
  'Western Union' and, 155, 206
Democratic Nouvelles Équipes Internationales (NEI), 159
democratic socialism, 117
Denmark, 58, 136
Deutsche Mark, 203
Dewey, Thomas E., 160
Dibelius, Otto, 98
dignity, 40, 92
Diktatfrieden, 96, 100
dirigisme, 101, 192
drawing rights, 170, 171, 172
Dulles, John Foster, 63, 93, 116
  chaired CJDP meeting in Cambridge, 162
  drove discourse on European unity, 160
  promoted a Christian agenda, 206
  relationship with Monnet of, 78
  supported the Truman Doctrine, 165
Düsseldorfer Leitsätze, 181
Dutch foreign policy, 185

Dutch foreign policy, 185
Dyson, Kenneth, 35, 182

Eastern Europe, 163, 166
Eco, Umberto, 9
École Libre des Hautes Études, 91
economic cooperation, 43, 58, 129, 137, 177, 178, 200
   Dutch focus on, 185
   as focus of Monnet and Clayton, 149
   Monnet planned European integration through, 188
Economic Cooperation Administration (ECA), 169, 170, 172, 177, 180, 202, 203
economic freedom, 74
economic growth, 21, 30, 75, 83, 144, 170, 193
economic humanism, 89, 104
economic imperialism, 71
economic integration, 177, 200
economic liberalism, 22, 207
economic nationalism, 2, 71, 177
economic policy, 29, 51, 88, 95, 113, 152, 164, 182, 183
economic reconstruction, 20, 164
economic stability, 120, 122
economic theory, 60, 170, 182
Economic Working Committee for Bavaria, 182
Economist, The, 86, 183
Edinburgh, 62
Einaudi, Luigi, 69, 85–8, 97, 104, 116, 137
Eisenhower, Dwight D., 81
Eliot, T. S., 158
Ellwood, David W., 35
embedded liberalism, 183
Emergency Economic Committee for Europe (EECE), 130
emotions, 9, 32, 44
   Bevin tapped a reservoir of, 153
   blueprints reflected, 9
   creation of trust and, 19
   drove American post-war leadership, 212
   ecumenical movement influenced, 207
   historical influence of, 15–16
   ideas, plans, and narratives are charged with, 18
   ideology based on, 212
   inherent in collective memory, 17
   narratives and, 19
   persuasion and, 19
   planning driven by, 101, 107
   role of in this book, 10
   study of historical phenomena through, 37
   unpredictability of, 17
   Western Europe a history of, 13
end of history, 4
England, 77, *See also* United Kingdom, Britain
   balance-of-payments deficit of, 133
   Dutch imports from, 186
   FRG took over economic role of, 184
   post-war economic situation of, 109
   Schumpeter on, 108, 109
Enlightenment, the, 3, 14, 35, 59
enterprise, 74, 164, 169, 192
entrepreneurship, 74
Enzensberger, Hans Magnus, 4
equality, 104, 138, 155
Erhard, Ludwig, 39, 52, 88, 89, 137, 148, 174, 181–3
escapism, 50, 105, 108, 110, 125
Eucken, Walter, 40, 51, 95, 97, 103
Eurafrique, 35
Euratom, 66
Europa (Klee), 24
Europe, 114, *See also* Western Europe
   after Soviet rejection of Marshall Aid, 161
   ambiguity and darkness fundamental to, 213
   American leadership and, 14
   American reconception of policy towards, 144
   Benelux plans for the reconstruction of, 146
   British relations with, 139
   Clayton's visit to, 133
   coal shortage in, 128
   Cold War as a determinant of, 129
   consensus for market integration in, 149
   economic reconstruction of, 20
   establishment of the ECSC in, 194
   failed attempts at federation of, 117
   food shortages in, 128
   the Great Depression and, 25
   importance of Germany for the future of, 184
   Kundera on, 215
   the Marshall Plan and, 129
   Marshall's task for the reconstruction of, 146
   need for United States aid of, 134
   Niebuhr on freedom in, 164
   the policy approach in, 110
   the post-European world and, 26
   present times of, 215
   radically different times signalled in, 214
   Soviet threat to stability in, 163
   United Kingdom's strategy in, 151

Index

uniting potential of Christianity in, 206
was able to circumvent the UN, 168
Western Union and, 155
willingness to die for, 215
the World Bank and, 135
Europe of European integration, the, 13, 15, 18, 31, 38, 52, 60, 67, 89, 215
European Believers (Van den Berg), 61, 166
European Central Inland Transport Organization (ECITO), 130
European Coal and Steel Community (ECSC), 38
  change towards regionalism and, 167
  EPU induced the establishment of, 205
  founding of, 189
  matched key interests of its members, 193–4
  as precursor of today's EU, 18
  regionalism set the stage for, 208
  shift from EPU to, 167
  West German re-entry and, 45
European Coal Committee (ECO), 130
European Convention on Human Rights and Fundamental Freedoms (ECHR), 58
European Customs Union Study Group, 176
European Economic Community (ECC), 35
European Economic Community (EEC), 36, 66, 228
'European experiment', the, 178
European integration
  'continentalisation' of, 205
  blueprints inspired the engineering of, 205
  control of process of, 17
  early stages of, 19
  EPU elevated discussions of, 203
  EPU induced a durable form of, 205
  GATT could not be the framework for, 199
  German confession furthered, 101
  historiography of, 31–8
  Hoffman's speech on, 178
  importance of for West Germany, 201
  incompleteness of economic and rational accounts of, 30
  institutional dynamics of, 32
  intellectuals not the architects of, 214
  lack of national control over, 33
  Monnet's mission for, 188
  never the result of a preconceived plan, 33
  as a political double-edged sword, 160
  is a political phenomenon, 14

scholarly debates on, 31
subsidiarity and, 84
surprising role of the FRG in, 201
trade liberalisation and, 161
United Kingdom could not be the driver of, 175
European Payments Union (EPU), 199–201, 202
  Anglo-American partnership was the main casualty of, 202
  ECA laid the groundwork for, 170
  elevated discussions about European integration, 203
  Europeanisation took the institutional form of, 205
  evolved into a bilateral affair, 203
  exerted its power as a bank, 203
  facilitated intra-European trade, 141
  factors for success of, 202
  founding of, 171
  position for the pound sterling in, 139
  Röpke's opposition to, 173
  served multilateral ambitions of the Western world, 203
  shift from OEEC to, 167
  shift to ECSC from, 167
  supplanted Finebel, 178
  unfit for role as monetary union, 203
  West German re-entry and, 45
European Recovery Plan (ERP), 168
  became a Western European affair, 136
  the Harriman Committee advised on, 148
  the 'how' of left to Europeans, 129
  the Paris Peace Conference and, 146
  policy issues arose during progress of, 27
  replaced the ECE, 135
  Röpke opposed the establishment of, 148
  United Kingdom led efforts to set up, 140
  United States embraced establishment of, 179
European Republic of Planning, 3, 5, 204, 209
European Rescue of the Nation-State, The (Milward), 31
European Union, 204
Europeanisation, 115, 140, 172, 179, 202–5, 207
Evangelische Kirche in Deutschland (EKD), 99, 145
exchange controls, 122, 126
exchange rates, 118, 119, 120, 126, 127, 128, 138
experiment, 82
export surpluses, 146

exports, 146, 172, 179, 183, 186
expressionism, 24

Fabianism, 72
'fake multilateralism', 173, 201
fascism, 39, 54, 64, 89
Federal Council of Churches of Christ in America, 63, 160
Federal Republic of Germany (FRG) as an answer to the German question, 53
Federal Republic of Germany (FRG)
  after segregation, 100
  Austrian School of economics and, 76
  break with the past of, 100
  durable European cooperation depended on, 178
  emerging centrality of, 205
  Eurafrique and, 36
  Europeanisation and, 179
  faced 'how' question about integration, 202
  Franco-German reconciliation was vital to, 174
  had no say in its own foreign affairs, 202
  influence of ordoliberalism in, 45, 174, 192
  as the motor of economic recovery and growth, 205
  multilateralisation and, 173, 201
  ordoliberal policy engineers and the creation of, 53
  reentry into Western European economy of, 200
  set boundaries of planners' supranational ambitions, 174
  supported free markets, 174
  surprising economic power of, 201
  took over England's economic role, 184
Federal Union, 72, 73, 78, 159
Federal Union Research Institute (FURI), 73
federalism, 73
federation, 116, 118
Fichte, Johann Gottlieb, 104
'Fight for Germany, The' (Niebuhr), 163
First World War, 2, 4, 9, 35, 43, 44
  American intervention in, 13
  Cassin's service in, 56
  disarray of Europe after, 49
  Einaudi's views on, 87
  false hope aroused during, 8
  hope aroused during, 214
  human rights failures after, 54
  Pope Benedict XV's action during, 91
  United States entry into, 116
  Western civilisation came under threat after, 60
fiscal policy, 134
Fitzgerald, F. Scott, 24
Foggy Bottom, 210
food shortages, 128
foreign affairs, 136, 139, 150, 162, 202
foreign policy
  of Adenauer, 193
  Bevin's goals for, 151
  effect of Marshall's speech on, 140
  impact of Marshall's speech on, 140
  lack of West German control over, 202
  of post-war America, 27
  Polanyi on demands of, 118
Foreign Secretary Halifax (E. F. L. Wood), 79
Four Freedoms, 57, 58, 59, 90
Fourteen Points, the, 23
fragmentation, 50
France, 66
  Acheson on, 187
  adherence to UDHR of, 55
  after the Munich Agreement, 78
  balance-of-payments deficit of, 133
  calls for a 'United States of Europe' and, 156
  collaboration with British of, 80
  colonial legacy of, 35
  consequences of defeat of, 82
  de Gaulle as prime minister of, 42
  declaration of war against Nazi Germany, 78
  division into Vichy and Free French, 81
  durable European cooperation depended on, 178
  during the Phoney War, 79
  economic relations with Germany, 190
  emergence of mixed economy in, 83
  fall of during Second World War, 17, 55
  ideas about European reconstruction of, 20
  impact of the Schuman Plan on, 191
  impact of UK currency devaluation on, 175
  impossibility of war with Germany, 193
  in interwar years, 39
  leadership of in early post-war period, 43
  membership in OEEC of, 136
  Monnet's proposal for West Germany and, 188
  partnership with United Kingdom of, 157
  planned federation with England of, 77
  plans for customs union of, 147
  plans for regionalised free trade of, 173

Index

post-war ideals originating in, 56
post-war inflation in, 134
power in the EPU of, 203
reaction to proposal for an Anglo-French union, 80
Rougier's activist role in, 65
signing of the Treaty of Brussels, 153
signing of Treaty of Dunkirk, 153
signing of UDHR of, 54
Spanish Civil War and, 65
suspected sincerity of US efforts on integration, 176
task of prioritising human rights left to, 54
unified coal and steel industries with Germany, 188
United Kingdom allied with, 156
United Kingdom's trade relations with, 151
at Versailles, 22
as a Western occupation force in Germany, 180
Franco, General Francisco, 65
Franco-German reconciliation, 13, 174, 201, 203
Frankfurter Dokumente, 181
free elections, 83, 181
free markets, 60, 71, 74, 76, 114, 174, 192
free trade, 123
  balance-of-payments issues furthered, 173
  of Bretton Woods system, 137
  Clayton on, 149
  contrast with planning of, 72
  differences of opinion on, 73
  embedded liberalism and, 183
  exchange rates and, 138
  factors contributing to focus on, 44
  freedom from exchange controls a condition for, 122
  impact of UK currency devaluation on, 175
  Keynes on balance-of-payments crisis and, 124
  need for customs union to ensure, 142
  not abandoned in post-war reconstruction, 123
  planners' promotion of, 30
  Wootton opposed Hayek on, 72
'free world', the, 112, 115, 177
freedom, 1, 14, 41, 86
  in the Atlantic Charter, 58
  the Austrian School seen as defenders of, 50
  Bevin on, 161
  Bonhoeffer Kreis called for, 96
  competition and, 103
  contrast with totalitarianism of, 72
  Croce on, 86
  economic concern with, 108
  economic integration and, 177
  Einaudi's views on, 87
  from want, 117
  German conceptions of, 104
  goals of security and, 157
  ideals as, 88
  interventionists on, 64
  Maritain on, 84
  as a myth of the welfare state, 83
  neoliberal views of, 68
  Niebuhr on, 94, 164
  political victories of, 4
  post-war ideals of, 55
  regulated markets and, 118
  sound money as aim of, 148
  state power and, 41
  as a value of Western Christianity, 190
  'Western Union' and, 206
  Western Union and, 155
Freiburg Circles, 93, 95
Freiburg School of Law and Economics, 97, 103, 182
Freiburger Konzil, 95
French Federation of Disabled War Veterans, 56
French Fourth Republic, the, 81
French Planning Commission, 142
French Revolution, 20, 59
French Revolution, the, 104, 112
French Third Republic, the, 82
French zone, the, 142
full employment
  Beveridge Report recommended, 72, 107
  exchange rates and the pursuit of, 120
  IMF aimed at, 173
  multilateralism prioritised the goal of, 114
  objective of an historical task, 121
  primacy of goal of, 109
  as priority of post-war economics, 117
  reconciliation with associated costs of, 124
  Röpke opposed, 201
  socioeconomic stability meant, 120
  worries of deflation and, 124
functionalism, 6, 31, 32, 41, 42, 50, 57, 107, 110, 116
futures, 1

Gasperi, Alcide de, 137
General Agreement on Tariffs and Trade (GATT), 137, 199, 204

GEORG (*Gemeinschaftsorganisation Ruhrkohle*), 194
German Guilt, The (Jaspers), 100
Germany, 7, 22, 51, 142, 169, 201, *See also* Federal Republic of Germany (FRG), West Germany, Nazi Germany
   Adenauer's 'great hope' for, 191
   after the fall of fascism, 54
   balance-of-payments deficit of, 133
   Barth on the errors of, 98
   Bevin's goals for, 151
   break with the past of, 100
   British occupation of, 138
   in Byrnes's Stuttgart speech, 151
   calls for a 'United States of Europe' and, 156
   Catholicism in, 91
   at the centre of Niebuhr's approach, 165
   during the London Six-Power Conference, 180
   during the Phoney War, 79
   economic and political problems of, 133
   economic reconstruction of Europe and, 20
   economic relations with France, 190
   ecumenical roots of reconciliation with, 207
   emotional charge of treatment towards, 44
   excluded from British-led Western Union, 156
   food shortages in, 148
   George Bell on the bombing of, 63
   guaranteeing a just peace for, 96
   historical views of freedom in, 104
   impact of the Germany Memorandum on, 185
   impact of the Schuman Plan on, 191
   importance for Western European stability of, 158
   importance to Dutch economy of, 186
   impossibility of war with France, 193
   integration as solution to economic and political problems of, 160
   the Morgenthau Plan and, 153
   as the most glaring problem in post-war Europe, 143
   Niebuhr's visit to, 163
   ordoliberal orientation of, 174
   ordoliberalism and, 90
   political imagination and, 1
   the Potsdam Conference and, 142
   reunification of, 4
   segregation of, 100
   signing the Anti-Comintern Pact, 65
   Treaty of Brussels and, 154
   unified coal and steel industries with France, 188
   United States military government in, 182
   US military government in, 164
   WCC aided reconciliation with, 166
'Germany memorandum'. *See* 'Memorandum on the allied and Dutch policies on West Germany'
Ghervas, Stella, 35, 159
Giraud, Henri, 81
Girton College, 162
Gleichschaltung (Nazification), 61
globalism, 143
God, 55, 69, 84, 87, 96, 97, 116, 160
gold standard, the, 118, 120, 121, 122
Good Society, The (Lippmann), 65, 69
government lending, 74
Great Depression, the, 25, 26
   caused the rise of Nazi Germany, 102
   currency devaluations amplified effects of, 120
   deflation amplified effects of, 120
   emphasised urgency of ecumenical action, 63
   fiction of self-regulating markets and, 118
   realising a better world after, 106
   Western civilisation came under threat after, 60
great persuasion, the, 60
Great Transformation, The (Polanyi), 104, 114, 118
Greece, 58, 136, 151
Großmann-Doerth, Hans, 97, 103
Guernica (Picasso), 23, 54
Guillebaud, Charles, 20
guilt, 15, 97, 98, 99, 145

Haberler, Gottfried, 170
Hague Congress of 1948, The, 58
Hallstein, Walter, 159
hard power, 14, 31
Harriman Committee, 147, 169, 170
Harriman, Averell, 169, 171, 203
Havana Charter, the, 137
Hayek, Friedrich, 66, 71, 73, 78
   against excessive planning, 214
   concerns about capitalism of, 117
   educated Bissell, 170
   as a member of the Austrian school, 50
   on social justice, 117
   on the United Kingdom, 109
hegemony, 59, 128
Hemingway, Ernest, 24

Index

Henriod, Henry-Louis, 63
Hertenstein, 159
historiography, 9, 18, 28, 30, 31–8
Hitler, Adolf, 7, 25, 44, 54, 64, 80, 81, 100
Hoffman, Paul, 169, 177, 203
hope, 8, 16, 19, 21, 23, 107, 206, 214
House of Commons of the United Kingdom, 154
Hromàdka, Josef, 166
Huber, Max, 63
human dignity, 70, 94
human nature, 211, 213
human rights, 4, 36, 57, See also rights
   at the core of France's political culture, 59
   Catholic Church aligned with, 145
   the Catholic church and, 22
   the Catholic church promoted, 206
   Catholic promotion of
   as a Christian concept, 41, 190
   Christian Democracy on, 92
   Christian unity and, 207
   development of structures of, 39
   in early post-war Europe, 43
   goals of security and, 157
   importance of safeguarding, 20
   Maritain's shift towards, 84
   mixed economy approach furthered, 83
   planning emphasised, 107
   post-war re-emphasis of, 54
   as a spiritual project, 55
   Western European promotion of, 58
Hungarian Press Bureau, 215
Hungary, 136, 166, 215
hunger, 41, 134, 164, 185
Husserl, Edmund, 103

Iberian Peninsula, 205
Iceland, 136
idealism, 214
ideas, 7, 9
   against socialism, 103
   of 'Atlantic civilization', 28
   battles of, 19
   became feasible and coherent policies, 3
   of Isaiah Berlin, 213
   of Bevin, 153, 161
   Bevin tapped a reservoir of, 153
   blueprints reflected, 9
   of Bretton Woods, 44
   are charged with emotions, 18
   in Cold War politics, 28
   confrontation between needs and, 107
   counterbalanced American planning, 192
   of the ECA, 170
   of economic cooperation, 137
   Einaudi's defence of, 88
   embedded nature of, 33
   of Erhard, 181
   of Europe's future, 37
   for European federation, 116
   of European integration, 215
   historical influence of, 15–16
   and the 'how' question of integration, 202
   injected into the 'European experiment', 178
   intellectual history a history of, 17
   of Keynes, 124, 126
   may produce emotions, 19
   for monetary regionalism, 141
   MPS as an incubator for, 201
   narratives and, 19
   OEEC and, 168
   ordoliberals needed to be practical with, 174
   in phases of integration, 205
   planners aimed to transform, 2
   planners' use of, 30
   planning and, 114
   political imagination and, 1, 2
   of Röpke, 174
   of Schumpeter, 105
   on trade blocs, 176
   Western Europe a history of, 13
   of White, 126
ideational reconciliation, 43
ideology
   adapted to practical policies, 116
   based on emotions, 212
   Christian responses to, 84
   churches' resistance to, 64
   democracy required a shift away from, 82
   European intoxication with, 37
   expectation that planning could regulate, 107
   multilateralisation was a substitute for, 113
   planners presented themselves as unsullied by, 29
   rationalism and, 3
   shift to policy from, 106
   social market economy as, 89
   WCC turned its attention to, 208
Ikenberry, John, 124
import surpluses, 146
imports, 109, 133, 146, 170, 179, 180, 186
inclusiveness, 215
India, 63, 166
individual freedom, 60
inflation, 108, 134, 141, 147

Institut Universitaire de Hautes Études Internationales (IUHEI), 104
Integral Humanism (Maritain), 84
integration
  benefits of in post-war Western Europe, 113
  as a counterforce to 'disintegrating' tendencies, 111
  ECSC as the start of, 194
  non-ideological approach of, 114
  as opposed to unification, 177
  sovereignty and, 141, 147
intellectual history, 17, 34
inter-elite persuasion, 19
intergovernmentalism, 31, 32, 161
international affairs, 13, 41, 155, 156
International Bank for Reconstruction and Development (IBRD), 146
International Clearing Union, 73
International Committee of the Movements for European Unity, 159
International Committee of the Red Cross, 63
international cooperation, 7
  Anglo-American partnership and, 112
  as an answer to the business cycle, 121
  as a Western post-war ideal, 36
  benefits of for Western Europe, 113
  Cassin's approach to, 57
  Catholic promotion of, 92
  characteristics of Western efforts for, 113
  Christian Democracy on, 92
  conversion of American ideas into practices of, 2
  Dulles's influence on politics of, 64
  during the Cold War, 44
  economic and monetary governance at the core of, 119
  in economic life, 70
  economic reconstruction and, 20
  end of the Cold War furthered, 4
  Europeanisation of Western Europe opposed, 140
  factors eroding the basis of, 2
  as a functionalist ideal, 110
  human rights and, 60
  ideas behind successful and durable policies of, 2
  irenic exercise of the churches furthered, 101
  Keynesianism between sovereignty and, 124
  mixed economy approach furthered, 83
  monetary policy and, 124
  Monnet's record of bringing about, 78
  move towards functionalism in, 57
  One World approach towards, 53
  planners' endorsement of, 30
  planning for social policies required, 41
  rationalism was at the heart of, 107
  reconciliation of ideals and needs in, 158
  reincorporation of West Germany furthered, 145
  remained a strictly Western affair, 28
  the Second World War catalysed, 112
  Temple an advocate of, 93
  use of American ideas in, 30
  Viner on, 121
  WCC fleshed out possibilities for, 166
international diplomacy, 187
international economy, 16, 72, 120, 126
International Exposition of Art and Technology in Modern Life, 54
international imperialism, 71
international investment, 120
International Missionary Council (IMC), 62, 63
international monetary and trade cooperation, 203, 205
International Monetary Fund (IMF), 137, 173, 199
international politics, 14, 19, 20, 23, 145, 151, 162, 166, 207
international relations, 9, 16, 113
  American focus in ecumenical movement on, 162
  the Benelux an example of, 157
  impact of free markets on, 71
  policy approach to, 50
  supranational approaches to, 64
  Western Union and, 155
International Studies Conference (ISC), 67
international trade, 2, 20, 118, 121, 127, 134, 137, 170, 202
International Trade Organisation (ITO), 135, 137, 138, 199, 204, 205
internationalism, 56, 71, 91
inter-war period, 25, 35, 107, 113
Intra-European Payments Scheme (IEPS), 171
intra-European trade, 138, 141, 170, 172, 173, 200
Ireland, 58, 136
Irenicism, 28, 89
Iron Curtain, 208
Iron Curtain, the, 185
isolationism, 143
Italian Christian Democratic Party, 91
Italy, 92
  Acheson on, 187

Index

Allied campaign to liberate, 8
balance-of-payments deficit of, 133
Catholicism in, 91
Christian Democratic response
  to Second World War in, 100
durable European cooperation depended
  on, 178
economic and political problems of, 133
ECSC stimulated growth in, 193
Einaudi fleeing from, 104
Einaudi nominated senator of, 86
Einaudi's presidency of, 87
Eurafrique and, 36
France's plans for free trade with, 173
inclusion in Western Union of, 156
membership in OEEC of, 136
post-war inflation in, 134
post-war liberal thinking in, 86
relations with United Kingdom of, 151
UK currency devaluation and, 175
at Versailles, 22

Japan, 65
Jaspers, Karl, 100, 159
justice, 57, 94, 164, 177

Kaiser, Wolfram, 18, 32
Kennan, George, 144, 165, 210
Keynes, John Maynard, 72
  on the balance-of-payments crisis, 124
  inspired the Bretton Woods system, 126
  opposed Hayek, 214
  overshadowed Schumpeter, 105
  policy paradoxes faced by, 119
  provided intellectual framework for
    Bretton Woods system, 126
  task of full employment and, 121
Keynesianism, 51, 60, 69, 75, 121, 125, 201
Kimber, Charles, 73
Kirchenkampf, 62
Klee, Paul, 24
Kohnstamm, Max, 184
Konzerne, 193
Kosseleck, Reinhart, 18
Kristallnacht, 95
Kundera, Milan, 215

La Riforma Sociale (LRF), 85
laissez faire economics, 67, 71
laissez faire liberalism, 75
League of Nations, 23, 26, 39, 56, 78, 92, 112, 150
Leffler, Melvyn, 49
Lend Lease Act, 123
Leningrad, 215

Leucht, Brigitte, 32
Lewis, Sinclair, 24
liberal interventionism, 76
liberalisation, 147, 170, 183
liberalism, 7, 28, 86
  Bissell was a promoter of, 170
  Catholic calls for strengthening of, 145
  clash between socialism and
    Keynesianism and, 51
  contraposition between socialism
    and, 71
  as the core of Western civilisation, 74
  in early post-war Europe, 43
  economic humanism and, 89, 104
  free markets and, 114
  German confession furthered, 101
  influence on Wootton of, 72
  key role played in uniting Western
    Europe, 52
  Lippmann on, 77
  Maritain's opposition to, 84
  Meade on, 138
  multilateralism and, 114
  of Niebuhr, 94
  ordoliberal views of, 75
  post-war confusion in, 163
  post-war reinvention of, 60
  rationality and, 213
  reconciliation between socialism
    and, 114
  schism within, 67
  Schumpeter on, 105
  search for new myths of, 82
  socialism and, 67
  struggle against planning of, 68
  UDHR and, 43
  in the Walter Lippmann Colloquium,
    66, 68
  watered down in social experiments, 83
liberty, 72, 74, 75, 92, 94, 118, 155, 161, 190, 206
Lieftinck, Pieter, 184
Life and Work movement, 62, 63, 94
Life magazine, 163
Lippmann, Walter, 23, 25, 65, 77, 83
London, 82
London Six-Power Conference, 180
'long telegram', the, 210
love, 155, 161, 206
Luce, Henry, 57
Lutheranism, 98
Luxembourg, 36, 136, 153, 156, 173, 178

MacMillan, Margaret, 22
Mannheim, Karl, 72

Schumpeter, Joseph 'The March into Socialism' and, 102
'March into Socialism, The' (Schumpeter), 102
Maritain, Jacques, 40, 55, 84, 91, 115, 206
Marjolin, Robert, 67, 142, 147, 172
market competition, 74
market economy, 52, 57, 70, 75, 76, 86, 89, 118
market integration, 128, 149, 167, 205, 208
market liberalism, 201
'Market or Planned Economy?', 181
Marshall Plan, 192
  the Atlantic Charter and, 107
  Clayton not focused on, 149
  in comparison to World Bank Loans, 135
  David Bruce and the administration of, 79
  EPU enhanced the liberalisation policy of, 203
  establishment of EPU and, 141
  establishment of the ECA and, 169
  European cooperation began after, 53
  first European talks on, 136
  goals of, 143
  illuminated a pathway for integration, 44
  Keynesian endorsement of, 124
  launch of, 17
  London Six-Power Conference and, 180
  as a milestone in regional approaches, 156
  mission of rebuilding Europe culminated in, 25
  Monnet not focused on, 149
  plan to allocate dollars of, 129
  policy issues arose during implementation of, 27
  reinvigoration of European trade and, 146
  Röpke on, 148
  Röpke opposed, 192
  shift in US foreign policy after, 144
  social market economy developed in the wake of, 52
  Soviet Union did not participate in, 136
  Soviet Union not invited to discuss, 136
  trade liberalisation a quid pro quo for, 161
  triggered Europeanisation, 172
  triggered shift away from UN power, 167
  United Kingdom's use of aid from, 109
  Western Union and, 155
Marshall, George, 129, 135, 140, 146
Marxism, 60, 95
mass unemployment, 121

Maurois, André, 66
Meade, James, 138, 152
'Memorandum on the allied and Dutch policies on West Germany', 184, 185
Milward, Alan, 3, 30, 31
Mitrany, David, 50, 107, 116, 188
mixed economy, 43, 76, 83, 96, 111, 114
moderation, 50, 110
Mollet, Guy, 66
Molotov, Vyacheslav, 136
monetary management, 121, 124, 205
monetary policy, 3, 17, 30, 119, 124
monetary union, 128, 203
Monnet, Jean
  advocated pooling sovereignty, 141
  after the Munich Agreement, 78–80
  on the aims of the ECSC, 194
  called for pooling coal and steel sectors, 160
  Cassin's strategy agreed with, 57
  Clayton's plan aligned with views of, 137
  drove forward blueprints for integration, 51
  Dulles's thoughts echoed, 64
  leadership of ECSC treaty negotiations, 193
  leadership of in European integration, 191
  on the OEEC, 168
  promoted pooling sovereignty, 147
  Schuman and, 188
  as special envoy of Roosevelt, 81
  translated Wilson's universal ideals into practice, 39
  was not focused on policy implementation, 149
Mont Pèlerin Society (MPS), 51, 68, 74, 88, 103, 137, 148, 192, 201
mood, 7, 17, 20
  of the 1940s, 105
  Christian Democracy was in tune with, 208
  the Congress of Europe marked changes in, 159
  ECSC was in tune with, 194
  in support of Keynesianism, 121
  reactivation of the Catholic church and, 22
  Schumpeter on, 106, 108
  spiritual unity of Europe and, 21
  study of historical phenomena through, 37
  US foreign policy matched, 144
Moravcsik, Andrew, 31, 32
Morgenthau Plan, 153

Index

Morgenthau, Henry, 113, 122
Moscow, 39, 49, 65, 136, 150, 165, 210, 215
Mouvement pour les États-Unis Socialistes d'Europe (MEUSE), 159
Moveable Feast, A (Hemingway), 24
Müller, Ludwig, 61
Müller-Armack, Alfred, 60, 69, 75, 88, 182
multilateralism, 29, 112, 113, 123, 172
  against American hegemony, 128
  against capital controls, 128
  blueprints of, 53
  developed Western European economic force, 173
  Dutch-West German relations and, 184
  as the essence of integration, 111
  failure of the ITO and, 138, 199
  free trade and, 138
  inconsistent with domestic planning, 204
  Keynes set in motion, 124
  made a social version of capitalism possible, 117
  post-war ideals of, 55
  setbacks for planners of, 137
  stripped away the utopia of free markets, 114
  the Truman Doctrine as bastion of, 129
  waning promises of, 199
  West Germany shaped, 201
multilateralization, 172, 173
Munich Agreement, the, 78
Mussolini, Benito, 64, 65, 86
Myrdal, Gunnar, 136

'Nächtliche Stimmen' ('Voices in the Night') (Bonhoeffer), 97
narratives, 16, 18, 19, 59
National Revolution (of Vichy France), 82
nationalism, 25, 39, 41, 112, 194
'Nature of a World Peace, The' (Einaudi), 85
Nazi Germany, 40, 61, 73, 78, 79, 80, 92, 102, 153, 182, *See also* Germany
Nazism, 39, 83
  ecumenical opposition to, 61, 62, 64
  is irreconcilable with Christianity, 84
  leftist opposition to, 91
  as an offspring of liberalism, 84
neoclassical economic theory, 95
neo-functionalism, 32, 34
neoliberalism, 51, 52, 117
  addressing social crisis of decline, 60
  appeal to France of, 77
  contraposition between corporatism and, 71
  development of, 60
  early weaknesses of, 72
  establishing the agenda for, 68
  in France, 81
  Niebuhr on, 95
Netherlands, The, 151
  Acheson on, 187
  diplomacy with United Kingdom of, 139
  durable European cooperation depended on, 178
  ECSC stimulated growth in, 193
  Eurafrique and, 36
  formation of Benelux customs union, 156
  French customs union plan matched the thinking of, 147
  the 'Germany Memorandum' and, 184
  impact of Erhard's economic policy on, 183
  impact of sterling devaluation on, 179
  membership in OEEC of, 136
  planned to counter threat of horizontal trade liberalisation, 170
  plans for regionalised free trade of, 173
  politics of, 183
  rejected proposal to join the sterling zone, 184
  signing of the Treaty of Brussels, 153
  trade agreement with West Germany, 183
  trade relations with England of, 186
  was reluctant to exclude themselves from Anglo-Saxon world, 175
New Deal experience, the, 73
New Deal, the, 5, 21
  as an example of non-ideological policy, 117
  functionalist thoughts about, 50
  as a global paradigm of policy, 49
  as the ideal example of social experiment, 82
  Lippmann on, 83
  Niebuhr's appreciation of, 94
  opponents of, 57
Niebuhr, Reinhold, 40, 94
  Biblical realism of, 94
  on blueprints, 42
  at the Cambridge Conference of Church Leaders, 162–5
  had foreseen a new bipolar world order, 167
  influence on Visser 't Hooft of, 94
  as an interventionist, 64
  involvement with WCC of, 93
  paradox on moral oversimplifications of, 97

Niebuhr, Reinhold (cont.)
  as a post-war Western intellectual, 214
  was a prolific publicist, 94
  sought a middle ground between neoliberalism and Marxism, 95
  summary of thoughts of, 94
  supported US charity, 207
  'Western Union' and, 206
Niemöller, Martin, 62, 98, 99
North Atlantic Treaty Organization (NATO), 27, 154, 177, 184, 185
Norway, 58, 136
Nuremberg Institute for Economic Studies, 182

Office of Strategic Services (OSS), 79
Office of the Special Representative (OSR), 169
Oldham, J. H., 63
'One World' approach to integration, 25, 166, 207, 208
Open Society and Its Enemies, The (Popper), 104
Operation Barbarossa, 91
ordoliberalism, 51, 60
  after Hoffman's speech to the OEEC, 179
  Christian Democracy and, 71
  core views of, 74
  counter movement to socialism and, 103
  ecumenical roots of, 90
  European cooperation based on, 201
  German confession furthered, 101
  growth of Christian Democracy and, 90
  growth of West Germany and, 89
  history of, 90
  influence in West Germany of, 45
  intellectual force of, 74
  key role played in uniting Western Europe, 52
  not identical to the Freiburg School, 103
  Röpke as mouthpiece of, 104
  schism within liberalism and, 67
  set apart from Keynesianism, 75
  shaped post-war German identity, 182
Organisation for European Economic Cooperation (OEEC), 141, 142, 147
  aimed to strengthen the European economy, 149
  archives of, 10
  attempt to address trade liberalisation of, 171
  Camps opposed trade liberalisation programme of, 176
  changed role after UK economic struggles, 191
  channelled ideas into concrete proposals, 168
  comparison between ECSC and, 194
  created momentum in first five years after the war, 168
  currency convertibility and, 173
  decline of, 180
  discussion of trade blocs of, 176
  downgraded its ambitions in 1949, 169
  drawing rights and, 172
  ECA as counterpart to, 169
  EPU remained within the framework of, 173
  faced challenge of achieving regional market integration, 149
  focus on exports of, 172
  generator of blueprints for European recovery, 168
  Hoffman's address to, 177
  impact of IEPS on, 171
  impact of UK currency devaluation on, 178, 180
  impacts of liberalised trade on, 170
  increasing dysfunction of, 177
  initial opinion of, 168
  monetary regionalism in, 141
  original members of, 136
  OSR was permanent US representation to, 169
  put in charge of ERP, 136
  shift to EPU from, 167
  signing of IEPS and, 171
  Stikker lobbied for a global solution, 139
  UK currency devaluation and, 175
  United Kingdom as culprit for the inefficacy of, 169
  United Kingdom led efforts to set up, 140
  United States endorsed after establishment, 179
  United States foreign policy and, 179
  West German delegates at Hoffman's speech to, 178
  West German re-entry and, 45
Oxford, 61, 62

Palm, Trineke, ix, 9
Paris, 39
  American writers and artists in, 24
  Americanisation in, 6
  centre of economic recovery shifted to Bonn from, 180
  during the interwar period, 24
  EPU marked a shift towards, 203
  first display of *Guernica* in, 54
  French Planning Commission at, 142

Index

intellectual figureheads' 1940 trip to, 78
Lippmann on a new Europe organized in, 39
talks on Marshall Plan in, 136
Walter Lippmann Colloquium in, 61, 65
Paris Peace Conference, the, 22, 23, 24, 146, 147
Parti Populaire Français, 66
Pastors' Emergency League, 62, 98
Patel, Kiran, 18
Pax Americana, 184
peace, 23, 24, 57, 82
  Cassin's advocacy for, 54, 56
  comforts of, 2
  demanded sacrifices in sovereignty, 42
  economic integration and, 177
  ERP and OEEC as instruments of, 179
  Europe desired, 20
  European federal unity as the backbone of, 92
  European Republic of Planning at the epicentre of, 209
  for Germany, 96
  imagining a better world during times of, 1
  low wages jeopardize, 70
  Nazy Germany and Stalinist Russia were threats to, 40
  in the post-Great War period, 23
  regional economic groupings were essential for, 153
  reincorporation of West Germany furthered, 145
  religious ideals and, 85
  shame motivated activism for, 153
  the Soviet Union posed a direct threat to, 150
  trans-Atlantic community aimed at, 14
  'Western Union' and, 155, 206
  winning the, 44, 57, 82
People and Freedom group, 91
Permanent Court of International Justice, 63
persuasion, 19, 20, 108
Pétain, Philippe, 80, 81, 82, 83
Phoney War, the, 78, 79
Picasso, Pablo, 23
Pineau, Christian, 66
planned capitalism, 3
planning
  against ideology, 107
  apolitical appeal of, 108
  contrast with free trade of, 72
  desire for stability and, 119
  driven by emotion, 107

during the Phoney War, 79
  emotions drove, 101
  emphasised human rights, 107
  as the essence of integration, 111
  fit well with centrist politics, 117
  Hayek's refraining from, 74
  ideas and, 114
  Keynesian endorsement of, 74
  liberalism's struggle against, 68
  multilateralism and, 204
  Niebuhr on the need for, 164
  political victories of, 4
  protects against the politicization of society, 106
  as a response to inequality and poverty, 112
  smashed illusions of, 128
  state intervention in, 29
  use of American ideas in, 30
  worries about an excess of, 214
Pleven, René, 80
pluralism, 84
Poland, 92, 136, 151, 161
Polanyi, Karl, 39, 114, 118–19
polarization, 50
policy
  apolitical outlook of, 50
  for Germany, 142
  non-ideological approaches to, 117
  post-war obsession with, 51
  shift from ideology to, 106
policy approach to international affairs, 50, 110
policy history, 17
politics, 107
politics of productivity, 144, 212
pooling, 140, 141, 147, 175
Pope Leo XIII, 61, 69, 90
Pope Pius XI, 61, 69
Pope Pius XII, 56, 91, 92, 145
Popper, Karl, 104
Porter, Cole, 24
Portugal, 136
post-European world, 25, 26
post-war era, 6, 14, 25, 28, 165, 191, 214
Potsdam, 4
Potsdam Conference, 142, 150, 151
poverty, 23, 25, 41, 112, 114, 117, 139, 152, 164, 178
power
  American commercial-economic, 164
  of Britain, 175
  communist monopolization of, 161
  is consolidated in capitalism, 70
  of the EPU, 203

248   Index

power (cont.)
  interventionists on, 64
  Marshall Plan triggered shift in, 167
  of post-war America, 27, 49
  of post-war France, 43
  as a psychological tool, 14
  of the United States, 8
  United States' geopolitical, 214
  of West Germany, 201
pragmatism, 72, 117, 123, 199, 205
Prague coup, the, 150, 161
price correction, 74, 192
price fixing, 74, 192
price mechanism, the, 68, 74, 108, 148, 201
price-setting, 194
proletarianisation, 74
prosperity, 4, 5, 14, 20, 28, 29, 30, 70, 179, 194, 204
protectionism, 85, 194
Protestant Reformation, the, 89

Quadragesimo Anno, 61, 69, 70

racism, 25, 116
Ransome, Patrick, 73
Rappard, William, 66
rationalism, 3, 50, 106, 107, 112, 214
rationality, 41, 119, 213
Rauch, Wendelin, 95
Rawnsley, Derek, 73
realism, 214
Realpolitik, 146, 163, 168
reason, 50
reconciliation, 15
  among Christian churches, 115
  between churches and parishioners, 162
  between socialism and laissez faire liberalism, 114
  between West Germany and Western Europe, 186
  Cold War blueprints and, 28
  ECSC would lead to, 194
  federal movements focused on, 159
  importance of ecumenical movement for, 207
  of left and right, 66
  originated in France, 56
  post-Great War Europeans turned a deaf ear to, 23
  Stuttgart meeting a harbinger of, 145
  WCC aided, 166
regionalisation, 128, 140, 167, 171, 173, 204
regionalism, 101, 141, 167, 203, 208

regulated markets, 118
religion, 21, 22, 29, 41, 57, 85, 87, 115, 144, 206
Rencontres International de Genève, 159
renewal, 19
Republic of Planning, 18, 21
Rerum Novarum, 61, 69, 70, 90
Respublica literaria, 3, 17, 204
revisionism, 31
revisionist realism, 32
Reynaud, Paul, 80
Rhineland, the, 65, 180, 181, 182, 190, 191
rights, 20, 41, 54, 55, 56, 57, 58, 93, 155, 160, 161, 206, *See also* human rights
Rivista di Storia Economica, 86
Road to Serfdom, The (Hayek), 72, 104, 214
Rockefeller Foundation, 77
Rolland, Romain, 88
Roman Christianity, 215
Roosevelt, Eleanor, 214
Roosevelt, Franklin Delano
  on Allied efforts in Africa, 81
  the Atlantic Charter and, 58, 59
  Kennan's relationship with, 210
  response to Munich Agreement of, 78
Röpke, Wilhelm, 39, 66, 67, 71
  argued for international aid for Germany, 148
  aversion to collectivism of, 75
  on coined freedom, 148
  on competition, 103
  correspondence with Lippmann of, 77
  deeply impacted West German policy-making, 192
  drove forward blueprints for integration, 52
  on economic humanism, 89
  on the EPU, 201
  Erhard implemented ideas of, 174
  on the 'European experiment', 178
  on 'fake multilateralism', 173, 201
  favoured a nationalist approach, 174
  growth of Christian Democracy and, 90
  influence in West Germany of, 104
  influenced Western European multilateralisation, 173
  as a leading ordoliberal, 103, 104
  Lippmann's views mirrored, 69
  on the Marshall Plan, 148
  met Lippmann in Geneva, 66
  most prominent ordoliberal, 74
  opposed Keynesian planning, 192
  opposed Keynesianism, 60
  opposed Labour government policies, 192

Index

opposed the EPU, 173
opposed the IMF, 173
as a leading ordoliberal post-war status of, 104
on *Quadragesimo Anno*, 70
relationship with Einaudi of, 104
supported currency convertibility, 173
on trade liberalisation, 172
views mirrored Pope Pius XI in *Quadragesimo Anno*, 69, 71
was concerned with the balance-of-payments problem, 172
Rougier, Louis, 65, 77
Rueff, Jacques, 67
Ruggie, John, 183
Ruhr, 151, 152, 189, 191, 193, 194
rule of law, the, 41, 83
Bonhoeffer Kreis called for, 96
Russian Orthodox Church, 166
Rüstow, Alexander, 39, 52, 67, 68, 70, 71, 77, 90, 103

Saar, 189, 193
Scandinavia, 151, 205, 211
scarcity, 184
School for Social Research, 82
Schuman Plan, 167, 189, 191, 195, 208
Schuman, Robert, 41, 159, 187, 188, 190, 193, 194
Schumpeter, Joseph, 51
against Keynesianism, 125
analysis of Western world of, 102
as apologist for capitalism and elitist liberalism, 105–7
on capitalism, 102
concerns about capitalism of, 117
defended individual freedom, 50
maddened by approaches to multilateralism, 138
as a member of the Austrian school, 50
membership in Austrian School of, 103
opposed Labour government policies, 192
pessimism of, 125
on planning, 108–11
policy paradoxes faced by, 119
on social justice, 117
on socialism, 102
thought functionalist plans were escapism, 50
was reluctant to openly address the social question, 71
Second World War, 8
American point of view of, 25
Bonhoeffer's poetic description of, 97
Cassin's intellectual status during, 56
Catholic involvement after, 145
developments responsible for integration during, 111
ecumenical responses to horrors of, 100
emergence of a smaller Europe from, 13
European cooperation and integration not created after, 36
false hope aroused during, 8
the Four Freedoms and, 57
functionalism a response to the misery of, 107
history of integration starts long before, 8
hope aroused during, 214
influence of American intellectual *avant garde* after, 24
influence of Kennan's writings after, 210
isolationists and interventionists on, 64
leadership of United States, United Kingdom, and France after, 43
Monnet's network expanded after, 79
move towards functionalism transpired during, 57
the New Deal and, 50
'new Europe' not created during or after, 5
political imagination and, 1, 2
the post-European framework ineffective after, 26
progress in years after, 5
reactivation of Catholic church during, 22
regional European plans advanced during, 200
religious aspects of, 116
as a religious war, 97
rise of Christian Democracy after, 60
roots of ordoliberalism during, 90
shift of European mood following, 37
United states supplied Europe with practical policies during, 8
secularisation, 60, 89
security, 157, 169
self-regulating markets, 118
shame, 153
Shortall, Sarah, 38, 55, 83
Simon, P. H., 79
simultaneity, 3
Skandal der Gleichzeitigkeit (Scandal of Simultaneity), 4
Smit, Peter-Ben, ix, 9
social charity, 70
social cohesion, 21, 41, 42, 107, 115, 121, 190, 204
social inequality, 25, 112, 114, 152

social justice, 30, 70
  Christian Democracy on, 92
  competition and, 103
  Hayek on, 117
  inter-war emphasis on, 83
  Keynesianism was in tune with, 125
  mixed economy approach furthered, 83
  neoliberal cynicism towards, 117
  reincorporation of West Germany furthered, 145
  shame motivated activism for, 153
social market economy, 52, 89, 90
social policy, 21, 69, 75, 104, 127, 183, 193
social question, the, 22, 43, 61, 65, 69, 71, 207
social welfare, 58, 73
socialism
  after the Bretton Woods Conference, 125
  Austrian school were denouncers of, 51
  battle between laissez faire capitalism and, 117
  the Catholic church and, 22
  choice between capitalism and, 110
  Christian unity broke with, 207
  clash between (neo-)liberalism and, 51
  Cold War politics and, 28
  contraposition between liberalism and, 71
  as a counter to competition, 102
  economic humanism and, 89, 104
  German confession furthered, 101
  ideas against, 103
  influence on Wootton of, 72
  liberalism and, 67
  multilateralism incorporated, 114
  Niebuhr signalled a clean break with, 163
  Niebuhr's sympathy for, 94
  ordoliberalism employed insights from, 52
  readjustment of Western Europe leads towards, 110
  reconciliation between liberalism and, 114
  Schumpeter on, 102, 105
  struggle of neoliberalism against, 69
  UDHR and, 43
  watered down in social experiments, 83
socioeconomic justice, 120
Söderblom, Nathan, 62
soft power, 15
solidarity, 36, 118, 189, 190, 193
Solzhenitsyn, Aleksandr, 215
Sombart, Werner, 103
sovereignty
  in the Bretton Woods system, 126
  can only be transferred through a function, 41
  Cassin sought to stifle, 56
  as a 'deadly myth', 87
  ECSC started a countermovement to, 194
  Einaudi sought to hasten the disappearance of, 85
  integration and, 141, 147
  Keynesianism between international cooperation and, 124
  as an obstacle to the 'One World' approach, 53
  Polanyi on foreign policy and, 118
  pooling of, 147
  possibility of pooling of, 141
  as a sine qua non for global monetary systems, 127
sovereignty-transfer, 160
Soviet Union, the, 135
  'atheistic' nature of, 165
  American crusade against, 144
  anti-atheistic campaign against, 165
  Catholic Church's opposition to, 145
  Churchill on, 157
  Cold War influence of, 129
  containment of, 165
  cooperation with United States of, 142
  customs union as response to threat from, 143
  did not participate in Marshall Plan, 136
  economic integration strengthened Western world against, 200
  fall of, 4
  Kennan on the totalitarianism of, 211
  Kennan's depictions of, 211
  London Six-Power Conference and, 180
  Nazi Germany alliance with, 91
  Niebuhr on, 163
  Niebuhr on opposition to, 164
  not invited to discuss the Marshall Plan, 136
  post-war arms production of, 49
  post-war GDP of, 49
  rejection of Marshall Aid of, 161
  religious front against, 144
  replaced the threat of Germany, 185
  schism between Western Allies and, 142
  as a threat to Western Europe, 150
  Trial of the Sixteen and, 150
  the Truman Doctrine and, 129
  US containment towards, 210
  use of the veto in UN by, 150
Soziale Marktwirtschaft (Social Market Economy), 89

Index

Spaak, Paul-Henri, 39, 58, 113, 159, 194
Spain, 65, 136
Spanish Civil War, the, 23, 65
Spengler, Oswald, 60
spiritual community, 21, 158
spiritual unity, 21, 158, 206
stability, 204
Stalinist Russia, 40
state control, 120, 121, 122, 126, 204
state intervention, 3, 29, 121
   in economic matters, 120
   Freiburg Circles on, 95
   neoliberal views of, 68
   neoliberalism and, 182
state-centric neoliberalism, 74
Steehouder, Jorrit ix, 10, 146, 171, 200
steel, 152, 160, 188, 189, 193
sterling, 128, 139, 157, 175, 178, 179
sterling crisis of 1947, 128, 157
sterling zone, 175, 184
Stikker, Dirk, 139
Stone, Shepard, 78
Stresemann, Gustav, 23
Studebaker Cars, 169
Sturzo, Luigi, 91
Stuttgart, 41, 99, 100, 151, 162, 163
'Stuttgart Declaration of Guilt', 99, 145
Stuttgart Declaration of Guilt, 207
subsidiarity, 84, 115, 201
supranationalism, 31
Sweden, 58, 62, 136
Switzerland, 66, 93, 94, 136, 159

tariffs, 123, 152, 170, 177, 192
taxation, 109, 134
Tehran, 150
Témoignage chrétien, 40, 55, 83, 84
Temple, William, 59, 93, 159
Tomlinson, Jim, 152
totalitarianism, 6, 41, 43, 54, 114, 163
   Isaiah Berlin on, 211
   Bonhoeffer Kreis opposed to, 97
   challenge to democracy of, 65
   Christian rhetoric against, 153
   contrast with freedom of, 72
   emotions tend towards, 212
   humanity's rise from struggle against, 54
   planning a form of, 74
   political defeat of, 4
trade, 146, 170
trade liberalisation, 161, 169, 170, 171, 174, 176, 177, 203, 205
traditional realism, 31, 32
'Tragedy of Central Europe, The' (Kundera), 215

trans-Atlantic cooperation, 16, 26, 37, 43, 137, 177
trauma, 153
Treaty of Brussels, 153, 154
Treaty of Dunkirk, 153, 156
Treaty of Versailles, the, 23
Treaty on the Final Settlement with Respect to Germany, 36
Trial of the Sixteen, 150
Triffin, Robert, 128
Trizone, 142, 156
Truman Doctrine, the, 22, 129, 130, 144, 165, 207
Truman, Harry S., 49, 129, 137, 144
trust, 19, 29, 176
truth, 145
Turkey, 58, 136

unemployment, 29, 55, 63, 69, 108, 109, 121, 134, 152, 193
Union Fédérale, 56
Union française, 35
Union of European Federalists, 159
Union of European Federalists (UEF), 159
United Kingdom, 44, 92
   Acheson opposed the interference of, 187
   the Atlantic Charter and, 58
   at the Cambridge meeting of CJDP, 162
   colonial legacy of, 35
   currency devaluation of, 175
   declarations of in the Atlantic Charter, 58
   diplomacy with the Netherlands of, 139
   economic relations with US of, 139
   economic retreat of, 178
   economic troubles of, 138
   erratic European policy of, 179
   exclusion from EPU of, 205
   failure of Western European customs union due to, 191
   feared trade liberalisation, 169
   financial sacrifices of, 185
   France allied with, 156
   Franco-German reconciliation and, 13
   indecisions about Cold War of, 151
   leadership of in early post-war period, 43
   membership in OEEC of, 136
   opposed drawing rights plans, 172
   on the outside of European integration, 68
   post-war GDP of, 49
   poverty and inequality in, 152
   relationship with United States of, 156
   resisted European cooperation, 140
   response of to currency devaluation, 176
   retreat from European leadership of, 192

United Kingdom (cont.)
  Schumpeter on, 108
  signing of the Treaty of Brussels, 153
  signing of Treaty of Dunkirk, 153
  Spanish Civil War and, 65
  strategy in Europe of, 151
  trade relations with France of, 151
  uncertainties after currency devaluation of, 180
  unrealistic self-image of, 157
  at Versailles, 22
  was no longer driving Western European cooperation, 178
  well placed to lead Western European consolidation, 156
  Western Union and, 154
  Western Union and the role of, 155
United Nations (UN), 76
  division in Europe and, 130
  ERP could not be a project of, 136
  Europe was able to circumvent, 168
  Europeans must implement aid outside of, 136
  the Marshall Plan and, 141
  the Marshall Plan triggered shift away from, 167
  Niebuhr's approach shifted away from, 165
  Soviet vetoes bogged down, 150
  the Truman Doctrine sidelined, 129
  United States relations with, 129
United Nations Charter, 150, 153
United Nations Economic Commission for Europe (ECE), 129, 130, 133, 135, 136, 167, 171
United Nations Monetary and Financial Conference. *See* Bretton Woods Conference
United Nations Relief and Rehabilitation Administration (UNRRA), 129, 135
United States, 8, 60, 65, 92, 156, 179
  1917 declaration of war of, 23
  accepting leadership of free world, 13
  allure of, 26
  as a beacon of hope, 8
  Isaiah Berlin on, 212
  Bevin sought independence from, 152
  at the Cambridge meeting of CJDP, 162
  Churchill on, 157
  Cold War influence of, 129
  Cold War policy of, 129
  control of over European integration, 17
  cooperation with Soviet Union of, 142
  declarations of in the Atlantic Charter, 58
  dominance of, 8
  economic relations with British of, 139
  either-or politics of, 28
  emotions drove post-war leadership, 212
  engagement of after Second World War, 49
  entry into First World War, 116
  European appropriation of ideas of, 30
  European Catholic views of, 91
  European need for aid from, 134
  failed establishment of the ITO and, 137
  fiction of self-regulating markets and, 118
  financial sacrifices of, 185
  goals of the Marshall Plan for, 143
  government appeal to citizens of, 134
  as an ideal to emulate, 214
  ideas about European reconstruction of, 20
  impact of economic policy goals of, 183
  imported food to Germany, 164
  influence of during interwar period, 24
  isolationists and interventionists in, 64
  Keynes on involvement of, 124
  leadership of in early post-war period, 43
  as a living example of optimism, 8
  must fund the recovery of Europe, 135
  the New Deal and, 50
  Niebuhr on free world ambitions of, 94
  as outside force on Western Europe, 179
  post-war arms production of, 49
  post-war GDP of, 49
  post-war hope hinged on, 27
  promoted Europeanisation, 179
  rebuilding Europe, 25
  relations with UN of, 129
  relationship with United Kingdom of, 157
  role in rebuilding Western Europe, 27
  role of in Western European reconstruction, 163
  stimulated economic integration in Western Europe, 200
  supplied Europe with practical policies during Second World War, 8
  trade relations with United Kingdom of, 152
  United Kingdom currency devaluation and, 175
  United Kingdom unafraid to oppose initiatives of, 175
  United Kingdom's relationship with, 156
  at Versailles, 22
  Western European societies spellbound by, 6
United States foreign policy, 22, 143
  'One World' approach of, 22

Index

charity as a principle of, 207
Clayton's conclusions about, 133
of containment, 165, 210
during liberalisation of West German imports, 179
economy as key area of, 164
end of the 'One World' approach in, 22, 53, 150, 154, 155, 163, 166, 205, 207
image of rationality of, 212
Marshall's speech marked a turning point in, 144
Niebuhr's consistency with aims of, 164
radical change in, 153
the Truman Doctrine and, 129
West German statehood as the main priority of, 143
Western European bloc formation a priority of, 187
United States Neutrality Act, 78
United States State Department, 135, 180, 200, 210
Universal Declaration of Human Rights (UDHR), 43, 54, 55, 56, 59, 166, 206, 207, 214
universalism, 23, 101
Uruguay, 92
utopia, 51, 106, 113, 116

valuta convertibility, 44, 171
van den Berg, Clemens ix, 10, 61, 92, 98, 99, 166, 167
Vansittart, Sir Robert, 80
Viner, Jacob, 104, 121
Visser 't Hooft, Willem, 40, 61, 63, 93, 94, 97, 98, 99, 166
von Mises, Ludwig, 50, 66, 104

'*Wahl-Lokomotive*' (election locomotive), 181
Walter Lippmann Colloquium, 61, 66, 67, 68, 74, 77, 103, 111
war debt, 134, 182
Warsaw, 215
weak state, 74
Weber, Max, 103
welfare state, the, 59, 68, 74, 75, 83, 107, 119, 183
Welles, Sumner, 25
Wells, H. G., 22, 72
West German Ministry of Economics, 89
West Germany, 60, 75, 145, 174, 182, *See also* Germany
   Acheson on, 187
   after segregation, 100
   blueprints for the foundation of, 181
   Catholic Church supported, 145
   as the centre of Western European bloc, 208
   Christian unity and, 207
   Christian values shaped the future of, 190
   discussions on trade blocs excluded, 176
   Erhard's position in, 181
   focus of the Dutch government on, 184
   French role in integration of, 187
   guiding principle of first governments of, 163
   as heart of Western Europe, 143
   in Hoffman's ideal of European integration, 178
   impact of EPU on, 178
   impact of the Germany memorandum on, 185
   impressive economic recovery of, 180
   influence of Röpke in, 104
   integration to Western Europe of, 186
   membership in OEEC of, 136
   Monnet's proposal for France and, 188
   Müller-Armack's influence on, 89
   multilateralisation and, 173
   ordoliberals shaped, 201
   as part of American shift towards 'building Europe', 141
   plans of French customs union with, 147
   politics superseded economics in, 193
   power in the EPU of, 203
   present at Hoffmann's speech to OEEC, 178
   prominence of Christian Democracy in, 89
   reconciliation between Western Europe and, 186
   reincorporation to Western Europe of, 145
   rise of Christian Democracy in, 145
   shaped Western European multilateralism, 201
   trade agreement with the Netherlands, 183
   truth, guilt, and reconciliation preceded establishment of, 145
   US liberalisation of imports into, 179
   Western bloc centred around, 166
   Weststaatsgründung of, 181
Westbindung, 100, 145, 202
Western Allies, 142
Western bloc, 151, 154, 165
Western bloc policy, 151
Western Christendom, 14
Western Christianity, 190
Western civilisation, 60, 74

254 Index

Western Europe. *See also* Europe
  'One World' approach foundered in, 166
  absence of currency convertibility in, 146
  Adenauer's views on, 191
  after Soviet rejection of Marshall Aid, 161
  America's role in rebuilding, 27
  Americanisation of, 30, 140
  avoiding a German threat to, 188
  benefits of multilateralism for, 113
  Bevin's assessment of, 155
  Bevin's relevance for building of, 152
  British outmanoeuvred in plans for, 139
  call for pooling coal and steel sectors of, 160
  Catholic calls for unification of, 145
  the Cold War required unity of, 185
  communism was a threat to, 150
  communism was winning ground in, 148
  countermovement to socialism in, 103
  demand for spiritual community in, 158
  developments responsible for re-design of, 111
  direct effect of Marshall's speech on, 140
  economic cooperation in, 149, 177
  ECSC was in tune with the mood of, 194
  ecumenical roots of cooperation in, 207
  Einaudi and Erhard as builders of, 88
  embedded liberalism and, 183
  the EPU and, 200
  erratic UK policy steered, 179
  Eurafrique and, 35
  Europeanisation of, 140, 202–5
  experimenting with capitalism and democracy, 83
  failed attempts at federation of, 117
  failed attempts to achieve cooperation in, 52
  French role in West German integration to, 187
  German market boosted the recovery of, 184
  German reentry to economy of, 200
  growth during Cold War of, 30
  growth of Christian Democracy in, 44
  Hoffman on economic integration of, 177
  ideas counterbalanced American planning in, 192
  illusion of British leadership in, 157
  impact of IEPS on, 171
  impact of the Germany memorandum on, 185
  impact of the Schuman Plan on, 191
  impacts of trade liberalisation on, 172
  importance of the US and Germany for, 158
  influence of Christian Democracy in, 45
  influence of Mont Pélerin Society on, 51
  integration of West Germany into, 186
  intra-European trade in, 146
  introduction of practices of international cooperation to, 112
  Keynes on productivity and growth in, 124
  liberalism and ordoliberalism played key roles in uniting, 52
  Marshall Aid a crucial lifeline for, 179
  move towards social version of capitalism of, 117
  need for a customs union in, 142
  Niebuhr focused on, 165
  Niebuhr on, 165
  Niebuhr on the Soviet Union in, 163
  planning of during post-war years, 40
  policy engineers of, 214
  pooling sovereignty in, 147
  possibility of pooling sovereignty in, 141
  post-war religious revival in, 115
  poverty and inequality in, 152
  promotion of human rights of, 58
  push towards bloc formation of, 137
  question about sovereignty and integration in, 141
  radical change in US policy towards, 153
  'readjustment by catastrophe' of, 110
  reconciliation between socialism and liberalism in, 114
  reconciliation between West Germany and, 186
  reconciliation of ideals and needs in, 158
  reincorporation of West Germany into, 145
  remained vulnerable to outside forces in late 1940s, 179
  rise of Christian Democracy in, 28, 60, 145
  Röpke's influence on multilateralisation in, 173
  shift towards regionalism in, 171
  stability of in post-war years, 28
  trade liberalisation in, 203
  trans-Atlantic cooperation in, 177
  Treaty of Brussels and, 154
  as a unit, 156
  United States' focus on, 135
  US stimulated economic integration in, 200
  the WCC aided cooperation in, 166

Index

the WCC on developing disconnect in, 165
WCC outmanoeuvred in the building of, 166
weakening of WCC in, 208
West Germany as heart of, 143
the Western Union and, 141
Western Union and, 155
Western Union of, 150
Western zones in Germany as part of, 143
Western European reconstruction, 19, 163
Western Germany, 45
Western Union, 54, 107, 141, 150, 152, 154, 156, 157, 158, 161, 162, 206
West-German Parliamentary Council, 181
Weststaatsgründung, 181
White, Harry Dexter, 120, 126
Willkie, Wendell, 25
Wilson, Harold, 137
Wilson, Woodrow, 8, 25, 214
winning the peace, 42, 82
Winter, Jay, 59
Wirtschaftslenkung und Marktwirtschaft (Müller-Armack), 90
Wirtschaftswunder, 52
Wootton, Barbara, 72, 76, 78
World Alliance for International Friendship Through the Churches, 63
World Bank, the, 135, 199
World Council of Churches (WCC), 38, 61, 93, 94, 98
  'One World' approach in, 166
  Americanisation of, 140
  demand for spiritual community led to, 159
  development of the Cold War weakened, 208
  Dulles's 1948 speech to, 206
  first meeting of Provisional Council of, 162
  founding of, 21
  global aims of, 166
  impact of Cold War on, 165
  impact of the Cold War on, 160
  incorporation of EKD into, 145
  India and China in, 166
  led the ecumenical movement of integration, 206
  overlooked the shift towards regionalisation, 167
  role in Cold War of, 165
  Stuttgart Declaration of Guilt and, 145
  success of in immediate post-war years, 207
  Temple as a pioneer of, 159
  turned its attention to global ideology, 208
  view of Dulles in, 160
  was outmanoeuvred in building post-war Western Europe, 207
  'Western Union' and, 206
world politics, 23, 150, 151
World Student Christian Federation (WSCF), 63
World War I. *See* First World War
World War II. *See* Second World War
Wurm, Theophil, 99

Yalta, 4
Yalta Conference, 142, 150

zeitgeist, 16, 17, 20, 75, 101, 107, 162